India's Policy Towards the European Union in the Post-Cold War Era

This book charts the remarkable evolution of New Delhi's engagement with the European Union (EU) from economic pragmatism to comprehensive strategic partnership. Through rigorous analysis of political dialogues, trade negotiations, and security cooperation from 1991 to present day, the book reveals how India progressively recognized the EU's collective weight in global governance, distinct from its bilateral ties with individual European states. The study highlights pivotal moments where Brussels' institutional influence and Delhi's great-power ambitions converged and explains limitations of their cooperation in the liberal order.

The volume will be of great interest to scholars of international institutions, comparative regionalism, and India's global strategy. Researchers examining how middle powers engage with hybrid actors like the EU – neither a traditional state nor a conventional international organization – will find this an indispensable case study. Policymakers navigating contemporary geopolitical realignments will gain critical insights into EU–India coordination on non-proliferation, climate action, and strategic autonomy debates.

Patryk Kugiel (PhD) is an Associate Professor at the University of Warsaw (Poland). He is also a Research Fellow at the Polish Institute of International Affairs in Warsaw. His research focuses on Indian foreign policy, South Asia and EU policy towards Asia and the Indo-Pacific. He is an author of dozens of academic articles, policy papers, book chapters, and a monograph on India's Soft Power: A New Foreign Policy Strategy (2016).

India's Policy Towards the European Union in the Post-Cold War Era
Partners in the Liberal Order?

Patryk Kugiel

LONDON AND NEW YORK

First published 2026
by Routledge
4 Park Square, Milton Park, Abingdon, Oxon OX14 4RN

and by Routledge
605 Third Avenue, New York, NY 10158

Routledge is an imprint of the Taylor & Francis Group, an informa business

© 2026 Patryk Kugiel

The right of Patryk Kugiel to be identified as author of this work has been asserted in accordance with sections 77 and 78 of the Copyright, Designs and Patents Act 1988.

The Open Access version of this book, available at www.taylorfrancis.com, has been made available under a Creative Commons Attribution-NonCommercial-NoDerivatives (CC-BY-NC-ND) 4.0 International license. Funded by University of Warsaw.

For Product Safety Concerns and Information please contact our EU representative GPSR@taylorandfrancis.com. Taylor & Francis Verlag GmbH, Kaufingerstraße 24, 80331 München, Germany.

Trademark notice: Product or corporate names may be trademarks or registered trademarks and are used only for identification and explanation without intent to infringe.

British Library Cataloguing-in-Publication Data
A catalogue record for this book is available from the British Library

ISBN: 978-1-041-17176-8 (hbk)
ISBN: 978-1-041-17232-1 (pbk)
ISBN: 978-1-003-68864-8 (ebk)

DOI: 10.4324/9781003688648

Typeset in Sabon
by KnowledgeWorks Global Ltd.

For MEGI and MARCEL

Contents

List of illustrations xi
List of abbreviations xiii

Introduction 1

1 The drivers of India's post-Cold War policy towards the European Union 14

  1.1 The legacy of historical relations with Europe 14
    1.1.1 India vis-à-vis the beginnings of European integration: 1947–1962 15
    1.1.2 Formalization of cooperation with the European communities: 1962–1973 17
    1.1.3 Period of intensified economic cooperation with the EU: 1974–1991 18
    1.1.4 Key lessons learned 20
  1.2 Redefinition of India's foreign policy goals after 1991 21
    1.2.1 The significance of the end of the Cold War for India's international strategy 21
    1.2.2 India's new foreign policy 24
    1.2.3 India's great power aspirations 26
  1.3 Pro-liberal economic reforms 28
    1.3.1 Reasons for the economic reforms 29
    1.3.2 Cautious liberalization of the economy 30
    1.3.3 Effects of economic reforms 31
  1.4 India's perception of the European Union 34
  1.5 Institutional constraints of stronger engagement with the EU 38

2 The decade of transition: The EU in India's
international strategy between 1991 and 2000   49
   2.1 India's policy goals towards the EU after the
        Cold War 49
        2.1.1 India's strategy towards the EU (2004) 51
   2.2 India's attitude towards deepening European
        integration and EU enlargement 54
        2.2.1 India's reactions to the establishment of the EU 54
        2.2.2 India's position towards the EU enlargement 57
   2.3 The EU as a difficult political partner 58
        2.3.1 Disputes over respect for human rights in India 62
        2.3.2 The situation in Kashmir as a source
               of tensions with the EU 63
        2.3.3 India–Pakistan conflict in relations with the EU 64
        2.3.4 India's nuclear programme and the
               crisis in relations with the EU 64
   2.4 The EU as a key economic partner 67
        2.4.1 India–EU trade in goods 67
        2.4.2 Investment flows and development cooperation 70
   2.5 Balance of the first decade 71

3 Era of engagement: Building India's strategic
partnership with the EU between 2000 and 2014   78
   3.1 The institutionalization of India's
        political cooperation with the EU 79
        3.1.1 A new beginning: India's policy towards
               the EU in the period 2000–2004 82
        3.1.2 The operationalization of the strategic
               partnership: 2005–2009 89
        3.1.3 The growing crisis in India's policy
               towards the EU: 2010–2014 92
        3.1.4 Criticism of the strategic partnership 94
   3.2 India's economic and social cooperation
        with the EU between 2000 and 2014 96
        3.2.1 The place of the EU in achieving
               India's economic objectives 96
        3.2.2 Negotiating a free trade agreement with the EU 99
        3.2.3 Economic cooperation 104
        3.2.4 Technological cooperation 114
        3.2.5 Socio-cultural contacts 116

3.3 Security cooperation 119
  3.3.1 The fight against international terrorism 119
  3.3.2 Combating piracy 124
  3.3.3 UN peacekeeping missions 125
3.4 Conclusions 126

4 Reinforced partnership: India's foreign policy towards the EU under the Prime Minister Modi (2014–2025)   137

  4.1 The rationale for growing role of the EU in Modi's foreign policy 138
    4.1.1 India's modernization agenda 138
    4.1.2 Trump factor in India's policy towards the EU 140
    4.1.3 The China threat and India–EU strategic convergence 143
  4.2 Deepening the strategic partnership with the EU 146
    4.2.1 Cold start in India's engagement with the EU: 2014–2015 146
    4.2.2 A new opening in India-EU partnership: 2016–2019 148
    4.2.3 Rejecting strategic hesitations towards the EU: 2020–2025 153
    4.2.4 Security cooperation 161
    4.2.5 Summary 162
  4.3 India's economic cooperation with the EU 164
    4.3.1 EU support for the modernization agenda 165
    4.3.2 Resumption of FTA negotiations 168
    4.3.3 Trade in goods and services 171
    4.3.4 Foreign direct investment (FDI) 174
    4.3.5 Scientific and technological cooperation and the role of the TTC 177
    4.3.6 Connectivity partnership and IMEC 179
    4.3.7 Migration and mobility 180
    4.3.8 International development cooperation 182
    4.3.9 Summary 184

5 India, the EU, and the liberal international order   191

  5.1 The EU in India's vision of reformed multilateralism 192
    5.1.1 India's difficult relationship with the LIO 192
    5.1.2 India's call for change 195
    5.1.3 India's offer to the EU 197

5.2　The EU as India's regional partner　199
　　　5.2.1　India, the EU, and SAARC　200
　　　5.2.2　India–EU cooperation in South Asian States　201
　　　5.2.3　India, the EU, and the Indo-Pacific　202
　5.3　Cooperation with the EU at the global level　205
　　　5.3.1　Reform of international institutions　206
　　　5.3.2　International trade negotiations　209
　　　5.3.3　International non-proliferation regime　213
　　　5.3.4　International climate-change negotiations　216
　　　5.3.5　Promotion of democracy and international protection of human rights　220
　　　5.3.6　International development cooperation　224
　5.4　Challenges and constraints in multilateral cooperation with the EU　227
　　　5.4.1　Historical differences: The legacy of colonialism and Cold War　228
　　　5.4.2　Economic divergence: Asymmetry in the socio-economic development　229
　　　5.4.3　Political and institutional differences　230
　　　5.4.4　Structural differences in the international system　232

Conclusions and the way forward　　　　　　　　　　　　　242

Index　　　　　　　　　　　　　　　　　　　　　　　　258

Illustrations

Charts

1.1	Export and import of goods from India in 1990–2000 (current prices, USD millions)	32
2.1	India's trade with the EU from 1991 to 2000 (Euro, million)	68
2.2	Official Development Assistance of European Institutions to India 1991–2000 (total aid, net disbursements, constant prices, millions of dollars)	71
3.1	India's trade with the EU from 2000 to 2014 (billion dollars)	104
3.2	EU share of India's foreign trade between 2000 and 2014 (in %)	105
3.3	India's main trading partners in the EU in 2000	107
3.4	India's main trading partners in the EU in 2014	107
3.5	FDI inflows into India from the EU 2000–2014 (US$million, current prices)	109
3.6	Major investors in India in 2014. (Cumulative value of FDI between 2000 and 2014, US$billion)	109
3.7	Major investors in India from the EU in 2014 (cumulative value between 2000 and 2014, value in US$billion)	110
3.8	EU Official Development Assistance to India 2001–2014 (net disbursements, US$million, constant prices)	114
4.1	India's merchandise trade with the EU from 2014 to 2025 ($billion, %)	172
4.2	India's major export partners in 2024–2025	173
4.3	India's major import partners in 2024–2025	173
4.4	EU direct investment inflows to India from 2014 to 2023 (US$billion)	175
4.5	Largest foreign investors in India (billion dollars, cumulative value of investments over the period 2000–2023)	176
4.6	Largest investors in India among EU members (cumulative value 2000–2023, US$billion, % in total)	176
4.7	Number of Indian nationals living in the EU27 between 1998 and 2024	182

4.8   EU Official Development Assistance to India, 2011 to 2023
      (€m, net disbursements)   183

Tables

3.1	Institutional structure of India–EU cooperation by 2014	80
3.2	List of India–EU summits from 2000 to 2014 and their main outcomes	84
3.3	India's major trading partners in 2000 and 2014	106
4.1	Institutional framework of India–EU strategic cooperation (as on June 30, 2025)	163

Abbreviations

ASEAN	Association of South-East Asian Nations
BJP	Bharatiya Janata Party (Indian People's Party)
BTIA	Broad-based Trade and Investment Agreement
CAPD	Cooperation Agreement on Partnership and Development
CCA	Commercial Cooperation Agreement
CDRI	Coalition for Disaster Resilient Infrastructure
CECA	Commercial and Economic Cooperation Agreement
CMP	Coordinated Maritime Presences
COP	Conference of the Parties
CRIMARIO	Critical Maritime Routes Indo-Pacific Project
EBI	European Investment Bank
EC	European Commission
EEC	European Economic Community
ESIWA	Enhancing Security Cooperation In and With Asia
FDI	Foreign Direct Investment
FTA	Free Trade Agreement
GATT	General Agreement on Tariffs and Trade
IMF	International Monetary Fund
IPCC	Intergovernmental Panel on Climate Change
IPOI	Indo-Pacific Oceans Initiative
ISA	International Solar Alliance
JAP	Joint Action Plan
LIO	Liberal International Order
MEA	Ministry of External Affairs
NSG	Nuclear Suppliers Group
ODA	Official Development Assistance
OECD	Organisation for Economic Co-operation and Development
RCEP	Regional Comprehensive Economic Partnership
SAARC	South Asian Association for Regional Cooperation
SDG	Sustainable Development Goals
UE	European Union
UN	United Nations

UNCTAD	United Nations Conference on Trade and Development
UNGA	United Nations General Assembly
UNSC	United Nation Security Council
WFP	World Food Programme
WTO	World Trade Organization

Introduction

The election of Donald Trump again as US president in November 2024 has raised concerns about a deepening crisis in the liberal international order and uncertainty in international cooperation.[1] States and organizations have begun to look more intensively for allies that can stop the negative impact of US unilateralism. India and the EU seemed to be some of the potential actors interested in defending and stabilizing multilateralism. Already during Donald Trump's first term in office, the EU recognized India as a partner with whom it wanted to "defend a rules-based international order".[2] Over the last 30 years, these two partners have built multifaceted and ever-growing strategic partnership. However, in order to assess whether India and the EU can defend the multilateral system, one must first understand India's approach to the EU. The purpose of this book is to examine three decades of Indian policy towards the EU to understand the potential for these actors to cooperate in protecting or changing the global order. India's economic, political, and strategic importance indicates that it is an actor that will play a growing influence not only for the EU, but also on the global economic and political stage.

This book analyses the evolution in India's policy towards the EU after the Cold War in the context of the realization of its superpower aspirations and the formation of a liberal international order. Framing the topic in this way first requires identifying the role of the EU in India's international strategy. India's motivations and factors influencing engagement with the EU need to be analysed. It is also necessary to examine India's attitude towards the existing international order and to reconstruct India's vision of the world and its thinking on international relations. This is to make it possible to assess to what extent the Indian approach coincides with that of the EU, to what extent India is satisfied with the existing global system and how much it wants to change it, or whether it is proposing its own alternative proposal for an international governance. The research process will also identify the main constraints and challenges to India's policy towards the EU and cooperation in shaping the international order.

Identification of the research area and objective of the work

This book traces the evolution of India's foreign policy towards the EU since the end of the Cold War to better comprehend the nature and potential of India–EU strategic partnership. Although India established diplomatic relations with the EU's predecessor – the European Economic Community – as early as 1962, it was the end of the bipolar world order and the subsequent changes both in India (economic liberalization) and in Europe (integration and enlargement) that ushered in a new era of Indian engagement with the EU. Over the next three decades, the EU's place in India's foreign policy strategy has moved from the margins to the centre. From being seen mainly as an economic bloc and an international organization with a marginal role in Indian strategic thinking, the EU became a valuable political actor and eventually a strategic partner. While still less important than other major powers or even the largest European countries, the EU has become a useful partner in securing India's economic aspirations and its security and strategic interests in Asia and beyond. This remarkable shift in India's approach to the EU from estrangement to engagement is comprehensively examined.

The book sheds more light on relations between one of the biggest economies and most influential global actors. These relations have not got enough attention in the past. Yet, India today is the rising global power, the most populous country, the fourth biggest economy, nuclear and military power and increasingly influential diplomatic actor. The EU is still the second biggest economy, technological and regulatory power, and despite Brexit and the war in its neighbourhood, or because of that, a re-emerging geopolitical player. Therefore, this is important to study cooperation between actors that will shape, separately or together, international system in decades to come. It is even more timely to comprehend that relationship when the US under Donald Trump fastened historical realignments in the world.

The partnership between India and the EU went through remarkable transformation over the last three decades expanding into new areas of cooperation and forging even more ambitious plans for future. With free trade area agreement and a new security cooperation in the sight, the India–EU partnership may be at the cusp of a new era. At the same time, pessimists say that this partnership is underperforming and is long on aspirations and short on deliveries. This makes the case for an in-depth analysis of strengths and weaknesses, opportunities, and limitations of this relationship more timely.

Interestingly, the book looks at EU–India relations from an Indian perspective. It examines the formation of India's policy towards the EU, tries to understand main motivations and factors influencing India's approach to European partner. It may seem a daunting task if not a bizarre ambition that a European author wants to explain India's policy on Europe. But it is also very important for Europeans to better understand expectations, goals, and limitations of India's engagement with the EU. It may help to enhance mutual understanding, avoid misplaced expectations, and draft a more realistic plans for future.

Scope of the book

The book includes a comprehensive analysis of India's policy towards the EU from 1991 to mid-2025. The first date, 1991, marks the beginning of economic reforms in India signifying greater openness to the global economy and the end of the Cold War, which resulted in a change in the country's foreign policy assumptions and directions. Importantly, 1991 can also be considered the symbolic beginning of the EU. Although the Treaty of Maastricht, which established it, did not enter into force until November 1, 1993, it was initialled while still in 1991, at the Summit of 11 December (and formally signed on February 7, 1992). This therefore makes it possible to consider 1991 as the beginning of important changes in both India and Europe and an opening of a new chapter in their relations.

The upper caesura of the work is the mid-2025. This not only keeps the book very timely but also includes recent historic moments in India–EU relations, like the visit of the whole European Commission to India in February 2025 and the start of the Strategic Dialogue in June, which highlights new quality of reinforced strategic partnership between the two. Long period of cooperation spanning over three decades provides a suitable perspective for drawing relevant conclusions.

India's policy towards the EU is analysed in three main dimensions – economic, political, and social. Analysis focuses at three levels of cooperation – bilateral, regional, and multilateral. At the global level, six specific regimes have been examined to find out synergies and divergences between the EU and India. Given the potential and importance of both partners, cooperation between them has a major impact on finding international solutions to major global challenges and the stability of the international order.

Literature review

Studies on India's policy towards the EU have not often been undertaken either in India or in Europe, until recently. Most research of India's foreign policy have focused on major directions of engagement or cross-cutting issues, which generally do not include the EU. India's bilateral relations with the major powers, such as US, Russia, or China, have most often been the subject of study, as well as with neighbours in South Asia such as Pakistan, or the analysis of selected issues, e.g. India's attitude towards the proliferation of weapons of mass destruction, climate change, or the fight against terrorism. It can be said that the EU occupies a marginal place in Indian literature on International Relations. Major books on foreign policy by Indian authors omit it completely or devote at most a few pages to it. Slightly more attention is given to the major European countries – especially the so-called Big Three – the UK, Germany, and France. It is only in the last few years that we have seen a growing interest in studying India's relations with the EU.

A review of the literature in terms of the book's theme makes it possible to distinguish two main groups of studies: (1) those analysing India–EU relations and (2) those analysing the impact of India–EU cooperation on the liberal international order.

Within the first group, the greatest contribution to the study of India's policy towards the EU has been made for decades by one major institution in India – the Centre for European Studies at Jawaharlal Nehru University in New Delhi. Researchers associated with this institute – Prof. Rajendra Jain,[3] Prof. Salma Ummu Bava,[4] Prof. Gulschan Sachdeva,[5] or Dr. Shreya Pandey[6] – have authored a number of articles and books on India's relations with the EU. In their reflections, they devote most space to political and economic relations, perceptions of the EU in India and cooperation on global challenges. It is only in the last few years that other Indian academia and think tanks have also begun to devote more space to the EU. The decision adopted at the EU–India Summit in Marseille in 2008 and expressed in the Joint Action Plan to financially support the establishment of European study centres and consortia of Indian and European universities studying EU–India relations played a positive role in this regard. This has resulted in the establishment of European centres at the University of Calcutta or Manipal, among others.[7] There is also a growing interest in the EU by Indian think tanks, including the Indian Council of World Affairs (ICWA), the Institute of Defense Studies and Analysis (IDSA), or the Observer Research Foundation (ORF), where positions on Europe have been established. This literature is complemented by European researchers analysing relations with India as one element of EU foreign policy.

Despite the growing interest in EU–India cooperation, a comprehensive analysis of India's post-Cold War policy towards the EU is still lacking. The closest to showing a long perspective on the whole India–EU relationship is a 2015 book edited by Pascaline Winiand, Marika Vicziana, Poonam Datar, *The European Union and India. Rehtoric or Meaningful Partnership?* – which, however, does not cover the last crucial phase of cooperation in the last decade.[8] Helpful in this regard are the collective works edited by R.K. Jain[9] and Philpp Gieg et al.,[10] which, however, are a collection of very different takes and subjective assessments of this relationship. Above all, there is a lack of monographs that analyse India's policy towards the EU. The exception here is a book by the former Indian Ambassador to European countries, Bhaswati Mukherjee, which is basically the only monograph published in recent years showing comprehensively the relationship with the EU from an Indian perspective, yet from a distinct diplomatic angle.[11]

Only over the last couple of years, there is a rising interest from journalists, researchers, and scholars in the India–EU relations, reflecting growing importance of that issue. This creates an expanding body of literature – mainly news in the press, policy papers from think tanks, and academic articles covering specific dimensions of the partnership. But available studies focus on some aspects or a short period and do not tell the whole story, with continuity and change of over 30 years of EU–India relations. This book aims to fill this gap and offers a more comprehensive analysis of that topic. It provides an in-depth analysis of practical cooperation in key areas. This will allow for a better understanding of India's approach to the EU and an indication of the convergence of goals and interests in a changing international order.

The second group of existing literature attempts to assess India's impact on the existing international order. Although most of the studies do not focus on cooperation with the EU in this regard, the conclusions drawn are of great relevance to the Union.

Defining India's attitude towards the liberal international order is far from obvious due to the ambivalence that characterizes it. Generally, one can identify three groups of opinions assessing the impact of liberal ideas on the Indian approach to this issue.[12] The first indicates that liberalism does not play a role in shaping India's vision of the world, and therefore, their foreign policy will be divergent and often contradictory to the approach of Western partners, including the EU. They see India as a revisionist power challenging the current status quo, with anti-colonial legacies and structural differences with the West standing in the way of changing this approach. Deepa Ollapally points out that India has a "deep seated postcolonial identity and near obsession with its autonomy", which means that its "commitment to the current order remains both instrumental and partial: it has not come around to seeing current liberal order constructed by the West as an end in itself, and is unlikely to do so".[13] The German researcher notes that India represents "different interests and norms in various policy fields" than those of Western countries – adding – "despite its democracy and economic opening-up after the end of the Cold War, India is not a natural partner of the West".[14] India does not want to join the current liberal order created by the West, but to change it according to its own vision (of a multipolar world) to end political and economic discrimination.[15] Others add that India is no less of a challenge to the US than China and "many Indian interests are closer to China than to the US".[16]

The second group of scholars believes that there is only partial convergence with Western states towards the international order, and India would only selectively want to cooperate in selected areas of the international system. Thus, it is possible to cooperate with India on a *case-by-case* basis on selected issues where the interests of the state require it, as India is primarily a "pivot power" (*swing state*) that can support the West or powers opposed to it depending on the assessment of benefits.[17] Indian scholar Salma Bava acknowledges that India's "socialization and buy into the current liberal order" means that it will "strive to sustain the existing global order since it has benefited from it", but at the same time she adds that "India challenges the rules of the global order by seeking change to the existing status quo in various institutions such as nuclear non-proliferation".[18] This approach is in line with the perception of India as a "reformist power" rather than a revisionist one, i.e. seeking change within the existing order.[19] In effect, India will act as both defender and destroyer of the liberal order, "as a rational, pragmatic actor, it will defend the liberal order where it suits its interests, and seek to change it – to suit its growing power aspirations".[20] Sumit Ganguly believes similarly, acknowledging that while "host of attributes should make India a staunch supporter of a global, liberal order", however, "since the days of its first prime minister, Jawaharlal Nehru, the country has been ambivalent about support for liberal/democratic principles and institutions abroad".[21]

Finally, a third group argues that India is guided by liberal ideas in its politics and will be interested in preserving and strengthening the liberal order. Leading Indian strategist Raja Mohan has for years portrayed India as a "responsible stakeholder" and an important partner of the West in solving the challenges of the modern age.[22] More recently, he believes that India should seek closer cooperation and coalition-building of democratic states supporting the existing system in the face of challenges emanating from authoritarian China.[23] Similarly, Samir Saran argues that India is one of the natural defenders of the liberal international order and can cooperate with the EU in this regard.[24] In general, the younger generation of Indian strategists often look to the EU as an important partner in reforming international institutions to improve their functioning and create new organizations and norms in emerging areas of international relations (such as the use of the internet, artificial intelligence, space) that have not yet been regulated.

This book will verify the existing lines of argumentation by analysing India's policy towards the EU in relation to the basic building blocks of the liberal order. It will be important in this context to examine the Indian approach to cooperation with the EU in several specific areas of multilateral cooperation. By showing the evolution of India's policy towards the EU, the analysis examines to what extent it may be motivated by the liberal paradigm. This should make it possible to answer the question of whether India can be seen by the EU as a *"like-minded partner"* and whether both entities can become pillars of a liberal international order.

A literature review has identified three major literature puzzles the book tries to address:

a No literature has taken a longer-term view to systematically explain the factors that have influenced India's policy towards the EU over the decades.
b Although there is an expanding literature discussing EU–India relations, there are few monographs that examine this relationship from an Indian strategic perspective.
c There is inconclusive discussion about possible impact of the India's cooperation with the EU on the liberal international order.

Research questions and hypothesis

Based on the analysis of the research to date, the following research questions were formulated:

1 Why did India decide after 1991 to intensify its cooperation with the EU and what factors shaped Indian policy towards the EU over last three decades?

2 What was the importance of cooperation with the EU for India in terms of realizing its superpower aspirations?
3 How does India's policy towards the EU affect the shape and sustainability of the liberal international order?

While addressing the first question, the book identified major factors and variables that have influenced the evolution of India's approach to post-Cold War relations with the EU. Secondly, it strives to show what role played the EU in achieving India's foreign policy objectives in the context of strengthening its international position. And finally, analysis will show what, if any, impact on the liberal international order has had India–EU partnership.

The book aims to prove the hypothesis saying that: *India is instrumental in using its relationship with the EU to accelerate its own economic development and realize its global power ambitions. Through closer cooperation with the EU, it wants to accelerate the reform of the liberal international order.*

Research methodology and methods

The study uses an inductive–deductive strategy and a variety of qualitative methods. The primary method is discourse analysis. It is based mainly on an examination of broad variety of primary sources (government documents, statements by politicians, official reports and strategies, election manifestos, bilateral documents agreed with the EU, documents adopted by the EU, etc.) and secondary sources (books, academic articles, press articles, analyses, etc.). Repeated conversations and interviews with leading Indian researchers on foreign policy and relations with the EU, diplomats and officials from both sides were helpful in understanding India's motivations and approach to the EU. In addition, the work draws on participant observation of events and processes in India and Europe that are important for the development of Indian–EU cooperation. The author has been following these relations for over 15 years, including participating in key expert dialogues (such as the EU–India Forum on Effective Multilateralism, EU–India Think Tank Twinning Initiative, and other seminars on the EU–India relationship) and the most important conferences on India's international strategy (e.g. all editions of the Raisina Dialogue in New Delhi since 2017).

The study includes six case studies of EU–India cooperation in multilateral arena. The case study allows for a more detailed analysis of selected phenomena or processes in order to identify certain regularities and general principles on this basis. The thesis focuses on examining examples of India's multilateral cooperation with the EU in relation to key international organizations and regimes that can be considered core elements of the liberal international order.[25] In the absence of a universally applicable list of such regimes, this study proposes an authoritative set of six international regimes that met two conditions: firstly, they constituted an important area of India's cooperation with the EU, and secondly, they are considered an essential element of the liberal order. In this way, a list of case studies was prepared, depicting India's cooperation with the EU vis-à-vis:

1 Global governance institutions (mainly in terms of UN, IMF, and World Bank reform)
2 Trade regime (India's and the EU's attitude to free trade and cooperation in international trade negotiations within the WTO)
3 Non-proliferation regime (relationship and cooperation between India and the EU in the main institutions and mechanisms – NPT and NSG)
4 Climate change regime (cooperation in international climate negotiations)
5 Regime for the protection of human rights and democracy (cooperation in the promotion of democracy and human rights)
6 The international development cooperation regime (cooperation in developing the architecture and principles of development assistance).

The analysis of these selected examples is helpful to identify more clearly the similarities and differences in India's and the EU's approaches to key international challenges and to indicate the potential for future cooperation in this regard. It has allowed to assess to what extent and under what conditions India engages in protecting and strengthening the liberal order and when cooperation with the EU in this regard occurs.

The study often refers to official statistical data. It was mainly used to illustrate the scale and trends in economic cooperation – trade, investment flows and development assistance. This has resulted in a number of graphs and charts depicting key processes and trends in India–EU cooperation. For the most part, data provided by the Indian Ministry of trade was used as a starting point, supplemented where necessary by data from Eurostat or international organizations (e.g. World Bank, UNCTAD).

Theoretical approach

India's policy towards the EU is analysed within the research perspective of neoliberal institutionalism theory. Representatives of this school of thought (e.g. R. Keohane) remain relatively close to realism and are sometimes referred to as "weak liberals".[26] According to them, states remain primary actors in international relations and act as a kind of "rational egoists" by supporting the creation of international institutions, norms, and conventions in order to reduce the anarchic nature of the international system and minimize fears and uncertainties about the intentions and behaviour of other actors.[27] States should therefore have an interest in protecting such a system that enhances the predictability of other states and facilitates international cooperation. In doing so, they are cooperative rather than confrontational and seek absolute rather than relative gains. This means that it is important to achieve one's own goal, regardless of whether other actors gain greater benefits. In this approach, support for international institutions, international law and a willingness to cooperate with other partners does not stem from an attachment to particular values or ideas, but from a belief that doing so is in the common interest. Neoliberal institutionalism is based on assumptions of rationalism and practicality, and its normative dimension is weaker than in other strands of liberalism.

It should be noted, however, that this approach is rarely used to analyse India's foreign policy, which is most often explained in terms of the realist theory. The choice of this perspective as the most appropriate for the study of India's policy towards the EU was determined by several specific considerations. Firstly, in India, it is still the state that is considered the primary actor and participant in international relations, and territorial integrity and almost absolute sovereignty are fundamental national interests. Neo-liberal institutionalism as "weak liberalism" therefore allows for such a state-centric analysis of Indian foreign policy. In the Indian worldview, states are rational actors operating in an anarchic international system for absolute gain. The overarching principles that define foreign policy are therefore rationality and pragmatism, as emphasized in the neoliberal approach.

Secondly, in India, all successive post-Cold War governments have placed the well-being of the people at the centre of their agenda, and consider the main goal to lift the population out of poverty and create the conditions for sustainable economic development. This results in the economization of foreign policy, becoming part of globalization processes and oriented towards cooperation with other partners. This leads to an increase in interdependence as an element that enhances state security.

Thirdly, India, after the end of the Cold War, is increasingly joining globalization and the US-led liberal international order, joining more regimes (functional orders), supporting multilateralism and standing up for international law. At the same time, it seeks to gain greater influence over international institutions, the creation and enforcement of international norms and standards. Building friendly and constructive relations with Western countries and the EU – i.e. the privileged and most influential actors in the international system – is, in this view, an extremely important condition for achieving India's strategic goals.

Fourthly, the adoption of a neoliberal approach is justified given the very object of the study – i.e. the policy towards the EU as a kind of supranational organization and economic partner of India. The content of this policy focused on economic matters, normative issues and multilateral cooperation within the framework of international institutions, i.e. the issues that occupy the most space within neoliberal institutionalism. Important in this regard was the sharing of democratic values and support for multilateralism in international relations, which led to the thesis of India's "natural partnership" with the EU.

Finally, neo-liberal institutionalism is helpful in analysing India's attitude towards the EU in the context of the liberal international order, understood as a set of rules, institutions and international regimes governing cooperation between states. Using this paradigm allows a better assessment of the convergence of India's goals at the level of the international system with the values promoted by the EU.

Neo-liberal institutionalism best combines the traditionally important assumptions of realism in India (e.g. about the role of the state, the anarchy of the international system, the role of material factors) with the changes in the post-Cold War approach to international relations resulting from India's integration into the global economy and increasing interdependence. Neo-liberalism, better than realism, can explain why India after 1991 engaged strongly in developing economic cooperation with its neighbours and major powers and became actively involved in activities within international institutions. Contrary to realism, India assumed that states should orient themselves towards cooperation rather than confrontation, and fostered efficient international institutions, free trade, or strong laws and norms governing international relations to this end.

Structure of the work

The book has been divided into five chapters covering the comprehensive overview of India's policy towards the EU over time and across different dimensions and levels of cooperation. It has taken a chronological linear approach to describing India–UE relations, though traditional and boring, was also necessary to show evolution and turning points in the relationship. Hence, while three chapters examines specific periods of cooperation, the first one focuses on the formation of India's policy towards the EU and the last on cooperation within the larger framework of Liberal Order.

The first chapter entitled **"The drivers of India's post-Cold War policy towards the European Union"** characterizes the main variables that have shaped India's approach to the EU since 1991. Five such factors have been identified – history, geopolitics, economics, perception, and diplomacy. Firstly, the book examines India's relations with the EU during the Cold War, in order to uncover the historical baggage of the relationship. Secondly, it shows how the geopolitical changes haves affected India's international strategy and worldview. Thirdly, it analyses the significance of economic liberalization in India for its cooperation with the EU. The fourth section overviews the changing perception of the EU in Indian elites and society. Finally, it examines India's diplomatic resources and capacities as a possible constraint on closer engagement with the EU.

The second chapter, **"'The decade of transition: the EU in India's international strategy between 1991 and 2000"**, looks at the beginning of the India–EU cooperation in the new era. The section begins by identifying EU's place in India's strategic objectives in the emerging world order. It then analyses India's reactions to the establishment of the EU, the deepening of European integration and the enlargement of the Union. The following section attempts to explain why the EU, initially seen as a natural democratic partner, became a serious political rival and adversary by the end of the decade. The impact of the situation in Kashmir and India's nuclear test on relations with the EU is analysed. It concludes with an overview of economic cooperation in the 1990s.

The third chapter, titled "**Era of engagement: building India's strategic partnership with the EU 2000–2014**", covers a critical period in India's policy towards the EU when it decided to engage its partner in a high-level, regular political dialogue and entered into a strategic partnership in 2004. The first section discusses the institutionalization of political dialogue into a range of mechanisms and formats – from annual summits to sectoral consultations – demonstrating the expanding scope of the partnership with Europe. The second section examines progress in the realization of India's economic interests and in technical and socio-cultural cooperation. It pays particular attention to the context, progress and suspension of the FTA negotiations and their impact on the overall partnership. Finally, it looks at emerging areas of security cooperation, such as maritime security and counter-terrorism.

The fourth chapter entitled "**Reinforced partnership: India's foreign policy towards the EU under the Prime Minister Modi (2014–2025)**" aims to demonstrate the transformative nature of India's engagement with the EU during the BJP rule in Delhi. It is divided into three parts. The first one describes three main reasons that drove the historic engagement with the EU – the launch of an ambitious modernization agenda, the assertive policies of China and the unpredictable policies of the US under President Donald Trump. The second section explains different phases in Modi's policy towards the EU – his initial suspicion of Europe, rediscovery of the EU and engagement in broad-based strategic and security cooperation. It discusses also the impact of the different responses to Russian aggression in Ukraine on the EU–India partnership. The third section provides an analysis of the role of the EU for economic interests, trade in goods and services, investment and aid flows, migration and mobility connectivity and technological cooperation.

The fifth chapter "**India, the EU and liberal international order**" shifts the focus to the regional and global levels. Firstly, it seeks to understand India's approach to the international liberal order and place of the EU in this context. Secondly, it analyses India's approach to the EU in the context of its interests in South Asia, and the Indo-Pacific. Finally, it examines practical outcomes of India's cooperation with the EU at multilateral fora. Six international regimes were selected that are seen as crucial elements of the LIO: 1. reform of international institutions; 2. international trade negotiations; 3. international nuclear non-proliferation regime; 4. international climate change negotiations; 5. promotion of democracy and international protection of human rights; and 6. international development cooperation. The final section provides an analysis of the limitations and challenges to closer cooperation with the EU at the global level.

The concluding part (Conclusions and the Way Forward) presents a summary of the research and main observations. This serves as material to propose predictions for future India–EU relations and to suggest some recommendations for European readers. This is where academic analysis meets practical observations of relevance to policy makers and business people. The book concludes by identifying key research gaps for further study.

Notes

1. H. Hurlburt, "Can the International Order Survive Trump 2.0?", Chattam House, 30 January 2025.
2. European Commission, High Representative of the Union for Foreign Affairs and Security Policy, *Joint Communication to the European Parliament and the Council*, "Elements for EU's Strategy on India – Partnership for sustainable modernisation and rules-based global order", Brussels, 20.11.2018 JOIN(2018) 28 final
3. R. K. Jain (ed.), *India and the European Union in a Turbulent World*, Singapore: Palgrave Macmillan, 2020; R. K. Jain (ed.), *Changing Indian Images of the European Union. Perceptions and Misperceptions*, Singapore: Palgrave Macmillan, 2019; R. K. Jain (ed.), *The European Union and South Asia*, New Delhi: Knowledge World Publishers, 2015; R. K. Jain (ed.), *India, Europe and Conflict Resolution in South Asia*, New Delhi: Knowledge World Publishers, 2015.
4. See, for example, U.S. Bava, "India and European Union: From Engagement to Strategic Partnership", *International Studies*, vol. 47, no. 2–4, 2010, pp. 373–386.
5. G. Sachdeva (ed.), *Challenges in Europe: Indian Perspectives*, Singapore: Palgrave Macmillan, 2019.
6. S. Pandey, *India and European Union: Perceptions of the Indian Print Media and Elites*, New Delhi: KWP, 2018.
7. R. K. Jain, "Indian Perceptions of the European Union", *International Journal*, vol. 1, no. 1, 2015 (Warsaw: Institute of International Relations, University of Warsaw), pp. 71–81.
8. P. Winand, M. Vicziany, P. Datar, *The European Union and India. Rehtoric or Meaningful Partnership?*, Cheltenhem: Edward Elgar, 2015.
9. R. K. Jain (ed.), *India and the European Union in a Turbulent World*, Singapore: Palgrave Macmillan, 2020.
10. P. Gieg et al. (eds.), *EU-India Relations. The Strategic Partnership in the Light of the European Union Global Strategy*, Cham: Springer, 2021.
11. B. Mukherjee, *India and EU. An Insider's View*, New Delhi: Vij Books India Pvt Ltd, 2018.
12. P. Kugiel, "India, the European Union and the Postwar Liberal Order", [in:] R. K. Jain (ed.), *India and the European Union in a Turbulent World*, Singapore: Palgrave Macmillan, 2020, p. 35.
13. D. M. Ollapally, "India and the International Order: Accommodation and Adjustment", *Ethics and International Affairs*, vol. 32, no. 1, 2018, p. 62.
14. T. Wojczewski, 'India in the World Order: Many Partners, No Allies', *GIDA Focus Asia*, no. 6, September 2016.
15. T. Wojczewski, "India's Vision of World Order: Multi-alignment, Exceptionalism and Peaceful Co-existence", *Global Affairs*, vol. 3, no. 2, 2017, pp. 111–123; and see T. Wojczewski, *India's Foreign Policy Discourse and Its Conceptions of World Order: The Quest for Power and Identity*, Abingdon, New York: Routledge, 2018.
16. G. J. Gilboy, E. Heginbotham, "Double Trouble: A Realist View of Chinese and Indian Power", *The Washington Quarterly*, vol. 36, no. 3, 2013, pp. 125–126.
17. D. M. Kliman, R. Fontaine, "International Order and Global Swing States", *The Washington Quarterly*, vol. 36, no. 1, 2013, pp. 93–109.
18. U. S. Bava, "India and the Global Order: Negotiating between Old and New Order", *International Studies*, vol. 54, no. 1–4, 2017, p. 22.
19. J. Zajączkowski, "India's Foreign Policy Following the End of the Cold War", [in:] J. Zajączkowski, J. Schottli, M. Thapa (eds.), *India in the Contemporary World: Polity, Economy and International Relations*, Delhi: Routledge, 2014.

20 P. Kugiel, "From Destroyer to Preserver? The Evolution of India's Position Towards the Liberal International Order and Its Significance for the EU-India Strategic Partnership", [in:] P. Gieg et al. (eds.), *EU-India Relations. Tre Strategic Partnership in the Light of the European Union Global Strategy*, Cham: Springer, 2021, p. 268.
21 S. Ganguly, "India in the Liberal Order", German Marshall Fund of the United States, 2013.
22 C. R. Mohan, "Rising India: Partner in Shaping Global Commons?", *The Washington Quarterly*, vol. 33, no. 3, 2010, pp. 133–148.
23 C. R. Mohan, "Putting Sovereignty Back in Global Order: An Indian View", *The Washington Quarterly*, vol. 43, no. 3, 2020, pp. 81–98.
24 S. Saran, "India's Role in a Liberal Post-Western World", *The International Spectator*, vol. 53, no. 1, 2018, pp. 92–108.
25 H. W. Maull (ed.), *The Rise and Decline of the Post-Cold War International Order*, Oxford: Oxford University Press, 2018, p. 4.
26 J. Czaputowicz, "Mapa współczesnego liberalizmu: neoliberalny instytucjonalizm, nowy liberalizm, liberalny interwencjonizm" ["Map of Contemporary Liberalism: Neoliberal Institutionalism, New Liberalism, Liberal Interventionism"], [in:] E. Haliżak, R. Ożarowski, A. Wróbel (eds.), *Liberalizm & neoliberalizm w nauce o stosunkach międzynarodowych: teoretyczny pluralism [Liberalism and Neoliberalism in the Study of International Relations: Theoretical Pluralism]*, Volume I, Warsaw: Rambler, 2016, p. 20.
27 R. O. Keohane, L. L. Martin, "The Promise of Institutionalist Theory", *International Security*, vol. 20, no. 1, 1995, p. 39.

1 The drivers of India's post-Cold War policy towards the European Union

A state's foreign policy does not arise in a vacuum. It is influenced by a range of internal and external factors, historical events and visions of the future, subjective perceptions of the partner and one's own place in the world, objective capabilities, and resources to pursue state's goals. In the case of India's policy towards the European Union (EU), long-standing historical ties, global events, and the processes triggered in both India and Europe by the end of the Cold War, as well as continuing institutional constraints, have played an important role. Five key factors influencing India's approach towards the EU will be examined more closely:

1 the history of cooperation with the European Economic Community (EEC) during the Cold War
2 the change in the international order after the Cold War
3 economic reforms in India
4 evolving perceptions of the EU in India
5 institutional constraints on India's policy towards the EU

1.1 The legacy of historical relations with Europe

India's relations with the EU did not begin only after 1991. On the contrary, they marked a new phase in a relationship that had begun much earlier. As early as March 2, 1962, India was the first country in Asia to establish diplomatic relations with the EEC, the predecessor of the EU. They were thus entering a new chapter of cooperation with 30 years of experience and institutional links, built on a foundation of much longer history of interaction with Europeans.

Historical contacts between India and Europe date back to ancient times and the expedition of Alexander the Great in the 4th century BC, followed by the development of the spice trade during the Roman Empire and the Middle Ages. They intensified with the discovery of the sea route to India in 1498. In the following decades and centuries, it was not only the British, but also the French, Dutch, and Portuguese who established their factories and eventually colonies in India. European missionaries, merchants, travellers, and

DOI: 10.4324/9781003688648-2
This chapter has been made available under a CC-BY-NC-ND 4.0 International license.

The Drivers of India's Post-Cold War Policy towards the EU 15

explorers followed through, inspired by material and spiritual wealth of the East. Since the 19th century, Europeans carried out extensive studies of Indian culture and religions. But Europe has also had widespread impact on the Indian thinking and worldviews. Suffice to say that many leaders of the independence movement, including Mahatma Gandhi and Jawaharlal Nehru, were educated in Britain and formed their political views under the influence of European Enlightenment thought. The history of Europeans' colonial past in India is still significant today in terms of mutual relations and perceptions.

Contemporary Indo-European contacts began with India's independence on August 15, 1947. While India inherited a fairly developed relationship with individual European states, particularly Britain, it paid less attention to cooperation at the supranational level. Three periods can be distinguished in the approach to European integration and regional organizations in Europe during the Cold War:

i 1947–1962 – covering the first contacts from independence to the establishment of diplomatic relations with the European Economic Community in 1962.
ii 1962–1973 – a decade of intensified cooperation from the establishment of diplomatic relations to the signing of the first trade agreement with the EEC in 1973.
iii 1974–1991 – a period of strengthening and consolidation of India's relations with the European Economic Community after the accession of Britain and until the end of the Cold War.

1.1.1 India vis-à-vis the beginnings of European integration: 1947–1962

The initial period of regional cooperation in Europe after the Second World War was met with limited interest by Indian political and intellectual elites.[1] For India, preoccupied with consolidating its young state and re-establishing difficult relations with its neighbours, events in Europe seemed "remote from concerns of India, or of Asia" and initial reactions towards the Communities were not very favourable.[2] Europe was at the bottom of the list of important international topics for the expert and academic community in Delhi.[3] Development in Europe was seen from three major perspectives:

1 Functional – as an interesting case study of regional cooperation
2 Economic – impact of European integration on India's economic interests
3 Political – European integration as a political process in the context of Cold War rivalry

If the first European attempts at integration, such as the establishment of the European Coal and Steel Community in 1951, the Western Union/ Brussels Treaty Organisation in 1948, the European Defence Community of 1952, or the Western European Union (WEU) in 1954, were of interest to anyone in India, it was primarily in functional terms, as a possible model or inspiration for integration processes and regional cooperation in Asia, or even the creation of a possible "Asian Union".[4]

Interest in European integration only increased with the signing of the Treaties of Rome creating EEC and EUROATOM in March 1957.[5] Although Indian politicians appreciated that this event had an important political dimension,[6] the economic impact was most important to them.[7] Indeed, the creation of a common market of six European countries and the unification of tariffs raised concerns in government and business circles that this would impede access to the EEC market and exacerbate the trade deficit that had been growing since 1948. It was even seen as "a new form of protectionism by European states".[8] Officials from the newly formed ECC Council of Ministers observed in 1958 that "the Indian Government has so far maintained a reserved, in certain cases, frankly hostile attitude toward the Treaty instituting the European Common Market".[9] In 1961, Prime Minister Nehru admitted that India has certainly not greeted the creation of the EEC with great enthusiasm. On the contrary, during a debate in the Indian Parliament in May 1962 around the issue of Britain joining the EEC, Nehru included the following assessment:

> The fact to be remembered is that the European common market may be good for those who are in it, and may be good—I do not know; it is not for me to judge—for United Kingdom. **It is not good for us. It will do us some harm**. More important than that, this is a first step in a particular direction, the direction being a certain measure of growing political solidarity between those countries. I do not know what this will lead to. But, **I fear it will not lead to anything good**. I am talking about political solidarity.[10]

In India, a critical stance towards the importance of European integration and concerns about the negative impact of European processes on global security and the economic interests of India and other developing countries prevailed. It was pointed out that this could lead to increased tensions between the superpowers and halt the process of emancipation of colonies from European influence. Prime Minister Nehru feared that "a relationship with the Community would probably lead to the continuation of colonial exploitation by other means".[11] According to a leading academician on this issue, Professor R. K. Jain, "a key factor in Nehru's thinking about the European Community was anti-colonialism, as three of the EEC members were colonial states – Belgium, France and the Netherlands".[12]

Moreover, Nehru "was apprehensive that if the Common Market became an inward-looking regional grouping and transformed itself into a rich man's club, the gap between developed and developing countries would become wider".[13] During the period of British accession to the ECC negotiations in 1962, Nehru argued in London that British membership of the EEC might aggravate tensions between East and West, while Defence Minister Krishna Menon described the organization as "an economic counterpart of the NATO and a protagonist of the Cold War".[14]

Indian concerns increased further when Britain made a formal request to join the EEC in July 1961 and began formal negotiations in November. This was a decisive factor in why India decided to engage more strongly with the Communities.[15] This is perfectly understandable given that at the time the UK was India's largest export market, far more important than all the EEC countries combined. According to 1962 figures, the British took as much as 37% of all Indian exports, while the six EEC countries combined received only 7% of its exports at that time.[16]

As a result, Nehru decided to act swiftly and as early as the autumn of 1961, India transferred from London to Brussels one of the two (besides Washington) senior officials responsible for the promotion of economic interests (Commissioner-General for Economic Affairs in Europe).[17] By November of 1961, the EEC gave its approval to an Indian request made back in 1959 for the opening of an Indian diplomatic mission. On March 2, 1962, the first Indian Ambassador to the EEC – Krishan Behari Lall – deposited his credential letters with the President of the EEC Commission in Brussels.

1.1.2 Formalization of cooperation with the European communities: 1962–1973

The establishment of diplomatic relations between India and the EEC in March 1962 was the first step towards formalizing cooperation at the supranational level. In April 1963, EEC Commission President Walter Hallstein visited Delhi for the first time ever. The prospect of the EEC's enlargement to the British, the rapid economic development of European countries and growing trade led India to pay more attention to European affairs. In the decade 1962–1973, three main objectives can be identified in India's policy towards the EEC:

1. Monitoring UK-ECC negotiations and ensure that the terms of UK accession into the EEC do not hit Indian economic interests.
2. Improving trade with EEC members.
3. Negotiating an agreement with the EEC to regulate and strengthen economic cooperation.

Although British accession was finally aborted in January 1963 as a result of France's veto, there was a widespread view among the Indian elite that Britain's eventual entry into the EEC was only a matter of time, and that with it would come a diminishing importance of the British Commonwealth of Nations.[18] As a result, by the time of British accession in 1973, India was busily seeking trade and economic concessions (transition periods, exemption from quotas, etc.) that took into account its previous privileges in the UK market.

India's second major objective was to improve terms of trade and access to the EEC common market. The main Indian demands included lowering tariffs on Indian products, reducing quantitative restrictions (e.g. quotas on selected goods) and other non-tariff barriers. Indian diplomats suggested that instead of assistance from Western Europe, India would simply prefer more favourable terms of trade, so that it was the growth in exports that would provide foreign exchange to cover imports and thus enable the country to accelerate its development. Prime Minister Nehru argued as early as July 1962 that "trade is better than aid".[19]

A broader justification for this view was provided by a young Indian economist who had just completed his PhD at Oxford University, Manmohan Singh (later Prime Minister of India from 2004 to 2014). In an article in 1963, he wrote that "When, therefore countries like India feel apprehensive [about the EEC], it is not because they are fundamentally opposed to the idea of European integration, but because they feel that certain aspects of arrangements for European integration suggest an inadequate appreciation of the needs of developing countries like India for higher export earnings for financing their development plans".[20] He also argued that the trade policies pursued by some EEC countries had "at least partly nullified the beneficial impact of [their] aid on India's economy", raising suspicions as to whether they were deliberately seeking to "stall the industrialisation of poorer countries".[21]

The way to improve trade problems and economic cooperation would be to negotiate a favourable trade agreement. As early as May 1962, the new Indian Ambassador to the EEC first made a proposal to start official negotiations for such an agreement. However, it was only on April 3, 1973, following the earlier accession of the UK, that the Council of the European Communities agreed to open negotiations for a trade agreement with India and approved the negotiating mandate of the Commission. The negotiations themselves were progressing rapidly and India's Commercial Cooperation Agreement (CCA) with the EEC was signed on December 17, 1973, in Brussels.

The CCA finally entered into force on April 1, 1974. Contrary to India's demands, however, it was limited to trade issues, although it left the door open for extending cooperation into new areas. Its main achievement was the creation of the EEC-India Joint Commission, which oversaw and monitored all trade and economic relations between the parties. The Commission's meetings gave India the opportunity to quickly raise difficult issues and expand practical cooperation into new areas, stimulating more frequent contacts between the two sides.

1.1.3 Period of intensified economic cooperation with the EU: 1974–1991

Britain's entry into the EEC and the signing of the first trade agreement in 1973 had a profound impact on India's policy towards the Communities. From an Indian perspective, British accession to the EEC changed the balance of power in the organization in their favour and increased the value of trade and economic ties with the EEC by leaps and bounds. At the same time, the Community became an important donor of development assistance to

India. It also led to an increased EEC interest in Asia, especially in the former British colonies, including the largest one, India. Apart from trade relations, policy towards the EEC also acquired a new political dimension.

Increasing access to the Common Market and reducing the trade deficit remained India's primary objectives in its relations with the enlarged EEC. Indian diplomats intensified lobbying for a reduction in tariff and non-tariff barriers, increased export quotas, and support for the promotion of Indian exports on the European market. In addition to trade, they paid increasing attention to extending cooperation to technical and development issues. At the same time, there was a growing realization on the Indian side that the trade deficit with the EEC was not only due to European tariff and non-tariff barriers, but also to the weakness of Indian producers and exporters.[22] A jointly commissioned report by the Commission and the Indian government on economic potential and complementarity (the so-called Smallman Report) published in 1975 indicated that "the main obstacle to increased trade is mutual ignorance" and the fact that both sides simply do not know each other's companies or products.[23] The report recommended, among other things, the establishment of an India Trade Center in Brussels, which actually took place in 1980 with financial support from the EEC ($1.5 million for three years).[24]

The adoption of the CCA trade agreement in 1973 and especially the joining of the UK to the EEC strengthened economic ties with India tremendously. Trade and investment with the EEC began to grow dynamically. The inclusion of the former British colonies as recipients of EEC-wide aid made development assistance an even more important dimension of the relationship. India became a beneficiary of more systemic European support, which complemented the food or humanitarian aid already being provided. ECC became the largest donor to India, ahead of the US and Japan and, according to some calculations, as much as 40% of all EEC financial and technical assistance to Asia, 34% of all food aid, 22% of humanitarian aid and 19% of economic support went to India in 1976–1988.[25]

Despite this progress, the Indian side increasingly suggested the need to negotiate a new, more ambitious economic agreement that would also include cooperation in additional sectors. Finally, negotiations began in June 1980 in Brussels and ended in April 1981. In June 1981, India and the EEC officially signed a second agreement, the Commercial and Economic Cooperation Agreement (CECA). The agreement, which came into force on December 1, 1981, opened up cooperation to a number of areas beyond trade, including investment promotion, scientific, technological, developmental, or industrial cooperation.

This contributed to further dynamic trade growth. Exports of goods from the EEC to India almost quadrupled between 1979 and 1989, while Indian sales within the EEC only doubled during this period. This meant that the deficit on the Indian side increased dramatically from ECU 170 million in 1979 to ECU 2902 million in 1989.[26] Indian researchers believed that the EEC's "protectionist measures", which are not favourable to development in the "third world", were responsible for this state of affairs.[27] Also, some European scholars acknowledged in 1988 that "India's poor trade performance with the European Economic Community (EEC) is due to both protectionist EEC policies and excessive state control in India in trade, industry and the public sector".[28]

Increasing economic cooperation has been accompanied by an intensification of political dialogue, including visits at the highest level. In April 1975, the President of the European Commission, Francois-Xavier Ortoli, visited Delhi,[29] and in 1978, India's Prime Minister Morarji Desai came to Brussels for the EEC's first visit. In May 1980, the new Commission President Roy Jenkins was in India again, followed by the next President Gaston Thorn in Delhi in October 1981.

In addition to the Joint Commission, which had existed since 1973 – the main platform for a regular review of India's cooperation with the Communities – additional mechanisms for contact began to emerge. In 1982, a political dialogue was initiated in the form of meetings between the so-called Troika of the European Economic Communities (comprising representatives of the country holding the Presidency of the Council at the time, the previous, and the next) and the Indian Foreign Minister. The EEC side also began to take a more serious interest in India and strengthen public diplomacy there.[30] Another milestone of cooperation was India's agreement to open an EEC Commission Representation in New Delhi. An agreement to this effect was signed by the two sides in 1981 and European Community diplomats began working in India in 1982.[31] Finally, contacts between parliamentarians from the European Parliament and the Indian Lok Sabha intensified.

1.1.4 Key lessons learned

As a result, by the end of the Cold War, India already had a legal framework for cooperation (CECA) and instruments for regular political (Troika meetings, permanent diplomatic representation) and economic (Joint Commission) dialogue. The EEC members were India's largest trading partner, accounting for 24% of India's exports and 32% of imports in 1992.[32] They were also the largest source of investment and development aid. This all made the EU a crucial partner for India at the onset of a new era.

At the same time, India accounted for only 0.5% of the exports of the EEC countries and 0.4% of its imports came from there. This created a huge imbalance in the relationship – the EEC of already 12 members was a much more important partner for India, than India was for the EEC.

The Cold War period in India's policy towards the EEC shows a steadily increasing intensity and widening scope of cooperation: from purely trade issues and development aid, to investment, technological, scientific, and industrial cooperation. Interestingly, it was India and not the EEC that was the more active party, putting forward new initiatives and demands, proposing an ever broader and more ambitious programme of cooperation. It took more than a decade for India to convince the ECC to conclude its first bilateral trade agreement (in 1973) and sought its rapid extension to economic cooperation (in 1981), opened its own embassy to the EEC in Brussels in 1962 – 20 years before the ECC opened its representation in Delhi (1982).

At the same time, bilateral contacts with European countries were already much more important than those at the EEC level. There was a strong perception in India that despite the progress of European integration, the Community was being torn apart by the conflicting interests of the member states. As one noted, "behind the façade of unity there are fierce and constant economic battles between EEC members seeking to promote their own narrow national interests".[33]

The experience of cooperation during the Cold War also left a strong mark on perceptions of the later European Union and burdened Indian policy with a baggage of suspicion and distrust. This had to impact future relations with the EU in several ways, including:

1 the treatment of the EU almost exclusively as an economic partner;
2 the perception of the Common Market as an instrument for the protection of the economic interests of European countries;
3 prioritization of the bilateral relations with the Member States over that with the Community institutions;
4 discouragement of European administration and its slowness in decision-making;
5 fear of an inward looking EU with no interest in developing countries;
6 an assessment of the EU as a junior partner to the US and part of a system of Western world domination.

1.2 Redefinition of India's foreign policy goals after 1991

The end of the Cold War marks an important caesura in the history of India and its foreign policy, including towards the European Union. The major consequences include:

1 A change in India's international strategy (objectives, directions, partners)
2 A change in the nature of India's foreign policy
3 The revival and strengthening of the country's major power aspirations.

1.2.1 The significance of the end of the Cold War for India's international strategy

In India, in the early 1990s, the end of the Cold War was assessed differently than in European countries. While, in Europe, the defeat of the USSR in the global competition with the US was welcomed with relief and joy as it brought an end to the division of the continent and the full independence of the states in Central Europe, in India it was a "traumatic" event assessed unfavourably for many reasons.[34] As a country close to the "bloc of communist states", India found itself in a sense in the camp of Cold War losers. The collapse of the USSR meant not only the loss of a major political ally in global institutions and an important economic and security partner, but also the failure of a particular economic model and the discrediting of socialism as an ideology. As Stephen Cohen has noted, "A generation ago India placed its chips on the Soviet Union, economic autarky and military might. It lost all three bets".[35] This gave rise to the need for new alliances and a change in the existing model of economic development.

With the end of bipolarity, India's non-aligned policy and the entire Non-Aligned Movement, which had hitherto been a key reference point in India's international strategy, was also losing relevance. This view was particularly articulated by politicians of the opposition Bharatiya Janata Party (BJP). In their election programme in 1991, they observed that US and USSR are no longer enemies, but partners with important global ramifications: "In the post-cold war period, neither the US needs the third world countries to contain communism nor does the USSR has any use now for its 'natural allies' in the developing world. As a result, non-alignment movement which was created against the backdrop of a bipolar world, has lost its relevance".[36]

The Western countries, with whom India had not always had the best relations in the past, gained predominance. A change in the international environment meant that "the West climbed much higher on the list of Indian foreign policy priorities", and indeed, India in the 1990s "turned towards the West" in search of "new markets, joint venture opportunities, sources of investment and advanced technology".[37] Some diplomats indicated that a change in international strategy should also include closer relations with the EU.[38]

From an Indian perspective, the consolidation of the US as the sole superpower – reaffirmed in the first Gulf War in 1991 – was not beneficial. India's traditional criticism of the imperial West and distrust of the US, as well as US reservations about India's nuclear programme, could not portend easy cooperation. The birth of the unipolar world, the Pax Americana, or the "unipolar moment"[39] meant that India's international position no longer depended on two powers, but on one – the one with which India had a troubled relationship. Similarly, it would mean more leverage of the US over its economic reforms and ensuring rapid economic growth. Much easier and more promising seemed to be the relationship with Europe in this context.

The sudden end of the Cold War found India unprepared for the changes this brought about.[40] The old foreign policy doctrine shaped by Prime Minister Nehru had become obsolete and India did not have a new strategy. Instead, the foreign policy-making elites had a problem in proposing India's role and place in the changed world. An analysis of the debates of MPs in the Indian Parliament in the early 1990s reveals a high level of uncertainty and unease about the basic tenets of India's international policy – the usefulness and role of the Non-Aligned Movement, the role of the UN and its reform, the relationship with the USSR, the emergence of a "unipolar world dominated by the West" where "there is a threat of the US dictating to the whole world what to do".[41]

Prime Minister N. Rao admitted in Parliament in September 1991 that "the events of recent years, even months, have been so rapid, so difficult to explain, that they have astonished the world" and that India is seeking a "new foreign policy framework", appealing to MPs of all parties in Parliament for unity in the search for a "consensus on India's new role in the future".[42]

Similarly, the Indian Ministry of External Affairs assessed in early 1992 that "the world stage has experienced dynamic changes [...] with far-reaching consequences for Indian foreign policy".[43] One of the "most serious developments" was considered to be "the disintegration of the structures of the Soviet Union and the emergence of the Commonwealth of Independent States". Diplomats noted that "the improvement in relations between the United States and the former USSR, the end of the Cold War and new diplomatic initiatives have made it possible to resolve several key problems" but added that "the reduction and elimination of tensions between East and West [...] have not solved the fundamental development problems faced by most developing countries".[44] A year later, the MEA indicated that "events in the countries of Eastern Europe and the former USSR will have a very significant impact on the evolution of the new international order".[45]

The sudden reorganization of the entire international system meant that foreign policy changes had to be implemented in many directions at the same time. Questions regarding the future of the Indian nuclear programme, economic policy, relations with Pakistan, relations with China and the US were still waiting to be answered. Redefining policy towards Europe was just one of many challenges, but not the most important one.

At the same time, international changes did not only mean new problems and threats for India. As one of India's most experienced diplomats, Shivshankar Menon, recalls, the view was popular among younger officials and political leaders that "the end of the bipolar world in 1989 liberated Indian foreign policy, creating more room for manoeuvre", although "senior diplomats perceived the changes as a threat to the established and comfortable ways of dealing with the world".[46] This "greater space" brought about by the end of the Cold War meant, according to Menon, "that we no longer had to choose between sides or make decisions with the inevitable antagonisms between powers in mind. From now on, it was possible for India to seek good and constructive relations with all the major powers". A similar, more optimistic interpretation was put forward by opposition BJP politicians, emphasizing that this "new situation is both a challenge and an opportunity, bringing new possibilities for increasing India's role in international relations".[47]

In these unprecedented circumstances, Indian diplomacy was quick to set new foreign policy objectives that remain relevant today. These included three main goals:

1 To strengthen the external and internal security of the country
2 To create favourable conditions for economic development
3 To enhance India's role in the international system

Already in 1992, the Indian Ministry of External Affairs (MEA) identified three main foreign policy objectives: (1) maintaining India's territorial integrity; (2) guaranteeing geopolitical security by creating a lasting environment of peace and stability in the region; and (3) building a framework for the economic prosperity of the population by promoting a healthy external economic environment.[48] A 1993 MEA report defined three similar main objectives of Indian policy: (1) preservation of India's identity as a pluralistic, democratic, and secular state; (2) territorial integrity; and (3) the welfare of our citizens.[49]

Ensuring external and internal security and improving the conditions for economic development have become permanent objectives of Indian foreign policy shared by all major political forces over the decades. For example, the Deputy Minister of Foreign Affairs in 2007 defined the three key objectives of Indian foreign policy as follows: "Firstly, ensuring a peaceful neighbourhood; secondly, relations with major powers; thirdly, focusing on the challenges of the future – i.e. food security, water, energy and the environment".[50]

In practice, this meant that improving security and stabilizing the situation in South Asia were of key importance for India. Therefore, in the 1990s, India emphasized improving cooperation with its neighbours in SAARC (known as the Gujral Doctrine – the then foreign minister) and launched the so-called Look East Policy in 1992, aimed at intensifying contacts with Southeast Asian countries or engaged in normalization process with China. Only later did relations with other partners, especially with superpowers, gain in importance, particularly in the context of supporting India's economic development.

The new international environment meant that India had to try to improve relations and get closer to its former rivals, the US and China, while maintaining close relations with Russia and its European partners. Breaking free from ideological constraints also meant establishing diplomatic relations with Israel in January 1992, while maintaining traditional support for the "Palestinian cause" and good relations with Iran. The end of the Cold War divisions strengthened hopes in New Delhi for a larger role in shaping international relations.

1.2.2 *India's new foreign policy*

India's foreign policy after the Cold War was characterized by several features that distinguished it from the previous period. These features include pragmatism, independence, its economization, and the stronger combination of soft and hard power tools.

Pragmatism has become the most characteristic feature and understood as the utilitarian and realistic subordination of external actions to the national interests of the state. In international politics, ideological or moral motivations have given way to expected economic and political benefits, or as Radha Kumar puts it, "normative goals have met Realpolitik".[51] This meant a greater tendency to act based on the calculation of costs and losses rather than attachment to specific values, ideologies or traditional obligations. India tried to assess the international situation soberly and choose solutions that could be of greater benefit to it. As David Mallone summarized this evolution, India changed from a "preacher to a pragmatist".[52]

The second characteristic of India's foreign policy, i.e. economization, was linked to pragmatism. This meant subordinating it to economic objectives. The creation of favourable conditions for economic development was a constant priority of diplomacy, shared regardless of changes in government. This required not only internal security and security in the immediate neighbourhood, but also an emphasis on developing economic cooperation with various partners, attracting foreign investment, soliciting new markets and ensuring that international regulations in various areas were favourable for accelerating economic development. This was a fundamental shift from the previous period, made possible only by a greater openness to economic cooperation with the world.

The third basic characteristic – independence – showed the greatest element of continuity. It derived from the policy of non-alignment, which was fundamental for India during the Cold War, but which no longer had any justification in the new conditions. However, it survived in a slightly modified form as the principle of "strategic autonomy". This meant that India still did not want to enter into formal alliances and agreements that would limit its independent foreign policy actions. Instead, it sought to establish and maintain good relations with all powers and important partners, often from opposing camps.

At the beginning of the 21st century, leading Indian researchers proposed to describe this policy as "non-alignment 2.0".[53] Increasingly, however, it began to mean a policy of *multi-alignment*,[54] i.e. a network of loose partnerships and cooperation groups with various partners, expanding opportunities for action and benefits. By not giving any of the partners excessive influence and not becoming dependent on any relationship, but "diversifying" the number of friendly "allies", India was to strengthen its "strategic autonomy". The same principle made India reluctant to sign agreements and accept legally binding obligations in any area (e.g. climate issues, non-proliferation).

Finally, the rejection of ideological constraints and a realistic approach to maximizing its international influence meant that India began to make more conscious use of both "hard" and "soft" sources of power (*soft power* and *hard power*) from the 1990s onwards. This represented a significant change in approach compared to the strategies used in previous decades, when India acted based on one of these elements. While the first Prime Minister, Jawaharlal Nehru, built the state's power position based on values, norms, and principles, his successors, with Indira Gandhi at the forefront, adopted a more realistic approach based on "hard power". However, after the Cold War, there was a growing awareness of other, non-material indicators of state power and tools of influence, referred to as *soft power*.[55] India, too, decided to make better use of its important assets in this dimension, such as its attractive culture, democratic values, and growing diaspora. Unlike in the past, both components – soft and hard – were to be developed in parallel and used to achieve foreign policy objectives in a "smart power" approach.[56] In other words, after the Cold War, India began to combine its former idealism, subsequent realism, and current pragmatism into a single coherent strategy.

1.2.3 India's great power aspirations

An important consequence of the international changes after 1991 was the revival of India's hopes and aspirations to realize its strategic goal of becoming a major power.[57] This has been a constant feature of Indian policy since independence, shared by all the country's leaders from Jawaharlal Nehru to Narendra Modi.[58] However, it was the end of the Cold War that created a unique opportunity for the old bipolar order to be replaced by a multipolar system in which India would play a central role. However, seizing this opportunity required a strengthening of resources and more active policies towards other powers.

India's aspirations stem from three Ps – Power, Prestige, and Predisposition. India's primary objective is to gain power in international structures in order to influence the creation of principles, norms, and rules of international cooperation, the shaping of institutions, and the international order in general. This was to ensure that the system would be fairer, i.e. that it would take greater account of its interests, but also that it would take a broader view of the Global South (developing) countries. Indian politicians recognized the importance of international institutions and their impact on the position, capabilities and relations between countries. In Indian political thought, India had been a "rules-taker" for too long and had to adapt to rules created by others.[59] This time, it wanted to became more of a "rules-shaper" and key decision maker, rather than a "rule breaker".[60] Only an international order in which India has a real influence would guarantee the creation of appropriate conditions for its security and development.

India's specific position in the international system after the Cold War suffered from something referred to by researchers as a "status inconsistency", i.e. the discrepancy between how a given country itself perceives its position and strength, and the importance and role assigned to it by external partners and the international order.[61] India's growing international role after the Cold War and its increasing material resources (economic, military) have boosted India's aspirations and efforts to gain recognition for its increased influence in global institutions. India did not want to dramatically change the current international order, but instead tried to realize its superpower ambitions within it.[62] However, the international system's unwillingness to accommodate India's aspirations meant that India turned to smaller (plurilateral) groupings such as BRICS, BASIC, IBSA, and G-20 to realize its ambitions and interests, including the pursuit of reform of existing international institutions.[63]

The Drivers of India's Post-Cold War Policy towards the EU 27

The second reason for India's aspirations to be a global power is Prestige, i.e., symbolic recognition of its status as a major power. According to T.V. Paul, this is no less an objective of national policy than ensuring security and prosperity.[64] Rohan Mukherjee proves that all emerging powers in history "were sensitive to their status in relation to existing powers" and even if they lacked military resources, they "valued their symbolic equality with the powers".[65] Hence, India (like other emerging powers before it) is striving to join certain exclusive clubs (e.g. the UN Security Council) in order to become "symbolically equal to the established powers", even if this means potential losses in material terms. It demands equal and fair treatment and equitable conditions of cooperation.

The third source of major power ambitions is India's special Predisposition, i.e. the belief that is has all the necessary qualities of a that special role. The enormous demographic and territorial potential, economic and military power, historical heritage, wealth of civilization, and promoted values mean that achieving major power status is no longer perceived as a privilege that someone can bestow on India, but as something it is entitled to. It is something that India naturally deserves, but which it has been unjustly deprived of. That is why in many international negotiations Indian statements express the belief in a "return to their rightful place".[66] All the more frustration is caused by India's exclusion from key international decision-making bodies (such as the UN Security Council) and the difficulties they face in trying to gain greater influence over global governance.

In India's worldview, great power aspirations do not stem from a desire for hegemony or global domination. On the contrary, the excessive power of one state over the international system was seen as a particular threat. The preferred worldview of Indian leaders is an order that is "inclusive, non-hegemonic (this also applies to China) and multipolar (i.e. with many poles of power)".[67] This is based on the belief that "multipolarity is good", because, as European experience suggests, "multipolar systems are generally more stable than systems dominated by one or two superpowers".[68] Promoting multipolarity would therefore reduce uncertainty in international relations and make the world a more just and peaceful place.

This preference for a multipolar system implied opposition and rejection of attempts to perpetuate a unipolar order with the hegemonic position of the US after the Cold War. Prime Minister Rao explained in September 1991 that his recent visit to Germany had made him realize that we did not live "in a unipolar world in all dimensions. While the world is unipolar in the military sense, it is multipolar and multicentric in the economic sense".[69] He pointed to many such centres, and while he acknowledged that India was not one of them, it was too important to be ignored by any other economic power.

Opposition to the unipolarity is therefore one area of possible cooperation with the European Union, as another potential major power. Although Indian experts give different numbers of centres of international order, they usually reserve one place to Europe in the broad sense (but not necessarily the

European Union). Hence, the establishment of a multipolar system, where India would occupy a central position, is closely related to the situation in Europe and the EU's willingness to take the place of an independent pole. The construction of such an order has become an important rationale for cooperation with the EU after the Cold War.

Great power ambitions were most openly articulated whenever the nationalist Bharatiya Janata Party (BJP) came to power. For instance, the party's 1998 election manifesto recognized the new opportunities that had arisen after the end of the Cold War, but also noted the "continuation of bad habits":

> We see a renewed tendency by some big powers to dominate and to impose conditionalities to advance their political and economic interest even if it is detrimental to others. There are also perceived notions of civilizational conflicts as also spurts in conflicts. This demands that India's national interest must be protected and pursued more vigorously. Our diplomacy must, therefore, be proactive rather than being merely reactive without sacrificing the values of peace, equality and cooperation. In the recent past we have seen a tendency to bend under pressure. This arises as much out of ignorance of our rightful place and role in world affairs as also from a loss of national self-confidence and resolve. **A nation as large and capable as ourselves must make its impact felt on the world arena.** A BJP Government will demand a premier position for the country in all global fora.[70]

As a result, BJP politicians have announced, among other things, opposition to attempts to "impose a hegemonic non-proliferation regime", rejection of "all attempts at political and economic hegemony", "ensuring that India's role and position in the world correspond to its size and capabilities", "intensive efforts to obtain a permanent seat on the UN Security Council, or the redirection of Indian diplomacy to serve the country's commercial and economic interests". On economic matters, the manifesto promised to make India an "economic global power" based on "economic nationalism" (*swadeshi*). The policy, referred to as "*India first*", was to mean, among other things, limiting the liberalization of the economy, allowing foreign investment only in selected sectors, maintaining a greater role of the state in the economy and a selective approach to the principles of international trade. One of the goals set was to "become a reliable partner in the development process of Asia and to develop relations on an equal footing with the world's major economic powers – the US, the EU and Japan – over the next five years".

1.3 Pro-liberal economic reforms

The end of the Cold War not only forced India to rethink its international strategy, but also its economic policy. The 1991 decision to initiate pro-market economic reforms was fundamental to India's policy towards the EU. This

"Copernican revolution in Indian economic policy" opened India up to foreign capital, investment, and trade to an unprecedented degree.[71] It brought the economic systems of India and the EU closer together and removed regulatory, administrative, and political obstacles to closer cooperation in many sectors.

As long as India pursued a socialist, centrally planned economy based on the idea of *swadeshi*, or self-sufficiency, cooperation with the free-market economies of Europe was not a high priority. India, which had been growing at a *Hindu rate of growth* of a few percent per year until the end of the Cold War, remained a poor and economically underdeveloped country. The country was also increasingly lagging behind the other "Asian tigers" and even China, which had attracted the interest of capitalist countries. India had always seemed to be a difficult and unattractive partner. With limited imports and a chronic balance of payments problem, it had a limited capacity to absorb European products. Nevertheless, it had a constant trade deficit with the EU and most of its previous policy towards Europe had focused on gaining greater access to the Community market. Now, opportunities for dynamic development of economic cooperation were opening up.

1.3.1 Reasons for the economic reforms

The end of the Cold War created an excellent opportunity for far-reaching economic reforms. This decision was influenced by a number of economic structural problems that had been building up over the years and had contributed to a serious crisis.[72] The immediate reason for the start of the economic transformation in 1991 was the balance of payments crisis, which threatened the country with bankruptcy. Raising over the years fiscal deficit, current account deficit, growing public debt and foreign debt led to situation of shrinking foreign exchange reserves, which by June 1991 were enough to cover the value of imports for two to three weeks.[73] India was threatened with insolvency and economic collapse.

In addition to the structural weaknesses of the Indian economy, a number of geopolitical factors influenced the decision to change the economic model. Firstly, the collapse of the communist bloc and the imminent disintegration of the USSR limited the possibilities of trading on favourable terms based on the conversion of the transferable rouble and rupee. In a symbolic sense, the defeat of the USSR and the socialist states in the global confrontation with the capitalist democracies called into question the economic model adopted by India.

Secondly, the first Gulf War in 1991 led to a significant increase in the price of oil, a commodity of which at least 70% in India is imported. At the same time, around 100,000 Indian workers were evacuated from Iraq, whose remittances were an important source of foreign currency for India. The reduction in the inflow of foreign exchange, combined with the higher purchase costs of imported oil, accelerated the balance of payments crisis.

Thirdly, the economic changes taking place in Asia played an increasingly important role. The Indian elite became increasingly aware that their economic model was distancing India economically from their Asian partners who had adopted capitalism. While India's economy was the largest in Asia in the early 1950s, accounting for 22.4% of the continent's GDP, this share had fallen to 12.1% by 1980. Compared to the Asian tigers and China, India seemed like a "sleeping elephant".[74] While India's share of the global economy was a modest 4.2% in 1950, it fell to 3.1% in 1973.[75] Similarly, its share of global trade shrank from 2.5% in 1950 to 0.55% in 1980, before rising slightly to 0.6% in 1990.[76] It became increasingly clear that the Indian model of socialism could not compete with either capitalist countries or socialist China. The end of the Cold War, the spread of the free market and globalization in many developing countries showed that there was not really any other alternative.

1.3.2 Cautious liberalization of the economy

In mid-1991, India made the historic decision to change its economic development model and open up to international trade and join globalisation. The new Prime Minister, Narasimha Rao, who had just taken over the reins of the minority government of the Indian National Congress after the May 1991 elections, decided to ask the International Monetary Fund for help. In response, he received a loan of $2.2 billion, but at the cost of meeting a number of conditions, including opening up the economy and adopting a package of reforms. As P. Chidambaram, the Indian Deputy Minister of Trade, justified India's new trade policy in the summer of 1991: "The world economy is changing rapidly and most countries, including developing countries and Eastern European countries, are preparing for the challenges of competing in an increasingly integrated, highly globalised world market. India cannot afford to ignore these changes. India can grow faster only as part of the global economy and not in isolation".[77]

In July 1991, the government presented a three-year plan for structural changes – the so-called New Economic Policy – covering not only fiscal policy, but also monetary, industrial, and agricultural policy. The aim of the "stabilisation package" was to improve the competitiveness, efficiency and productivity of the Indian economy. The changes were presented as "modifying" the current system, which had lost its "vitality", and as measures leading to the recovery of macroeconomic stability and credibility.[78] The broad programme of action also included the liberalization of the visa and trade regimes, further changes in industrial policy, gradual privatization, the introduction of partial rupee convertibility, facilitation of capital flows and the admission of private entities in the banking sector. The government tried to reduce the budget deficit by rationalizing public spending, while at the same time reducing taxes in accordance with the recommendations of international institutions.

Some profitable companies were earmarked for privatization, and a public-private partnership model was introduced. Government control was reduced, and companies were granted greater autonomy. In the financial sector, credit instalments were deregulated, access to credit was facilitated, and the development of state and private banks was encouraged. The capital market was liberalized, and in 1993, the Stock Exchange in Mumbai, the economic capital of the country, began operating. The rupee was allowed to devalue, initially by 20%, and finally, in March 1992, full convertibility of the national currency was introduced. Further steps were taken to reduce state spending on subsidies for agriculture, food, and fuel.

At the same time, it should be emphasized that India's opening to the world was not complete and unconditional. India was not a "testing ground" for the Washington Consensus and, unlike the countries of Latin America or Central Europe at the time, it did not introduce drastic reforms, sometimes referred to as "shock therapy".[79] India also did not adopt the export-based economic development model popular in many Asian countries. Inclusion in global trade progressed slowly and the influx of foreign investment remained much lower than in China, for example. Domestic consumption and a growing middle class became the driving force of the Indian economy. Indian growth depended more on the export of services than on the export of goods. This led some economists to talk about the "Bombay Consensus", a unique Indian development model between the Washington Consensus and the Chinese model.[80]

In India, large state-owned companies and thriving private corporations coexisted and thrived. According to Christof Jafferflot, the essence of the reforms of the 1990s was to dismantle the system of regulations and licences (the so-called License Raj) that had previously hampered the development of private enterprise.[81] This allowed the natural energy of the Indians to be unleashed and their love of business to be exploited. In the following years, this had a particular impact on the development of the service sector, where the role of the state was the smallest and where the activity of private capital had the greatest scope for action.

1.3.3 Effects of economic reforms

The extensive reforms introduced since 1991 have quickly stabilized public finances, accelerated economic growth and improved foreign confidence in India. By 1993, the deficit had been reduced to 4.8% of GDP (from 7% in 1991) and inflation had been cut from almost 14% in 1991 to 4% in 2000. Foreign exchange reserves, which stood at $5.8 billion at the end of March 1991, rose steadily to $25.2 billion in March 1995 and $38 billion in March 2000.[82] Economic growth rebounded from a 1979 low of 1% in 1991 to 5.5% in 1992 and 7.6% in 1995, to reach a record 8.8% in 1999.[83] Overall, the Indian economy grew at an average annual rate of 5.6% of GDP in the decade from 1991 to 2000, which was significantly better than the average for the global economy

Market-oriented reforms, a huge domestic market, and a large labour supply have increased foreign investors' interest in India. In the following years, foreign investment began to flow into the country, although at a much lower level than in the case of China. While only $73 million in investments were recorded in 1991, this figure rose to $253 million a year later and $974 million in 1994. From that year on, investments began to grow faster, reaching $3.6 billion in 1996.[84] In the following years, they decreased slightly (due to the crisis in Asia and sanctions against India), but at the end of the decade, they started to grow again. Nevertheless, even in the best year, they accounted for only about 10% of investments in China during that time.

Opening up to globalization and international trade caused a dynamic development of the exchange of goods and services in India, not only increasing its value, but also broadening the commodity and geographical structure. After 1993, exports picked up considerably, with an annual growth rate of 20% between 1993 and 1996. Overall, in the last decade of the 20th century, India's exports increased from 17.7 billion dollars in 1991 to 42.4 billion dollars in year 2000, while imports jumped from 20.5 billion dollars to 51.5 billion dollars, creating a deficit of almost 10 billion dollars deficit. (see Chart 1.1.)[85] During this time, India's share of global goods imports increased slightly from 0.56% to 0.77%, and in the case of exports – from 0.5% to 0.65%.

Although initially imports did not grow as dynamically as exports, which improved the trade balance, in the following years the negative trend was

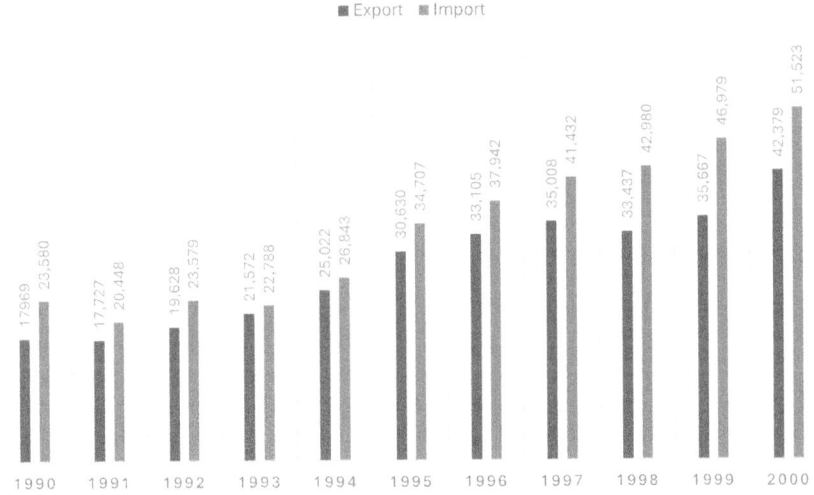

Chart 1.1 Export and import of goods from India in 1990–2000 (current prices, USD millions)

Source: UNCTAD. International Trade Statistics. Author's compilation. https://unctad.org/statistics Accessed 20.03.2021.

confirmed and the negative trade balance reached $106 billion in 2018 (i.e. 3.2% of GDP). However, this was less of a problem than during the Cold War, as these deficits were offset by an inflow of foreign currency through the growing value of private remittances from emigrants, investments, or development aid, as well as a positive balance in trade in services.

All in all, between 1990 and 2014, India's imports increased almost 20-fold, while exports increased 18-fold. By comparison, global trade in goods increased only fivefold over the same period.

However, trade in services has become a hallmark of India since the 1990s. Service exports more than tripled between 1991 and 2000 from just under $5 billion to $16.7 billion, while service imports increased from just under $6 billion to $19.1 billion.[86] India's share of global service exports increased from 0.6% to 1.1%, and the change for imports was from 0.6% to 1.3%.

The liberalization of the economy contributed to the realization of India's fundamental strategic goals. It was possible to accelerate economic growth and improve the socio-economic conditions of the population. In the following decades, tens of millions of Indians were lifted out of poverty. The poverty rate (calculated by World Bank at 3 USD a day in PPP terms), which in 1993 affected almost half of the country's population (47.5%, i.e. approx. 400 million people), fell to 27% in 2011 and below 5% in 2022.[87] The overall situation in India improved in terms of socio-economic development indicators (Human Development Index), as well as the state of infrastructure and access to basic services (electricity, clean water, etc.). The size of the middle class, and therefore the potential consumer base, increased. Last but not least, the attractiveness of the Indian economy improved, increasing India's international prestige and importance.

Since the end of the 1990s, India has been rapidly catching up with the global economy, especially with OECD countries and other emerging markets in Asia. Between 1991 and 2012, the Indian economy grew on average two to three times faster than the rest of the world. Among the major economies, only China grew faster than India, continuing to increase its lead over its neighbour and regional rival. However, what is important from India's point of view is that its international position in relation to other major economies has improved. While at the end of the Cold War it was the 15th largest economy in the world, by 2010 it was already the 7th largest. Taking purchasing power parity (PPP) into account, India has improved its position from 5th to 3rd, behind only the US and China. Similarly, India's share of global GDP increased from 1.22% in 1991 to 1.42% in 2000 and 2.65% in 2010. This gave Indian leaders an increasingly strong argument in realizing their superpower ambitions.

As a result, the liberalization of the economy combined with changes in the international order also forced natural changes in India's foreign policy. Other countries from the Non-Aligned Movement or former partners from the communist bloc, which themselves felt capital shortages, could not be a key source of investment and technology. In a capitalist economy, the richest countries, especially those in Western Europe and the US, had to be natural choice for India. There, India could naturally also look for receptive markets and sources of investment. This is where many ordinary Indians dreamt of emigrating to and living in. The West, including the EU, also became a point of reference and a natural economic partner for many in India.

1.4 India's perception of the European Union

Another element that determined the attitude of the Indian authorities and society towards the European Union was knowledge, perception and emotional attitude. As indicated above, this attitude was shaped by a fairly long relationship with the EEC and an even longer colonial heritage. The way in which the EU was evaluated as a partner was also influenced by mutual connections, changes in Europe itself and investments in relationships.

At the beginning of this period, just after the Cold War, the European Union was an extremely unknown and misunderstood partner in Indian society and was rarely present in Indian media or public debate. For the indocentric Indian media, Europe remained a distant and unattractive topic, which translated into its low visibility and significance in India in the following decades.[88] Research conducted in the first decade of the 21st century on the perception of the EU in India indicated a "serious information deficit".[89] When the media did take an interest in European affairs, they focused primarily on the larger countries, and only in the second step would pay any attention to the supranational dimension of the EU. Perceptions in India were further distorted by the fact that events in Europe reached Indian audiences mostly through the British, and therefore more Eurosceptic, lens.[90] In addition, one should be aware that during the Cold War, some Indian observers viewed Europe through the prism of Soviet propaganda. Only after 1991 was it possible for the perception of European affairs to free itself from British and Russian influences.[91] Despite this, Indians generally did not distinguish between the EU and Europe, as for them the Union "only expressed the collective identity of Europe" and did not have its own separate identity.[92]

For those Indians who were aware of the European Union, it was perceived primarily as a regional organization and economic bloc. It was not a political actor, nor a security partner nor even a normative power. A number of studies and analyses over the years have shown that despite the intensification and broadening of the scope of cooperation on political issues in the 1990s, the EU appeared only in discussions on economic and trade cooperation, development aid, and technology.[93] An analysis of the EU's visibility in the Indian press in 2010 confirmed that information on this subject "is modest" and that the Union, if it appears at all, is rather superficial, being mentioned most often as an "economic actor", which shows that this aspect of the relationship is "the strongest and most visible".[94]

Much less attention and recognition was given to the EU as an actor in the fields of security, defence, and foreign policy. Shreya Pandey pointed out that Indian readers' c of the EU's global political role "borders on ignorance and ambiguity", which is due to the fact that "the Indian press refuses to recognise the EU as a relevant actor in political affairs".[95] Although the Indian media's interest in the EU increased with the intensification of contacts since the first summit in Lisbon in 2000, especially on the occasion of subsequent summits, changes in perception were slow.

Even after the establishment of the strategic partnership in 2004, the image of the EU changed little. As a 2006 survey of the Indian press shows, the EU was "a topic of little importance in the Indian social, political and cultural debate".[96] The economic crisis in Europe after 2008 and the stalemate in bilateral relations since 2012 have further reduced interest in the EU and given the news a negative tone.[97] The Indian media gave EU internal affairs "the lowest and the furthest priority" because, as Jain and Pandey pointed out in 2010 – the topic is "boring as a Brussels landscape" and the EU is "simply not sexy enough to arouse emotions and interest of Indian newspapers".[98] A British researcher analysing the attitude of Indian elites pointed out that the EU "ranks at the bottom of India's list of partners" in a multipolar world. The changes introduced after the adoption of the Maastricht Treaty also did little to change the perception of the Union. Other studies of the Indian media in 2015 confirmed that the EU appeared least frequently among the regional powers surveyed, and also less frequently than the member states.[99]

An even more critical and dismissive attitude towards the EU prevailed in academic and expert discourse.[100] The Community was often seen in a negative light – as a tool for protecting the market of European countries, as part of the selfish West, which pursues a policy of "exploitation of developing countries" and perpetuates the "current unjust world order based on inequality".[101] Its approach to the promotion of democracy, human rights and international trade was criticized, pointing to double standards and hypocrisy in foreign policy and interference in the internal affairs of other countries.[102] The EU's migration and asylum policy in the 1990s was criticized for attempting to strengthen "Fortress Europe" out of fear of immigrants.[103]

At the same time, the Union's political role and international significance were underestimated. Indian experts considered the Union to be a "weak, divided and non-influential" international actor with limited foreign policy and security competencies.[104] The EU's limited power in matters relevant to India (e.g. the fight against terrorism, arms sales) meant that India preferred to pursue its interests at a bilateral level, directly with individual EU member states.[105] A series of crises, from the 2008 financial crisis to the UK referendum on leaving the EU, reinforced the image of a weak and internally divided Union.[106]

In addition, the complex and lengthy decision-making mechanisms in the EU were often a source of frustration and disappointment for Indian partners. As early as the 1970s, when the EU still only consisted of six member states, the pace of negotiations on a trade agreement irritated Indian diplomats, who complained that the EEC was so slow in discussions with India that it "would put a snail to shame".[107] The situation became even more complicated with the expansion of the number of countries in the Council to 15, 25, or 28.

Very pragmatically, Indian diplomats and politicians therefore preferred to bypass the EU level and settle the most important issues first with the largest and most important countries in the Union, namely the UK, Germany, and France. It was at this level that concrete decisions on European investment, military cooperation, and security could be made. Moreover, European leaders themselves encouraged their Indian partners to bypass the EU level or to leave the most delicate and sensitive issues to the EU, such as talks on human rights and democracy. At the same time, Indian observers have raised the charge of misperception of India in Europe, where the stereotype of exotic India still persists and where there is an "unfair impatience" in assessing the slow pace of Indian economic reforms, which does not take into account the enormous development challenges it faces.[108]

Despite the low level of knowledge about the EU, it should be noted that a more positive attitude towards the EU prevailed among the Indian society. In a public opinion survey in India in 2007, the majority of respondents viewed EU-India relations positively – 58% believed they were improving and 33% believed they were stable.[109] However, the EU was not mentioned as a priority partner for India, and the most important areas in which the EU has an impact on India were economic issues (trade, business, finance), CO_2 emissions, human rights and democracy, and development aid.[110]

Another study from 2015 showed that respondents had rarely heard of the EU and knew it the least among the countries included in the study (US, China, Japan, Russia, Brazil), while the majority (2/3) had a positive attitude towards the Union (although less than in the case of the US and Japan).[111] Interestingly, the survey showed that few Indians believed in the EU's role in strengthening world peace and security, and fewer people wanted EU leadership in the world than India, the US, Russia, or Japan. Another survey from the turn of 2013 and 2014 showed that only 34% of Indians had a positive perception of the EU, much less than the US (56%), Japan (49%), Russia (45%), and even China (35%).[112]

A major problem was the lack of knowledge about the EU. The European Union was not researched, studied, or taught at Indian universities and think tanks until the end of the 20th century. Little more attention was paid to Europe, which was traditionally considered the least important region, far behind India's Asian neighbours, Africa, the US, and the USSR. European studies in India began in 1964 as a research programme (awarding doctoral degrees) within the Department of Politics and International Organisations at the Indian School of International Studies (ISIS) in Delhi.[113] When ISIS merged with Jawaharlal Nehru University in 1970 (School of International Studies JNU), a Master's and MPhil programme on European affairs was offered for the first time. The former faculty was divided into several small departments. Due to ideological restrictions during the Cold War, the Centre for Western Europe and American Studies dealt with Western Europe and

America, while the Centre of Eastern Europe and Soviet Studies dealt with Eastern Europe and the Soviet Union.

This situation persisted until the end of the 20th century, when the Centre for Western European and American Studies at JNU in Delhi was the only place in a country of 900 million people where European affairs were studied. The focus was on the largest European countries, and the European Union was treated as a secondary entity. This was despite the fact that the EU was India's largest trading and investment partner as an economic organization. When the Indian government allocated financial support in 1996 for the creation of 23 regional studies departments in 19 public universities, JNU remained the only one of 150 universities to offer European studies.[114] As such, it was the main place for debates on European topics, organizing lectures and conferences, and publishing the only publications in India on the European Union.

The EU was actually the organization to change this situation as part of its rapprochement with India after the Cold War. In the 1990s, it donated six million euros to set up four European studies centres in four parts of India – in Kolkata, Goa, Bangalore, and Delhi.[115] The centres were to benefit from visits by European lecturers. In the following decades, the promotion of academic and expert cooperation became an important area of the Indo-EU partnership. The EU financed the creation of Jean Monnet Chairs in European studies at Indian universities and the creation of consortia of Indian and European universities.

A similar lack of interest and expertise in European affairs was long exhibited by Indian think tanks, which play an important role in the public debate on foreign affairs. Until the end of the 20th century, none of them had not only a programme but even a single position on European affairs. For example, at the Institute of Defence Studies and Analysis (IDSA), the main centre affiliated with the Ministry of Defence, European issues were marginally covered as part of the Eurasian Programme, where most experts dealt with Russia and the post-Soviet area. It was not until 2023 that the first analyst for Europe was hired, Dr Swasti Rao. In the prestigious Indian Council of World Affairs, which is affiliated with the Ministry of External Affairs, it was not until the beginning of the second decade of the 21st century that the first position of analyst for Europe was created (Dr Dinoj Upadhayay). Other private institutions have also recently begun to create separate positions for Europe/the EU. The Observer Research Foundation played a special role here, as it began to devote a lot of space to Europe in its activities and maintained analytical positions on the EU.

The efforts and changes of recent years are making up for the huge backlog and neglect in learning about and understanding the European Union. Hence, researchers have been pointing out for years that one of the fundamental problems in India's policy towards the EU is the mutual lack of knowledge and understanding of the partners.[116] Little has changed since the 1970s when the authors of the Smallman Report came to similar conclusions, already recommending the intensification of promotional activities at that time.

The EU's presence and image in the Indian media and public debate has only started to change more noticeably in the last decade. This has been linked to the intensification of the political dialogue after 2016 and a more regular exchange of visits, including more frequent trips by Indian representatives to Europe. European topics appeared more frequently in the Indian media and analytical studies (also due to the crises afflicting Europe), occupied more space at conferences on international affairs (e.g. Raisina Dialogue), additional chairs of European studies began to appear at universities, and think tanks had more experts specializing in Europe. A significant change in the perception of the EU, from an exclusively economic actor to a "greater political role", is shown by a study of the media coverage of the 13th EU-India Summit in October 2017.[117] The fact that the summit took place after a long break and under changed international circumstances led the Indian media to give the EU more credit by showing "that the strategic partnership is becoming more important than ever" and is moving beyond traditional trade issues "towards strategic matters".[118] This impression was further reinforced in the following years, especially on the occasion of the 2020 and 2021 summits, when a number of Indian authors pointed out the "strategic convergence" of both sides with regard to China, the fight against the COVID-19 pandemic or cooperation in the Indo-Pacific.

There has been an interesting shift in interest and attitudes towards the EU among Indian experts, journalists, and the general public. The EU has become a better known and appreciated partner for India. From being seen solely in terms of economic cooperation, it is more often seen as a serious political and strategic partner. Though still a little-known entity, it enjoys growing interest and appreciation. This shift reflects and follows changes in the official relationship between India and the EU.

1.5 Institutional constraints of stronger engagement with the EU

Two additional elements conditioned India's ability to engage more closely with the EU during this period: Changes of leadership and the institutional limitations of Indian diplomacy.

Firstly, the post-Cold War period saw the beginning of a process of fragmentation of the party scene and political instability in India. The 1989 elections ended the period of dominance of the Indian National Congress (INC), which had ruled the country almost continuously since independence. By 1999, five general elections to the federal parliament had been held and eight different governments had come to power. The right-wing Bharatiya Janata Party (BJP) became the main rival of the INC. Regional parties, which not only governed the individual states independently, but also gained significant support in general Indian elections and thus influence on decisions made in Delhi, strengthened their position and importance. The transition from a one-party to a multi-party system meant that coalition governments, often comprising more than 10 or 20 parties, became a new norm.

The necessity to form such broad coalitions and to take into account the interests of diverse partners seeking to promote the interests of individual regions or social groups has made it much more difficult to pursue effective domestic and foreign policies.[119] When making decisions, the government had to take into account not only the voices of the political opposition or regional parties, but also the very active media and public opinion,[120] civil society,[121] experts,[122] corporations, and Indian business.[123] The need to take into account the voices of many internal actors was one of the factors slowing down the pace of liberal reforms and opening up the economy. This often resulted in the delay or cancellation of strategic investments and complicated the plans of foreign investors. For example, opposition from a regional party in Bengal has for years been holding back the settlement of the border dispute with Bangladesh, and the coalition parties' resistance to the nuclear deal with the US almost led to the fall of the Manmohan Singh government in 2008.

Public concerns, fuelled by opposition parties and pressure groups, limited the scope for concessions and hampered negotiations on a free trade agreement with the EU. The opposition of Indian farmers and the car and pharmaceutical manufacturers' lobby were among the key barriers to an agreement. Also, on the multilateral level, accusations of betraying the national interest hardened the Indian negotiating position in international climate and trade talks at the WTO, distancing it from the positions adopted by the European Union. Tanvi Madan shows that it was precisely the pressure from various internal interest groups and public opinion that made that Indian negotiators preferred no agreement to a difficult compromise at the WTO, leading to the failure of the Doha Round in 2008, and similar concerns and internal tensions hampered the adoption of a more flexible negotiating position at the Copenhagen Climate Summit in 2009.[124]

It was not until the BJP won the elections twice with a landslide victory in 2014 and 2019 that the central government was strengthened and was able to push through more decisive domestic reforms and foreign policy measures. The independence from the coalition partners gave Prime Minister Modi more power and enabled him to take a more active stance towards the EU. Also, his personal charisma and ambitions played a role in getting more dynamic policy towards Europe.

The second, perhaps more important challenge for India's policy towards the EU were the limitations resulting from the modest human and financial resources of the Indian diplomatic apparatus.

Immediately after the end of the Cold War, the Indian Ministry of External Affairs (MEA) had 139 Resident Missions/Posts abroad, while the total sanctioned strength of the Indian Foreign Service (IFS and IFS B) at headquarters and Indian Missions/Posts abroad was 3,409, of which less than half were career diplomats.[125] For years, pundits have pointed to the limited "software" of Indian diplomacy, especially when compared to other great powers like Russia or the US.[126] India's foreign service was far smaller than those of major Asian countries such as China and Japan, and similar in size to the small city-state of Singapore.[127] The understaffing meant that India had limited capacity to engage with its partners and deal with the ever-growing and increasingly complex issues of international cooperation.

Despite repeated calls for reform, this problem has become more acute as India's reach and ambitions have expanded over the past decades. By 2024, the MEA cadre strength at headquarters and missions abroad stood at 4,628, with one of the largest diplomatic networks in the world.[128] Today, India has diplomatic missions in 203 countries and territories and additional posts in international organizations. But while the diplomatic footprint has grown exponentially, the addition of a thousand more people to the IFS over 30 years has further stretched resources to deal effectively with a more complicated and expanded scope of international relations. And out of 4.5 thousand personnel, only about 1,000 are diplomats, suggesting a disconnect between India's foreign policy ambitions and its current diplomatic infrastructure.[129]

This general bottleneck in the Indian system has naturally had a chilling effect on its cooperation with the EU. At a basic level, this is also reflected in the form of a modest diplomatic representation in Europe, which hampers the ability to engage in a multifaceted and sustained dialogue with the EU. In 2015, Pascaline Winand noted that "the Indian embassy in Belgium, Luxembourg and the European Union, with 60 staff, is small compared to European embassies and some Asian embassies".[130] Ten years later, the situation is even worse. At the beginning of 2025, the list of Indian staff dealing with the EU and two countries in the embassy contains 30 names.[131] Requests by the author to the embassy for information on the exact number of diplomats working on the EU have not been answered, possibly reflecting the limited capacity of staff to respond to an ever-increasing number of enquiries. India's representation looks particularly bleak when compared to the presence in Brussels of other major players such as the US or China.

The situation is no better at the MEA headquarter in Delhi. At the end of 2024, there were seven officers in the MEA's Western Europe Division, dealing with 13 Western European countries (including heavyweights such as the UK, Germany, and France) plus the European Union.[132] Moreover, the MEA's internal organization had long made it difficult to work effectively with the EU, which was not seen as having the same priority as its largest member states. Confusingly, while the EU was the responsibility of the Secretary (West) together with many other Western and Eastern European countries, the UK, France, and Germany were the responsibility of the higher-ranking Foreign Secretary, together with other P5 countries.[133] This not only symbolically demonstrated the lower status of the EU to India vis-à-vis its largest members, but also created practical obstacles to access to the higher echelons of power in the Indian government. It was only under EAM S. Jaishankar in the late 2010s that some changes were introduced to elevate the EU in the structure of the Indian MEA. Today, while there is still a distinction between the UK, France, and Germany (under the portfolio of Foreign Secretary, Vikram Misri) and other European partners, including the EU (Secretary-West, Tanmaya Lal), the oversight and supervision of the entire Europe-West Division has been elevated directly under the Minister of External Affairs.[134] This small change illustrates the rising profile of the EU in Indian foreign policy and has practically facilitated contacts with the Minister to accelerate strategic dialogue.

However, the persistent understaffing of Indian diplomacy means that a limited number of officials have to deal with an ever-increasing number of issues, covering wide areas of specialization, from trade to energy, environment, human rights, culture, science, and technology, political issues, security cooperation, multilateral cooperation, as well as, more recently, AI, data computing, or space. Despite the fact that Indian diplomats are highly professional and well qualified to do their job, they simply do not have the time and resources to engage in multiple meetings, discussions and lengthy negotiations with another bureaucratic machine like the EU. This leaves even less space for Indian officials to engage with complex European institutional partners and lobby for Indian interests among key stakeholders in the European Commission, the European Parliament or the Council of the European Union (composed of Member State ministers for specific sectors), but also among non-officials such as journalists, opinion leaders, trade unions, NGOs, or business associations.

The disparity in human resources between the European and Indian sides is also reflected in other dimensions, from parliamentarians to the business community. While a Delegation for South Asia was formed in the European Parliament in the 1990s and a separate Delegation for India in the 2000s, there is still no similar parliamentary group on the EU in the Lok Sabha. As a result, while visits to India by members of the European Parliament do take place from time to time, there is much less interest in the EU from the other side. Similarly, while the EU helped establish the European Business and Technology Centre (EBTC) in Delhi in 2008, there is no dedicated representation of Indian business in Brussels. Although there was an attempt in the 1980s to establish a Community-supported India Trade Centre in Europe, this experiment was short-lived and discontinued. While Indian business organizations such as the Confederation of Indian Industries (CII) or the Federation of Indian Chambers of Commerce and Industries (FICCI) have recently been organizing more dialogues and business summits with European counterparts, they do not have a permanent presence in Brussels to lobby for their interests.

One of the ideas to overcome these structural bottlenecks in engagement with the EU has been to outsource some elements of diplomacy to think tanks. This has accelerated in recent years, with many private and public think tanks engaging in some form of dialogue with Europeans to discuss EU-India issues. A particular role has been played by the Observer Research Foundation, which has been instrumental in giving more space to European issues in public debate in India. This is best illustrated by the development of its flagship international relations conference – the Raisina Dialogue – co-organized with the MEA. While at the first Raisina Dialogue in 2016 Europe was not on the agenda at all, at the second conference in January

2017, there was only one side event on EU-India relations, funded by the EU project, with a limited presence of European diplomats and experts. In the following years, however, European guests, including European Commission President von der Leyen or the EU's top diplomat Joseph Borell and many foreign ministers of European member states, dominated Raisina's numerous sessions. Thanks to Raisina and the ORF, Europe moved from the margins to the centre of expert discussions in Indian strategic circles.

Similarly, it can be said that the growing EU-India partnership has created space for more direct interactions and forums between professionals, business people, academics, and activists from India and the EU. The widening of the pool of participants in the dialogue with the EU beyond diplomats has allowed the impact of institutional constraints in the MEA to be minimized to some extent and official relations to be enriched with new ideas and input from outside. Nevertheless, official foreign policy must have depended on the skills and extra commitment of Indian diplomats. And enhancement of Indian diplomatic software is still pending with a potential for new openings also in policy towards the EU.

Notes

1 P. Winiand, "Fearing European Unity and Yearning for Asian Cooperation: The Early Years", [in:] P. Winand, M. Vicziany, P. Datar (eds.), *The European Union and India. Rhetoric or Meaningful Partnership?*, Cheltenhem: Edward Elgar, 2015, pp. 14–40.
2 R. K. Jain, "Initial Indian Perceptions of the European Union", [in:] R. K. Jain (red.), *Changing Indian Images of the European Union. Perceptions and Misperceptions*, Singapore: Palgrave Macmillan, 2019, p. 37.
3 R. K. Jain, "European Studies in India", [in:] R. K. Jain (ed.), *India and Europe in the New Millenium*, New Delhi: Radiant Publishers, 2002, p. 125.
4 H. Venkatasubbiah, "Prospects of an Asian Union", *India Quarterly*, vol. 5, no. 3, July-September 1949, pp. 212–228; K. M. Panikkar, "Regionalism and World Security", *India Quarterly*, vol. 2, no. 2, May 1946, pp. 120–124; G. Mookerjee, "Steps Toward European Unity", *India Quarterly*, vol. 5, no. 3, July-September 1949, pp. 235–243.
5 R. K. Jain (ed.), *Changing Indian Images of the European Union. Perceptions and Misperceptions*, Singapore: Palgrave Macmillan, 2019, p. VI.
6 B. P. Adarkar, "Political Aspects of European Integration", *India Quarterly*, vol. 19, no. 2, 1963, p. 157.
7 R. K. Jain, "Initial Indian Perceptions of the European Union", [in:] R. K. Jain (red.), *Changing Indian Images of the European Union. Perceptions and Misperceptions*, Singapore: Palgrave Macmillan, 2019, p. 38.
8 B. Mukherjee, *India and EU. An Insider's View*, New Delhi: Vij Books India Pvt Ltd, 2018, p. 11.
9 Quoted in: P. Winand, M. Vicziany, P. Datar, *The European Union and India. Rhetoric or Meaningful Partnership?*, Cheltenhem: Edward Elgar, 2015, s. 14.
10 Jawaharlal Nehru, Prime Minister's Statement in Lok Sabha on Foreign Affairs, Replying to the debate on the Ministry of External Affairs' grants, the Prime Minister Shri Jawaharlal Nehru made the following statement in Lok Sabha on Foreign Affairs on May 14, 1962 [w:] *Foreign Affairs Record*, vol. VIII, no. 1, January 01, 1962, p. 234. https://mealib.nic.in/?pdf2550?000

11 R. K. Jain, "Jawaharlal Nehru and the European Economic Community", *India Quarterly*, vol. 71 no. 1, 2015, p. 11.
12 R. K. Jain, "Jawaharlal Nehru and the European Economic Community", *India Quarterly*, vol. 71 no. 1, 2015, p. 10.
13 R. K. Jain, "Initial Indian Perceptions of the European Union", [in:] R. K. Jain (red.), *Changing Indian Images of the European Union. Perceptions and Misperceptions*, Singapore: Palgrave Macmillan, 2019, p. 38.
14 Quoted in: P. Winand, M. Vicziany, P. Datar, *The European Union and India. Rhetoric or Meaningful Partnership?*, Cheltenhem: Edward Elgar, 2015, p. 51.
15 R. K. Jain "India and Britain's First Application to Join the European Community, 1961–1963", *India Quarterly*, vol. 77, no. 1, 2021, p. 60.
16 P. Winand, M. Vicziany, P. Datar, *The European Union and India. Rhetoric or Meaningful Partnership?*, Cheltenhem: Edward Elgar, 2015, p. 45.
17 R. K. Jain, "Initial Indian Perceptions of the European Union", [in:] R. K. Jain (red.), *Changing Indian Images of the European Union. Perceptions and Misperceptions*, Singapore: Palgrave Macmillan, 2019, p. 13.
18 R. K. Jain, "India and Britain's First Application to Join the European Community, 1961–1963", *India Quarterly*, vol. 77, no. 1, 2021, p. 73.
19 Quoted in: R. K. Jain, "Jawaharlal Nehru and the European Economic Community", *India Quarterly*, vol. 71 no. 1, 2015, p. 11.
20 M. Singh, "India and the European Common Market", *Journal of Common Market Studies*, vol. 1, no. 3, March 1963, p. 265.
21 M. Singh, "India and the European Common Market", *Journal of Common Market Studies*, vol. 1, no. 3, March 1963, p. 265, 271.
22 S. S. Mehta, "India's Economic Relations with the European Economic Community", *India Quarterly*, vol. 33 no. 281, 1977, pp. 284–286.
23 P. Winand, M. Vicziany, P. Datar, *The European Union and India. Rhetoric or Meaningful Partnership?*, Cheltenhem: Edward Elgar, 2015, p. 120.
24 Economic missions, participation in trade fairs and scientific-technical contacts also became more frequent. For example, as early as 1978 the Commission organized three conferences on solar energy with companies from India and the EEC.
25 P. P. Winand, M. Vicziany, P. Datar, *The European Union and India. Rhetoric or Meaningful Partnership?*, Cheltenhem: Edward Elgar, 2015, p. 137.
26 Data by D. K. S. Bora, N. K. Sah, "Indo – EC Relations: Retrospect and Prospects", *India Quarterly*, vol. 50, no. 1/2, (January–June 1994), p. 65. ECU is special currency used in the transaction in the ECC at that time.
27 B. Vivekanandan, "The European Economic Community: Unity and Solidarity a Distant Dream", *India Quarterly*, vol. 37, no. 2, 1981, p. 220.
28 B. Knall, W. Veit, "Indo-European Cooperation in an Interdependent World: An Overview and Analysis", *Internationales Asienfomm*, vol. 19, no. 3–4, 1988, pp. 295–315.
29 He was the third President of the ECC Commission to visit India in the span of 12 years, after first President W. Hellenstein's travel to Delhi in 1963 and second – Jean Rey in April 1970.
30 In 1975, Member State diplomats in Delhi first proposed the establishment of a European Commission Press and Information Office and increased promotion of EEC information. In 1977, the Commission, in cooperation with the embassies of the Member States, organized for the first time a film festival of EEC countries, Images of Europe.
31 Government of India, Ministry of External Affairs, *Annual Report 1982–1981*, New Delhi 1982.
32 D. K. S. Bora, N. K. Sah, "Indo – EC Relations: Retrospect and Prospects", *India Quarterly*, vol. 50, no. 1/2 (January–June 1994), p. 67.

33 B. Vivekanandan, "The European Economic Community: Unity and Solidarity a Distant Dream", *India Quarterly*, vol. 37, no. 2, 1981, p. 213.
34 C. R. Mohan, *Crossing the Rubicon: The Shaping of India's New Foreign Policy*, New Delhi: Viking, 2003, p. 117.
35 S. Cohen, *India: Emerging Power*, New Delhi: Oxford University Press, 2004(first edition 2001), p. 54.
36 BJP Election Manifesto 1991, Bharatiya Janata Party, New Delhi, 1991, p. 350
37 R. K. Jain, "India and the European Union: Challenges and Opportunities", [in:] R. K. Jain (ed.), *India and Europe in the New Millennium*, New Delhi: Radiant Publishers, 2000, p. 89.
38 V. K. Grover, "India – The Need for a Post Cold War Foreign Policy and the Importance of the EU", *India Quarterly*, vol. 57, no. 1, 2001, pp. 171–176.
39 Ch. Krauthamer, "The Unipolar Moment", *Foreign Affairs*, vol. 70, no. 1, 1990/1991, pp. 23–33.
40 E. Kavalski, "Venus and the Porcupine: Assessing the European Union-India Strategic Partnership", *South Asian Survey*, vol. 15, no. 1, 2008, p. 66; R. Kumar, "India as a Foreign Policy Actor – Normative Redux", *CEPS Working Document*, no. 285/February 2008, p. 5.
41 Lok Sabha Debates, vol. V, no. 49, September 18, 1991. Parliament of India, p. 116.
42 Lok Sabha Debates, vol. V, no. 49, September 18, 1991. Parliament of India, p. 133.
43 Ministry of External Affairs, Government of India, Annual Report 1991–1992. New Delhi, 1992, p. I.
44 Ministry of External Affairs, Government of India, Annual Report 1991–1992. New Delhi, 1992, p. I.
45 Ministry of External Affairs, Government of India, Annual Report 1992–1993. New Delhi, 1993, p. 60.
46 Sh. Menon, India and Asian Geopolitics: The Past, Present, Penguin, New Delhi, 2021, p. 188.
47 BJP Election Manifesto 1991, Bharatiya Janata Party, New Delhi, 1991.
48 Government of India, Ministry of External Affairs, Annual Report 1991–1992, New Delhi, 1992, p. II.
49 Government of India, Ministry of External Affairs, Annual Report 1992–1993, New Delhi, 1993, p. 1.
50 Sh. Menon, 'The Challenges Ahead for India's Foreign Policy', Speech by the Indian Foreign Secretary at the Observer Research Foundation, Ministry of External Affairs, Government of India, New Delhi 10 April 2007.
51 R. Kumar, "India as a Foreign Policy Actor – Normative Redux", *CEPS Working Document*, no. 285, 2008, p. 4.
52 D. Malone, *Does the Elephant Dance? Contemporary Indian Foreign Policy*, New Delhi: Oxford University Press, p. 47.
53 See: S. Khilnani et al., *Nonalignment 2.0: A Foreign and Strategic Policy for India in the Twenty-First Century*, New Delhi: Centre for Policy Research, 2012.
54 Ch. Jaffrelot, W. P. S. Sidhu, "From Pluralism to Multilateralism? G-20, IBSA, BRICS and BASIC", [in:] W. P. S. Sidhu, P. B. Mehta, B. Jones (eds.), *Shaping the Emerging World. India and the Multilateral Order*, Washington D.C.: Brookings Institution Press, 2013, p. 319.
55 J. S. Nye, *Soft Power: The Means to Success in World Politics*, New York: Public Affairs, 2004.
56 P. Kugiel, *India's Soft Power: New Foreign Policy Strategy*, Abingdon, New York: Routledge, 2017.
57 See B. R. Nayar, T. V. Paul, *India in the World: Searching for Major Power Status*, New Delhi: Cambridge University Press, 2004; J. Zajączkowski, *Indie w stosunkach międzynarodowych [India in International Relations]*, Warsaw: Wydawnictwo Naukowe Scholar, 2008.

58 T. V. Paul, *The Unfinished Quest, India's Search for Major Power Status from Nehru to Modi*, New York: Oxford University Press, 2024.
59 B. R. Nayar, T. V. Paul, *India in the World: Searching for Major Power Status*, New Delhi: Cambridge University Press, 2004.
60 P. S. Sidhu, P. B. Mehta, B. Jones (eds.), *Shaping the Emerging World. India and the Multilateral Order*, Washington D.C.: Brookings Institution Press, 2013.
61 D. Malone, R. Mukherjee, "Dilemmas of Sovereignty and Order: India and the UN Security Council", [in:] W. P. S. Sidhu, P. B. Mehta, B. Jones (eds.), *Shaping the Emerging World. India and the Multilateral Order*, Washington D.C.: Brookings Institution Press, 2013, pp. 170–172.
62 D. Malone, R. Mukherjee, "Dilemmas of Sovereignty and Order: India and the UN Security Council", [in:] W. P. S. Sidhu, P. B. Mehta, B. Jones (eds.), *Shaping the Emerging World. India and the Multilateral Order*, Washington D.C.: Brookings Institution Press, 2013, p. 166.
63 Ch. Jaffrelot, W. P. S. Sidhu, "From Pluralism to Multilateralism? G-20, IBSA, BRICS and BASIC", [in:] W. P. S. Sidhu, P. B. Mehta, B. Jones (eds.), *Shaping the Emerging World. India and the Multilateral Order*, Washington D.C.: Brookings Institution Press, 2013, p. 333.
64 T. V. Paul, *The Unfinished Quest, India's Search for Major Power Status from Nehru to Modi*, New York: Oxford University Press, 2024, p. 8.
65 R. Mukherjee, *Ascending Order. Rising Powers and the Politics of Status in International Institutions*, Cambridge, MA: Cambridge University Press, 2022, p. 25.
66 A. Narlikar, "Peculiar Chauvinism or Strategic Calculation? Explaining the Negotiating Strategy of a Rising India", *International Affairs*, vol. 82, no. 1, 2006, p. 59.
67 Ch. Ogden, "Great Power Aspiration and Indian Conceptions of International Society", [in:] J. Gaskarth (ed.), *China, India and the Future of International Society*, London, New Year: Rowman and Littlefield International, 2015, p. 57.
68 Sh. Menon, India and Asian Geopolitics: The Past, Present, Penguin, New Delhi, 2021, p. 366.
69 *Lok Sabha Debates*, vol. V, no. 49, 18 September 1991. Parliament of India, p. 135.
70 *BJP Election Manifesto 1998*, Bharatiya Janata Party, BJP, New Delhi 1998, p. 192.
71 S. Domżalski, *Indie w gospodarce światowej. Słoń, który pragnął latać, [India in Global Economy: An Elephant that wanted to Fly]*, Warsaw: Wydawnictwo Asian Century, 2017, p. 157.
72 G. Bywalec, *Reformy ekonomiczne i polityczne a rozwój gospodarczy Indii (1991–2012) [Economic and Political Reforms and Economic Growth in India 1991-2012]* Lodz: Wydawnictwo Uniwersytetu Łódzkiego, 2015, pp. 97–103.
73 S. Domżalski, *Indie w gospodarce światowej. Słoń, który pragnął latać [India in Global Economy: An Elephant that wanted to Fly]*, Warsaw: Wydawnictwo Asian Century, 2017, p. 163.
74 S. Bhutani, 'India – a rising superpower?', *Homo Politicus. Rocznik Politologiczny [Political Review]*, vol. 1, 2006.
75 A. Madison, *The World Economy: Historical Statistics*, Paris: Development Centre Studies, OECD Publishing, 2003, p. 263.
76 H. S. Chopra, S. K. Bhattacharya. "India-EU Interface: Changing Perspectives on Cooperation for Economic Development", *India Quarterly*, vol. 53, no. 3/4, 1997, p. 106.
77 Statement by Minister on Trade Policy, Part 2(Other than Questions and Answers), Lok Sabha Debates, Parliament of India, 13-Aug-1991, p. 499
78 Ch. Ogden, *Indian Foreign Policy: Ambition and Transition*, Cambridge: Polity Press, 2014, p. 57.
79 See N. Klein, *The Shock Doctrine. How Contemporary Capitalism Uses Natural Disasters and Social Crises*, New York: Metropolitan Books, 2007.
80 G. Das, "The India Model", *Foreign Affairs*, July/August 2006.

81 Ch. Jaffrelot, "India, and Emerging Power, but How Far?" [in:] Ch. Jaffrelot (ed.), *Emerging States. The Wellspring of a New World Order*, London: Hurst & Company, 2008, (translated from French by Cynthia Schoch), p. 78.
82 Report on Foreign Exchange Reserves, Reserve Bank of India, 06 July 2005
83 World Bank data, GDP growth (%), India, World, (20.03.2020)
84 The World Bank, Foreign direct investment, net inflows (BoP, current US$), Foreign direct investment, net outflows (BoP, current US$), (Accessed 20.12.2020).
85 UNCTADStat, Merchandise: Total trade and share, annual, United Nations Conference on Trade and Development, (20.03.2020)
86 UNCTADStat, Services (BPM5): Exports and imports of total services, value, shares and growth, annual, 1980–2013 (Discontinued)
87 World Bank Indicators, Poverty headcount ratio at $3.00 a day (2021 PPP) (% of population) – India, (Accessed 20.07.2025)
88 S. Pandey, "The Visibility and Perceptions of the EU in the Indian Print Media, 2009–2010", [in:] R. K. Jain (ed.), *Changing Indian Images of the European Union. Perception and Misperception*, Singapore: Palgrave Macmillan, 2019, pp. 79–92.
89 R. K. Jain, S. Pandey, "Public Attitudes and Images of the EU in India", [in:] R. K. Jain, *Changing Indian Images of the European Union. Perception and Misperception*, Singapore: Palgrave Macmillan, 2019, p. 106.
90 R. K. Jain, S. Pandey, "The European Union in the Eyes of India", *Asia Europe Journal*, vol. 8, no. 2, 2010, p. 207.
91 C. R. Mohan, "Indo-Pacific and Delhi's New Europolitik", [in:] Ch. Echle, J. Klien (eds.), *Panorama – Insights into Asian and European Affairs*, Singapore: Konrad-Adenauer-Stiftung, 2022, p. 76.
92 K. Lisbonne-de Vergeron, *Contemporary Indian views of Europe*, London: Royal Institute of International Affairs, 2006, p. XII.
93 R. K. Jain, S. Pandey, "The Public Attitudes and Images of the European Union in India", *India Quarterly*, vol. 68, no. 4, October–December 2012, pp. 331–343; R. K. Jain, S. Pandey, "Perceptions and Visibility of the European Union in India: A Study of the Media, Elites, and Public Opinion", [in:] J. Zajaczkowski, J. Schottli, M. Thapa (eds.), *India in the Contemporary World*, New Delhi: Routledge, 2014, pp. 385–406; K. Lisbonne-de Vergeron, *Contemporary Indian Views of Europe*, London: Royal Institute of International Affairs, 2006.
94 S. Pandey, "The Visibility and Perceptions of the EU in the Indian Print Media, 2009–2010", [in:] R. K. Jain (ed.), *Changing Indian Images of the European Union. Perception and Misperception*, Palgrave Macmillan, 2019, p. 90.
95 S. Pandey, "The Visibility and Perceptions of the EU in the Indian Print Media, 2009–2010", [in:] R. K. Jain (ed.), *Changing Indian Images of the European Union. Perception and Misperception*, Singapore: Palgrave Macmillan, 2019, p. 90.
96 L. Fioramonti, "Different Facets of a Strategic Partnership: How the EU is Viewed by Political and Business Elites, Civil Society and the Press in India", *European Foreign Affairs Review*, vol. 12, no. 3, 2007, pp. 349–362.
97 N. Chaban, O. Elgström, "The Role of the EU in an Emerging New World Order in the Eyes of the Chinese, Indian and Russian Press", *Journal of European Integration*, vol. 36, no. 2, 2014, pp. 170–188.
98 R. K. Jain, S. Pandey, "The European Union in the Eyes of India", *Asia Europe Journal*, vol. 8, no. 2, 2010, p. 207.
99 PPMI, *Analysis of the perception of the EU and EU's policies abroad. Final Report*. Vilnius: Public Policy and Management Institute, 2015, p. 117
100 For more information, see: S. Pandey, *India and European Union: Perceptions of the Indian Print Media and Elites*, New Delhi: KWP, 2018; R. K. Jain (ed.), *Changing Indian Images of the European Union. Perception and Misperception*, Singapore: Palgrave Macmillan, 2019.

101 B. Vivekanandan, "The West Viewed from India", [in:] B. Vivekanandan, D. K. Giri (eds.), *Contemporary Europe and South Asia*, New Delhi: Concept Publishing Company, 2001, pp. 240–247.
102 A. N. Ram, "India and the European Union in the New Millennium", [in:] R. K. Jain (ed.), *India and the European Union in the 21st Century*, New Delhi: Radiant Publishers, 2002, pp. 1–24; R. K. Jain, S. Pandey, "Indian Elites and the EU as a Normative Power", *Baltic Journal of European Studies*, vol. 3, no. 3, December 2013, pp. 105–126; R. K. Jain, "India, the European Union and Human Rights", *India Quarterly*, vol. 73, no. 4, 2017, pp. 411–429.
103 R. K. Jain, "Fortifying the 'Fortress': Immigration and Politics in the European Union", *International Studies*, vol. 34, no. 2, 1997, pp. 163–192.
104 S. Gulshan (ed.), *Challenges in Europe: Indian Perspectives*, Singapore: Palgrave Macmillan, 2019, p. 2; P. Winand, "A Partnership Between Two Large Elephants? Opportunities and Challenges in India-EU Relations", [in:] P. Gieg et al. (eds.), *EU-India Relations. The Strategic Partnership in the Light of the European Union Global Strategy*, Cham: Springer, 2021, p. 117.
105 K. Lisbonne-de Vergeron, *Contemporary Indian Views of Europe*, London: Royal Institute of International Affairs, 2006, p. 12.
106 K. Sibal, "India and Europe: Perceptions and Misperceptions", [in:] R. K. Jain (ed.), *Changing Indian Images of the European Union. Perception and Misperception*, Singapore: Palgrave Macmillan, 2019, pp. 61–79.
107 Quote: P. Winand, M. Vicziany, P. Datar, *The European Union and India. Rhetoric or Meaningful Partnership?*, Cheltenhem: Edward Elgar, 2015, p. 91.
108 J. N. Dixit, "India and Europe: Perceptions and Misperceptions", [in:] R. K. Jain (ed.), *India and Europe in the New Millennium*, New Delhi: Radiant Publishers, 2000, p. 84.
109 R. K. Jain, S. Pandey, "Public Attitudes and Images of the EU in India", [in:] R. K. Jain (ed.), *Changing Indian Images of the European Union. Perception and Misperception*, Singapore: Palgrave Macmillan, 2019, p. 104.
110 R. K. Jain, S. Pandey, "Public Attitudes and Images of the EU in India", [in:] R. K. Jain (ed.), *Changing Indian Images of the European Union. Perception and Misperception*, Singapore: Palgrave Macmillan, 2019, p. 105.
111 PPMI, *Analysis of the Perception of the EU and EU's Policies Abroad. Final Report*. Vilnius: Public Policy and Management Institute, 2015, pp. 110–111.
112 Pew Research Center, *Indian Reflect on their Country and the World*, Washington: Pew Research Centre, 2014.
113 R. K. Jain, "European Studies in India", [in:] R. K. Jain (ed.), *India and Europe in the New Millenium*, New Delhi: Radiant Publishers, 2000, p. 124.
114 R. K. Jain, "European Studies in India", [in:] R. K. Jain (ed.), *India and Europe in the New Millenium*, New Delhi: Radiant Publishers, 2000, p. 127.
115 R. K. Jain, "European Studies in India", [in:] R. K. Jain (ed.), *India and Europe in the New Millenium*, New Delhi: Radiant Publishers, 2000, p. 133.
116 P. Kugiel, "A Challenge for EU Public Diplomacy in India: Why the Union Needs a Europe House", *Policy Paper*, vol. 4, no. 174, 18 November 2019; P. Winand, "A Partnership Between Two Large Elephants? Opportunities and Challenges in India-EU Relations", [in:], P. Gieg et al. (eds.), *EU-India Relations. The Strategic Partnership in the Light of the European Union Global Strategy*, Cham: Springer, 2021, p. 114; R. K. Jain, "The European Union as a Global Power: Indian Perceptions", *Perspectives*, vol. 20, no. 2, 2012, pp. 31–44; R. K. Jain, S. Pandey, "The Public Attitudes and Images of the European Union in India", *India Quarterly*, vol. 68, no. 4, 2012, pp. 331–343.
117 N. Babalova, I. Goddeeris, "Towards a Stronger Political Ties? The EU's Shifting Image in the Indian Media during the EU-India Summit of October 2017", [in:]

R. K. Jain (ed.), *Changing Indian Images of the European Union. Perception and Misperception*, Singapore: Palgrave Macmillan, 2019, p. 115.
118 N. Babalova, I. Goddeeris, "Towards a Stronger Political Ties? The EU's Shifting Image in the Indian Media during the EU-India Summit of October 2017", [in:] R. K. Jain (ed.), *Changing Indian Images of the European Union. Perception and Misperception*, Singapore: Palgrave Macmillan, 2019, p. 133.
119 P. Chitalkar, D. M. Malone, "Democracy, Politics, and India's Foreign Policy", *Canadian Foreign Policy Journal*, vol. 17, no. 1, March 2011; T. Madan, "What in the World Is India Able to Do? India's State Capacity for Multilateralism", [in:] W. P. S. Sidhu, P. B. Mehta, B. Jones (eds.), *Shaping the Emerging World. India and the Multilateral Order*, Washington D.C.: Brookings Institution Press, 2013.
120 S. Baru, "The Growing Influence of Business and Media on Indian Foreign Policy", *ISAS Insights*, no. 49, 5 February 2009.
121 A. Malik, R. Medclaf, "Indian's New World: Civil Society in the Making of Foreign Policy", Sydney: Lowy Institute for International Policy, May 2011.
122 C. R. Mohan, "The Making of Indian Foreign Policy: The Role of Scholarship and Public Opinion", *ISAS Working Paper no 73*, National University of Singapore, Institute of South Asian Studies, 13 July 2009.
123 T. Madan, "What in the World is India Able to Do? India's State Capacity for Multilateralism", [in:] W. P. S. Sidhu, P. B. Mehta, B. Jones (eds.), *Shaping the Emerging World. India and the Multilateral Order*, Washington D.C.: Brookings Institution Press, 2013, pp. 103–104.
124 T. Madan, "What in the World is India Able to Do? India's State Capacity for Multilateralism", [in:] W. P. S. Sidhu, P. B. Mehta, B. Jones (eds.), *Shaping the Emerging World. India and the Multilateral Order*, Washington D.C.: Brookings Institution Press, 2013, pp. 104–107.
125 Ministry of External Affairs, Annual Report 1991–1992, New Delhi, 1992, pp. 83–84.
126 D. Markey, 'Developing India's Foreign Policy Software', *Asia Policy*, July 2009.
127 S. K. Rana, *Asian Diplomacy: The Foreign Ministries of China, India, Japan, Singapore, and Thailand*, Baltimore: Johns Hopkins University Press, 2008.
128 Ministry of External Affairs, Annual Report 2023, New Delhi, 2024, p. 333.
129 G. Mohan, "India's Foreign Policy Ambitions are Big, yet the Size of the Foreign Service has Remained Static": Constantino Xavier on India's Union Budget 2025, India Today, 31.01.2025.
130 P. Winand, M. Vicziany, P. Datar, *The European Union and India. Rhetoric or Meaningful Partnership?*, Cheltenhem: Edward Elgar, 2015, p. 178.
131 MEA 2025, Embassy of India to Belgium Luxemburg and European Union, https://www.indianembassybrussels.gov.in/listofofficers.php (Accessed 02.02.2025).
132 Ministry of External Affairs, Organisation Structure, https://www.mea.gov.in/organization-structure.htm (Accessed 11.02.2025).
133 P. Winiand, "Fearing European unity and yearning for Asian cooperation: The Early Years", [in:] P. Winand, M. Vicziany, P. Datar, *The European Union and India. Rhetoric or Meaningful Partnership?*, Cheltenhem: Edward Elgar, 2015, p. 177.
134 Ministry of External Affairs, Organisation Structure, https://www.mea.gov.in/organization-structure.htm (Accessed 11.02.2025).

2 The decade of transition
The EU in India's international strategy between 1991 and 2000

Changes in the international order and reforms in India after the Cold War created the perfect conditions for closer cooperation with the EU. At the same time, however, India's rapprochement with Europe was neither automatic nor inevitable. Historical experience, ideological, economic, or structural differences stood in the way, resulting in different perspectives on a range of international challenges. The implementation of India's policy toward the EU was also influenced by the dynamic developments in Europe and South Asia itself in the 1990s, which prompted both sides to focus their attention on their immediate neighbourhoods.

This chapter first reconstructs the place of the EU in India's international strategy and foreign policy objectives towards the EU after the Cold War. It does so by looking at statements of Indian representatives and experts and the only official document explaining India's approach to the EU released in 2004. This chapter also analyses in detail the reactions and evaluations in India of the processes of deepening and widening European integration. The next sections present the evolution of political and economic cooperation until the end of the 20th century. The most important points of contention in relations with the EU, which hindered the realization of Indian objectives, are presented. Finally, the achievements of the "lost decade" in relations with the EU are assessed.

2.1 India's policy goals towards the EU after the Cold War

No coherent document explaining comprehensively and explicitly the goals and objectives of policy towards the EU emerged in India in the 1990s. Scattered documents from India's Foreign Ministry and statements by politicians and experts provide insight into this vision. They show that Europe was certainly not among the primary partners. That place was occupied, for obvious reasons, by its neighbours in South Asia, the largest countries in Asia and the major powers – the US, Russia, and China. The government's new initiatives towards Asia that emerged during this period (e.g. *Neighborhood First* towards South Asia, *Look East Policy* towards ASEAN) were not accompanied by any special strategy for relations with European partners.

DOI: 10.4324/9781003688648-3

This chapter has been made available under a CC-BY-NC-ND 4.0 International license.

If the attention of Indian leaders has already turned to Europe, it has been more about relations with the largest European countries – Britain, France, and Germany – than about the nascent supranational structure. The EU, and even more broadly Europe, also made almost no appearance in the election manifestos of the main Indian parties from 1989 to 1999. Only the BJP's programme before the victorious 1998 elections, in a lengthy passage on foreign policy, mentioned the EU as one of the partners with whom India "will seek to strengthen political and economic relations".[1]

The EU's place in India's post-Cold War foreign policy was marked by its position as India's largest trading partner, as well as a major source of investment and development assistance. This gave it a key role in supporting India's economic reforms and to ensure rapid economic growth and poverty reduction. Foreign investment, aid, or cutting-edge technologies were to come largely from Europe. The European common market, which was already a major export destination, remained as attractive as it was difficult for Indian entrepreneurs. At the same time, interest in Europe as a labour emigration destination for Indian workers was growing. India's economic goals vis-à-vis the EU after 1991 were largely a continuation of efforts already underway for several decades vis-à-vis the EEC. However, as India opened up to globalization, the intensity and quality of cooperation was to change. India's most important specific economic objectives vis-à-vis the EU in 1990s included:

1. Improving access to the Union market by reducing tariff and non-tariff barriers
2. Increasing Indian exports and addressing trade imbalance with the EU
3. Getting European investments
4. Ensuring the continuation of development assistance
5. Developing scientific and technological cooperation to enable technology transfer
6. Increasing access to the EU labour market through visa liberalization

Although the EU was seen primarily as an economic partner, closer cooperation was also intended to serve India's strategic interests. Firstly, in the new international environment, there was a growing awareness in India that material prosperity and economic strength were prerequisites for being recognized as a global power. Accelerating economic growth through closer cooperation with the EU would therefore serve the country's superpower ambitions.

Secondly, India watched with some hope the post-Cold War deepening of European integration process and the emergence of the EU as a security and foreign policy actor. In Delhi, it was hoped that this would lead to the emancipation of Europe from US influence and its emergence as an independent centre of power in the international system. In this context, the EU was seen as a prospective partner interested in building a multipolar international order, where both India and Europe would constitute independent poles.

Thirdly, the EU, as a powerful economic bloc and the most successful regional organization, has been an important force in international organizations and multilateral negotiations. For India seeking to increase its voice in these institutions and influence in setting international rules, cooperation with the EU became a necessity. More frequent consultations on international issues would sensitize European partners to Indian concerns and interests facilitating the spread of Indian demands and perspectives.

Finally, the Union, as a political and economic actor, has had a significant impact on India's regional challenges like Pakistan's policies and the terrorist threat. Throughout the 1990s, India was forced to counter Pakistani interference in Kashmir and sought to portray the situation itself in terms of cross-border terrorism. In Delhi, it was hoped that an understanding of Indian concerns by other democracies would generate international pressure on Pakistan, thereby improving security in the immediate neighbourhood.

2.1.1 India's strategy towards the EU (2004)

The first and only Indian official strategy towards the EU was presented only in the next decade, on August 27, 2004.[2] It was the first time that India had issued such a document to any foreign partner. It outlined the most comprehensive vision of relations with the EU to date, explaining Europe's place in India's international strategy and its interests and expectations towards the Union. It set out Indian policy for the coming years and has not been updated since. The document was adopted by the newly formed United Progressive Alliance government of Prime Minister Manmohan Singh, who took office in the spring, and was a response to the EU's earlier strategy towards India published in June, which proposed upgrading relations to a strategic partnership.[3]

The extensive Indian text (31 pages) described India's position in detail in seven key areas of cooperation, most of which overlapped with the proposals contained in the EC Communication: (1) international cooperation; (2) a common strategy in Asia; (3) strengthening the economic partnership; (4) trade and investment; (5) science and technology; (6) development cooperation; and (7) mutual understanding.[4]

India welcomed the EU's desire to develop a "strategic partnership" between the two sides" (Paragraph 2). It acknowledged that with "the EU's emergence as a major geopolitical and economic force in the new world order", the time had come to formalize India's approach to the EU "so that a coordinated and mutually reinforcing strategy can be evolved". Europe is presented as "an important political and strategic actor influencing the international power equations, affecting major international political and economic developments". It is particularly emphasized that "the membership of countries of the EU in the United Nations and other multilateral fora makes it a **desirable partner for India**, in influencing many dimensions of collective international cooperation in the spheres of security, development, and globalization".

Appreciating the historical changes in the EU, the Indian authors recognized that "the most important result of EU enlargement was that it decisively erased the vertical fault lines that divided the European continent for over half a century". Furthermore, they expressed their belief that enlargement would not adversely affect the effectiveness of EU institutions, stating that "the expansion of geographical borders and demographic diversity, together with the ability to synthesise the divergent goals and approaches of member states into a coherent whole, ensured its emergence as one of the most important poles of a multi-polar world" (Paragraph 2).

The authors also emphasized the "identical views" on "strategic priorities and issues of vital importance to both sides", including support for multilateralism, combating terrorism, belief in democracy, human rights, pluralism of society, freedom, independence of the judiciary, and the media. It was here that the EU was first described as a **"natural partner"**. The document states that, given its commitment to multilateralism, the EU is "a natural partner for a country like India with multicultural, multi-religious, multi-ethnic, and tolerant society" (Paragraph 3).

The Indian side also explained how it understands a "strategic partnership":

> It is admittedly a level of relationship higher than that maintained by either side with non-strategic partners, and immune from the vicissitudes of either side's relationship with a third party. We see it as a relationship of sovereign equality, based on comparative advantage and a mutuality of interests and benefits, intended to promote the prosperity and well-being of the peoples of India and of the European Union. It visualises prior consultations with each other on international political, economic, military and security issues of mutual interest, particularly on areas of divergence, in a spirit of cooperation, accommodation and mutual respect. A strategic partnership between India and the EU is special, because the two sides share values, and not just interests (Paragraph 2).

The document highlights India's economic reforms, its enormous potential for development, its commitment to democracy and multilateralism, its aspirations for permanent membership in the UN Security Council, and the role it is assigned to play "even beyond its immediate neighbourhood". The growing ties with other regional organizations on different continents and India's "growing political and strategic influence and capabilities" are cited as justification for a "strategic partnership" with the EU.

The Indian side responded positively to a number of EU proposals to strengthen institutional dialogue in a number of areas, including "formal, institutionalised dialogue on cooperation in the UN and UN-related matters", high-level dialogue on peacekeeping operations, conflict management and post-conflict reconstruction; religious extremism and fundamentalism, a Joint Working Group on Biotechnology; a Joint Working Group on Phytosanitary

Standards and Non-Technical Barriers to Trade; and an Energy Panel, suggesting additional subgroups on clean coal technology and solar energy.

India also put forward its own proposals, not previously raised by the EU side, to establish a Joint Working Group on regions of interest to the parties (the Middle East, Iraq, and Afghanistan were mentioned); to upgrade and expand the mandate of the Joint Working Group on Terrorism to a Joint Group on Security Cooperation; create separate channels of communication between the EU Counter-Terrorism Coordinator and Europol with their Indian counterparts; establish a separate Joint Working Group to examine and discuss the opportunities and challenges for India arising from the EU's enlargement in 2004 to include ten Central European countries. India also indicated its readiness to negotiate agreements on air transport, maritime transport, and joining the Galileo project.

India took the opportunity not only to highlight its interests and objectives, but also to mark its "red lines" that it would not tolerate being crossed. In political matters, this concerned discussions on human rights and democracy. Indian diplomats emphasized that "India believes that the issue of human rights is solely within the national domain" and proposed that matters of interest to both sides "be taken up informally in Brussels or in New Delhi", bearing in mind that these issues "in which public opinion and the media have an overriding interest and where distortions need to be corrected, could be effectively addressed in the future". Recalling that "both sides are unequivocally committed to democratic principles and institutions", they cautioned that neither side "should adopt 'a prescriptive approach on either side" (paragraph 10).

Another "red line" concerned trade issues and linking them to social issues or environmental protection, both bilaterally and multilaterally. Indian diplomats pointed out that concern for the environment should take into account "the respective needs and concerns of the countries at different levels of economic development", and that past attempts to link trade and environmental issues, which were used for protectionist purposes, would meet with "India's 'principled opposition" (Paragraph 51).

India also hoped for greater understanding in the areas of nuclear cooperation and the fight against international terrorism. The document recalled that "India was among the first countries to be targeted by terrorists [...] and for over two decades we have been victims of repeated and senseless violence", pointing out that the EU "has been through similar experiences in the last few years, and particularly after 9/11". The strong threat of terrorism to democratic countries and the agreement that "terrorism cannot be justified under any circumstances" should help to strengthen cooperation in this area, including leading to "concrete steps" towards the adoption of the Comprehensive Convention on International Terrorism (paragraphs 14–15).

As transpires from this document and former discussions shows that India had not only economic expectations towards the EU, but saw it also as a political and multilateral partner. In general, one can point at three broad aims in Indian policy to the EU after the Cold War. By cooperation with the EU, India wanted to:

1. Accelerate its economic development and modernization of the country
2. Advance its rise as a global power and regional leader
3. Change the international order towards a multipolar system.

2.2 India's attitude towards deepening European integration and EU enlargement

India's approach to the EU after the Cold War was greatly influenced by the historical changes taking place in Europe at the time. The countries of Western Europe were, along with the US, the main winners of the Cold War, with enormous influence on international politics and economics. The democratization of the post-communist countries and the integration processes in the European Economic Community (EEC) provided an opportunity to unite the entire continent. The establishment of the EU on February 7, 1992 (which entered into force in 1993), comprising 12 member states, determined further integration and closer cooperation also in foreign and defence policy. In 1995, the EU expanded with the addition of three more countries (Austria, Sweden, and Denmark), and preparations for another enlargement into Central Europe gained momentum. The EU as a whole was the world's largest economic bloc and a key source of investment and modern technology, thus resources necessary for India, opening up to international trade, capital, and know-how.

Although India already had a long tradition of cooperation with the European Communities, this cooperation had so far focused on trade and development assistance. The creation of the EU as a political entity opened up the opportunity to develop partnerships in new areas as well. When planning policy towards the EU, Indian policymakers had to take into account that the subject of the policy was undergoing constant and fundamental changes. The direction of change in Europe strengthened the argument for treating the Community as a separate and independent partner in external relations. This section takes a closer look at the reaction of Indian authorities to the emergence of the EU and the deepening of integration and the initiated process of enlargement to additional countries.

2.2.1 India's reactions to the establishment of the EU

In India, preparations for deeper integration and the establishment of the EU were followed closely. India's foreign ministry assessed in 1992 that the Maastricht Summit meeting on December 9 and 10, 1991, was "a watershed in the history of Europe in the post-World War II era'" adding that "the European Community embarked on a new chapter in its move towards the creation of a political, economic and monetary union".[5] Diplomats in Delhi noted plans to adopt a common euro currency by 1999, the will to introduce a common security and foreign policy, and the creation of a European Economic Area with EFTA that will include 380 million people. They noted that the European Community, "which is already India's largest trading and economic partner, offers additional opportunities for even closer cooperation with India".[6] They also stated that "India has observed with satisfaction the positive reaction in Western Europe to the new economic policies and liberalization measures taken in India".[7] A year later, when the ratification process of the Maastricht Treaty encountered some delays, the Indian Ministry of External Affairs assessed that "the political and economic integration of Europe, despite the difficulties experienced along the way, requires India to take this factor into account in its relations with Western European countries".[8]

Indian politicians at the time, led by the country's prime minister, spoke positively about European integration. Prime Minister Narasimha Rao argued after a visit to Germany in September 1991 that India could count on many friends in Europe and allayed fears about deepening the common market. During a debate in the Indian parliament, he said that he had "been assured that India will not be left outside this imagined fortress to be built in Europe in 1992" – adding – "that India will have access to this fortress".[9] Positive views also prevailed among Indian parliamentarians from different political options. For example, in one of the foreign policy debates in mid-1991, Sudarshan Roy Choudhury of the Communist Party of India (Marxist) estimated that in 1992, "there will be a new Europe, a stronger Europe".[10] M.V.V.S. Murthy of the regional Telugu Desam Party pointed to the tremendous changes taking place in Europe (German unification, the emergence of the Common Market), claiming that "Europe is rapidly emerging as an important political and economic force on the world stage" and that India "should recognize these changes and make efforts for closer political and economic relations with the European Communities".[11] As he added, "the European Common Market, which is expected to come into being in 1992, will provide an opportunity to boost trade with European countries" and presents a "golden opportunity" to increase exports. All in all, Delhi's assessment was that "the rapid integration process of the European Economic Community is likely to improve its importance as another major centre of economic strength".[12]

At the same time, the advancing European integration after the Cold War attracted increasing interest in Indian opinion-making circles. It can be said that unlike in the 1950s, this time processes in Europe were viewed with greater optimism. Popular opinions were that a more united and richer Union would be able to open up more to Indian exports.[13] Unlike with the creation of the EEC, this time analysts hoped that the economic impact of the creation of a single market for India (such as the introduction of free movement of goods, capital, people, harmonization of standards, increased competitiveness) could be beneficial, as it meant the elimination of many physical (e.g. border controls), technical (separate certificates, standards), and fiscal (additional fees) barriers to trade with European countries.[14] It was expected that economic development, improved living standards for Europeans, and increased consumption would lead to increased demand for raw materials, consumer goods, and other products that are absent or in short supply in Europe, creating opportunities for improved exports from India.

The introduction of a single GSP trade preference system for the entire common market, instead of quotas set for individual member states, or the harmonization of technical standards were supposed to increase export opportunities for Indian companies. It was pointed out that the changes in Europe "give India a fair playing field" provided, however, that it produces "goods of adequate quality and cheaper".[15] Therefore, Indian analysts also pointed to increased product competition in the EU market and urged Indian authorities to take measures to "improve the competitiveness of Indian exports". On the other side, competition from European producers in third markets was a concern. Overall, however, according to these authors, "the prospects for India's relations with the EU are good", there is "great potential for export growth to the Community market", and "the new Europe presents great interests, challenges, and opportunities for countries like India".[16] They also hoped for a greater influx of industrial investment and technology from Europe. The introduction of the euro common currency in 1999 was also viewed positively. This was expected to create additional opportunities for India to export to the integrated European market, especially for high-tech products, but also to increase the possibility of raising capital for Indian companies.[17]

In addition to new hopes for improved economic relations, political integration of the EU was of great interest. Changes in Europe were viewed favourably, as an opportunity to strengthen political partnerships in the post-Cold War world. It was hoped that a more united EU could become an independent actor in international relations and a counterweight to unfettered US dominance. Indian Ministry of External Affairs, while recognizing that "the world was perceived as unipolar with the United States becoming the most influential politic-military power", rejected proposals to define the international situation in "uni-dimensional terms".[18] It further suggested that attention should also be paid to other "centres of power", and alongside China or Japan, it included here "politically assertive Europe integrating itself in socio-economic terms" as one of "potent influence in conduct of foreign affairs".

The perception of the EU as one of the centres of the emerging multipolar international order has become a constant and important part of Indian perception. After the EU's 1995 enlargement, Indian diplomats emphasized "the emergence of the EU as an influential political actor and the consolidation of the EU's common foreign and security policy".[19] Also, some experts were optimistic about the EU's efforts to build a European security and defence policy, assessing that while the road to success is long and challenging, "the decision has been made" and a certain "boundary has been crossed, and the Europeans can no longer return to the position of comfortable irresponsibility they occupied for more than four decades".[20] Leading Indian security expert Brahma Chellaney assessed in 2000 that "an economically and politically united Europe could potentially emerge as an independent power centre".[21] And while he noted that the security situation in Europe and India's neighbourhood are radically different, "if you put security in a broad sense Europe and India share many interests".

However, the EU's function as a security actor was seen as a potential and rather distant possibility. In this regard, individual member states, mainly those offering modern armaments or military technology, remained priority partners for India. Clear evidence that the EU's security aspirations were ignored is provided by the annual reports of India's defence ministry, which in the 1990s did not mention the EU as a cooperation partner at all.[22]

2.2.2 India's position towards the EU enlargement

Indian experts assessed that "enlargement and deepening [of integration] are complementary goals, not mutual challenges".[23] While the increase in the number of EU members by three countries of "old Europe" from 12 to 15 in 1995 did not arouse particular interest, as it was seen as something natural, the preparations in the 1990s for the EU's great enlargement to Central Europe were studied with greater curiosity in Delhi.[24] One of the earliest texts referring to the prospect of accession of post-communist countries opined with optimism as early as 1992 that the possible enlargement of the EU to Central European countries would lead "to the emergence of a huge economic zone of 500 million people", which would include 40% of India's exports and create additional opportunities.[25] The entire process of democratic and economic transformation and achievements in the various Central European countries, including Poland, was also followed with some appreciation.[26] However, already in the early 1990s, there was an awareness among experts that successive enlargements of the EU would increase differences between members, which would create "different speeds and levels of integration", which could lead to a "Europe of different speeds".[27]

A matter of special interest was the impact of greater EU focus on the east of the continent on India's economic interests. Therefore, Indian authorities commissioned a number of studies of the possible impact of enlargement on their economic interests. Among others, the Ministry of Foreign Affairs in 1998, the Indian Institute of Foreign Trade in 1998, and a little later (in 2003) the major business organization FICCI presented their opinions on the matter.

The general conclusions of all the studies were positive. The 1998 study pointed to the small contribution of the candidate countries to India's trade with the EU and assessed that "the negative impact of their accession will be marginal or non-existent", while the overall impact may be favourable for two reasons: The EU's common tariff is generally lower than that applied to Central European countries to date, and secondly, accession should trigger rapid economic growth in this part of Europe and therefore will increase their demand for products, including those from India.[28] Slightly more downsides were found by the later FICCI study, mainly in the extent of trade diversion within the Community, increasing competition of goods and services from companies of the new member states.

In the 1990s, there was a fairly popular concern that the risk for India was a reduction in the value of development assistance from the EU, as a result of directing more support to accession countries from Central Europe. According to one author, "Western Europe has discovered its Third World right on its doorstep – in Eastern Europe, which will now have a higher priority for financial flows, technology transfer and market access".[29] India, however, has received clear assurances that aid to it will not be compromised in any way. Overall, Indian researchers assessed that the eastern enlargement of the EU "presents an opportunity to increase trade and investment flows".[30]

Similarly, Indians did not expect negative consequences of enlargement on political cooperation with the EU. As one of India's leading experts on European affairs, Prof. R. K. Jain, explained it was highly unlikely that enlargement will lead in the near future to a sudden or significant change in the nature or content of the strategic and political dialogue India has with the EU. This was mainly due to the new members' little impact of the Union's foreign policy, especially on issues of importance to India like non-proliferation and dual-use technologies. As Prof. Jain assessed, "Central and Eastern European countries will tend to conform to the dominant approach in the Union on these issues".[31] The impact on relations with the EU would not be great, not least because the region lost its traditional ties with India after the Cold War and became a marginal economic and political partner.[32]

However, the traditional concerns voiced a few decades earlier by Prime Minister Nehru about "an *inward looking Europe*" and that "a united Europe, will be a fortress Europe" returned. This time it was supposed to be because enlargement would "bring the EU closer to problem areas on the periphery of its new borders both in the east and in the south, and thus could reinforce trends towards a more Eurocentric Europe".[33] The fact that the enlargement of the Union to include such a large number of countries that are at a different level of development meant a number of serious challenges regarding the functioning of institutions, adaptation to EU laws, labour mobility, common agricultural policy, etc.[34] Observers also pointed out that increasing the number of members could complicate the Union's activities, weaken its effectiveness, and negatively affect its ability to lead the world.[35]

2.3 The EU as a difficult political partner

Positive international context after the Cold War opened up new opportunities for closer engagement of India with the EU. Though both sides were quick to intensify contacts and form a new framework of more equal partnership, relations soon lost momentum, and then spiralled down into a major crisis. India found the EU as a problematic political partner, not interested too much in bilateral ties, complicated institutionally and not understanding India's complex environment, both internally and it its region.

Three main phases can be distinguished during this period:

1 **Redefinition of India's policy towards the EU from 1991 to 1994.** During this time, India was focused on stabilizing the domestic situation and rebuilding relations with its neighbours in South Asia and Southeast Asia. Changes in Europe were observed and efforts were made to create a new institutional and legal framework for bilateral cooperation with the EU culminating in the adoption of the Cooperation and Partnership Agreement in 1993.
2 **Growing crisis in bilateral relations between 1995 and 1998.** A deepening political instability and the deteriorating state of democracy in India stunted the process of political engagement with the EU. Tensions reached a climax in May 1998 when India conducted nuclear weapons tests, which drew condemnation from many European countries and the EU itself.
3 **Rebuilding relations in 1998–2000.** Immediately after the Indian tests began a period of reassessment of EU–India cooperation, when India sought acceptance of its decision to "nuclearize" and return to normal relations. This led to intensified cooperation and the first India–EU summit in 2000.

The changes in Europe and India brought by the abrupt end of the Cold War called for renewed contacts and discussion of new opportunities for cooperation. It was not without reason that the first foreign visit made by the new Prime Minister Narasimha Rao was to Germany in September 1991, and two months later, he also visited France – two major member states of the transforming EU. Talking to members of parliament about the results of his visit to Germany and his talks with Chancellor Helmut Kohl, Prime Minister N. Rao stressed, "the special significance" of the fact that the Chancellor expressed his desire "to draw India closer to the New Europe that is emerging".[36]

The revival of cooperation with major EU/EEC members has been accompanied by greater attention to relations at the EU level. The dialogue on political and international issues, developed in previous decades, with the India–EC Joint Commission and the India–EC Troika meetings at the core, was fast revitalized. Already in November 1991, a meeting of the Joint Commission was held in New Delhi.[37] A month earlier, Vice President of the European Commission Frans Andriessen visited India, and the purpose of the meeting with India's Trade Minister was to discuss multilateral trade issues. A European Parliament delegation also visited India in November. In March 1992, an India–EC Troika meeting took place in Delhi, where European ministers assured the Indian side that the Community's focus on developments in Central and Eastern Europe "should not be seen as diminishing their interest in developing countries, including India".[38]

New international conditions and historical changes in India and the EU made it necessary to update the legal basis for cooperation. India wanted the new agreement with the EU to strengthen the equality of the parties and create room to expand the dialogue into new areas. It wanted relations with the EU to move from the "cooperation" stage to the "partnership" stage.[39] This view was shared by the European Commission, which in September 1992 asked the Council to authorize the start of negotiations for a new agreement with India.

The talks continued for a year and finalized on December 20, 1993, in signing the *Cooperation Agreement on Partnership and Development between the European Community and the Republic of India* (CAPD).[40] Formally, the agreement came into force on August 1, 1994. The Indian Foreign Ministry estimated that the agreement was intended to "build India's economic capacity to interact more effectively with the EU".[41]

Simultaneously, with the adoption of the CAPD, the EU and India also signed a Political Statement on December 20, 1993. MEA observed that two documents "symbolized the high importance that both sides attach to significantly strengthening and expanding mutually beneficial cooperation between the EU and India".[42]

The CAPD was one of the so-called "third-generation" cooperation agreements adopted by the Union at the time, which, in addition to purely commercial or economic issues, included political commitments to certain rights and standards. As a result, the very first article indicated "respect for human rights and democratic principles"[43] as the "basis" and "essential element" of the agreement. This meant that in the event of a violation of these provisions, the agreement (and thus also the transfer of development assistance funds, which took place on its basis) could be suspended. The document identified 18 areas of cooperation, covering trade issues, investment, intellectual property, and added new sectors such as tourism, culture, cooperation in electronics, telecommunications, combating drug addiction, or satellite technology. It heralded cooperation in human capital development, including through education and greater private sector participation in relations. It provided the basis for closer scientific and technological cooperation, joint research and projects, and set the direction and framework for future development cooperation, which was to focus on supporting underprivileged groups (such as women) and underfunded sectors (health care). Protection of the environment and the indication of high standards in this regard was also an important element. Finally, the agreement retained the Joint Commission (established by the 1981 Agreement) as the primary body responsible for implementing the agreement, and left the door open for cooperation in new areas not mentioned in the text, and for which only "mutual consent" would be needed.

The issues of political cooperation, however, were rounded out by a separate yet short Political Declaration adopted at the same time. It reaffirmed the commitment of both sides to the defence of democracy, human rights, and diversity. It listed a broad set of areas of cooperation, such as combating terrorism, drug trafficking, and non-proliferation of nuclear weapons.[44] While this political document was intended to indicate that the relationship goes beyond the traditional scope of cooperation, the non-binding nature of the declaration and the language of both documents confirmed that the economy remains the core area of the relationship.[45]

Soon India welcomed another proof of growing EU's interest in Asia – adopted in 1994 by European Commission document titled: "Towards the New Asia Strategy".[46] It recommended that the Union rapidly increase "its economic presence in Asia" and "develop political dialogue" and engage more "in non-confrontational dialogue of equals", especially with priority partners that included India. The EU strategy indicated a "rediscovery of Asia" and was an expression of the EU's "new Asia policy".[47] It created good conditions for the development of India–EU cooperation, including on non-economic issues. It sent a signal that while China is the Union's main interest, more attention should also be paid to India.

Indeed, in the second half of the decade, the European Commission began to prepare the first stand-alone EU strategy towards India. The document was presented in June 1996 proposing the creation of an "enhanced partnership".[48] It promised, among other things, to intensify political dialogue, establish working groups in selected sectors, improve coherence of action with member states, and strengthen contacts between social organizations, trade unions, universities, or the media.

India appreciated the Commission's initiative, describing it as a "positive development" that enabled it to focus on the means of fully tapping the potential for cooperation.[49] Indian diplomats hoped for the support of European partners in minimizing security threats in South Asia. They stressed that the end of the Cold War era and "the increasing political and economic integration of West European nations into the EU, as well as India's deregulation and opening up of the economy, created the basis for further development of bilateral relations based on complementarity of interests and mutual benefit".[50] They added that India has made "sustained efforts" to strengthen the EU's understanding on issues of vital concern to India, both regional and global".[51]

This first EU strategy towards India gained the approval of the European Council in December 1996. However, the European Parliament stood in the way of its implementation, expressing its positive opinion only 26 months later, in early 1999.[52]

By then, however, India–EU relations had been in crisis for some time. Since 1994, there had been growing tensions over the situation in India and India's policies in the region. In addition, since 1995, there was an escalating political crisis and a series of elections in India, resulting in the lack of a stable government as peer partner for the EU. Although by the end of the 1990s, India continued dialogue through Troika meetings[53] and exchanges of parliamentarians,[54] the optimistic atmosphere of the early part of the decade quickly gave way to escalating disputes. Tensions over several major issues stood in the way of more fruitful cooperation with the EU in 1990s:[55]

1 concerns over human rights in India
2 situation in Kashmir

3   intensification of the India-Pakistan dispute
4   India's nuclear programme

2.3.1   Disputes over respect for human rights in India

The issue of India's human rights record and the quality of India's democracy has become a new and rather surprising challenge for political cooperation with Europe. The deterioration of democracy, the inter-religious riots in Ayodhia in 1992, the anti-Muslim pogroms in Mumbai in 1993, increasingly high-profile reports of human rights violations by security forces in Kashmir or police brutality attracted interest in Europe. Increasingly, some European NGOs, media, and politicians, including members of the European Parliament, criticized India for violations of children's rights and child labour, violence against women, persecution of minorities or failure to comply with labour law standards.

India was forced to explain the violations of human rights and complained about the lack of understanding of its internal situation. Indian diplomats have argued that the slow improvement in standards to protect the rights of workers or children is not due to a lack of will, but a lack of resources and capacity. According to them, it is not that the Indian authorities consider work to be the best occupation for children and poor working conditions to be more desirable, it is just that it takes time and rapid economic development to make changes in this regard.[56] Contrary to European expectations, such reforms cannot be imposed by top-down regulations and administrative setting of the highest standards, but required a long time and broad socio-economic changes. As the former Indian ambassador to Europe, A. N. Ram, explained, "no country more than India wishes to eradicate the endemic and pervasive evils of child labor, caste and gender discrimination, and to provide equal constitutional guarantees and opportunities for all its citizens. Indeed, the Indian Constitution is a model document in this regard".[57] He pointed out, however, that the "incomplete and even superficial" understanding in the EU and especially in the European Parliament of "the social environment in India and the problems of more than 5,000 years of Indian society" does not serve mutual relations well. He stressed that these problems "are deep-rooted" and their solution "takes time". As such, Ram explained, what India expects from European friends is "understanding and support to effect change as quickly as possible", rather than lecture or punish, and it will be helpful if the EU "adopts a more pragmatic and helpful approach".[58]

India has been particularly critical of attempts to link human rights issues with trade cooperation or aid. Making trade preferences conditional on meeting certain labour or environmental standards seemed too many in India to be unfair and a form of interference in internal affairs. Indian partners were very reluctant to any attempt to condition development assistance. As even one European expert admitted in the late 1990s: "All in all, in all three dimensions – political, economic and development cooperation – the EU is exerting pressure and wants to set the agenda. The EU is flexing its economic and political muscles. So too is it part of development policy, where, despite the rhetorical emphasis on mutual interests, it is the EU that selectively shapes the content, speed, and directions of cooperation".[59] This approach has bred distrust in India and worsened relations.

2.3.2 The situation in Kashmir as a source of tensions with the EU

The issue of human rights was closely linked to the second challenge of the 1990s in India's relations with the EU, i.e. the unstable security situation in Kashmir. Protests broke out in this Indian state and disputed territory between India and Pakistan in the late 1980s, which quickly turned into an anti-India insurgency supported from Pakistan. The central government responded with force and deployed hundreds of thousands of paramilitary forces and the military to the region to quell resistance and restore control. However, some separatist organizations backed by Pakistani intelligence have taken up arms against Indian forces, increasingly using terrorist methods.[60]

The deterioration of the situation in Kashmir was influenced by changes in the region. The withdrawal of Soviet troops and the end of the jihad against the "infidel" Soviet soldiers caused some seasoned mujahedeen to support the fight against India in Kashmir. As a result, the situation in the region remained tense throughout the 1990s. Indian security forces equipped with special laws guaranteeing their immunity (Armed Forces Special Power Act, AFSPA) were accused of committing extrajudicial killings, torture, and other crimes. It is estimated that the conflict in Kashmir forced some 100,000 people (mostly Hindus in the initial phase of the conflict) to flee, and tens of thousands were killed. The European Parliament, in a 2008 resolution, called on the Indian government to conduct an impartial investigation to verify reports that mass graves have been found in Kashmir, where at least several hundred dead have been discovered.[61] Human rights violations and regional instability have become since mid-1990s one of the main issues of contention in US and European relations with India.

However, while the EU approached the issue from the side of respecting human rights, India presented it in terms of fighting terrorism and taking care of the security of the state and citizens. As such Indian side reacted negatively to criticism from the EU (especially the European Parliament) and raising the issue in bilateral relations, it tried instead (unsuccessfully) to convince the EU to condemn Pakistan for supporting separatist forces and "cross-border terrorism". It was disappointed by Europe's lack of support in its fight against Islamic terrorists.

India has also taken a number of steps to respond to European counterparts' accusations and increase transparency in its human rights activities: Among other things, it established an independent Human Rights Commission, held elections in Kashmir, and organized a visit for European diplomats to the region. At the same time, it has criticized the West for "double standards" and cooperation with other countries with greater human rights violations.[62]

2.3.3 India–Pakistan conflict in relations with the EU

The third issue, related to the previous challenge was the Pakistan–India dispute. India fought three wars with Pakistan (in 1947, 1965, and 1971), and a major crisis in 1987 almost turned into another conflict. The high scale of tensions continued throughout the 1990s due to the unstable situation in Kashmir and Pakistan's support for the Kashmir "cause". Pakistan's leaders sought to publicize human rights violations in the region and internationalize the dispute with India, including in the UN arena and in relations with the EU.

India sought to block these actions and persuade the EU to get Pakistan to stop interfering in Indian affairs. It expected the Union to condemn Pakistan's support for terrorism and to unequivocally back it in this dispute. Failure of Europe to understand India's security concerns, and to support it in dealings with Pakistan India, fed disappointment and distrust.

The EU has looked at the Kashmir issue in the context of human rights violations by Indian forces and the pacification of the region. It urged both sides to resolve the dispute and offered mediation. The EU's Asia strategy n 1994 cited the Pakistan–India conflict as a major source of instability in Asia requiring attention. This positioning of India and Pakistan as equal parties with legitimate rationales aroused frustration in Delhi, which felt itself to be a victim of Pakistan's campaign to use non-state actors in its foreign policy.

Only the reaction of European countries to the outbreak of a limited war on the Siachen glacier near the town of Kargil in the Indian part of Kashmir in the summer of 1999, triggered more understanding in Delhi. The Indian ministry was pleased to see that the European countries appreciated India's "restrained" reaction and recognized that the "situation had been caused by cross-border infiltration and violation of the Line of Control" by Pakistan.[63] This had indicated, according to India, "the trend of warming and deepening of relations with the EU and its member countries".[64] This allowed trust to improve in subsequent years and made India–Pakistan relations less of a problem for cooperation with the EU.

2.3.4 India's nuclear programme and the crisis in relations with the EU

But the most serious challenge that negatively affected India's relations with the EU in the 1990s was the issue of its nuclear programme. India was one of the last countries in the world (along with Pakistan or Israel) not to accede to the 1967 Nuclear Non-Proliferation Treaty (NPT), which banned the possession of such weapons from all but five powers possessing them before that date. India has also ultimately rejected the possibility of signing two important treaties that had been negotiated in the 1990s: the Comprehensive Nuclear-Test Ban Treaty (CTBT) and the Fissile Material Cut-off Treaty (FMCT). At the same time, it did not want disputes over these issues to negatively affect economic cooperation with Europe or its access to advanced technologies.

Therefore, Europe's stance on the issue was of great importance to India. EU members, including two nuclear powers, France and the UK, were signatories and major supporters of the NPT and promoters of the signing of the CTBT. They were also members of several non-proliferation regimes that control the trade in fissile materials and devices that could be used to produce nuclear weapons, including the Nuclear Suppliers Group (NSG) formed just in response to India's 1974 "peaceful" nuclear test. The EU as a whole strongly supported international non-proliferation efforts. In the 1990s, it also supported US policies aimed to *"cap, roll-back and eliminate"*) India's nuclear programme.[65] This became a source of tension and distrust between the EU and India. In 1995, the India became subject to (European Council decision of December 19, 1994) Community regulations on the restriction of trade in so-called "dual-use goods", which meant that it became an important actor limiting India's access to cutting-edge technology.[66]

India has had a nuclear programme since the 1960s and had a de facto capability to produce nuclear weapons since the first test explosions in 1974. However, it did not take advantage of this capability by applying a voluntary moratorium on nuclear testing and continuing to call for universal and complete nuclear disarmament. This policy of "keeping the nuclear option open" was portrayed as a policy of Indian "self-restraint" and allegiance to the goals of universal denuclearization.[67] Indian politicians considered a non-proliferation regime that sanctioned the possession of nuclear weapons by some and denied this right to other states (*nuclear have's and have nots*) as discriminatory and a form of "nuclear apartheid".[68] This gave rise to "fundamental differences" in the approach of India and European countries, which, taking advantage of the US nuclear umbrella, changed their approach in the 1990s from seeking nuclear disarmament to non-proliferation.[69]

Increased pressure from the West and the negotiation of additional treaties that would close the nuclear option meant that the time to make a decision was shrinking. Eventually, the situation was decided unequivocally by the new right-wing Indian People's Party (BJP) government led by Atal B. Vajpayee. On May 11 and 13, 1998, India conducted five nuclear test explosions in the Rajasthan desert, after which it declared itself a nuclear state. In response, Pakistan conducted its tests on May 28.

The situation has triggered one of the most serious crises in India's relations with the West. In the first reaction, the EU – acting through Britain holding the rotating Presidency in the European Council – expressed "dismay" at the news of Indian nuclear tests, and was "concerned about the risk of nuclear and missile proliferation".[70] Several EU member states coordinated their response and jointly issued demarches (formal diplomatic protests) in New Delhi. Yet, the reaction was not that strong like major power. The US condemned India (and Pakistan) for the move and imposed sanctions. In June, a joint statement criticizing India and calling for the abandonment of nuclear weapons was jointly signed by the US, Britain, and China. However, at the same time, the US engaged in the most intensive diplomatic talks with India in history, which eventually led to the normalization of relations and a historic India–US rapprochement.[71]

The EU and European countries were equally concerned about India's action. However, despite a principled stance on nuclear issues, Europe's approach appeared divided. Sweden, Denmark, or the Netherlands joined the US in condemning India's tests and suspended their aid programmes and wanted the EU to take a strong stance. However, others like Spain and especially France showed more understanding of the Delhi government's decision, recognizing that India, which is not a member of the NPT, had no obligation to refrain from entering in possession of these weapons.[72] Moreover, France, following in the footsteps of the US, soon engaged in bilateral talks with India and was the first European country to establish a "strategic partnership" in September 1998.

Eventually, divisions within the EU softened the focus of the Union's criticism, which was limited to two European Council declarations on May 25 and June 8–9.[73] In the first declaration, the EU "condemned" India's underground nuclear tests, deeming them a "serious threat to international peace and security and global efforts towards non-proliferation and nuclear disarmament".[74] Union urged India, among other things, to join the NPT and sign the CTBT, threatening otherwise to consider excluding India from the EU's GSP trade preference scheme and withholding loans from the World Bank. It praised Pakistan's "restrained response", (which has yet to respond with tests of its own two days later) promising increased development assistance.

India's reaction was swift and decisive. Just a day later, a foreign ministry spokesman, referring to the EU declaration, stated that "any suggestion that India should conform to international regimes or face economic consequences is unacceptable".[75] He reminded that "Indian policy is carried out only by the national leadership and no one else and is meant to serve India's interests", and any suggestion by foreign partners containing "warnings" or "ultimatums" is unacceptable. He recalled India's "impeccable record on disarmament" and scoffed at the fact that "these suggestions come from countries that themselves possess nuclear weapons or enjoy a nuclear umbrella".

Director of the government think-tank IDSA Jasjit Singh warned shortly after the nuclear tests against escalating rhetoric from European partners, pointing out that this "would only lead to polarized relations between the world's largest democracy and Western liberal democracies", and asserted that India's "containment strategy" simply won't work in the current international climate, and that India is capable of withstanding even the largest economic sanctions. Instead of confrontation, he recommended that Europe take the path of adapting and accommodating India to new conditions.[76]

Following the Pakistan's tests on 28 May, the European Council adopted declarations on Indian and Pakistani nuclear tests on June 8–9, 1998, and on June 15–16, 1998, adopted conclusions on Indian and Pakistani nuclear tests, in which demanded that both India and Pakistan sign the CTBT as it stands and move to ratify it, and called India and Pakistan, to adhere to the NPT as it stands, without any modifications. On June 18, 1998 the European Parliament adopted resolution in which it strongly condemned the tests and called on India and Pakistan to refrain from further tests and to accede immediately and unconditionally to the NPT "without any modifications" and to the CTBT.[77] On October 26, European Council adopted Common position, in which focus shifted however, to support contribution to the promotion of non-proliferation in South Asian region and confidence-building measures among India and Pakistan.[78]

In the end, the EU as a whole did not impose sanctions on India, as the US or Japan did. Individual measures were taken by some European countries, such as the Netherlands, Switzerland, Norway, Sweden, and Denmark, which halted their own development assistance programmes and introduced arms export restrictions. Though political dialogue with India has been frozen for some time, it resumed soon with the EU–India Troika ministerial meeting on November 13, 1998, in New Delhi. Indian Foreign Ministry officials noted with some satisfaction in 1999 that "while most countries in Western Europe and the EU expressed reservations about the tests, the specific reactions of individual countries were far from homogeneous".[79] Although the EU's action was thus ultimately limited to only critical political statements and diplomatic pressure, the issue seriously spoiled the atmosphere of cooperation.

The situation was improved by India's declaration of voluntary moratorium on further tests, adoption of a doctrine of "*no-first-use of* these weapons" (known as the "*no-first-use policy*"), announcement of a total ban on nuclear exports and announcement of cooperation with the NPT regime as a non-member state. India also explained its decision by the unique security situation in the region (where two neighbours – China and Pakistan possessed nuclear weapons) and the defensive nature of these weapons as a "deterrent.

India's assertive but also cooperative stance soon had a positive effect. In a subsequent resolution in 1999, the European Parliament special report, usually critical of India, noted that "India deserves more attention than it received before the tests"[80] and called for strengthening cooperation. In its Resolution in June 1999, finally, the European Parliament supported the idea of the Commission to establish with India an "enhanced partnership".[81] It was also increasingly clear to the Europeans that forcing India to give up its weapons and "roll back" its nuclear programme was impossible. Following the example of the US and France, the EU, too, as a result, began to listen more carefully to India's security concerns and eventually showed more understanding of Indian arguments. Quite quickly, intensive talks and a new reset in relations took place, despite differences in the assessment of the nuclear issue.

2.4 The EU as a key economic partner

2.4.1 *India–EU trade in goods*

Indian liberalization has lifted a number of restrictions and opened the door to comprehensive economic cooperation with the EU. In many key areas, it was possible to record serious progress in the 1990s. India–EU trade began growing rapidly as early as 1993 (up 20.24% year-on-year) and maintained a high growth rate until 1998, when it declined for the first time (-1.74% year-on-year).[82] Overall, the value of all trade doubled from 1991 to 1999, from less than €10 billion to more than €20 billion and €25.7 billion in 2000 (see Chart 2.1).[83] Although India bought more than it sold to EU markets, the deficit was no longer as large as during the Cold War.

Despite the increase in trade volume, it is worth noting that the EU's share of India's total merchandise trade began a slow decline. While the ratio was 27.71% at its peak in 1991, it dropped to 25.41% in 1997 and 26.32% in 1998.[84] This was due to the fact that India, which was opening up to the world, also began to cooperate more with other countries in Asia and the Persian Gulf, while the US was also strengthening its position. Still, the EU was the largest export market for India.

India's largest trading partners in the EU were Germany (in 1998 accounted for 21.82% of EU-15 trade with India), the UK (21.53%), Italy (12.82%), Belgium (12.67%), and France (10.32%).[85] The first five countries accounted for as much as 80% of India's trade with the "15", which shows a high concentration of cooperation with selected partners. It is also worth noting the declining importance of the UK in India's trade. While its share in the EEC's trade with India reached 59.52% in 1970, it decreased to 21.53% in 1998. Germany and continental Europe as a whole were becoming more important partners for India.

The main products exported to the Union from India at the time were textiles and clothing (38.8% in 1997), engineering products (13.5%), agricultural products (13.3%), and precious stones and jewellery (10%). In

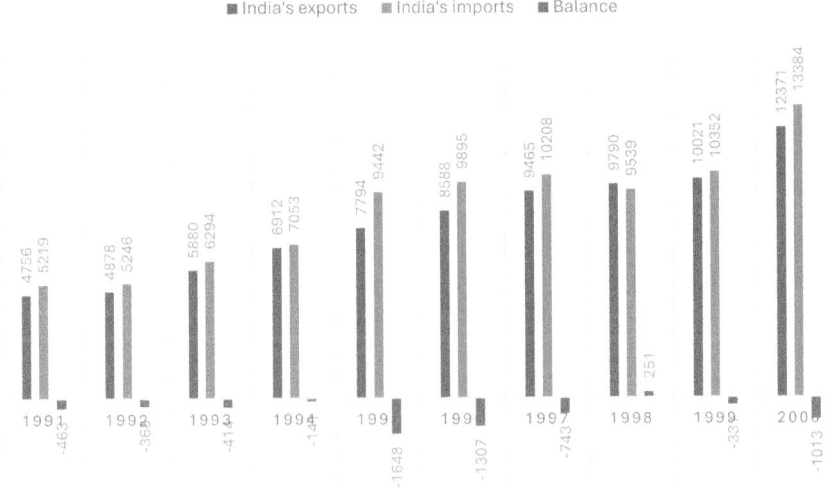

Chart 2.1 India's trade with the EU from 1991 to 2000 (Euro, million)

Source: Eurostat. Comext database. International Trade. Author's own compilation. Accessed 20.03.2021.

contrast, India mainly bought engineering products (42.5%), precious stones and jewellery (28.5%), chemical products (11.3%), and metals and minerals (10.7%) from Union countries. India thus continued to sell mainly low-processed products to the Union, while buying machinery and equipment. Jewellery products were a separate category due mainly to the formation of trade in this area between Belgium and India.

However, the increase in trade was also accompanied by increasingly serious disputes and accusations. India continued to demand easier access to the common market, which it saw as "very difficult to penetrate". Indian exporters complained about "unclear EU regulations and business practices" and "an excess of non-tariff barriers" and "non-technical barriers to trade", including meeting exorbitant technical standards, holding appropriate licenses, environmental certificates, or geographical indications, etc. [86]

While Indian researchers admitted that tariffs in the EU are significantly lower than in India (average tariffs in the EU at 3–4%, while in India they were at 30%), they argued that the problem is not the tariffs themselves, but a host of non-tariff restrictions (such as anti-dumping fees, quotas, etc.)[87] They pointed out that despite the fact that under the WTO, developed countries have pledged to convert non-tariff barriers into tariffs by 2005, even before this has happened, they are already erecting new forms of restrictions to protect the market. Others stressed that "although such non-tariff barriers are more delicate in their application, they have the same potential to block market access as more official and quantifiable tariff measures".[88]

The main barriers to entry into the EU market included sanitary and phytosanitary standards, product packaging and labelling requirements, quota arrangements, or anti-dumping and countervailing proceedings. Over time, environmental standards and requirements for working conditions began to play an increasingly important role. On the basis of these measures, exports of Indian textiles (quota restrictions), seafood (banned in 1997 for failure to meet phytosanitary standards), stainless steel (anti-dumping proceedings and countervailing duties of 25.5%), among others, were restricted or stopped in the 1990s. Particularly unauthorized was the use of anti-dumping proceedings (e.g. against cotton fabrics and bedding in 1994) as a tactic to stall product entry and increase costs for exporters.[89] India increasingly viewed these regulations as protectionist measures to protect European producers from competition from cheaper suppliers from developing countries.

As one researcher noted with disappointment, "to expect the EU to practice free trade as it teaches about it in the near future is to remain under an illusion".[90] Among the reasons cited for this situation were the asymmetrical nature of the relationship (the EU for India is much more important than India for the EU), the concentration of the European market on a few major countries, the competition of Indian exports with products with which there is already strong intra-EU trade, too little diversification of Indian exports.

On the other hand, India also had to fend off increasingly serious allegations from the EU. European partners raised the problem of unusually high tariffs and continuing restrictions on market entry or investments in certain sectors, as well as insufficient protection of intellectual property rights or unfair competition resulting from lower standards and access to cheaper raw materials. Increasingly, disputes with the EU moved to international forums (WTO), where India and the EU mostly presented opposing positions.[91]

2.4.2 Investment flows and development cooperation

In contrast, capital cooperation strengthened in the 1990s. Between 1994/4 and 1996/7, only the four largest European economies (Britain, Germany, the Netherlands, and France) invested $925 million in India – the most among all foreign investors.[92] In 1995/6 alone, the EU invested $281.7 million, almost 100 million more than the second-ranked US ($192 million) or the third (Japan – $60.9 million).

In the first four years after liberalization, FDI from the EU flowed in slowly to increase dynamically only after 1996. Indian researchers pointed to several possible reasons for the low investment interest from European companies: (1) market instability, (2) political instability, (3) lack of transparency, (4) discrimination between local and foreign investors, (5) failure to grant MFN status to foreign companies, (6) lack of freedom of choice in the area of activity, (7) lack of a level playing field, and (8) insufficient protection of intellectual property.[93]

At the same time, it is worth noting that while the value of investments from EU countries grew in the 1990s, their importance in the inflow of all investments declined. If EU countries were the source of 69% of FDI inflows in 1981, by 1996, their share had already fallen to 18.84%.[94] At that time, the share of the US, for example, in FDI inflows increased from 20.61% to 27.01%.

Development cooperation remained an important area in India's relations with the EU. Contrary to some fears, India remained an important recipient of EU aid. In the 1990s, it was the largest recipient in Asia. In contrast, at the same time, changes in Central Europe and growing needs in Africa caused India to fall further down the list of countries receiving the most ODA. Still, for India, the Union (Commission and member states) was the main source of aid.

After the end of the Cold War, there were significant changes in this cooperation: The value of aid increased significantly and project aid was replaced by sectoral budget support. Between 1993 and 2000, the EU provided 837 million euros to India, mainly for government programmes in two areas: basic health care and basic education, as well as for projects supporting development in rural areas and environmental protection (see Chart 2.2.)_.[95]

In total, European Institutions provided $940 million to India as ODA in the decade 1991–2000.[96] This placed them among several of the largest ODA donors, albeit with a small share in the total funds received by India. In addition to this, major donors for India were the UK, Germany, or the Netherlands, further strengthening the EU's position as a collective partner. However, much more important sources of financial support were multilateral institutions (World Bank, UN), as well as Japan.

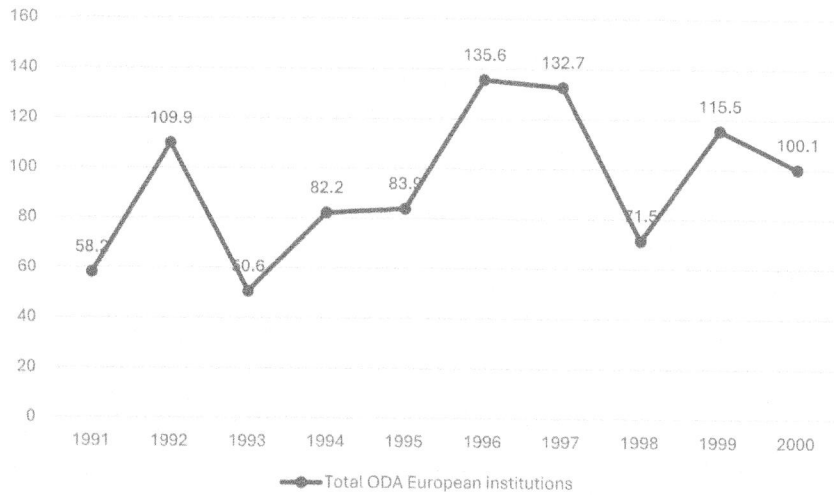

Chart 2.2 Official Development Assistance of European Institutions to India 1991–2000 (total aid, net disbursements, constant prices, millions of dollars)

Source: Own compilation based on: OECD.Stat, Official Development Assistance (ODA) https://stats.oecd.org/

2.5 Balance of the first decade

In conclusion, the end of the Cold War forced an attempt to redefine India's international strategy and change its economic policy. A number of factors favoured taking a more active policy towards the EU. In the context of the realization of the country's superpower ambitions, closer relations with the EU – an economic power and a deepening political integration at that time – took on greater significance. The liberalization of the Indian economy and integration into the processes of globalization were raising the value of the Union as an economic partner. The rapprochement between India and Europe was served by the spread of liberal international order, where democratic systems of governance were gaining importance. The expansion of the free market in the world's largest democracy was expected to make it more like European countries, just as happened with post-communist states in Central Europe.

Despite these positive conditions, the balance of the first decade after the end of the Cold War in India's policy towards the EU is mixed. From India's perspective, some of the assumptions or expectations of the EU proved to be excessive and impossible to meet. At the same time, however, the first post-Cold War years cannot be described as a "lost decade". Rather, it should be described as a period of transition and preparation for more fruitful strategic cooperation in the future. India, like the EU, used this time to get its domestic affairs in order and in its immediate neighbourhood. Secondarily, it has only had to reinvent itself in the changed international order and arrange relations with the major powers, including Europe.

The greatest progress has been achieved on economic front. India's economic opening to the world and faster GDP growth have caused trade with the EU to increase significantly, and India has boosted exports to the EU market. This has significantly reduced India's deficit in merchandise trade. European investments and technology also flowed to India in a wider stream, yet at much smaller scale than to China.

While much progress has been made economically, political cooperation has encountered unexpected problems. Disputes over India's nuclear programme, the conflict with Pakistan, and the situation in Kashmir have worsened the atmosphere of India–EU relations and prevented closer cooperation. Perhaps most surprisingly, democracy – which was supposed to be the element that brought the two sides together and facilitated mutual understanding – turned out to be a significant source of tension and misunderstanding.

While the EU has finally begun to take India more seriously, it has not supported India's aspirations to play a greater role in the region and in global politics. Not only has the EU failed to formally recognize India as a global power worthy of a permanent seat on the UN Security Council, but it has accepted India's exclusion from the Europe–Asia–ASEM dialogue. To the disappointment of the Indians, the EU chose China as its main partner in Asia, despite systemic differences. What irritated Delhi even more, it was not China, but India that also became the object of European criticism in the context of human rights. The community of political systems has thus not played a major role, in India's relations with the EU, contrary to the expectations.

At the same time, India's more assertive stance has begun to yield tangible benefits. Faster economic development (and eventually nuclear testing) strengthened India's position vis-à-vis the EU. While India was a difficult and unattractive partner for Europe at the beginning of the decade, by the turn of the millennium it was still a difficult but more desirable partner. There was a growing realization in the EU that India should be treated as a priority partner and that a conversation should be held on strategic issues, including the difficult ones of counter-terrorism or non-proliferation of nuclear weapons. Increasingly intense political contacts and stronger economic ties were about to pay off.

India gained an additional partner in international politics, in addition to European countries, which watched its economic transformation quite favourably. Although India still preferred contacts at bilateral level, it tried to engage Union where it saw the greatest opportunities (trade, investment, development assistance). At the same time, Indian politicians found the EU's moralistic style of policy-making and detachment from the realities faced by the Indian state, in terms of terrorist threats or the fight against poverty, increasingly problematic.

India managed to lay the groundwork for closer relations in the future and made progress in many dimensions of cooperation. Tensions over human rights violations in Kashmir or India's nuclear programme, which complicated cooperation, has eased by the end of the decade. The end of the Cold

War and the historical changes in India and Europe have indeed opened a new phase in Indian policy towards the EU. India's goals previously limited to trade issues and development assistance have now broadened to include political affairs as well. Relations have been elevated from the level of economic contacts to a "political partnership" preparing the ground for a "strategic partnership".

Notes

1 *BJP Election Manifesto 1998*, Bharatiya Janata Party, BJP, New Delhi, 1998, p. 193.
2 Government of India, Ministry of External Affairs, *EC Communication Titled "An EU-India Strategic Partnership"– India's Response*, New Delhi, August 27, 2004.
3 Commission of the European Communities, *An EU-India Strategic Partnership. Communication from The Commission to the Council, the European Parliament and the European Economic and Social Committee.* Com(2004) 430 Final, {Sec(2004) 768}, Brussels, 16.6.2004.
4 Government of India, Ministry of External Affairs, *EC Communication Titled "An EU-India Strategic Partnership"– India's Response*, New Delhi, August 27, 2004.
5 *Annual Report 1991–1992*, Ministry of External Affairs, Government of India, New Delhi, 1992, p. I.
6 *Annual Report 1991–1992*, Ministry of External Affairs, Government of India, New Delhi, 1992, p. 46.
7 *Annual Report 1991–1992*, Ministry of External Affairs, Government of India, New Delhi, 1992, p. I.
8 *Annual Report 1992–1993*, Ministry of External Affairs, Government of India, New Delhi, 1993, p. 5.
9 *Lok Sabha Debates*, vol. V, no. 49, September 18, 1991. Parliament of India, p. 135.
10 *Lok Sabha Debates*, vol. V, no. 49, September 18, 1991. parliament of India, p. 159.
11 *Lok Sabha Debates*, vol. V, no. 49, September 18, 1991 Parliament of India, pp. 172–173.
12 *Annual Report 1991–1992*, Ministry of External Affairs, Government of India, New Delhi, 1992, p. VI.
13 P. Winand, M. Vicziany, P. Datar, *The European Union and India. Rehtoric or Meaningful Partnership?*, Cheltenhem: Edward Elgar, 2015, p. 143.
14 D. K. S. Bora, N. K. Sah, "Indo – EC Relations: Retrospect and Prospects", *India Quarterly*, vol. 50, no. 1/2 (January–June 1994), p. 68.
15 D. K. S. Bora, N. K. Sah, "Indo – EC Relations: Retrospect and Prospects", *India Quarterly*, vol. 50, no. 1/2 (January–June 1994), p. 68.
16 D. K. S. Bora, N. K. Sah, "Indo – EC Relations: Retrospect and Prospects", *India Quarterly*, vol. 50, no. 1/2 (January–June 1994), p. 75.
17 A. Q. Khan, M. Faiyaz, "The Euro – Implications and Opportunities for Global Trade: A Focus on India", *India Quarterly*, vol. 56, no. 1–2, 2000, p. 47.
18 Government of India, Ministry of External Affairs, *Annual Report 1992–1993*, New Delhi, 1993, p. 1.
19 Ministry of External Affairs, Government of India, *Annual Report, 1994–1995*, New Delhi, 1995, p. 64.
20 S. Barrow, "European Security and Defence Identity: Challenges and Opportunities", [in:] R. K. Jain, H. Elsenhans (eds.), *India, Europe and the Changing Dimensions of Security*, New Delhi: Radiant Publishers, 2006, p. 297.

21 B. Chellaney, "European and Indian Security in the New Millennium", [in:] R. K. Jain (ed.), *India and Europe in the New Millennium*, Delhi: Radiant Publishers, 2000, p. 102.
22 See Ministry of Defence, Government of India, *Annual Report, 1991–2000*.
23 R. K. Jain, "European Organizations After the Cold War", *India Quarterly: A Journal of International Affairs*, vol. 49, no. 1–2, January 1993, p. 48.
24 R. K. Jain, "Eastward Enlargement of the European Union: Issues, Problems, and Challenges", [in:] R. K. Jain (ed.), *The European Union in a Changing World*, Delhi: Radiant Publishers, 2002, pp. 46–80.
25 D. K. S. Bora, N. K. Sah, "Indo – EC Relations: Retrospect and Prospects", *India Quarterly*, vol. 50, no. 1/2 (January–June 1994), p. 68.
26 R. K. Randhawa, "Poland in Transition: Successes in the Initial Phase", *India Quarterly*, vol. 58, no. 1, 2002, pp. 139–152.
27 R. K. Jain, "European Organizations After the Cold War", *India Quarterly: A Journal of International Affairs*, vol. 49, no. 1–2, January 1993, p. 46.
28 R. K. Jain, "India and EU Enlargement", [in:] R. K. Jain, H. Elsenhans, A. S. Narang (eds.), *The European Union in World Politics*, Delhi: Radiant Publishers, 2006, p. 182.
29 R. K. Jain, "European Development Aid Policies in the 1990s: Implications for India", *India Quarterly*, vol. 52, no. 3, 1996, s. 39.
30 R. K. Jain, "India and EU Enlargement", [in:] R. K. Jain, H. Elsenhans, A. S. Narang (eds.), *The European Union in World Politics*, Delhi: Radiant Publishers, 2006, p. 190.
31 R. K. Jain, "India and EU Enlargement", [in:] R. K. Jain, H. Elsenhans, A. S. Narang (eds.), *The European Union in World Politics*, Delhi: Radiant Publishers, 2006, p.181.
32 P. Kugiel, D. Upadhyay, "India and Central and Eastern Europe: Post-Cold War Engagement", *International Studies*, vol. 54, no. 1–4, January–October 2017.
33 R. K. Jain, "India and EU Enlargement", [in:] R. K. Jain, H. Elsenhans, A. S. Narang (eds.), *The European Union in World Politics*, New Delhi: Radiant Publishers, 2006, p. 180.
34 R. K. Jain, "Eastward Enlargement of the European Union: East European Perceptions and Perspectives", *India Quarterly*, vol. 57, no. 1, 2001, ss. 181–185.
35 U. S. Bava, "India and European Union: From Engagement to Strategic Partnership", *International Studies*, vol. 47, no. 2–4, 2010, pp. 373–386.
36 *P. V. Narasimha Rao: Visit to Federal Republic of Germany, Part 2(Other Than Questions and Answers), Lok Sabha Debates*, Parliament of India, September 13, 1991, p. 511.
37 *Annual Report 1991–1992*, Ministry of External Affairs, Government of India, New Delhi, 1992, p. 44.
38 *Annual Report 1992–1993*, Ministry of External Affairs, Government of India, New Delhi, 1993, p. 71.
39 P. Winand, M. Vicziany, P. Datar, *The European Union and India. Rehtoric or Meaningful Partnership?*, Cheltenhem: Edward Elgar, 2015, p. 147.
40 Cooperation Agreement Between the European Community and the Republic of India on Partnership and Development, *Official Journal of the European Communities*, L. 223, August 27, 1994.
41 *Annual Report, 1993–1994*, Ministry of External Affairs, Government of India, New Delhi, 1994, p. 65.
42 *Annual Report, 1993–1994*, Ministry of External Affairs, Government of India, New Delhi, 1994, p. 65.
43 Cooperation Agreement Between the European Community and the Republic of India on Partnership and Development, *Official Journal of the European Communities*, L. 223, August 27, 1994.

44 See F. Cameron, "India and the EU: A Long Road Ahead", [in:] H. Pant (ed.), *Indian Foreign Policy in a Unipolar World*, London: Routledge, 2009.
45 E. Kavalski, "Venus and the Porcupine: Assessing the European Union-India Strategic Partnership", *South Asian Survey*, vol. 15, no. 1, 2008.
46 *Towards a New Asia Strategy, communication from the Commission to the Council*, COM (94) 314 final, Brussels, July 13, 1994.
47 B. Gaens, "The Development of the EU's Asia Strategy with Special Reference to China and India: Driving Forces and New Directions", [in:] B. Gaens, J. Jokela, E. Limnel (eds.), *The Role of the European Union in Asia. China and India as Strategic Partners*, Farnham: Ashgate, 2009, p. 74.
48 *EU-India Enhanced Partnership, Communication from the Commission*, COM (96) 275 final, June 26, 1996.
49 *Annual Report 1996–1997*, Ministry of External Affairs, Government of India, New Delhi, 1996, p. 61.
50 *Annual Report 1996–1997*, Ministry of External Affairs, Government of India, New Delhi, 1996, p. 61.
51 *Annual Report 1996–1997*, Ministry of External Affairs, Government of India, New Delhi, 1996, p. 61.
52 P. Winiand, "The Rise of Asia and India from 1990s to the 21st Century", [in:] P. Winand, M. Vicziany, P. Datar (eds.), *The European Union and India. Rehtoric or Meaningful Partnership?*, Cheltenhem: Edward Elgar, 2015, p. 154.
53 For example, the eighth round of India-EU Troika talks was held in Paris on April 6, 1995, and the ninth meeting was held in New Delhi on March 4, 1996. Ministry of External Affairs, Government of India, *Annual Report 1995–1996*, New Delhi, 1996, p. 75.
54 In 1996, a Friends of India Group, consisting of 60 members, was formed in the European Parliament. Members of the Delegation for South Asia also traveled to India (e.g. in December 1995) – *Annual Report 1995–1996*, Ministry of External Affairs, Government of India, New Delhi, 1996, p. 75.
55 P. Bhattacharya, "European Political Co-operation and South Asia: From Indifference to an Institutional Dialogue", [in:] B. Vivekanandan, D. K. Giri (eds.), *Contemporary Europe and South Asia*, New Delhi: Concept Publishing Company, 2001, pp. 77–92.
56 R. N. Ram, "India and the European Union in the New Millennium", [in:] R. K. Jain (ed.), *India and the European Union in the 21st Century*, Delhi: Radiant Publishers, pp. 6–7.
57 R. N. Ram, "India and the European Union in the New Millennium", [in:] R. K. Jain (ed.), *India and the European Union in the 21st Century*, Delhi: Radiant Publishers, p. 7.
58 R. N. Ram, "India and the European Union in the New Millennium", [in:] R. K. Jain (ed.), *India and the European Union in the 21st Century*, Delhi: Radiant Publishers, p. 7.
59 P. Sutton, "New Directions in the Development Policy of the European Union", [in:] B. Vivekanandan, D. K. Giri (eds.), *Contemporary Europe and South Asia*, New Delhi: Concept Publishing Company, 2001, p. 117.
60 S. Ganguly, *The Crisis in Kashmir: Portents of War, Hopes of Peace*, Cambridge, MA; New York: Woodrow Wilson Center Press; Cambridge University Press, 1998.
61 *European Parliament resolution of July 10, 2008 on allegations of mass graves in Indian-administered Kashmir*, European Parliament, Brussels, 2008.
62 R. K. Jain, "European Development Aid Policies in The 1990s: Implications For India", *India Quarterly*, vol. 52, no. 3, 1996, s. 45
63 *Annual Report 1999–2000*, Ministry of External Affairs, Government of India, New Delhi, 2000, p. 57.

64 *Annual Report 1999–2000*, Ministry of External Affairs, Government of India, New Delhi, 2000, p. 57.
65 See G. Perkovich, *India's Nuclear Bomb: The Impact on Global Proliferation*, Berkeley, London: University of California Press, 1999.
66 R. K. Jain, "India and the European Union: Challenges and Opportunities", [in:] R. K. Jain (ed.), *India and Europe in the New Millennium*, New Delhi: Radiant Publishers, 2000, pp. 89–99.
67 J. Singh, "India, Europe and Non-proliferation: Pokharan II and After", *Strategic Analysis*, vol. 22 no. 8, 1998, p. 1116.
68 J. Singh, "Against the Nuclear Apartheid", *Foreign Affairs*, September/October 1998.
69 J. Singh, "India, Europe and Non-proliferation: Pokharan II and After", *Strategic Analysis*, vol. 22 no. 8, 1998, p. 1116.
70 Quoted in: *Disarmament Conference Members Condemn Indian Nuclear Tests*, Press Release, DCF/332, United Nations, Geneva, May 15, 1998.
71 On this historical process leading to US-India rapprochement, see S. Talbott, *Engaging India: Diplomacy, Democracy, and the Bomb*, Washington: Brookings Institution Press, 2004.
72 S. Baroowa, "The Emerging Strategic Partnership between India and the EU: A Critical Appraisal", *European Law Journal*, vol. 13, no. 6, November 2007, p. 737.
73 Council of the European Union, *Conclusions of the 2097th General Affairs Council Meeting of May 25, 1998*, Brussels, May 25, 1998; Council of the European Union, *Conclusions of the 2104th General Affairs Council Meeting of June 8–9, 1998*, Brussels, June 09, 1998.
74 Council of the European Union, *Conclusions of the 2097th General Affairs Council Meeting of May 25, 1998*;
75 *Following is the text of a statement issued by the Official Spokesperson of the Ministry of External Affairs in New Delhi on May 26, 1998 regarding Statement Issued by the European Union at Foreign Minister's Level*. Vol. XLIV, no. 5, 1995 INDIA. India's Security.
76 J. Singh, "India, Europe and Non-proliferation: Pokharan II and After", *Strategic Analysis*, vol. 22 no. 8, 1998, p. 1120.
77 Resolution on nuclear testing by India and Pakistan adopted by the European Parliament on 19 June 1998, European Parliament, Strassburg, 19.06.1998.
78 Common Position of 26 October 1998 defined by the Council on the basis of Article J.2 of the Treaty on European Union on the European Union's contribution to the promotion of non-proliferation and confidence-building in the South Asian region, *Official Journal L 290, 29/10/1998*
79 *Annual Report 1998–1999*, Ministry of External Affairs, Government of India, New Delhi, 1999.
80 European Parliament, Report on the Communication from the Commission on EU-India Enhanced Partnership (COM (96)0275-C4-0-0407/96), Committee on Foreign Affairs Security and Defense Policy, EP 226.781/fin, February 18, 1999.
81 European Parliament, Resolution on the Communication from the Commission on EU- India Enhanced Partnership (COM(96)0275 C4-0407/96), *Official Journal C 175, 21/06/1999 P.*
82 N. Kurian, "India-EU Economic Relations: Problems and Prospects", [in:] B. Vivekanandan, D. K. Giri (eds.), *Contemporary Europe and South Asia*, New Delhi: Concept Publishing Company, 2001, p. 125.
83 Eurostat, European Commission, (Accessed 20.03.2021).
84 N. Kurian, "India-EU Economic Relations: Problems and Prospects", [in:] B. Vivekanandan, D. K. Giri (eds.), *Contemporary Europe and South Asia*, New Delhi: Concept Publishing Company, 2001, p. 126.

85 Eurostat, data as in: P. Winand, M. Vicziany, P. Datar, *The European Union and India. Rehtoric or Meaningful Partnership?*, Cheltenhem: Edward Elgar, 2015, pp. 126–127.
86 P. Winand, M. Vicziany, P. Datar, *The European Union and India. Rehtoric or Meaningful Partnership?*, Cheltenhem: Edward Elgar, 2015, p. 154.
87 H. S. Chopra, S. K. Bhattacharya. "India-EU Interface: Changing Perspectives on Cooperation for Economic Development", *India Quarterly*, vol. 53, no. 3/4, 1997, s. 120.
88 N. Kurian, "India-EU Economic Relations: Problems and Prospects", [in:] B. Vivekanandan, D. K. Giri (eds.), *Contemporary Europe and South Asia*, New Delhi: Concept Publishing Company, 2001, p. 128.
89 N. Kurian, "India-EU Economic Relations: Problems and Prospects", [in:] B. Vivekanandan, D. K. Giri (eds.), *Contemporary Europe and South Asia*, New Delhi: Concept Publishing Company, 2001, p. 132.
90 N. Kurian, "India-EU Economic Relations: Problems and Prospects", [in:] B. Vivekanandan, D. K. Giri (eds.), *Contemporary Europe and South Asia*, New Delhi: Concept Publishing Company, 2001, p. 123.
91 See R. K. Jain, H. Elsenhans (eds.), *India, the European Union and the WTO*, New Delhi: Radiant Publishers, 2006.
92 N. Kurian, "India-EU Economic Relations: Problems and Prospects", [in:] B. Vivekanandan, D. K. Giri (eds.), *Contemporary Europe and South Asia*, New Delhi: Concept Publishing Company, 2001, p. 122.
93 H. S. Chopra, S. K. Bhattacharya. "India-EU Interface: Changing Perspectives on Cooperation for Economic Development", *India Quarterly*, vol. 53, no. 3/4, 1997, s. 115.
94 H. S. Chopra, S. K. Bhattacharya. "India-EU Interface: Changing Perspectives on Cooperation for Economic Development", *India Quarterly*, vol. 53, no. 3/4, 1997, s. 115.
95 A. Coulon, "European Union Development Cooperation in India", [in:] S. A. Wulbers (ed.), *EU-India Relations: A Critique*, New Delhi: Academic Foundation, 2008, p. 17.
96 Data from OECD.Stat, Aid (ODA) disbursements to countries and regions [DAC2a] Total ODA Gross disbursements, Constant prices, $million. https://stats.oecd.org/ (Accessed 22.12.2022).

3 Era of engagement

Building India's strategic partnership with the EU between 2000 and 2014

At the turn of the Millennium India engaged the EU in the high-level dialogue since 2000, launched the Strategic Partnership in 2004, and set up broad and multifaceted institutional architecture of cooperation. The relationship, which had hitherto focused on trade, economic, and development issues, acquired a political and strategic dimension. While economic interests continued to dominate India's policy towards the EU, it has already gone beyond trade to include dialogue on regional issues and global challenges, security issues such as counter-terrorism, and piracy. By the end of this period, cooperation lost momentum showing limitations of the partnership.

The rapprochement with the EU was facilitated by a favourable international context and positive developments in India and Europe at the beginning of the new era. The 1999 elections brought a stable National Democratic Alliance (NDA) coalition government led by the Indian People's Party (BJP) ending the period of political instability of the 1990s. The new Prime Minister Atal B. Vajpayee portrayed India as a more assertive state pursuing superpower ambitions. The positive effects of economic reforms and the absence of strong sanctions after the 1998 nuclear tests meant that India's international standing improved significantly. The accelerating globalization and the good state of the highly developed economies were creating demand for export goods and IT and business services that were soon to become India's hallmark. The launch of the global "war on terror" in 2001 made India's local fight against terrorists in Kashmir suddenly part of a global effort by the international community. It also accelerated the removal of the recent Western sanctions imposed after the nuclear tests and made South Asia, a hitherto marginal region, a key area for global security.

The consolidation of a liberal international order with the key role of the US as the sole superpower and the progressive democratization processes around the world meant that India had to pay more attention to cooperation with the West. In doing so, the economic and political importance of the EU as a partner was growing. A period of economic growth and a deepening process of regional integration forced India to engage more not only individual European countries, but also to the EU as a separate entity.

DOI: 10.4324/9781003688648-4

This chapter has been made available under a CC-BY-NC-ND 4.0 International license.

India therefore responded positively to signals from Brussels indicating a desire for a new opening and closer cooperation. Three phases in the cooperation with the EU can be distinguished

1 2000–2004 – the "new opening" and preparation of the strategic partnership.
2 2005–2009 – operationalization of the partnership.
3 2010–2014 – increasing disillusionment and growing crisis in cooperation with the EU.

This chapter analyses India's cooperation with the EU in three dimensions – political, economic, and security. Firstly, it details the development of political relations on the basis of the expansion of the institutional framework of cooperation. It then characterizes the intensification of economic cooperation. Finally, it discusses the new areas of strategic and security cooperation.

3.1 The institutionalization of India's political cooperation with the EU

During the period 2000–2014, a multi-faceted and comprehensive institutional framework for India's cooperation with the EU was established. The highest level of contact became the annual India–EU Summits. They were the ones that set the agenda, served to discuss key bilateral and global issues, mobilized to expedite the negotiation of concrete agreements and prepare new initiatives that could be announced by politicians. They also helped to foster mutual understanding between the parties and to give visibility to the relationship. Over the years, the Summits have been the main opportunity for Indian media or experts to take an interest in the EU.

At the lower level, the main mechanisms responsible for the implementation of the Summits and the day-to-day management of the partnership were the annual Ministerial Meetings on political issues (India–EU Troika Meetings since 1993, and since 2010 EU–India Ministerial Meetings) and the Joint Commission on economic issues. Supporting the work of ministers and discussing more specific issues have been the annual Foreign Policy Consultations (Foreign and Security Policy Consultations since 2011) at the level of Secretaries of State and the biannual meetings of senior officials (SOMs) and the sub-committees of the Joint Commission. The institutional architecture of official contacts was complemented by thematic and sectoral dialogues. More technical and specialised issues were discussed by junior officials and experts in joint working groups. Outside the official structure, but in close connection and association, there were platforms for contacts between civil society and business representatives. By 2014, this whole complex structure counted more than 30 different mechanisms within three areas: (1) political and strategic, (2) economic, and (3) socio-economic dialogue (Table 3.1).

Table 3.1 Institutional structure of India–EU cooperation by 2014

India–EU Summits (since 2000)

Political and strategic dialogue	Economic dialogue	Civil society dialogue
1 India–EU Troika Meetings (1993–2010)	1 Joint Economic Commission (1993)	1 EU–India Business Summit (2000)
2 EU–India Ministerial Meetings (2010)	a Subcommission on Trade (1993)	2 EU–India Round Table (2000–2009)
3 India–EU Policy Planners Dialogue (1998)	b Subcommission on Economic Cooperation (1993)	3 EU–India Think Tank Network (2000)
4 Foreign Policy Consultations (2011)	c Subcommission on Development Cooperation (1993)	4 India–EU Civil Society Internet Forum (2005)
5 Senior Officials Meetings (1998)	i Working Group on Agriculture and Marine Products (2000)	5 India–EU Information Society Dialogue (2005)
6 Dialogue on countering international terrorism (2000)	ii Working Group on Telecomunications (2000)	6 EU–India Business Round Table (2005)
7 Dialogue on disarmament and non-proliferation (2004)	iii Working Group on Textiles (2000)	7 EU–India Forum on Effective Multilateralism (2009 –2013)
8 Dialogue on Human Rights (2004)	iv Working Group on Consular Issues (2000)	
9 EU–India Security Dialogue (2005)	v Working Group on Environment (2000)	
10 Dialogue on Pluralism and Diversity (2005)	vi Working Group on WTO (2000)	
11 Dialogue on UN peacekeeping and peace-building (2005)	vii Working Group on Food Processing Industries (2005)	
12 Dialogue on countering piracy (2011)	viii Working Group on SPS/TBT (2005)	
13 Political dialogue on culture (2010).	ix Working Group on Pharmaceuticals and Biotech	
14 Consultations on cybersecurity and cybercrime (2011)	x Working Group on Engineering (2010)	
	2 High-Level Economic and Commercial Dialogue (2000)	
	3 Energy Panel (2004)	
	a Working Group on Coal and Coal Cleaning Technologies (2005)	
	b Working Group on Energy Efficiency and Renewable Energy (2005)	
	c Working Party on Fusion Energy (2005)	
	d Working Group on Oil and Gas (2006)	

(*Continued*)

Table 3.1 (Continued)

India–EU Summits (since 2000)

Political and strategic dialogue	Economic dialogue	Civil society dialogue
	4 EU–India Environment Forum (2005) 5 Regular Macroeconomic Dialogue (2005) 6 Dialogue in the Sector of Civil Aviation (2005) 7 Comprehensive Dialogue on Migration Issues (2005) 8 Policy Dialogue on Employment and Social Security (2005) 9 Dialogue on Intellectual Property Protection (2005, 2006) 10 Dialogue on Regulations in Services Policy (2005) 11 Dialogue on Financial Services (2006, 2010)	

Source: Author's own elaboration based on the documents from the India–EU Summits, MEA Annual Reports, 2000–2014.

The expansion of the institutional framework for cooperation indicated India's growing engagement with the EU and laid a strong foundation for a strategic partnership.[1] It also reflected the ever-growing spectrum of issues where India saw the need for closer contacts. It allowed for detailed discussion and better mutual understanding of the parties' positions on bilateral and international issues ranging from trade to migration, counter-terrorism to climate negotiations. For India, this meant an opportunity to present its perspective, concerns, and needs in key areas to one of the world's major economies. As the Indian expert assessed, "more extensive engagement with the European superpower has intrinsic value, even if it does not narrow the differences or produce immediate results, since it does facilitates greater clarity and understanding of each other's perspective and approaches toward bilateral, regional and global issues".[2]

3.1.1 A new beginning: India's policy towards the EU in the period 2000–2004

The key event that opened a new phase and set the direction for India's cooperation with the EU was the first Leaders' Summit in Lisbon in June 2000. Participation in this meeting was important for India for several reasons. Firstly, it was seeking an end to international ostracism and normalization of relations with Europe after the 1998 nuclear tests, which would have been *de facto* recognition of its new nuclear-state status. Secondly, an important objective was to present the Indian position on Pakistan's support for terrorist organizations in Kashmir and aggression in Kargil a year earlier. Thirdly, it enhanced the prestige and international standing of India, which had become the second country with which the EU had launched bilateral summits (after China in 1998). After all, the Indian authorities hoped to boost economic cooperation, increase investment inflows, and stimulate economic contacts. For the new Indian government under the leadership of the BJP, distrusted in the West, it was also an opportunity to set out its expectations and give cooperation its preferred direction.

Therefore, when Antonio Guterres, Prime Minister of Portugal, the country holding the rotating Presidency of the Council of the EU, proposed that a meeting at the EU level be organized on the occasion of the Indian Prime Minister's bilateral visit to Lisbon, the Indian authorities took up the challenge.[3] In addition to the host, the first EU–India Summit on 28 June in Lisbon was attended by Indian Prime Minister Atal B. Vajpayee and EU leaders – President of the European Commission – Romano Prodi and Secretary General and High Representative for the Common Foreign and Security Policy – Javier Solana along with several ministers from both sides.

The main outcome of the summit was the adoption of a Joint Declaration entitled "EU–India Partnership in the 21st Century". Both sides declared that "in the 21st century the EU and India shall build a new strategic partnership founded on shared values and aspirations". The normative basis for cooperation included "shared universal values of democracy and the respect for human rights, rule of law and fundamental freedoms", and the promotion of "international peace, stability and security".[4]

The short document (only 5 pages and 22 paragraphs) provided a synthetic overview of the state of the relationship and a long list of concrete proposals for joint actions and initiatives to strengthen cooperation in a number of areas, included in the Agenda for Action, attached to the declaration. It was agreed that EU–India Summits would continue on a regular basis and be held alternately in Europe and India, with the next one scheduled for 2001 in New Delhi. There were also to be annual meetings of foreign ministers and bi-annual Senior Officials Meetings. It was announced, inter alia, to launch a dialogue of eminent personalities in the form of EU–India Round Table and a dialogue of experts in the form of EU–India Think Tanks Network. The summit was accompanied by the EU–India Business Summit, creating a platform for direct contacts with European companies and an opportunity for India's economic promotion in Europe.

According to the Indian Ministry of Foreign Affairs, the summit "highlighted the convergence of perspectives" of the partners and marked "the beginning of a process of building a strategic partnership".[5] From a hindsight, it is even seen as a "watershed moment in the evolution of the relationship".[6] The Union gained greater visibility and relevance not only as an economic partner, but also as a political one. This paved the way for more top-level meetings in the following years.

Until 2010, summits were held regularly every year, alternating between India and Europe. This allowed to maintain contacts at the highest level and set the direction for cooperation. The Summits provided an opportunity to sign new agreements and declarations and launch new formats of cooperation. A list of the outcomes of each Summit is presented in Table 3.2.

The most important were the Summits in 2004 in The Hague, in 2005 in New Delhi, and in 2008 in Marseille. The second EU–India summit in Delhi in 2001 brought the Science and Technology Cooperation Agreement. The third meeting in Copenhagen in 2002 almost broke down due to excessive criticism of India in the context of human rights and democracy violations by the Prime Minister of Denmark, the country holding the EU Presidency. The fourth summit in New Delhi in 2003 became famous for the fact that it took place at all, which was uncertain in view of the last-minute cancellation of the arrival of the Italian Prime Minister Silvio Berlusconi, acting as President of the European Council. Nevertheless, even these less successful Summits have perpetuated the practice of dialogue and kept the dynamic of cooperation alive by bringing partners closer together.

The 2004 Summit in The Hague was a key step in cooperation. It was preceded by important developments in Europe and India that ultimately contributed to the success of the leaders' meeting. Firstly, in May 2004, general elections were held in India, which the ruling Indian People's Party (BJP) unexpectedly lost, and the United Progressive Alliance (UPA) coalition led by

84 *India's Policy Towards the EU in the Post-Cold War Era*

Table 3.2 List of India–EU summits from 2000 to 2014 and their main outcomes

I.P.	Date and place	Main documents signed	Main initiatives announced
1	June 28, 2000 Lisbon	1. Joint Declaration	1. EU–India Summits 2. Ministerial Meetings 3. Senior Officials Meetings 4. EU–India Round Table 5. EU–India Think Tank Network 6. Working group on countering international terrorism 7. High-level dialogue on WTO 8. High-level economic and commercial dialogue 9. Joint working group on environment 10. Institute of Environment Technology in India
2	November 23, 2001 New Delhi	1. Joint Communique Second India–EU Summit 2. Agreement for Scientific and Technological Cooperation between the Government of the Republic of India and the European Community 3. Declaration Against International Terrorism 4. Joint India–EU Vision Statement on Development of the Information Society and Information & Communication Technology 5. Financing Agreement between the European Community and the Republic of India,	
3	October 10, 2002 Copenhagen	3rd EU–India Summit, Joint Press Statement	
4	November 29, 2003 New Delhi	1. 4th EU–India Summit – Joint Press Statement 2. India-EU Customs Cooperation Agreement 3. Financing Agreement for EU-India Trade and Investment Development Programme	

(*Continued*)

Table 3.2 (Continued)

LP.	Date and place	Main documents signed	Main initiatives announced
5	October 8, 2004 The Hague	Joint Press Statement for 5th India–EU Summit	11 Dialogue on disarmament and non-proliferation 12 Energy Panel 13 EU–India Environment Forum 14 EU–India Security Dialogue 15 High-Level Trade Group
6	2005 New Delhi	1 Political Declaration on the India–EU Strategic Partnership 2 The India–EU Strategic Partnership: Joint Action Plan	16 Dialogue on Pluralism and Diversity 17 Dialogue on UN Peacekeeping and Peace-building 18 Comprehensive Dialogue on Migration 19 Regular Macroeconomic Dialogue 20 India–EU Civil Society Internet Forum 21 India–EU Information Society Dialogue 22 Dialogue in the Sector of Civil Aviation 23 India–EU Initiative on Clean Development and Climate Change 24 EU–India Business Round Table 25 Consultations between Europol and Central Bureau of Investigation 26 Working Group on Food Processing Industries 27 Joint Working Group on SPS/TBT 28 Working Group on Pharmaceuticals and Biotech 29 Policy Dialogue on Employment and Social Security 30 Dialogue to Discuss IPR Policy, Regulatory Issues, Implementation, and Enforcement 31 Dialogue on Regulatory Policy, including related to services
7	October 13, 2006 Helsinki	India–EU Summit Joint Statement	

(Continued)

Era of Engagement 85

86 *India's Policy Towards the EU in the Post-Cold War Era*

Table 3.2 (Continued)

LP.	Date and place	Main documents signed	Main initiatives announced
8	November 30, 2007 New Delhi	1 Joint Statement issued after the 8th India–EU Annual Summit 2 Agreement for Scientific & Technological Cooperation (renewed) 3 MoU on Multi-Annual Indicative Programme 2007–2009	32 European Business and Technology Centre (EBTC) in New Delhi 33 Working Group on engineering sector including automotive industry; 34 Dialogue on sustainable industrial policy
9	September 29, 2008 Marseille	1 EU–India Joint Press Communique 2 Global Partners for Global Challenges: the EU–India Joint Action Plan (JAP), 3 Horizontal Civil Aviation Agreement 4 Joint Work Programme, EU–India Co-operation on Energy, Clean Development and Climate Change	35 Dialogue on Financial Services 36 Political Dialogue on Culture 37 Dialogue on Counter-Piracy
10	2009 New Delhi	Joint Statement issued after India–EU Summit	
11	2010 Brussels	1 EU–India Joint Statement 2 India–EU Joint Declaration on International Terrorism 3 Joint Declaration on Culture	38 Dialogue on Cyber-Security
12	2012 New Delhi	1 India–EU Joint Statement 2 India–EU Joint Declaration on Enhanced Cooperation on Energy 3 Joint Declaration on Research and Innovation Cooperation 4 MoU between Eurostat and Ministry of Statistics and Programme Implementation	

Source: Own compilation based on EU–India summits' documents between 2000 and 2014.

the Indian National Congress took power. Manmohan Singh, an economist and author of the liberal reforms of the early 1990s, became the new Prime Minister. The new government, where the Prime Minister was a Sikh, the head of the ruling party had Christian roots (Sonia Gandhi) and the President was a Muslim (A. P. J. Abdul Kalam from 2002–2007) symbolized India's diversity and tolerance and the vitality of its democracy, much appreciated by the liberal European elites.

At the same time, historic changes were taking place in Europe. In May 2004, ten new countries from Central Europe, mostly new democracies, former communist bloc states, joined the EU. The EU has grown from 15 countries to 25, its population has increased by nearly 100 million people, and its borders have expanded eastwards to reach Ukraine and Belarus. The Indian Ministry of External Affairs (MEA) noted that "the ongoing changes in the EU – which is our largest trading partner and source of investment – have direct implications for India".[7]

At the same time, the Union has shown a growing interest in cooperating with India. The first European Security Strategy ("A Secure Europe in a Better World"), adopted by the European Council in December 2003, identified India, alongside China, Japan, and Canada, as a country with which "we should particularly seek to develop strategic partnerships".[8] In June 2024, the European Commission presented a vision for the further development of relations with India, including a proposal to launch a "strategic partnership".[9]

The Commission's communication was already the second strategy towards India (the first was presented in 1996), and together with a more detailed working document of more than 40 pages, analysed the main challenges, opportunities, and expectations for EU–India cooperation in the international, economic, and development fields. It proposed strengthening cooperation in five areas: (1) improved international cooperation; (2) enhanced economic partnership; (3) development cooperation; (4) mutual understanding; and (5) development of institutional architecture. In line with the new EU Security Strategy, the Commission called for a "renewed strategic partnership to promote an *effective multilateral* approach", as well as enhanced cooperation in conflict prevention and post-conflict reconstruction, non-proliferation of weapons of mass destruction, the fight against terrorism and organized crime, migration, democracy and human rights, peace, prosperity, and stability in South Asia.

In response to the European document, the Indian government prepared its own document in August 2004, accepting the proposal to establish a strategic partnership.[10] As a result, the EU Council Decision of October 11, 2004, endorsed the Commission's June proposals on relations with India. The Foreign Ministers of the 25 Member States supported the EC's assessment that "there is great potential for developing the content of the EU–India relationship in several key areas".[11] Finally, on October 28, a positive recommendation was also expressed by the European Parliament, identifying a dozen-specific recommendations.[12] All these steps prepared the ground for a historic meeting at the highest level.

The fifth India–EU summit took place in The Hague on November 9, 2004. Indian Prime Minister, Manmohan Singh before departing for Europe noted that India and the EU are "natural partners" and that their relationship is based on "shared values: democracy, pluralism, rule of law, free media and independent judiciary".[13] He noted with satisfaction that the European Commission had proposed a strategic partnership in "recognition of India's growing stature and influence", and that the meeting in The Hague would formalize a higher level of relationship. He also appreciated the importance of the enlarged Union as "an important political and strategic actor on the international stage".

The main outcome of the summit was to elevate the relationship to the level of a "strategic partnership", although the statement itself does not make a direct and clear statement to this effect.[14] It does, however, announce concrete steps in this direction, with a view to preparing jointly by the next Summit an EU–India Action Plan and a new Joint Political Declaration based on the positions of the Commission, the Council, and the Indian response.

The statement highlighted the "excellent atmosphere" of the Summit and substantial results".[15] It described the EU and India as "the largest democracies in the world" and recalled that their "partnership is based on a strong foundation of shared values and beliefs", enumerating in this context "democracy, pluralism, the rule of law and multilateralism". Progress in bilateral cooperation, regional and multilateral issues were discussed, and several new dialogue mechanisms were established (see Table no 3.2).

The Indian authorities assessed the outcome of the Summit well. Prime Minister Manmohan Singh, still at the press conference in the Hague, assessed the meeting as "historic", where "the India–EU strategic partnership was successfully launched".[16] He reiterated the two sides as "natural partners" and noted that the joint statement "captures the desire of both India and the EU to give strategic depth to our relationship". An Indian MEA publication to the national press after the summit highlighted the symbolic benefits and recognition of India's growing role, stressing that the summit with the EU at The Hague, "placed India in a special category of countries" as the EU's strategic partner status is "an honour hitherto reserved for the world's five major powers – the US, Canada, Russia, China, and Japan".[17] The same article pointed out that the summit's findings "make it clear that both sides will take up a coordinated fight against terrorism, a major source of worry for India for a long time". For his part, External Affairs Minister Natwar Singh, addressing the expert community in Delhi shortly after his return from The Hague, emphasized (besides the issues of terrorism and the economy) "the commitment of Europe and Asia to the common interest of strengthening multilateralism", which had become particularly necessary "in the aftermath of events in Iraq".[18] In this sense, he noted, "the EU will seek external assistance to strengthen multilateralism and countries such as India (but also China and ASEAN) are seen as increasingly important promoters of this idea".

3.1.2 *The operationalization of the strategic partnership: 2005–2009*

In the months that followed, India engaged in the creation of a joint action plan and the implementation of the Hague Summit. The focus was on operationalizing the strategic partnership and launching new dialogue mechanisms. The first meeting of the Energy Panel was held in Brussels on June 20, 2005, at the deputy ministerial level and established three working groups: (1) Coal and Coal Cleaning Technologies, (2) Energy Efficiency and Renewable Energy, and (3) Fusion Energy, including on India's participation in the ITER project. On November 12, 2005, the Environment Forum was launched in New Delhi. Parliamentarians' contacts were intensified.

The sixth India–EU Summit in New Delhi on September 7, 2005, was crucial in formalizing the "strategic partnership" and further institutionalizing cooperation. Two important documents were adopted: The Political Declaration on the India–EU Strategic Partnership, which replaced the 1993 Political Statement, and the Joint Action Plan (JAP), the first joint multi-year strategy to guide cooperation for three years.[19] It was also the first such document adopted by India jointly with a foreign partner. Until then, Action Plans were attached to Joint Declarations and announced annually for the coming year only.

The Declaration recognized the EU and India – "the world's two largest democracies sharing common values and beliefs" – as "natural partners in the modern inter-connected world".[20] It announced deepened cooperation in three areas: (1) political dialogue and cooperation; (2) economic dialogue and cooperation, trade and investment; and (3) bringing together people and cultures. The JAP elaborated on these tasks in detail (in 21 pages) by identifying dozens of proposals for initiatives and projects at bilateral and multilateral levels.[21] It announced over a dozen new consultation mechanisms and initiatives, including the launch of an EU–India Security Dialogue at senior official level to discuss key regional and global security, disarmament, and non-proliferation issues.

The plan also announced the completion of the negotiation of agreements to allow India's participation in the European Galileo project and the International Thermonuclear Reactor (ITER) initiative, as well as a maritime transport agreement and exploring the possibility for a horizontal aviation agreement. It also pledged, among other things, to continue talks on human rights and democracy, effective multilateralism, or closer cooperation between the EU and SAARC.

The implementation of the JAP was to be assessed annually at successive summits, and a comprehensive review was announced in three years' time in 2008. Prime Minister Singh, at the Business Summit held on the same day, expressed satisfaction at the adoption of the document, which "covers not only political aspects of the relationship, but most importantly, economic cooperation" stressing that "we see the EU as a natural partner in our economic development".[22]

The adopted declarations have given a new dynamic to India's cooperation with the EU. Already at the 15th Joint Commission Meeting in New Delhi on October 24–25, 2005, it was decided to set up a High-Level Group on Trade to explore the possibility of an EU–India Free Trade Area. In December 2005, India joined the ITER project as a full member. The first meeting of the Security Dialogue, announced in the Plan, was held in New Delhi on May 22, 2006, on the margins of a meeting of high-level officials.[23] The positive dynamics of cooperation led raised expectations to further "deepen the relationship"[24] and the need to move beyond trade issues and focus on developing security cooperation.[25]

A new impetus was given to economic cooperation. At the seventh EU–India Summit in Helsinki on October 13, 2006, leaders endorsed the recommendations of the report of the High-Level Trade Group and decided to "swiftly launch negotiations for a Broad-based Trade and Investment Agreement" (BTIA).[26] An important development in relations was the opening of another level of cooperation at the inter-regional level. The EU acknowledged India's support in SAARC's decision to have the Union join as an observer of the organization, while India was admitted to ASEM (Asia–Europe Meetings) that year.

Prime Minister Singh at the Helsinki Summit portrayed India and the EU as "indispensable pillars of the new multipolar world order" and "natural partners" calling on them "to work together to respond to issues of globalization, terrorism, proliferation, energy, and the environment".[27] He asserted that "an international order based on well-defined rules and effective institutions is in our vital interest". He also expressed satisfaction with the decision to support the negotiation of a trade agreement, expecting the talks to be finalized within two years. Referring to the recent terrorist attacks in Mumbai and London and Madrid, he pointed to common terrorist threats.[28] He also emphasized the importance of civilian nuclear power in achieving climate policy goals, at a time when important talks were underway in the Nuclear Suppliers Group for India to pave the way for finalizing a nuclear deal with the US.

In April 2007, the EU Council adopted a negotiating mandate for the European Commission to start FTA talks with India. Negotiations were formally launched in June 2007 in Brussels, and a second round took place in October 2007 in New Delhi.

Inter-parliamentary contacts were developing. In April 2007, for the first time ever, the President of India visited the European Parliament, addressing MEPs.[29] In turn, a separate Delegation for relation with India was created in the new European Parliament, replacing the earlier South Asia Delegation, highlighting the greater interest in India by European politicians. The group's chairperson, Neena Gil, visited India in August 2007. Still, Indian parliamentarians saw no need in setting up any EU group.

The eighth India–EU summit in New Delhi on November 30, 2007, did not bring new institutional arrangements or important policy decisions. Of greater significance was the ninth India–EU Summit in Marseille on September 29, 2008. The meeting resulted in the issuance of a Joint Communiqué, an updated Joint Action Plan, the signing of the Horizontal Civil Aviation Agreement, the launch of the Joint Working Programme on Energy, Clean development and Climate Change, and the inauguration of the European Business and Technology Centre in New Delhi. The updated Joint Plan of Action appreciated the "improved political cooperation" or "doubled trade" over the past five years and identified new opportunities for cooperation in three areas: (1) promotion of peace and comprehensive security; (2) promotion of sustainable development; and (3) promotion of research and technology, cultural, and people-to-people exchanges.

However, shortly after this successful summit, events and processes occurred that worsened the international environment and negatively affected India's policy towards the EU. On November 26, ten terrorists from the Pakistani-origin Lashkar-e-Toiba organization launched a three-day attack on several sites in Mumbai, killing more than 160 people. This Indian "September 11" re-established the issue of terrorism as the most important security challenge for India and worsened relations with Pakistan, halting the peace dialogue that had been ongoing since 2004. In the spring of 2009, India held general elections, but these consolidated the power of the UPA coalition led by the Indian National Congress. Prime Minister Manmohan Singh remained in office for a second term, but his position grew weaker and weaker in the coming years, limiting the government's willingness to take risks in foreign relations. Most importantly, the international financial crisis that began in the US in 2008 has soon hit the EU particularly hard, triggering a multi-year economic crisis.

The 10th anniversary India–EU Summit took place in New Delhi on November 6, 2009. However, it was held in the more difficult circumstances of the economic crisis and ahead of the Copenhagen Climate Summit in December 2009. Although economic and climate issues took a dominant place in the deliberations, the parties failed to reach a common position on these issues.[30] India succeeded in putting a caveat in the record that the fight against climate change should take into account the "overriding priority of poverty alleviation and socio-economic development in developing countries", treat "mitigation and adaptation to climate change" equally, and secure "financial and technological assistance to developing countries". The EU unequivocally expressed its "strong condemnation of the Mumbai terrorist attacks" and stressed the "utmost importance in bringing justice to the perpetrators of these cowardly acts". In this context, the EU and Member States expressed full support for India's application to join the Financial Action Task Force (FATF) and announced that negotiations for a cooperation agreement between Europol and Indian counterparts would be accelerated. Regional issues discussed included cooperation between SAARC and the EU, the future of Afghanistan, Myanmar/Burma, Nepal, Iran, and ASEM. Key bilateral negotiations and issues were discussed.

3.1.3 The growing crisis in India's policy towards the EU: 2010–2014

Since 2010, India's relations with the EU have been losing momentum and relevance. The international economic crisis hit the economies of European countries hard, making the EU more compelled to deal with its own problems. India, which continued to maintain a rapid growth rate, feared a decline in investment inflows and impeded access to the European market. At the same time, however, piling up economic problems and political tensions meant that the Manmohan Singh government paid less attention to foreign affairs, including relations with Europe, during its second term.

The next India–EU Summit took place in a new institutional setting. On December 1, 2009, the Lisbon Treaty on the functioning of the EU entered into force. From the point of view of external partners, it was important to replace the rotating presidency of a Member State by a permanent President of the European Council. The position of top European diplomat, called High Representative for Foreign Affairs and Security Policy, who was also the Vice-President of the European Commission, was strengthened. Foreign partners, including India, no longer had to conduct arrangements with biannually changing representatives of Member States, but with permanent EU officials. Summits with third countries were no longer to be held in the capital of the country holding the presidency, but in Brussels, the capital of the EU. The establishment of the European External Action Service on December 1, 2010 was to lead to the professionalization of EU foreign policy. At the same time, the Delegation of the European Commission in New Delhi was renamed the Delegation of the EU. Another change was the replacement of the previous EU–India Troika Meetings with Ministerial Meetings, where the Indian Minister's partner was the High Representative for Foreign Affairs and Security Policy.

In India, the institutional reforms were perceived positively as a step to reduce intra-EU competence disputes and facilitate relations with external partners. Indian diplomats expressed the expectation that the changes introduced by the treaty would "strengthen the functioning of the EU institutions and help improve foreign policy coordination among member states".[31] Moreover, it was expected that "as the EU's scope of authority expands, it will naturally enable cooperation between India and the EU on a wider range of bilateral, regional, and global issues of importance to both sides".[32]

The eleventh India–EU Summit took place only at the end of the year, on December 10, 2010, in Brussels. In an extremely brief statement, bilateral, regional, and global issues were discussed. The most important outcome of the meeting for India was a clear condemnation of terrorism and a call on Pakistan to "swiftly bring to justice all perpetrators, authors and facilitators of the Mumbai attacks". The parties adopted a second Declaration on

Combating Terrorism. The overall cooperation was increasingly weighed down by the difficulties in negotiating the BTIA.

In 2010, cooperation continued through existing mechanisms, such as the Security Dialogue (June 8 in Brussels) or the meetings of high-level officials (October 21 in Brussels). For the first time, the EU was represented by the High Representative for Foreign and Security Policy, Catherine Ashton, in the new format of a ministerial meeting (June 21 in New Delhi). In April 2010, members of the Delegation for India to the European Parliament visited India. It was also the second time that a meeting of experts and academics called the Forum on Effective Multilateralism was held in Brussels on October 11–12, 2010, by the Indian Council for World Affairs (ICWA) and the EU Institute for Security Studies (EUISS), an EU think-tank.

Evidence of the growing disenchantment with cooperation was the fact that a bilateral India–EU Summit was not held in 2011 for the first time since 2000. This was mainly due to delays in the FTA negotiations, as well as internal problems within the EU and India. Nevertheless, cooperation took place through established mechanisms (2011 saw a security dialogue, a meeting of high-level officials, an energy panel). At the same time, despite the absence of a summit, new forms of cooperation were introduced in 2011. Firstly, on November 15, 2011, the Foreign Policy Consultations were inaugurated in New Delhi at the level of Secretaries of State and their counterparts in the EU EEAS (or Heads of Department in the case of Commission) to exchange views on key regional and global issues. Secondly, on October 20, Indian experts participated for the first time in the EU–India Consultation on Cyber Security and Cyber Crime. Finally, the first meeting of experts on combating piracy was organized in New Delhi on November 16, 2011.[33] All these forms of dialogue were to be incorporated into the architecture of cooperation at the forthcoming leaders' meeting.

The 12th India–EU Summit was finally held in New Delhi on February 15, 2012. The leaders expressed in a statement their "satisfaction" with the deepening of the comprehensive relationship. The most important bilateral issue was the negotiation of the BTIA trade agreement, which the politicians said had recorded "significant progress" in all areas and which "is now close to completion".[34] After the meeting, the Indian Prime Minister assured of "extremely productive and wide-ranging talks held in a friendly and amicable atmosphere".[35]

2012 saw another Foreign Policy Consultation (July 20 in Brussels) and a second Cyber Security Consultation (in New Delhi on October 26). In May, the first round of negotiations for an agreement on the research and development of peaceful uses of nuclear energy took place.[36] In January 2013, dialogues on macroeconomic issues and on financial services took place in Delhi. Contacts between parliamentarians and experts continued (4th India–EU Forum on Effective Multilateralism, in Brussels October 23–24, 2012). Although successive rounds of trade agreement negotiations took place in 2012 and 2013, it became increasingly clear that the talks had stalled.

In 2013 India–EU summit did not take place again. One of the reasons was the lack of a breakthrough in the BTIA negotiations. The loss of political will to meet was indicative of a growing crisis and mutual relationship fatigue. India, too, was increasingly affected by the economic downturn and political problems, including a leadership crisis. In the last years of the Congress government, its domestic policy was characterized by stagnation, inertia, and lack of resolve and will to undertake difficult reforms, while its foreign policy was defined by low activity, lack of a clear vision, and a broader perspective.[37]

The escalating dispute between Italy and India over the 2012 arrest of two Italian sailors in the Indian Ocean, accused of murdering Indian fishermen, also created an increasingly bad atmosphere for cooperation. In a gesture of solidarity with Italy, the EU was not interested in pursuing a bilateral summit. For the Indian side, this showed that, despite the entry into force of the Lisbon Treaty, bilateral relations with an EU member continue to have an overwhelming influence on cooperation with the EU as a whole.

Despite the absence of the Summit, contacts continued at lower levels. New elements in India–EU cooperation in 2013 include the launch of the Policy Dialogue on Culture on April 18, 2013, in New Delhi (in line with the 2010 Declaration on Culture) and the signing of the India–EU MoU on Competition on November 21 in New Delhi, for the exchange of information and improved cooperation on the implementation of competition law. A second dialogue on anti-piracy was held at the EU naval base in the UK in September 2013 and a second meeting of high-level officials on education and multilingualism was held in Delhi on April 13.[38]

With parliamentary elections in India and the European Parliament scheduled for spring 2014, issues of cooperation with the EU were receding into the background, and the postponed bilateral Summit had to await the emergence of new leadership in Europe and India.

3.1.4 Criticism of the strategic partnership

After initial optimism, in recent years, there has been growing disappointment at the meagre tangible results of cooperation and growing criticism of the India–EU "strategic partnership". The impression in both India and Europe that the summits were focused on expanding cooperation formats rather than on solving specific problems was reinforced. While the "strategic partnership" developed mainly in the rhetorical layer, it fared less well in the content dimension of the partnership. Hence, some critics described the "strategic partnership" merely as a "charade".[39]

Indeed, the results of the strategic partnership in the first decade proved disappointing. By 2014, three bilateral agreements had been signed, and not in the most important areas: science and technology (2001), customs cooperation (2003), and civil aviation (2008). Alongside these, successes include several non-binding political declarations (on terrorism twice in 2001 and

2010; culture in 2010; on Enhanced Cooperation on Energy in 2012; and on Research and Innovation in 2012), as well as some technical documents on financing development programmes or cooperation on clean energy, etc. Negotiations on key agreements dragged on for years exceeding successive deadlines. Despite many assurances and calls for the rapid finalization of the talks, an agreement on maritime transport (negotiated since 2001), the development of a satellite navigation programme (2003), and cooperation on research and development in the peaceful uses of nuclear energy (2005) could not be agreed. Implementation of civilian aviation agreement signed in 2008 was delayed by years, and failed negotiations of the BTIA further strengthened the impression of that the partnership cannot deliver substantial outcomes.

The impressive list of dialogue mechanisms were not fully functional. Some of proposed formats have never kicked off, others went dormant, while many continued discussions without any breakthrough. In India, the impression was reinforced that the creation of further consultation mechanisms was an end in itself and the only outcome of cooperation. It was pointed out that a long list of objectives resembles a "wish list" and, without the right tools and funding, may not lead to the expected results. The ambitious agenda of the Joint Action Plan adopted in 2005 and updated in 2008 was described as "long on shared fundamentals and abstract political objectives but short on specifics and deliverables, and devoid of timelines".[40] The lack of joint initiatives in multilateral fora and the focus on economic issues meant that the partnership did not really acquire the strategic dimension that was announced.[41]

Indian experts had already warned that unproductive meetings with EU bureaucrats, could soon discourage Indian politicians from summits with more "information exchange" and "consultation" than decision-making and called for a "de-bureaucratization" of the strategic partnership suggesting that it was time to "move from dialogue and consultation to a higher level of concrete commitments in a rapidly changing Asia".[42] One expert's characterisation of the EU–India partnership as an "arranged loveless marriage" has become a popular symbol of a disappointing relationship.[43] It has become apparent that the creation of consultation mechanisms alone is not enough to overcome existing differences of interest and to break down the parties' historical mistrust.

Reasons cited for the limited progress in this relationship included the lack of understanding of India in the EU, the focus in Europe on China, the ambitions of smaller EU states to play a greater role in relations with India and the preference of larger member states to develop bilateral cooperation, and the problem of leadership in the EU, meaning tensions and divergences between short-term goals and national rivalries made it difficult to develop a coherent position.[44] Major European countries were strongly engaged in bilateral cooperation with India, forming bilateral strategic partnerships and looking after their own economic and security interests. Sensitive topics (such as human rights, climate protection) were relegated to the EU level, while bilateral relations focused on areas transferring real benefits (trade, investment, security).[45]

The practice of bilateral summits, and both before and after the Lisbon Treaty, confirmed the huge role that individual, even the smallest member states, can have on the EU–India partnership. Indian politicians felt that cooperation with the Community as a whole could be held hostage to individual member states' disputes with India, as was the case with the Copenhagen summit in 2002 or the Italian marine case after 2012. Opposition from individual states blocked EU support for India joining the NSG before 2008 or adopting a civil nuclear cooperation agreement and stood in the way of symbolic support for the country's aspiration for a permanent seat on the UN Security Council. This reinforced the practice of the Indian authorities to prioritize relations with the major European countries – Germany, France, and the UK. Relations with the EU were seen as complementary and additional to bilateral cooperation. Impasse in trade negotiations over BTIA exhausted initial enthusiasm and cast a shadow over the whole partnership. Cooperation with the EU was relegated to lower priority for Indian government.

3.2 India's economic and social cooperation with the EU between 2000 and 2014

Despite the challenges in building a strategic partnership, intensification of political contacts fostered the development of economic cooperation. Trade grew dynamically during this period and European companies became an important source of direct investment in India. At the same time, relations were extended to technological, scientific and educational cooperation, energy transition, or transport development. The declining importance of development aid from Europe was accompanied by a growing role for remittances from Indian migrants. The EU has been an important partner in achieving the country's economic and social objectives – to continue modernization, to maintain rapid growth rates, and ultimately lift millions of citizens out of poverty and provide them with the conditions to realize their potential.

3.2.1 The place of the EU in achieving India's economic objectives

In the 21st century, India has continued its gradual integration into the global economy to speed up its economic development. Successive five-year plans and trade policies heralded the modernization of the country and the transformation of the economy through increasing exports and participation in global trade, accessing new markets and technologies, and attracting investment in the industrial sector.[46] Economic cooperation with foreign countries was to play an important role in India's development and was to serve several key objectives: increasing exports, attracting investment and capital, creating jobs, and modernising the country. The EU could play a key role in all these areas. In the fiscal year ending March 2000, the EU was India's largest trading partner, accounting for 22.38% of imports and as much as 26.26% of exports.[47] Merchandise trade with the 15 member states amounted to $21.4 billion.

More frequent contacts with EU representatives allowed India to be promoted as an economic partner, but also to raise its own expectations and interests. For example, Indian Foreign Minister Yashwant Sinha pointed out during a lecture at the University of Athens in 2003 that "problems between India and the EU in the form of non-tariff barriers against Indian products must be resolved immediately".[48] He recommended that the EC should instead use more "constructive remedies" as envisaged by the WTO's treatment of developing countries. He proposed that both sides recognize each other's export surveillance agencies so as to facilitate trade, especially in agricultural products. Another important demand of India was mutual recognition of workers' qualifications, which would facilitate the mobility of professionals and facilitate the provision of services. He called for greater investment by companies in both directions, closer cooperation in science and technology (especially in the IT, biotechnology, pharmaceutical, and chemical sectors). Highlighting India's rapid development, he proposed that "the EU should seize the benefits of investing in a new, dynamic, creative and reborn India".

The fullest picture of India's economic objectives vis-à-vis the EU was contained in India's August 2004 response to the EC's proposals for the establishment of a strategic partnership. The document presented a long list of India's offensive and defensive interests. It detailed 13 sectors as offering the greatest potential for closer cooperation.[49] In particular, it emphasized the need to increase access to the EU market and reduce non-tariff barriers for Indian exports of food, textiles, and clothing. The analysis of the problems of an ageing Europe was accompanied by a presentation of the human capital of young India and a call for the EU to make "adjustments to its migration policy in order to sustain its economic efficiency and productivity levels". The paper called for "liberal and hassle-free movement of natural persons" and criticized the policies of some EU Member States that "maintain restrictions which are practically impossible to fulfil for setting up business by developing countries. "India attaches", the document states, "a high priority to the issue of mutual recognition of qualifications of Indian and EU professionals"". It also emphasized the huge opportunities for European companies arising from investment in infrastructure: power generation, transmission and distribution, construction of ports, motorway networks, privatisation of airports, urban development; food processing, medical services, the banking and insurance sector, or ICT. European investments should not only "facilitate the transfer of capital, but also the know-how and state-of-art technology". The signing of the strategic partnership was therefore intended, according to the Indian side, to help remove existing problems in economic cooperation and realize its potential.

Indian Prime Minister Manmohan Singh speaking at the EU–India Business Summit in New Delhi in 2005 described the EU as "a natural partner in our economic development" and referred to the reforms he initiated liberalizing the Indian economy in the 1990s. However, he pointed to the strong impression of Indian entrepreneurs that "the European market is becoming increasingly difficult to penetrate" because as tariff barriers disintegrate, then "non-tariff barriers suddenly come up".[50] Highlighting India's dynamic economic growth, he noted with concern that the EU's share of Indian trade and investment was steadily declining, crowded out by other Asian economies, and urged European entrepreneurs to "reverse this trend by re-discovering the new India that we are in the process of creating" so that they "don't miss this bus!".

At the same time, he portrayed India's vast human capital – "recognised world over– as an opportunity for the EU, where demographic shifts will widen the gap between the availability of skilled workers and the needs of economies and which can benefit from the services of "young Indian workers and professionals". He pointed out that a "liberal and easy [visa] regime allowing the free movement of natural persons" would create a "win-win relationship with the European Union."[51] He called for more European investment in Indian infrastructure – energy, roads, railways, ports, airports. He also raised India's other traditional demand in the multilateral talks in the Doha Round of the WTO, pointing out that "our developmental imperatives require accommodation of our concerns by developed countries" and demanding market access for agricultural and industrial products and services. Asserting his willingness to work with the EU for the successful conclusion of the Doha Round negotiations, he recalled that "the poor countries of the world have a vested interest in strengthening the rules-based, non-discriminatory a multi-lateral trading system".

At a subsequent summit in Helsinki in 2006, addressing EU business representatives, Prime Minister Singh emphasized India's rapid economic growth and enormous potential while pointing to a number of reforms he had undertaken that increased the attractiveness of doing business there (e.g. revision of the patent law, enhancing protection of intellectual property, enactment of the Right to Public Information Act, reduction of red tape for opening a business).[52] He again encouraged European entities to participate in the "investment boom that is taking place in India" and to set up research and development centres. The Union and India were to cooperate in developing a *knowledge industry*. European companies – according to him – should become an active partner in India's "historic transformation" and help tap the "dormant potential" of cooperation.

For his part, at his last EU–India summit in February 2012, Singh stressed that India attaches "great importance to the EU's participation in our growth agenda, especially infrastructure development, the development of clean energy technologies, innovation, research development, and training".[53] Once again, the Indian Prime Minister very clearly highlighted the problem in facilitating people-to-people exchanges, travel of tourists, businessmen, skilled workers, and other categories.

In addition to the potential for increased bilateral cooperation, India also looked to the EU as an important partner in shaping international regulations and standards to better serve Indian interests. Alongside increasingly fierce disputes with the EU in international trade negotiations at the WTO, Indian diplomats have been careful to ensure that European proposals to combat climate change or develop modern technology do not harm developing countries.

As can be seen, there are several well-established themes running through these statements and documents, which were important objectives for India vis-à-vis the EU. These include in particular:

1 Increasing access to the EU market, especially by reducing non-tariff barriers
2 Encouraging greater European investment in India, particularly in infrastructure and the manufacturing sector
3 Enabling access to the EU labour market for Indian professionals, through visa liberalization, recognition of qualifications.
4 Increasing technology transfer and joint development research
5 Protecting the rights and privileges of developing countries in multilateral negotiations

3.2.2 Negotiating a free trade agreement with the EU

Awareness of the untapped potential for economic cooperation and existing barriers to accessing the EU market prompted India to negotiate an FTA. The European market of 500 mln people, with an average GDP per capita of over €25,000, had strong purchasing power. An additional impetus was the prospect of losing access preferences to the EU under the GSP scheme, which was available to the least developed countries. India's main asset and bargaining chip in economic talks with the EU was, in turn, its own huge and hitherto closed market of over one billion people.

At the beginning of the new century, talks on enhancing economic cooperation and reducing barriers were held by India within the Joint Economic Commission (and its sub-committees and working groups), as well as at EU–India business summits held since 2000. Recognising insufficient progress in improving relations, the 2002 Summit set up a special initiative, the Trade and Investment Development Programme (TIDP), to which the EU contributed €14 million, to facilitate cooperation through the provision of training, technical assistance and equipment.

At the Sixth Summit in 2005 in The Hague, it was decided to set up a High-level Group on Trade (HLGT), which was to examine, among other things, the possibility of adopting a free trade agreement. The results of the report were already presented at the next summit in Helsinki in October 2006, recommending the launch of negotiations for an ambitious and comprehensive agreement covering not only trade but also investment. The authors estimated that such an arrangement would bring tangible benefits to both partners, including that it was expected to boost India's GDP growth by 0.6% in the short term and 1.6% of GDP in the longer term.[54] The broadly positive effects of an agreement for both sides were also pointed out by other independent studies of the consequences of signing an FTA emerging at that time.[55]

The agreement to start negotiations at the Helsinki Summit rekindled hopes that the talks would be finalized quickly. The HLGT met twice more in 2006 and early 2007, preparing the ground for formal negotiations. Finally, negotiations of the Broad-based Trade and Investment Agreement (BTIA) formally began in June 2007 in Brussels. Prime Minister Singh initially estimated that the negotiations should take two years.[56]

The comprehensive and ambitious agreement was to lead ultimately to a substantial reduction or complete elimination of tariffs for most trade of goods and services, and also covered investment, government procurement, intellectual property rights, geographical indications, competition policy, and others. It was to cover min. 90% of trade, both in terms of exchange value and tariff lines. From the outset, however, the parties had divergent approaches to the level of ambition and scope of the agreement.

India's objectives were limited and focused on trade and investment facilitation, primarily removing trade and non-tariff barriers, increasing access to the European market, and boosting investment flows to India.[57] The Union insisted that the agreement should also cover access to government procurement, investment protection, guarantees for the protection of intellectual property rights and competition policy, as well as sustainability issues.

If the agreement came into force, it would be the largest free trade agreement between a developing country and a bloc of highly developed countries (North-South FTA). Entering the talks was quite a challenge and a breakthrough for India in particular. After all, it had traditionally been sceptical of regional trade agreements and preferred multilateral negotiations in the WTO. It was only the impasse at the WTO that prompted it to gradually change its own policy and increase its interest in Regional Trade Agreements (RTAs). Although India at that time already had the first RTAs with several countries in Asia and was preparing others with Japan or Australia, none were as comprehensive as the agreement with the EU.

Apart from the huge asymmetry in the level of economic development between the EU and India, an additional problem was the differing level of market protection. Although India had been clearly reducing tariffs since the 1990s, they remained at much higher levels than in the EU, in some sectors (e.g. alcohol) reaching 150%. The reduction or elimination of tariffs would therefore require greater concessions on the Indian side. This posed a major political challenge for the government to explain to its own people why it was granting concessions in market access to some of the richest and most technologically advanced economies in the world. At the same time, the reduction in European market access tariffs, which were among the lowest in the world anyway, had relatively less benefit.

India therefore sought preferential treatment and greater concessions from the EU in other areas. The starting proposal at the beginning of the negotiations was that the EU should cover more tariff lines than India, which if it opened 90% of all tariffs, then the EU should do so for 95%.[58] Indian diplomats considered such a solution "fair" pointing precisely to the huge differences in the level of socio-economic development.[59] This argument, however, was not understood by the EU side, which emphasized the principle of reciprocity. The relatively small benefits of tariff reductions, on the other hand, led India to pay more attention to the removal of non-tariff barriers, particularly the reduction of onerous application of sanitary and phytosanitary standards (SPS) and technical barriers to trade (TBT).

India's other offensive interests have been in the services sector, particularly under the so-called Mode 4 of the General Agreement on Trade in Services (GATS) (i.e. provision of a service by the periodic presence and work of persons originating from one member country in the territory of another member country) and Mode 1 (provision of a service from the territory of one country to the territory of another country). On the first issue, India sought streamlining of visa issuance, work permits, and recognition of qualifications. On the second issue, India was particularly keen to be recognized as a *data secure nation*. It was important for increasing access to the EU market for IT and business services companies, sectors in which they had a comparative advantage.

There was a much longer list of defensive interests, i.e. matters where India would like to retain increased protection of its own market. These ranged from trade (e.g. certain categories of agricultural products, the automobile sector or liquor) to services (banking, wholesale retail, financial, accounting, and legal services). Product categories that required further protection were placed on a "negative list" or "sensitive list" and were excluded from tariff reductions or subjected to longer transition periods.

India was also reluctant to accept EU proposals to link trade with environmental or human rights protection. There were also differences over procedural issues. It was India that was keen to maintain the confidentiality of the negotiations and limit the information reaching the public, due to fears of public protests and criticism from the opposition. As the Indian negotiator recalls, "there is a tradition in India of maintaining the confidentiality of international negotiations [...] fear of the media, press, and parliament is built into the Indian system and results in fear of powerful criticism if one is perceived to be making concessions to the developed EU".[60]

The first round of formal BTIA negotiations took place on June 26–27, 2007, in Brussels, following the adoption of the negotiating mandate for the EC by the EU Council in April. Decisions were made at the level of India's Trade Minister and the EU Trade Commissioner, and the talks themselves were conducted by the designated lead negotiators. Two more rounds were held in 2007, allowing Indian and EU leaders at a summit in November to praise the "progress made" and assert a "willingness to further intensify negotiations".[61] At the next summit in September 2008 they "recognized the importance of concluding negotiations quickly".[62] Prime Minister Singh, at a press conference after the meeting, said that the EU and India had agreed to "work to complete the negotiations by the end of 2008". When the deadline was not met, a year later at a summit in Delhi in November 2009, the leaders reiterated their willingness to "expedite the talks so that the agreement is adopted as soon as possible".[63]

At a subsequent summit in Brussels in December 2010, Indian and EU representatives noted the "significant progress recorded during recent negotiations" and even announced agreement on the "contours of a final package".[64] A new date for the completion of the talks was indicated this time as "spring 2011". Despite the failure to meet this deadline as well and the increasingly difficult international environment, the parties remained positive and confident of ultimate success also at the next summit in February 2012. The leaders assured that "negotiations on an ambitious and balanced package are close to completion" and that the relevant ministers "will monitor the progress of the negotiations with a view to their speedy completion".[65] The Indian diplomat leading the negotiations mentioned that there was "broad agreement on 94% of the tariff lines" and that a deal was within reach, contingent on a final package.[66] More caution was shown in his statement by the Indian Prime Minister, who noted in 2012 that the negotiations "involve complex issues" and stressed that India and the EU were seeking "solutions that are practical, beneficial, and acceptable to both sides". At the same time, he announced that they could be concluded "as soon as possible".[67]

The talks were already having to proceed under increasing time pressure. Indian negotiators felt that they had to conclude by mid-2013 at the latest in order to have the agreement adopted in time for the European Parliament elections and the change of EU leadership in spring 2014.[68] At the same time, public and political resistance to the deal with the EU was growing in India. The loudest protests came from the powerful business lobbies of the automotive or pharmaceutical companies. Strong opposition and attacks on the government were voiced by the main opposition party BJP, threatening the loss of millions of jobs for small vendors or the influx of cheap alcohol from Europe. India's opponents of the BTIA were also succoured by some European NGOs, who believed that the signing of the agreement was in the interests of big business but would actually "increase poverty, inequality, and environmental degradation in India".[69] The Indian government, weakened by successive corruption scandals and faced with the prospect of elections in spring 2014, was no longer able to make the concessions expected by the EU, which on the other hand was unwilling to lower its own expectations and offer new concessions.

Despite this, there were still further attempts in 2012 to overcome the impasse in negotiations. On June 25, India's Deputy Trade Minister and the head of the EC's DG-Trade met in Brussels to discuss contentious issues, and a day later, on June 26, Trade, Industry and Textiles Minister Annand Sharma and EU Trade Commissioner Karl de Gucht met.[70] Their subsequent meetings took place in April 2013 in Brussels and in May 2013 in Paris on the sidelines of the OECD conference.[71] The lack of progress meant that the talks reached a deadlock.

Negotiations of the agreement were formally suspended in April 2013, although the Indian side indicates that the latest 16th round of negotiations took place on May 13, 2013, in New Delhi.[72] According to EU data, there were a total of 12 full-fledged negotiating rounds,[73] and the difference may be due to the different qualification of the different meetings, especially in the last phase of the process. Indeed, the negotiations consist of various formats of talks, including meetings of experts between official rounds, meetings of chief negotiators, and meetings at the highest ministerial level, not all of which formally marked negotiation rounds.

The official reason for the discontinuation of the trade agreement discussions was the "divergence in the level of ambition" of the parties and the lack of progress in key areas.[74] The Indian side claims that the negotiations stalled since 2013 because "the EU withdrew from the negotiations under differences in asks and give-aways, especially in some tracks with high sensitivity for India"[75].

Although most issues had been agreed when negotiations broke down, the most contentious issues remained unresolved. India continued to refuse to accept significant reductions in tariffs on cars and car parts, as well as wines and spirits. It also maintained restrictions on access to financial services, banking, and retail trade. In turn, India's demands for liberalization of labour mobility rules and data-secure country were not satisfactorily addressed by the EU. Disparities remained over access to government procurement, geographical indications, or intellectual property protection. On the latter, India did not agree to arrangements going beyond the general WTO standards on intellectual property rights of the so-called TRIPS.

The inclusion of clauses on labour rights and environmental standards in the agreement also remained a bone of contention. The Union required such elements in all its FTAs, citing public expectations and the need for ratification of the agreement by the European Parliament, which is particularly sensitive to these issues. Indeed, in a European Parliament resolution of March 26, 2009, parliamentarians called on the EC to "include an ambitious chapter on sustainable development as an essential element of the FTA", pointing out, among other things, the requirement for India to ratify core International Labour Organisation conventions, an end to child labour, forced labour, respect for workers' rights and democracy, and human rights.[76] The fact that, under the Lisbon Treaty, the European Parliament had gained the right to ratify international agreements meant that the Commission had to take MEPs' advice seriously.

The suspension of the BTIA talks impacted negatively on the overall India–EU relationship, becoming, for many, evidence of the structural divergence and façade of the strategic partnership. This was all the more important as trade negotiations had dominated bilateral relations since 2007, and progress on this issue encouraged increasingly close cooperation in other areas as well. The fiasco on this issue meant that interest in cooperation declined on both sides. Therefore, opinions began to be increasingly voiced to separate the difficult trade negotiations from cooperation in other areas, where more progress was being made. According to some commentators, the strategic partnership should not become "hostage" to the BTIA talks.[77] Indian experts also called for greater realism in the negotiations, arguing that "it is high time to stop striving for the perfect deal".[78]

3.2.3 Economic cooperation

Despite the absence of an FTA, economic cooperation between India and the EU developed dynamically during this period. The value of trade between 2000 and 2014 increased nearly fivefold from $21.4 billion in 2000 to almost $100 billion ($98.727 billion) in 2014, (see Chart 3.1.)[79] and cumulative EU investment in India increased from $0.5 billion to $64 billion.[80]

Trade in goods remained the most important element of the relationship. The value of trade grew steadily until 2009, when the financial crisis in Europe caused a decline from $82.2 billion to $74.6 billion. The following year, however, trade returned to a rapid growth trajectory reaching a historic level of almost 110 billion dollars in 2011 since it began to decline again in subsequent years. This was mainly due to economic slowdown in most European countries.

Importantly, both India's exports and imports fluctuated at a similar rate. As a result, India's trade with the EU remained balanced. At the same time,

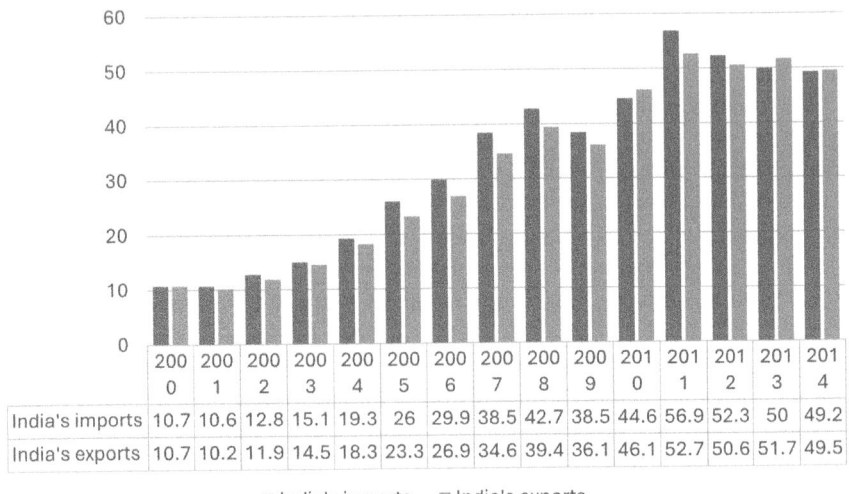

Chart 3.1 India's trade with the EU from 2000 to 2014 (billion dollars)

Source: own compilation based on: Government of India, Ministry of Commerce and Industry, Trade Statistics, Export Import Data Bank, (accessed 20.03.2021)

this meant that India managed to close its historic trade deficit. Increasingly, it also began to run a small surplus.

While the value of trade grew dynamically, another worrying trend was clearly evident during this period – the declining share of the EU in India's total merchandise trade. It declined from 22.5% in 2000 to 13% in 2014. The EU's share of India's exports fell from 24% to 16%, while its share of imports fell from over 21% to less than 11% (see Chart 3.2).[81] According to experts, this illustrated the increasing openness and integration of India's economy into the global economy, particularly its growing contacts with countries in East Asia, Southeast Asia, and the Gulf region.[82] It also meant that India's trade growth rate with the EU was not keeping pace with the growth rate of India's overall trade, and European economies were not able to take full advantage of the expansion taking place in the Indian economy.

This is perfectly illustrated by the changes in India's list of major trading partners (see Table 3.3). While in 2014 the EU as a whole remained India's largest trading partner, only one member country – Germany – remained among the top 10 bilateral partners. Noteworthy is the spectacular rise in China's position – from tenth place in 2000 to first place in 2014, as well as the importance of other Asian countries from the Gulf (UAE, Saudi Arabia) and Southeast Asia (Singapore, Malaysia, Indonesia). It can be said that just as the UK was losing its position as India's largest trading partner to other European countries after World War II, the EU was losing its dominant position in India's trade to other emerging economies in Asia after the Cold War.

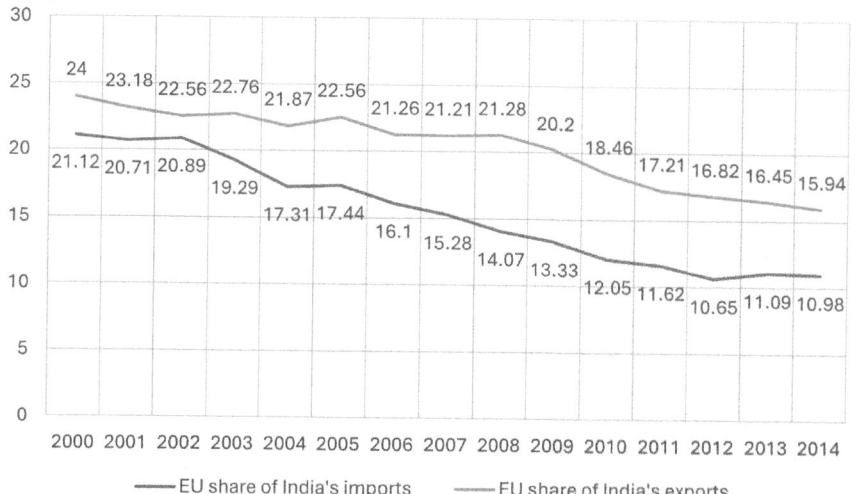

Chart 3.2 EU share of India's foreign trade between 2000 and 2014 (in %)

Source: own compilation based on: Government of India, Ministry of Commerce and Industry, Trade Statistics, Export Import Data Bank, (accessed 20.03.2021)

Table 3.3 India's major trading partners in 2000 and 2014

	Major partners and value of trade in goods	
	2000 r.	2014 r.
1	EU ($21.4 billion) US ($12.3 billion)	EU ($98.7 billion) China ($72.3 billion)
2	UK ($5.4 billion)	US ($64.2 billion)
3	Belgium ($4.3 billion)	United Arab Emirates ($59 billion)
4	Germany ($3.7 billion)	Saudi Arabia ($39.2 billion)
5	Japan ($3.6 billion)	Switzerland ($23.2 billion)
6	Switzerland ($3.6 billion)	Germany ($20.3 billion)
7	Hong Kong (3.5 billion)	Hong Kong ($19.2 billion)
8	United Arab Emirates ($3.2 billion)	Indonesia ($19 billion)
9	Singapore ($2.3 billion)	South Korea ($18.1 billion)
10	China ($2.3 billion)	Malaysia ($16.9 billion)

Source: Own compilation based on: Government of India, Ministry of Commerce and Industry, Trade Statistics, Export Import Data Bank, (accessed 20.03.2021)

Interestingly, while the importance of the EU to India's trade was declining, India's share of EU trade was growing, albeit from a low starting point. In 2000, merchandise exports to India accounted for only 1.4% of total exports outside the EU, rising to 2.1% in 2014.[83] The corresponding figures for imports from India were 1.2% in 2000 and 2.2% in 2014. While this did not fundamentally change the asymmetry in the position of the two parties, the trend was definitely in India's favour in the long term.

Another important feature of India's trade with the EU was the concentration of exchanges on a few major European economies. Although the EU counted in 2014 28 countries, only a few still mattered for India. As shown in Chart 3.3, in 2000, six countries – the UK, Belgium, Germany, Italy, France, and the Netherlands – accounted for 86% of the EU's trade with India and the other 9 EU members together generated only 14% of India's merchandise trade.[84] In 2014, the same group of 6 countries generated 80% of trade with India, while the remaining 22 member states accounted for a total of 20% of their trade with the EU.

The high concentration of trade with a few partners has also reinforced India's need to nurture cooperation with the largest members of the Union rather than with the Community as a whole. Thus, it is one of the reasons for India's preference for bilateral contacts. It is worth noting the significant changes in the position of India's largest partners (see Chart 3.4). The UK, which alone generated as much as ¼ of the EU's trade with India at the beginning of the 21st century, fell to third place in 2014 with a share of 15%. Germany has taken over the EU's leading place, with its share rising from 17% to 21%. Belgium retained its second position, but with a smaller share, mainly due to its traditional trade in jewellery and precious stones. The Netherlands and France increased their share in trade with India, as did the largest countries outside the top six – Spain or Sweden.

India's main trade partners with the EU in 2000.

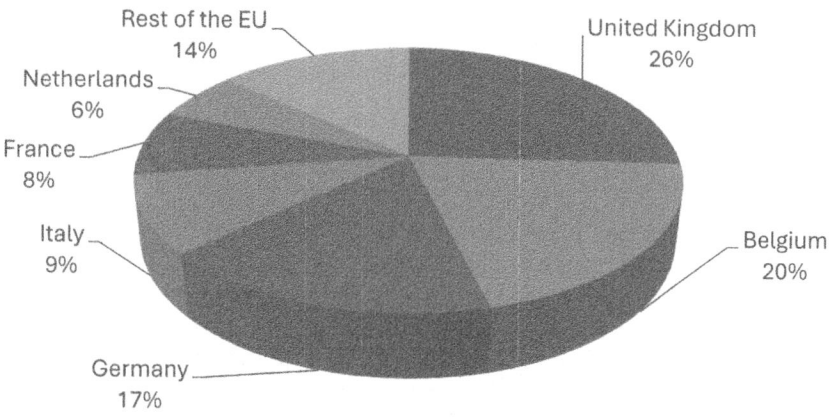

Chart 3.3 India's main trading partners in the EU in 2000

Source: Own compilation based on: Government of India, Ministry of Commerce and Industry, Trade Statistics, Export Import Data Bank, (accessed 20.03.2021)

In contrast, there has been little impact on trade patterns from the EU's enlargement to the East after 2004. In total, the 13 "new" Member States accounted for 5% of EU trade with India in 2014.[85] This share has increased only slightly since 2004. From India's point of view, trade with countries such as Poland and Bulgaria was therefore of tertiary importance.

On the positive side, there has been an increase in diversity and complementarity in the exchange of goods with the EU. The main goods traded were manufactured products, including machinery, transport equipment,

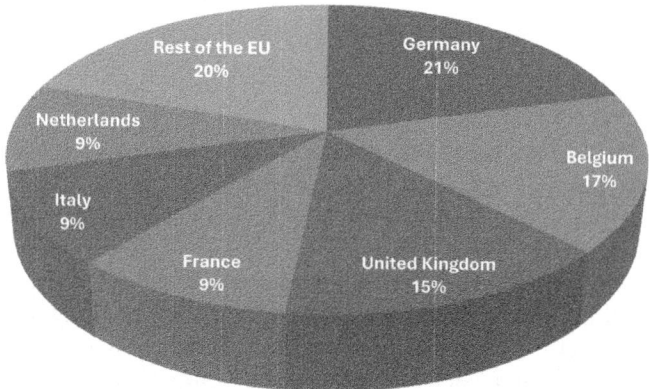

Chart 3.4 India's main trading partners in the EU in 2014

Source: Own compilation based on: Government of India, Ministry of Commerce and Industry, Trade Statistics, Export Import Data Bank, (accessed 20.03.2021)

and others. India's major export items were ready-made garments, precious stones and jewellery, pharmaceuticals, organic chemicals, leather products, vehicles, and machinery. The major import items were precious stones and jewellery, machinery, electronics, chemicals, iron, steel, and aluminium. Similar commodities included in both lists indicate a significant share of intra-industry trade.

3.2.3.1 Trade in services

Trade in services has played an increasingly important role in the Indian economy in the 21st century. The EU was a significant contributor, accounting on average for more than 10% of India's services trade. According to Eurostat data, India's services trade with the EU was €24.7 billion in 2014, including sales of services to the EU28 of €12.55 billion and purchases from the EU of €12.2 billion.[86] This gave India a slight surplus of €345 million. India had a favourable balance of trade with most European countries, with the exception of Ireland (a deficit of as much as €1.8 billion). India's main partners in services imports were the UK (€2.8 billion), Ireland (€1.9 billion), Germany (€1.8 billion), France (€1.4 billion), and Denmark (€920 million). In services exports, the UK (€3.4 billion), France (€1.7 billion), and the Netherlands (€1.5 billion) were the most important.[87]

According to OECD sources, on the other hand, India's services exports to the EU almost tripled in the decade between 2003 and 2013 from about $5 billion to $14.8 billion, and services imports similarly rose to $16 billion.[88] Regarding the structure of services trade, it is worth noting that India's exports to the EU in 2013 were dominated by three sectors: ICT services (18.58%, $2,768 million), travel (16.70%, $2,487 million), and transport (15.90%, $2,368 million). The structure of service imports from the EU is also similar, with three sectors accounting for more than half of imports: transport (27.75% or $4.675 million), IT services (13.85% ($2.333 million), and tourism (12.07%, $2.032 million).

3.2.3.2 Investment cooperation

The EU remained the leading source of investment for India. The value of EU direct investment inflows (FDI) increased from just over $0.5 billion in 2000 to over $8 billion in 2014 (Chart 3.5). 2011 witnessed a historic level of investment of over $15 billion.

In total, the cumulative value of investment from the EU between January 2000 and December 2014 amounted to $64,068.40 million, representing 26.78% of all FDIs.[89] This was therefore more than investments from the US, Japan, Singapore combined.[90] The Union was second only to Mauritius, whose position, however, was due to its favourable tax and legal regulations, causing many companies to channel their investments through that country (see Chart 3.6.). Thus, in reality, FDIs from the EU could have been much higher.

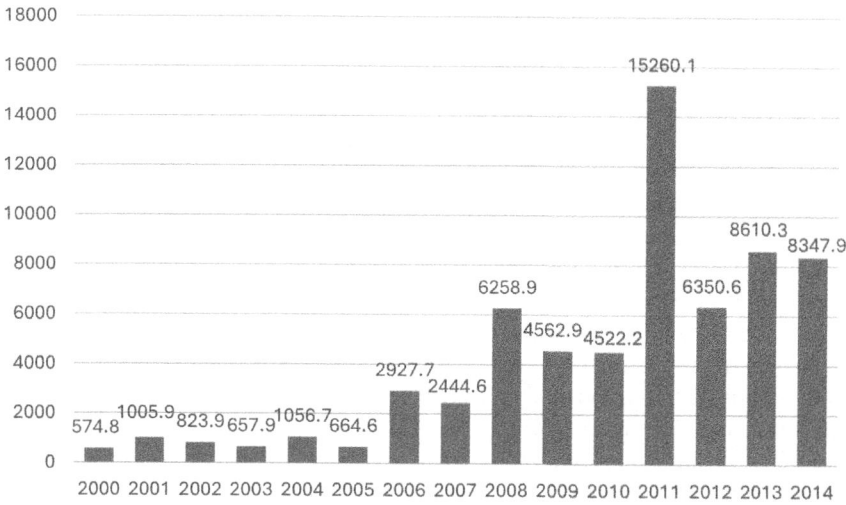

Chart 3.5 FDI inflows into India from the EU 2000–2014 (US$million, current prices)

Source: Own compilation based on: Government of India, Ministry of Commerce and Industry, Department of Promotion of Industry and Internal Trade, (accessed 20.03.2021)

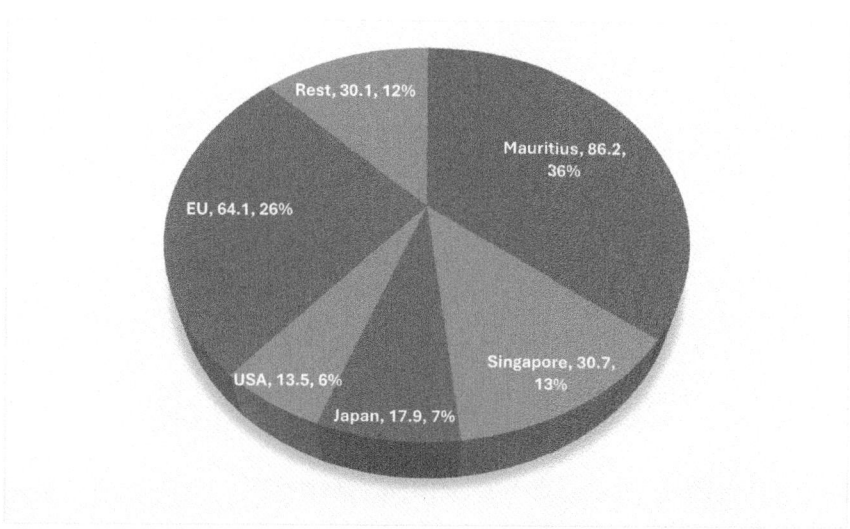

Chart 3.6 Major investors in India in 2014. (Cumulative value of FDI between 2000 and 2014, US$billion)

Source: Own compilation based on: Government of India, Ministry of Commerce and Industry, Department of Promotion of Industry and Internal Trade, (accessed 20.03.2021)

India was becoming an increasingly attractive destination for foreign investment for European companies. Although India's share of total investment outflows from the EU remained small, it increased from 0.12% of the total in 2001 to 1.67% in 2012.[91] India was less attractive than the US – the traditional location of European investment – but also other emerging economies – China, Brazil, or Turkey. From an Indian perspective, however, this indicated a strong potential for increased capital inflows from the EU to India.

Among EU members, companies from the UK collectively invested the most in India, at $22 billion, accounting for as much as 34% of total investment from the EU. This was followed by entities from the Netherlands, Cyprus, Germany, and France. In total, nine European countries accounted for 95% of all investment from the EU in India (Chart 3.7), while only five EU members (UK, Netherlands, Cyprus, Germany, France) accounted for 80% of EU investment. This confirmed the special importance of these major European partners for India. The high position of Cyprus in this area was due, as in the case of Mauritius, to preferential tax and legal regulations; hence, some European companies made investments in India from branches registered in this country.

EU investment was concentrated in several sectors: primarily services (13% of total EU FDI), chemicals (12%), construction (8%), automotive (7%), and pharmaceuticals (7%). Most went to three regions of the state: the Mumbai area, the capital New Delhi, and in the southern state of Karnataka.[92]

Interestingly, investment was no longer only flowing from Europe to India, but the opposite direction – from India to the EU – was also becoming increasingly important. Indian private corporations were already so strong

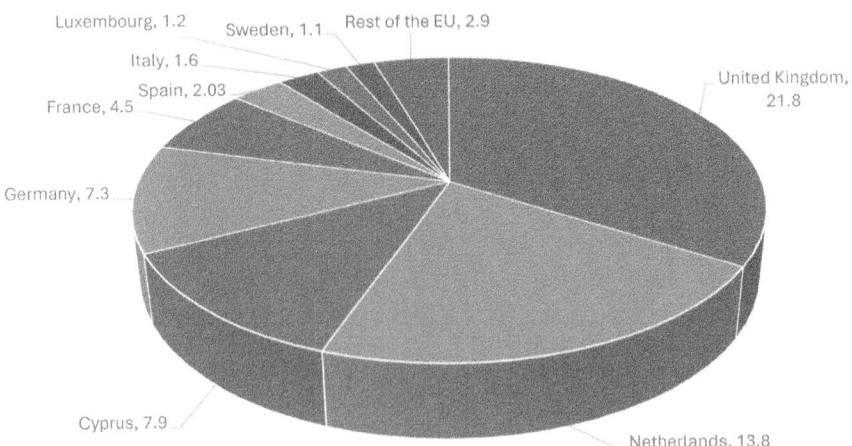

Chart 3.7 Major investors in India from the EU in 2014 (cumulative value between 2000 and 2014, value in US$billion)

Source: Own compilation based on: Government of India, Ministry of Commerce and Industry, Department of Promotion of Industry and Internal Trade, (accessed 20.03.2021)

that they themselves were looking for profit opportunities and new markets in developed countries. Indian investments in Europe went into the IT and business services, construction, automotive, or steel sectors. For the most part, Indian companies used acquisitions of existing companies so as to gain new markets and technologies. The purchase of the British conglomerate Jaguar by the Indian automotive giant TATA became symbolic. Occasionally, Indian entrepreneurs faced resistance from their European partners, which, as in the case of the purchase of the steel company Arcelor by one of the richest Indians Lakshmi Mittal, gave rise to accusations of racial discrimination.[93]

3.2.3.3 Migration and private remittances

Over time, the migration of Indian citizens to the EU and private *remittances* (*remmitances*) from Europe to the homeland also became increasingly important economically. The origins of the Indian diaspora in Europe were linked to the European, mainly British (but also French, Dutch, Portuguese, Danish) colonial heritage. However, during the Cold War Indian migrants remained concentrated almost exclusively in Britain, due to historical, linguistic, legal, or economic ties.[94] This was also due to restrictive migration laws in continental European countries, which remained closed to migration from Asia until the 1980s.[95] As a result, Indians at this time began to migrate in large numbers to the US or Canada, which had previously opened up to Indian migration, rather than to Europe.

At the beginning of the 21st century, the number of people of Indian origin in Europe was estimated to be around 1 million, but they overwhelmingly lived in the UK. It is only since the end of the Cold War that they have begun to explore more eagerly continental countries, members of the EU, such as Italy and Germany. The number of Indian nationals migrating annually to the EU grew from 12,000 in 1996 to over 102,000 in 2010 before falling to 64,000 in 2012.[96] In total, 670,000 Indian migrants were already living in the EU in 2012, making them the fifth largest group of foreigners in the EU (behind Turks, Moroccans, Albanians, and Chinese). In addition to the UK, (54% of Indians in 2013), Italy (19%), Germany (8%), and Spain (5%) have risen in importance as a migration destination in Europe. A new phenomenon in the last decade is the dynamic growth of the Indian diaspora in Central Europe.[97]

In economic terms, Indian migrants nowadays became an important source of capital – *remittances* as well as investments and knowledge about Europe for their compatriots at home. India by the end of the 20th century had become a country with one of the largest numbers of citizens living abroad in the world and, as a result, one of the largest recipients of remittances from migrants. In 2010, for example, over $50 billion flowed into India from members of the diaspora, the most of any country in the world. Along with the surplus in services trade, remittances have been an important means of supplementing the trade deficit and mitigating the country's current account deficit.

Although the importance of Europe as a source of remittances from migrants has been declining since the 1970s, following the opening of rich and receptive labour markets in the Gulf countries or increasing emigration to the US and Australia, it has still retained an important role. According to available estimates, in 2009–2010, remittances from Indians in Europe amounted to $8 billion, i.e. 15% of all remittances flowing into India and the equivalent of 0.6% of India's GDP.[98] The vast majority of this amount (75% or $6 billion) came from the UK. However, the importance of Germany, or France, was growing. In addition, Non-Resident Indians (NRIs) in Europe held in Indian banks in 2010 $7.8 billion, or 18% of all deposits held by NRIs. Apart from the UK, an important source of NRI savings held in India was Germany, and to a lesser extent Italy, France, and Spain. As can be seen, the economic factor was also an important source of pressure from successive Indian governments to facilitate legal migration to Europe.

3.2.3.4 Development aid

Development cooperation has remained another dimension of economic contact with the EU, although its importance has steadily declined. In 2003, the nationalist BJP government made a historic shift towards accepting foreign aid in a bid to mark India's growing ambitions and new international role. Therefore, the new guidelines adopted in September 2003 restricted the acceptance of bilateral aid to only the six largest donors: Japan, the UK, Germany, the US, Russia, and the EU. The rest of the countries were allowed to terminate their support or channel it through international organizations or by directly supporting individual projects or civil society. In 2005, however, the new M. Singh government slightly modified these rules by expanding the list of support donors to include all G8 members and those countries that will provide support of min. USD 25 million per year. Nevertheless, India's rapid economic development meant that many donors were ending their aid programmes in the country. The EU, which was one of the main and traditional donors of aid to India, continued for a few more years.

At the beginning of the new millennium, EU aid focused on helping India achieve the Millennium Development Goals (MDGs), including in particular the reduction of extreme poverty. In 2002 the Commission first adopted a multi-year Country Strategy Paper (CSP) for India for the period 2002–2006. Recognizing that the overarching challenge in the country over the next decade would be to lift 200–300 million people out of poverty, the document identified poverty eradication as a key objective.[99] This was to be achieved by continuing assistance in two social sectors: education (co-financing of the SSP's central "Education for All" programme) and health (co-financing of the National Rural Health Mission), as well as environment. In addition to supporting central programmes, the Union started to cooperate at the regional level, supporting the same sectors through "Partnerships for Progress" with selected states (Rajasthan and Chhattisgarh).

The second objective of the strategy was to support India in "carrying out a second generation of economic reforms" to create a more conducive environment for economic development and bilateral cooperation. Specifically, the EU wanted to share its experience in economic governance and help India in its efforts to integrate regionally and with the global economy.[100] To this end, a special Trade Development and Investment Programme was set up with a budget of €14 million.

The third objective was to increase cultural understanding through closer contacts between civil society, scientists, students, and experts. Aid money began to fund scholarship programmes, academic exchanges, expert contacts, or business projects. In addition, as part of humanitarian aid, the EU supported a programme to increase resilience to natural disasters. The Union's support was to be implemented at three levels – in cooperation with central authorities, partnerships with selected states, and through civil society and NGOs.

The establishment of a strategic partnership treating India and the EU as equal partners and the Indian authorities' new policy towards development assistance led to important changes in the subsequent Country Strategy 2007–2013. The Commission suggested that this strategy should be regarded as "transitional", reflecting a progressive shift from development assistance to support for sectoral policy reforms and economic cooperation.[101] It predicted that given India's rapid development, the need for development assistance was likely to decrease.

At the same time, it pointed out that India "inhabits two worlds at the same time" and there are still vast areas of poverty and powerful challenges. Union's response to this ambiguity was to take two-pronged approach. One objective of support, receiving 70% of the funds, remained the implementation of the MDGs, including through continued sectoral support to the social sectors – education and health. The second objective, receiving the remaining funds, was the implementation of the Joint Action Plan, including in particular economic dialogue, cultural, academic exchanges, and civil society. In this way, the Union provided funding for some of the projects envisaged in the implementation of the Strategic Partnership.

The total EU budget for development assistance in India for the period 2000–2006 was €430 million. In the next budget perspective for the period 2007–2013, the EU has provided €470 million for development assistance to India.[102] In total, it is estimated that from 1976 to 2007 India has received more than $2 billion in aid from the EU.[103] According to OECD data, for the period 2001–2014 alone, EU institutions have provided net official development assistance (ODA) to India amounting to $1693.5 million. (See Chart 3.8)[104]

For the Indian authorities overall, development cooperation with the EU was already of limited importance. Despite the significant value of all international aid, given the scale of the country, it has not played a great role. For example, between 1991 and 1999, all development aid to India did not exceed 0.5% of its GDP.[105] Indian politicians have traditionally argued that India does not need aid just fairer terms of trade and economic cooperation.

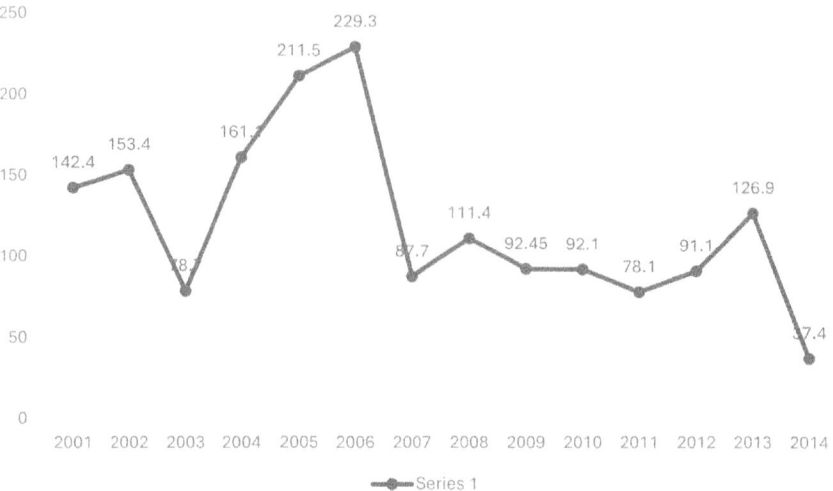

Chart 3.8 EU Official Development Assistance to India 2001–2014 (net disbursements, US$million, constant prices)

Source: Own compilation based on: OECD.Stat, Aid (ODA) disbursements to countries and regions [DAC2a] Total ODA Gross disbursements, Constant prices, USD million. https://stats.oecd.org/ (accessed 22.12.2022)

Some observers believe that the EU has "prematurely shifted from development cooperation focused on poverty eradication to economic cooperation".[106] However, given India's growing aspirations, including a desire to change its perception from aid recipient to aid donor, this shift was in line with Indian expectations. Of greater concern to Indian politicians were the EU's attempts to link aid to trade policy and condition it on changes in labour laws or environmental standards. Experts also pointed out the inconsistency and selectivity of the EU's approach to fighting poverty. "It is paradoxical that while the EU is pursuing policies that support the poor", an Indian expert noted, "it is at the same time supporting free trade, which is unlikely to benefit all sections of society since global trade is dominated by multinational corporations".[107] They also accused the EU of "selectively interpreting the principles of multilateralism", as despite WTO injunctions, "the EU continues to protect sectors hugely important to India, such as agriculture, leather and textiles, through non-tariff barriers, and anti-dumping measures".

3.2.4 Technological cooperation

For India, science and technology represented "the most promising area of India–EU relations".[108] Increasing S&T cooperation was also one of the first and most tangible results of rapprochement with the EU. Already at the first summit in 2000, it was announced that negotiations would be accelerated and that a science and technology cooperation agreement would be adopted quickly, "not only to expand the frontiers of our knowledge, but also to help respond to the challenges of poverty, disease, and hunger".[109]

Indeed, the agreement was already signed in 2001 at the second India–EU summit in New Delhi. This allowed, among other things, the launch of joint research programmes and the participation of Indian scientists in the EU's 6th Framework Programme, which funds joint scientific projects. The cooperation was managed by an established Steering Committee, which set priorities, objectives, and lines of action. At the same time, the Summit adopted a Joint Vision Statement on the development of the information society and information and communication technologies, recognizing India's special competence in this area. The Indian side also expressed interest in joining the EU's flagship projects: the Galileo satellite navigation programme and the International Thermonuclear Experimental Reactor Project (ITER), which is expected to lead to large-scale production of energy from controlled nuclear fusion, and in which only a few countries – the US, Japan, Russia, China, and South Korea – participated.

The 2003 summit announced the start of negotiations on Galileo, but these dragged on for years without success. By contrast, India was formally accepted into the ITER programme on December 6, 2005. The entry into force of the agreement was still extended until October 24, 2007, and it was only on November 27–28, 2007, that a representative of India was able to attend the ITER Governing Board meeting for the first time, fully initiating membership in the initiative. At the same time, discussions began on cooperation between India and the European atomic agency EUROATOM on fusion research, which would complement the ITER agreement.[110] Space exploration became an additional area of technological cooperation, and the two entered into discussions in 2005 to negotiate an agreement between the respective space agencies in the EU and India.

India has been supportive of cooperation on modern technologies used in the economy, looking forward to joint projects and technology transfer. In 2004, workshops were launched in four economic sectors: automotive engineering, genomics, life sciences, and nanotechnology. India also became an important partner in another – the EU's Seventh Framework Programme. The S&T Cooperation Agreement was renewed in 2007, and a working group on the engineering sector was set up in 2009.

Technology cooperation took centre stage at the 2012 Bilateral Summit. Among other things, it adopted the Joint Declaration on Research and Innovation Cooperation, which promised to increase the scale, scope, and impact of collaborative research and establish a "Research and Innovation Partnership" to address common societal challenges and ensure better convergence between India and European countries.[111] It was also announced to deepen cooperation between space agencies – the Indian Space Research Organisation (ISRO) and the European Space Agency (ESA) in space exploration, new technologies, and applications, including through the signing of the ISRO–ESA Agreement for cooperation on Earth Observation and Climate Change.

Climate change issues became a key area of technological cooperation. The Indian side hoped that the EU, with its vast experience, technology, and capital in the field of environmental protection, could "provide solutions to Indian problems".[112] Huge potential for cooperation was indicated in the fields of renewable energy, wind, solar, hydroelectric, or biomass combustion.[113]

Already at the first summit in 2000, India proposed the establishment of a joint Institute of Environmental Technology in Delhi. Although the idea was revisited again in 2001, ultimately nothing came of this proposal. India proposed in 2004, as part of a strategic partnership, to set up an Energy Panel with several working groups to develop cooperation on green technologies. Such a mechanism was indeed set up at the 2004 summit, and in the following years, several working groups began to operate under it: on coal and coal cleaning technologies (2005), on energy efficiency and renewable energy (2005), on fusion energy (2005), and on oil and gas (2006). The aim of the cooperation was to "ensure a safe, secure, accessible and sustainable energy supply".[114]

The 2005 Joint Action Plan Summit announced the launch of the India–EU Initiative on Clean Development and Climate Change and the organization of the EU–India Environment Forum. The theme of the 2007 business summits and Roundtable of the business community was "sustainability and the use of modern technology".[115] In 2008, the European Business and Technology Centre (EBTC) was established in New Delhi. The centre, funded by the EU, was to explore opportunities and promote scientific, technical, and business cooperation between European and Indian partners in four areas: energy, environment, biotechnology, and transport.

The 2009 summit launched the Joint Working Programme on Energy, Clean Development, and Climate Change. There was also a proposal to develop a joint flagship project on solar energy for the first time. In 2012, in turn, the Joint Declaration on Enhanced Cooperation in Energy was signed, announcing the intensification of joint activities.

These various initiatives soon also began to yield tangible benefits in the form of cooperation between researchers and entrepreneurs and additional funding opportunities for innovative technologies. For example, in 2011, the European Investment Bank provided a €200 million loan to India's ICICI Bank to finance renewable energy projects contributing to climate change mitigation.[116] New financing opportunities were also provided by Member States' development banks and FP7 programmes open to researchers in India.

3.2.5 Socio-cultural contacts

An important objective of India's policy towards the EU was to facilitate people-to-people contacts and cultural and educational cooperation. To some extent, this was intended as a response to the existing information deficit and little mutual knowledge. The Indian authorities lamented that "despite the tremendous changes that the Indian economy and society have gone through in the last two decades, the image of the country in Western minds has changed little" and it was imperative "that a coordinated effort is made to improve India's visibility in the EU and change the way India is perceived in European countries".[117] India proposed a number of initiatives in the 2004 document in this regard: The implementation of a scholarship programme for Indian students in Europe, the establishment of an Institute of Indian Studies in Brussels, increased exchanges and cooperation between parliamentarians, improved cultural cooperation, e.g. through the organization of a Cultural Week to accompany bilateral summits, or increased cooperation between journalists, e.g. through the establishment of an India–EU Information Centre to support journalists' contacts and the dissemination of information on India.[118] India also saw this as a necessary investment in its own human capital: student education, academic exchanges, training, and sharing of experiences. The positive attitude from the EU meant that a separate priority on people-to-people contacts was a distinct and one of the main dimensions of India–EU cooperation since the first summit in 2000.

Education was another important area of cooperation for India. The EU financially supported the universal primary education (SSA) programme as part of its development assistance. Between 2002 and 2006, it allocated €200 million – the largest share of its total development assistance to India to this programme, and continued support until 2014. A new and ultimately more important element became cooperation at the tertiary level, something India was particularly keen on. In 2003, the EU announced €33 million for a scholarship programme for Indian students.

As a result, since 2004, Indian nationals have been able to participate in the EU's Erasmus Mundus programme, which funded Master's and PhD-level studies for international students. By 2009, around 2,500 Indian students had benefited from the programme, making them the largest group of beneficiaries among all countries. In total, almost 4,000 Indian citizens (students and lecturers) benefited from Erasmus Mundus mobility programmes between 2004 and 2014, the highest number of any non-EU partner (ahead of Russians, Chinese).[119] In addition, the EU Education Fair in India began to be organized periodically from 2006, with Member States presenting their study offers. Indian students began to increasingly choose not only to study in the UK – the traditional destination for education abroad – but also the continental countries – Germany, France, or Poland.

The EU also started to support the development of studies on the modern EU and India. In India, it funded several Jean Monnet European Centres (Jean Monnet Chair), including, among others, at the prestigious Jawaharlal Nehru University in New Delhi. In addition, it was agreed at the 2005 summit that the EU would also support the establishment of centres for the study of contemporary India in European universities. One such centre, thanks to the programme, was established in 2010 at the University of Warsaw carrying out research and offering a study programme on South Asia and India in English. It has also enabled the establishment of a network of partnerships with European and Indian universities involved in joint research, conferences, publications, academic, and student exchanges. In total, several such institutions have been established in Europe. With financial support from the EU, European Studies Centres have in turn begun to be established in Indian universities.

From the beginning, India has sought closer cultural cooperation. The Hague Summit in 2004 adopted a joint declaration on cultural relations and announced increased cooperation between parliamentarians from the European and Indian Parliaments as well as political parties, trade unions, business associations, universities, and civil society. A second declaration on culture was adopted at the summit in 2010. At that time, it was also announced that a Political Dialogue on Culture would be launched, which took place in 2013.

Finally, initiatives to bring entrepreneurs and companies from both sides together played an important role from an Indian perspective. Already the first Lisbon Summit was accompanied by the EU–India Business Summit. It was organized periodically by the main business organizations in India and the Member States and provided a forum for talks, networking by EU and Indian companies. Organized as a side event to a meeting of political leaders, it generally brought together the heads of major companies and the highest representatives of India and the EU. In addition, a separate roundtable of the business leaders, EU–India Business Roundtable was launched in 2004. It provided a more expert and consultative body for political leaders on economic issues. The European Business and Technology Centre, established in 2008 in Delhi, has played an important role in bringing together entrepreneurs from both continents, as well as chambers of commerce and business (including the European Chamber in Delhi, which has existed since 1982).

Initiatives involving civil society, opinion leaders, and experts have played an important role in promoting mutual knowledge and understanding. In particular, great importance is attributed to the Round Table, which was launched in parallel to the first summit in 2000 on the initiative of Chris Patten, then EU Commissioner for External Relations, and Jaswant Singh, India's Minister of External Affairs. The forum comprised 30 eminent personalities (15 from each side) – representatives from business, industry, trade unions, research centres, NGOs, the media, and the Ministry of Foreign Affairs. On the European side, it was entirely made up of representatives from the European Economic and Social Committee (EESC), with the ESCC President as co-chair on the EU side. On the Indian side, on the other hand, there was no fixed composition of members, but the chairman from the Indian side was appointed by the Prime Minister of the country. This function was held from the beginning till 2008 by one of the more experienced Indian officials N.N. Vohra. After his resignation from this role following his assumption of the office of the Governor of the State of Jammu and Kashmir in 2008, the Roundtable lost its relevance and finally ended its activities in 2009. Nonetheless, the impact of this forum was positively acknowledged in India, particularly for bringing civil society together, better presenting issues of importance to India and increasing understanding of "the role, functioning, and influence of civil society within the EU".[120]

The tasks of the Roundtable were taken over by an initiative of the official think tanks of the EU (the EU Institute for Security Studies, EUISS) and India (the Indian Council for World Affairs (ICWA). Both institutions have since 2009 organized an annual EU–India Forum on Effective Multilateralism (EU-ISS) with the participation of experts and think tank representatives from across Europe and India, as a platform to discuss key international challenges and opportunities for cooperation. As a result, four joint conferences were organized between 2009 and 2013 and two publications were produced, assessing the achievements and progress of the EU–India partnership. To some extent, the cooperation of official institutes was intended to replace the unrealized proposal to create a permanent network of EU and Indian think tanks. Such an announcement was already made at the 2000 summit and repeatedly made (e.g. in the Joint Action Plan in 2005), but a permanent mechanism did not emerge until 2014.

3.3 Security cooperation

Although trade has been the "cornerstone of the EU–India partnership", as noted in 2003 by Pascal Lamy, EU Trade Commissioner, new important areas of cooperation have emerged over the years. The 2005 Joint Action Plan assessed that "the India–EU relationship has grown dynamically from a trade- and economy-driven relationship to one that already encompasses all areas of activity".[121] Particular progress and new opportunities were opened up by the entry into force of the Lisbon Treaty in 2009.

For India, a country with unregulated borders and a difficult neighbourhood, facing both traditional and non-traditional threats, security cooperation is a key foreign policy dimension. The EU, seen primarily as an intergovernmental economic organization, has long appeared as an unimportant partner in this regard. Lacking its own army, defence industry, intelligence services, or even a police force, India did not take the EU seriously. Nevertheless, EU's attempts to develop a European Security and Defence Policy (ESDP) and to create its own forces subject to EU structures were watched with interest in Delhi, but progress in these matters was judged to be disappointing.

Despite these limitations in the area of "hard security", the Union has gradually become an interlocutor for India in at least three dimensions of security policy: counter-terrorism, combating maritime piracy, and cooperation in UN peacekeeping missions.

3.3.1 The fight against international terrorism

At the beginning of the 21st century, terrorism was one of the most important threats to India's security, and cooperation in this area was an important dimension of external relations, including with the EU. India had for years been a target of attacks by terrorist groups and had tried to alert the global community. India's Prime Minister A. B. Vajpayee speaking at the UN in September 1998 identified terrorism as the most important global threat "that affects us all equally" and which "can only be defeated by organised international action".[122] A year before the September 11, 2001, attacks in the US, the Indian Prime Minister in the same venue called "upon the international community to act against terrorism before it is too late".[123] At the next UN General Assembly, already after the attacks in New York, Prime Minister Vajpayee reasserted India's commitment to fighting terrorism and warned against trying to find any justification or explanation for acts of terror: "We must firmly rebuff any ideological, political or religious justification for terrorism", he argued, "We should reject self-serving arguments seeking to classify terrorism according to its root causes and therefore justifying terrorist actions somewhere while condemning it elswhere".[124]

In order to gain the support of Western democracies for their demands and to enhance cooperation in the fight against terrorism, Indian politicians invoked a particular convergence and commonality of democratic values. In 2000, the Indian Prime Minister indicated that "terrorism feeds on violence against innocent people and seeks to undermine pluralistic, open societies".[125] Condemning the "barbaric terrorist act of 9/11", Indian Prime Minister A. B. Vajpayee stressed that "such acts represent an arrogant rejection of the values of freedom and tolerance, which democratic and pluralistic societies cherish".[126]

Counter-terrorism cooperation has emerged as an important theme in all India–EU summits since 2000. The two sides have also adopted two joint declarations (in 2001 and 2010) on cooperation in the fight against terrorism. As early as 2000, a Joint Working Group on Terrorism was set up, where discussions between specialists and exchanges of information were to take place. In 2004, India proposed to raise its profile and broaden its scope by setting up a Joint Working Group on Security Cooperation, and invited a representative of the EU Counter-Terrorism Coordination Office to participate. The 2005 Joint Action Plan identified the "fight against terrorism and organised crime" as one of the main tasks under priority 2: political cooperation and dialogue. Both sides expressed condemnation of the terrorist acts taking place in India and the EU and agreed that terrorism has no excuse. The Action Plan listed nine specific tasks that both sides should undertake in this area:

1 Closer cooperation within the UN framework for the implementation of all UNSC resolutions in this regard;
2 Establishing contacts between the Indian and European Coordinator on Terrorism;
3 Fight against drug trafficking;
4 Support for entry into force of the International Convention for the Suppression of Acts of Nuclear Terrorism and the International Convention on International Terrorism;

5 Cooperation in reducing terrorist access to financing and money laundering, including consideration of the standards adopted by the Financial Action Task Force (FATF);
6 Cooperation in the preparation of a comprehensive counter-terrorism strategy within the UN framework;
7 Promoting cooperation between Europol and the Indian Central Bureau of Investigation;
8 Establishing a Eurojust contact point in India;
9 Expanding the EU–India dialogue to also cover the links between terrorism and drug trafficking, document security, illicit arms trafficking, and cyber-terrorism.[127]

However, despite these ambitious plans, cooperation on counter-terrorism has not gone far beyond joint declarations and technical expert talks. It was not possible to sign a cooperation agreement between Indian and EU security agencies by 2014, nor to establish a sustainable dialogue mechanism between the relevant services. Interaction between the national terrorism coordinators was initiated during a visit to India in 2006 of Gilles de Kerchove, EU Terrorism Coordinator, but these were sporadic and did not translate into new joint initiatives. Work at the UN on the International Convention on International Terrorism, which India was keen to see, also failed to get off the ground because of differences in the definition of terrorism in Europe and India and doubts about how to combat the threat. Many European countries were critical of forceful solutions, with the additional problem of the death penalty in force in India. It was because of EU reservations about Indian actions that assurances were added to the joint documents that "the fight against terrorism must be carried out in accordance with the UN Charter and the relevant principles of international law".[128]

Several agreements that would have facilitated cooperation in this area failed to be adopted. India proposed, for example, an extradition agreement with the EU. In this way, a single document would have covered extradition issues from 27 countries, also filling the gaps in bilateral agreements. The Union has also not signed a Mutual Legal Assistance (MLA) agreement with India, or financial flows related to counter-terrorism investigations (SWIFT), which would have significantly facilitated cooperation in combating terrorist threats. There is also no agreement on the sharing of airline passenger data (PNR), although the Union had such agreements with the US, Australia, and Canada.[129]

Indian politicians complained about the lack of understanding in Europe of the difficult internal and regional circumstances in which Indian forces, fighting separatist and terrorist organizations supported from abroad, operate. In Delhi, it was hoped that the terrorist attacks in the US in 2001 would change the attitude of the Europeans towards counter-terrorism and allow for a better mutual understanding in this regard. This conviction was reinforced by the President of the European Commission, Romano Prodi, who, speaking in New Delhi two months after the attacks in New York, admitted:

"Terrorism has threatened India for many years and you have often warned us of the danger of it spreading to the rest of the world. Events have proved you right. We in Europe will listen more closely to India in future".[130] Despite these assurances, Indian concerns and expectations were not taken much more seriously in the years that followed.

Expectations of convergence in the assessment of terrorism increased after the subsequent attacks in Europe – in Madrid in March 2003 and in London in July 2005. However, the European response was different and less forceful than the American response in 2001. In India, it was read as too soft and focused on the social processes and causes of radicalization, rather than the physical elimination of threats. As a result, despite these events, differences in approach to counter-terrorism have remained. Exposure to attacks in Europe, however, has meant that European criticism of the situation in Kashmir has quietened down, and the subject has ceased to come up in bilateral talks since at least 2008.[131]

Particularly disappointing was the EU's reluctance to strongly condemn Pakistan-sponsored cross-border terrorism against democratic India. India accused its neighbour of a deliberate policy of using non-state actors and terrorist groups to destabilize it and waging a "war of attrition through a thousand cuts". EU decisions to increase development aid to Pakistan in December 2008 – shortly after the Mumbai attacks by the Pakistani Lashkar-e-Toiba organization, or giving it trade preferences under the GSP system, were even perceived as rewarding Pakistan's policies.[132] The lack of direct condemnation of Pakistan and the groups it supports in the joint statement of the first EU–India summit after the Mumbai attacks, held in November 2009, was received with considerable disappointment in Delhi.[133] Indian diplomats had to content themselves, in effect, with more veiled criticism of Pakistan's policies and general references to the country in joint documents.

It was not until the 2010 joint summit statement that Indian expectations were met and for the first time Pakistan was mentioned by name, calling on it to punish the perpetrators of the Mumbai attacks. In contrast, the Declaration on Combating Terrorism, while not explicitly referring to Pakistan used language typical of Indian diplomacy, calling to "encourage all countries to deny safe haven to terrorists and to dismantle terror infrastructure on the territories under their control".[134] At a subsequent summit in 2012, India and the EU agreed on "importance of Pakistan's cooperation with countries in the region to eliminate terrorism and dismantle terrorist networks" and called for "the perpetrators of the November 2008 Mumbai attacks to be brought to justice expeditiously"".[135]

For the Indian side, a major constraint in its policy towards the EU was not only its different approach to counter-terrorism methods, but above all the EU's limited competences in this area. These ultimately boiled down to two areas – coordination of national policies in this regard and regulations.[136]

The Union adopted its own definition of terrorism in December 2001 and legislation allowing for the creation of a list of terrorist organizations whose resources, financial assets, and economic resources were frozen in the EU. In 2003, regulation was adopted to allow a more effective fight against terrorist financing. The EU supported India's accession to the Financial Action Task Force (FATF). But the EU could not offer India what it needs most – intelligence.[137]

Despite these limitations, counter-terrorism cooperation with the EU has brought some benefits to India. Overall, it gained another important international forum to present its threat perception and expectations in this regard. It have received legitimacy and support, even if only moral support, for its counter-terrorism efforts. Presenting the situation in Kashmir in the context of counter-terrorism no longer aroused criticism in Europe. At the political level, the EU gradually increased pressure on Pakistan to take more effective action against extremist groups on its territory.

A concrete achievement was the inclusion of some organizations considered to be terrorist in India on the relevant EU list. From the outset, this included two lesser-known and already inactive Sikh organizations seeking to create an independent Khalistan in the Indian state of Punjab – Babbar Khalsa and the Khalistan Zindabad Force (KZF). In 2003, Lashkar-e-Toiba, the main Pakistani organization active in Kashmir, was added to the Union's list, and in 2005 – Hizbul Mujahidin – Kashmir's largest armed Islamist organization. In 2006, the Tamil Tigers (actually the Liberation Tigers of Tamil Eelam, LTTE), an organization active in Sri Lanka but responsible, among other things, for the assassination of Indian Prime Minister Rajiv Gandhi in 1991 and outlawed in India, were added to the EU sanctions list. In subsequent years, the EU added one more Sikh organization, the Sikh Youth Forum. Although the EU list ultimately captured fewer organizations threatening India than the corresponding lists in the US or UK, it brought India and the EU closer to a common threat assessment. It also made foreign funding for these organizations more difficult and provided political support for India.

India was also positive about the technical discussions of the relevant services. An Indian diplomat involved in the Joint Working Group between 2000 and 2004 estimated that it allowed for the presentation and better understanding of existing and new threats in Europe and South Asia and facilitated contacts between the relevant services.[138] However, the importance of this format was limited by the fact that in parallel, India was running similar working groups at bilateral level with selected major EU members. It was there that the most crucial information and warnings about planned attacks were shared, making the EU level only complementary.

In the face of limited progress in traditional counter-terrorism cooperation, India showed a willingness to share experiences in counter-radicalization. It was emphasized that despite having the world's largest Muslim minority, Indian Muslims are extremely resistant to extremist slogans and do not join global groups promoting jihad.[139] According to Indian diplomats, "a democratic India with a constitution based on recognition of pluralism and protection of minorities can serve as a model for the EU grappling with 'Islamic radicalization'".[140] An additional increasingly important area of discussion and exchange of experience has been terrorist activities on the Internet and the security of communications infrastructure. The long-standing dialogue on terrorism has increased mutual understanding and facilitated closer cooperation in the years to come.

3.3.2 Combating piracy

The emergence of a new threat in the first decade of the 21st century in the form of pirate attacks in the Indian Ocean has put the subject of maritime security on the Indian policy agenda. India carries about 95% of its trade by sea and the country's energy security also depends on the security of its raw material supply.[141] Hence, India was interested in enhancing the security of sea lanes of communication (SLOCs) off the coast of Africa or the Middle East.

Earlier cooperation with the EU was hampered by the EU's low interest and lack of presence in the area of maritime security. Although the EU had a specific foreign and security policy strategy towards East Asia, as one expert noted, "it seemed that Europe had forgotten that the link between Asia and the Pacific and Europe was the Indian Ocean".[142] Thus, it was only with the emergence of modern-day pirates in this strategic body of water and the launch of the first EU-flagged naval mission – EU NAVFOR Somalia (Operation Atalanta) in late 2008 that brought India's attention to the EU in a new context. The launch of another naval mission in 2012 off the African coast – EUCAP Nestor – involving the strengthening of the naval capabilities of five African states, further enhanced the EU's attractiveness as a new player in the region.

The opportunity for contact arose in 2009 when India joined the international effort under the auspices of the UN in the Indian Ocean and sent its own ships there. They also joined the Contact Group on Piracy off the coast of Somalia as a founding member (along with the EU). Both the EU and India also became members of the SHADE (Shared Awareness and Deconfliction) multilateral initiative, established in Bahrain in December 2008, which provided coordination and information sharing between the various countries and coalitions involved in counter-piracy. The interaction of maritime operations in the region opened up new opportunities for cooperation. As a result, maritime security, which had not featured at all in earlier contacts, found its way onto the agenda of bilateral summits. So far, neither the joint communiqués nor the 2005 and 2008 action plans have mentioned maritime security as an area of cooperation, nor the Indian Ocean as a region where the interests of both sides converge.

For the first time, reference to this topic was made at the 2010 summit. It was agreed to have dialogue and cooperation on "security and defence, including, in the context of maritime operations to combat piracy and more broadly to implement UNSC resolutions".[143] Even more space was devoted to this issue at the next summit in 2012. India and the EU agreed to held regular discussions aimed at "enhancing cooperation on anti-piracy efforts", and agreed "in principle" to cooperate in "the escorting of World Food Programme shipments", strengthening regulations of "privately contracted armed security guards and "to share piracy-related information in a systematic manner".[144] Back in November 2011, the first meeting of experts on counter-piracy took place in New Delhi and it was decided to continue such cooperation in a regular format. In September 2013, a second counter-piracy dialogue took place at an EU naval base in the UK.

However, what was to be a promising area of partnership suddenly turned into one of the most serious tensions in the history of India–EU relations. The crisis erupted after commandos providing security aboard the civilian Italian ship *Enrica Lexie* shot dead two Indian fishermen off the coast of Kerala in southern India in March 2012, taking them for pirates. The arrest of the two soldiers and the long legal and diplomatic battle between Italy and India also left a strong negative mark on India–EU relations, leading to a freeze in relations in many areas for several years. The situation got more complex especially in 2014 when an Italian, Federica Mogherini, became the head of EU diplomacy and thus, in the perception in Delhi, the crisis in India–Italy relations, became an India–EU crisis.[145]

The little progress achieved in the area of maritime security also had a much deeper basis. According to experts, they were due to "differences in security culture, threat perception as well as lack of strategic trust".[146] In addition, the fact that the EU did not have a specific maritime security strategy at the time, focused on normative and civilian challenges, and did not share the Indian threat from China, all meant that it was not a particularly valuable partner for the Indian side. India preferred to continue to cooperate in the Indian Ocean with individual member states (France, the UK) that had a visible military presence in the region and were more willing to work together. An example of the difficulties of cooperation in the maritime area was the protracted negotiations of a maritime transport agreement, which started in 2003 and did not lead to an end.

Nonetheless, observers pointed to the still great potential for cooperation in areas such as joint exercises and patrols, training and capacity building of the countries of the region in maritime security, strengthening adaptation to climate change, countering the proliferation of weapons of mass destruction, strengthening multilateral solutions, and the ability of navies to cooperate.[147]

3.3.3 UN peacekeeping missions

India viewed cooperation with the EU in UN peacekeeping missions as an uncontroversial proposition that would enhance its image as a global power supporting a multilateral system with a central role for the United Nations. Historically, India has been among the largest sources of military personnel in UN operations. EU members, on the other hand, have been the most generous source of funding, and a number of European countries have also maintained their own military and civilian contingents in a number of UN missions. Therefore, this topic was discussed at an early stage of India–EU relations.

Already at the first bilateral Summit in 2000, the willingness to work together to "strengthen the international security system, namely the UN, and to support it in its peace-keeping efforts" was indicated.[148] Similarly, a year later, the EU and India pledged to "strengthening UN's capacity to play its role in development and maintenance of international peace and security", pointing to the "growing importance of both India and the EU in the UN, including our contribution to UN Peacekeeping and international peace and security".[149]

In 2004, the Indian government stressed that India's strength was its experience in "conflict management and post-conflict reconstruction', proposing to start a dialogue with the EU at the high officials level to identify specific areas of cooperation.[150] It put forward the offer that the Centre for United Nations Peacekeeping (CUNPK), established four years earlier in New Delhi, should become "a useful entity for closer cooperation in training and coordination between EU and Indian components in UN missions".

Indeed, the 2005 Joint Action Plan listed cooperation in peacekeeping operations and post-conflict assistance as one of the priority areas of cooperation. It announced consultations prior to conferences and discussions on the subject at the UN and even proposed the creation of a special bilateral Dialogue on UN peacekeeping missions. Such a mechanism was supposed to help develop and identify specific areas of cooperation on six specific issues.[151] A new version of the Joint Action Plan adopted three years later listed among the additional activities "the organization of seminars and the exchange of best practices on civilian and military peace initiatives, including those in Africa".[152]

Although similar assurances were repeated in subsequent declarations and joint documents, cooperation in this area remained limited and did not move beyond the planning stage. Issues of peacekeeping missions came up in discussions between representatives of both sides at various levels, including the Security Dialogue, but no joint initiatives or cooperation projects in specific UN missions emerged. Bilateral cooperation between training institutions as well as joint training for third-country nationals remained limited. The potential of the India' based Centre for United Nations Peacekeeping for the exchange of experience and training of EU personnel was not realized. Structural differences in the equipment and organization of the training centres, the different training philosophies of the EU and developing countries, as well as the lack of trust and reluctance of Indian representatives and military officers to cooperate with European institutions stood in the way of closer cooperation.[153]

3.4 Conclusions

Summing up the period 2000–2014, it is fair to say that India's policy towards the EU in the 21st century has significantly evolved into new areas and forms of cooperation. As Indian diplomats noted in 2013 "especially since the Lisbon Treaty in 2009, relations with the EU have expanded with a special emphasis on political and security cooperation".[154] However, cooperation in most of these areas has been limited to successive meetings, consultations, and information exchange.

India's policy towards the EU between 2000 and 2014 evolved from cautious engagement and widening of the scope of the relationship to growing disillusionment and discouragement. Nonetheless, during this period, a multi-level and complex network of institutionalized relationships involving more than 30 dialogue mechanisms was built, and the policy and approach towards the EU went beyond economic issues to include political, strategic, and security cooperation. The EU remained India's most important trading partner and major source of investment, and the trade agreement under negotiation was expected to allow further strengthening of cooperation. Yet, the EU was still not a true Strategic Partner.

The most visible results of engagement with the EU were achieved in technological and socio-cultural cooperation. Indeed, during the period under review, a number of joint scientific and research projects were launched, academic cooperation, student exchanges, and business community contacts were strengthened. The Union began to have a greater presence in India's expert debates, in the media, and in the academy. The establishment of multifaceted networks of relationships was expected to bring more tangible benefits to Indian policy in the years to come.

Security cooperation, crucial from India's point of view, has taken up more space since 2000 and has allowed regular dialogue to begin in many areas. However, it has not yielded many tangible benefits, joint projects, and initiatives. The time has been used for the partners to get to know each other better, mitigate differences, and present their own priorities. India gained some concessions from the EU on non-proliferation (support for an exception in the NSG), terrorism (e.g. inclusion of several anti-India terrorist organisations on the EU sanctions list) and undertook initial contacts between intelligence services and navies. However, limited examples of joint action on maritime security, UN peacekeeping operations, or counter-terrorism activities confirmed the observation that India and the EU were "pursuing parallel rather than joint" strategies on security issues.[155]

Despite the historic transformation and expansion of India's partnership with the EU, Indian politicians and strategists became increasingly critical of the new partner over time. Tired of successive meetings without tangible results, Indian leaders showed a diminishing interest in cooperation with the EU. The post-2008 economic crisis in Europe further reinforced the impression of the EU's declining relevance and agility as a global actor. Around 2012, it became clear that the partnership was in serious crisis. The suspension of the FTA talks in 2013 was the result and confirmation of this mutual disillusionment. It sealed the impasse, which was further overshadowed by the Italian–Indian dispute over the issue of Italian marines. At the same time, the EU's relative position as an important economic partner of India was diminishing in favour of countries in Asia.

Representatives of leading think tanks from India and Europe assessed in 2012 that bilateral summits were too formal and lacked smaller and flexible cooperative groups able to propose more concrete actions.[156] The overly bureaucratic nature of cooperation was also a problem. As Pascaline Winand assessed: "The general impression is of complex, unwieldy, internally divided, and underfunded bureaucracies, both on the Indian and EU side, with competent diplomats and representatives, but who lack both regular top-level contacts and sufficiently accessible knowledge of each other".[157]

Despite the institutional and thematic expansion of cooperation, there was a widespread perception that the EU and India had little in common beyond "commercial interests",[158] and that "the lack of shared interests on a number of issues will continue to limit cooperation".[159] The two sides often had different objectives and cooperation was hampered by different challenges and mutual perceptions.[160] As a result, this "paradoxical partnership" was judged to be "neither very strategic nor really a partnership" and likely to remain "one of *non*-strategic *un*partnership for a foreseeable future".[161] Building partnerships based on shared values rather than interests seemed naïve and unrealistic and needed to be rethought.[162] It was pointed out that in order to give a strategic dimension to the partnership, it was time to move from dialogue to joint action.[163] The hopes raised during this period and the subsequent disillusionment represented the valuable lesson with which India was entering the next phase of cooperation with the EU after 2014.

Notes

1 U. S. Bava, "India and European Union: From Engagement to Strategic Partnership", *International Studies*, vol. 47, no. 2–4, 2010, pp. 373–386.
2 R. K. Jain, "Engaging the European Superpower: India and the European Union", [in:] B. Gaens, J. Jokela, E. Limnell, (eds.), *The Role of the European Union in Asia: China and India as Strategic Partners*, The International Political Economy of New Regionalisms Series, Farnham: Ashgate, 2009, p. 186.
3 B. Mukherjee, *India and EU: An Insider's View*, New Delhi: Vij Books, 2018, p. 76.
4 Council of the European Union, *EU-India Summit. Lisbon, 28 June 2000 Joint Declaration*. Conseil/00/229, Brussels, June 28, 2000, 9552/00 (Press 229).
5 Government of India, Ministry of External Affairs, *Annual Report 2000–2001*, New Delhi, 2001, p. 61.
6 Government of India, Ministry of External Affairs, *India-EU Bilateral Relations*, October 2019, https://mea.gov.in/Portal/ForeignRelation/India-EU_Bilateral_Unclassified_-_Oct_2019.pdf.
7 Government of India, Ministry of External Affairs, *Annual Report 2004–2005*, New Delhi, 2005, p. IV.
8 Council of the European Union, *European Security Strategy. A Secure Europe in a Better World*, (15895/03, PESC 787), Brussels, December 08, 2003, p. 16.
9 Commission of the European Communities, *An EU-India Strategic Partnership. Communication from The Commission to the Council, the European Parliament and the European Economic and Social Committee*. Com(2004) 430 Final, {Sec(2004) 768}, Brussels, 16.6.2004.
10 Government of India, Ministry of External Affairs, *EC Communication Titled "An EU-India Strategic Partnership"– India's Response*, New Delhi, August 27, 2004.

11 Council of the European Union, *Council Meeting General Affairs and External Relations General Affairs, PRESS RELEASE 2608th*, Luxembourg, October 11, 2004.
12 European Parliament, *European Parliament Recommendation to the Council on EU-India Relations (2004/2195(INI)), EU-India Relations*, P6_TA(2004)0044, Strasbourg, October 28, 2004.
13 Government of India, Ministry of External Affairs, *Statement by Prime Minister Dr. Manmohan Singh on the Eve of his Departure to The Hague for 5th India-EU Summit*, November 08, 2004.
14 Government of India, Ministry of External Affairs, *Joint Press Statement for 5th India-EU Summit*, New Delhi, November 08, 2004.
15 Government of India, Ministry of External Affairs, *Joint Press Statement for 5th India-EU Summit*, New Delhi, November 08, 2004.
16 Government of India, Ministry of External Affairs, *Opening Remarks of Prime Minister Dr. Manmohan Singh at the Press Conference with the Dutch PM and EU Leaders at The Hague*, November 08, 2004.
17 Government of India, Ministry of External Affairs, *Europe as a Partner*, Articles in Indian Media, November 10, 2004.
18 Government of India, Ministry of External Affairs, *Address by External Affairs Minister Shri K. Natwar Singh at the Seminar Organized by the Observer Research Foundation, New Delhi on "Europe and Asia: Perspectives on the Emerging International Order"*, New Delhi, November 19, 2004.
19 Government of India, Ministry of External Affairs, *Annual Report 2005–2006*, New Delhi, 2006, p. 73.
20 Government of India, Ministry of External Affairs, *Political Declaration on the India-EU Strategic Partnership*, New Delhi, September 07, 2005.
21 Council of the European Union, *The India-EU Strategic Partnership: Joint Action Plan*, Brussels, September 07, 2005, 11984/05 (press 223).
22 Government of India, Ministry of External Affairs, *Keynote Address by Prime Minister Dr. Manmohan Singh at the India-EU Business Summit*, New Delhi, September 07, 2005.
23 Government of India, Ministry of External Affairs, *Annual Report 2006–2007*, New Delhi, 2007, p. 95.
24 See N. M. Abbasi, "EU – India: Looking Towards Deeper Relations", *Strategic Studies*, Vol. 23, no. 4, 2003, pp. 52-77.
25 G. Sachdeva, "India and the European Union: Broadening Strategic Partnership Beyond Economic Linkages", *International Studies*, vol. 45, no. 4, 2008, pp. 341–367.
26 Government of India, Ministry of External Affairs, *India-EU Summit Joint Statement*, Helsinki, October 13, 2006.
27 Government of India, Ministry of External Affairs, *PM's Opening Statement at 7th India-EU Summit*, October 13, 2006.
28 Government of India, Ministry of External Affairs, *Statement at the Press Conference at 7th India-EU Summit*, October 13, 2006.
29 Government of India, Ministry of External Affairs, *Annual Report, 2007–2008*, New Delhi, 2008, p. 80.
30 Government of India, Ministry of External Affairs, *Joint Statement Issued After India-EU Summit*, New Delhi, November 06, 2009.
31 Government of India, Ministry of External Affairs, *Annual Report 2009–2010*, New Delhi, 2010, p. 88.
32 Government of India, Ministry of External Affairs, *Annual Report 2010–2011*, New Delhi, 2011, p. 86.
33 Government of India, Ministry of External Affairs, *Annual Report 2011–2012*, New Delhi, 2012, p. 90.
34 Government of India, Ministry of External Affairs, *India-EU Joint Statement*, February 10, 2012, para. 4, s. 1.

35 Government of India, Ministry of External Affairs, *Media Statement by PM during 12th India-EU Summit*, New Delhi, February 10, 2012.
36 Government of India, Ministry of External Affairs, *Annual Report 2012–2013*, New Delhi, 2013, p. 70.
37 J. Zajączkowski, "India's 2014 General Election: Significance for Domestic and Foreign Policy", *International Relations*, vol. 51, no. 1, 2015, pp. 184–191.
38 Government of India, Ministry of External Affairs, *Annual Report 2013–2014*, New Delhi, 2014, p. 69.
39 C. Jaffrelot, "India and the European Union: The Charade of a Strategic Partnership", *CERI-Focus*, March 06, 2006.
40 B. Von Muenchow-Pohl, "India and Europe in a Multipolar World", Carnegie Endowment for International Peace, *Article*, August 23, 2012, p. 2.
41 P. Kugiel, "EU-India: A Non-strategic Partnership', *Polish Diplomatic Review*, vol. 12, no. 2, 2011, p. 60.
42 G. Sachdeva, "India and the EU: Time to de-bureaucratize Strategic Partnership", *Strategic Analysis*, vol. 33, no. 2, 2009, p. 207.
43 G. Khandekar, "The EU and India: A Loveless Arranged Marriage", *FRIDE Policy Brief*, no. 90, August 2011.
44 S. Baroowa, "The Emerging Strategic Partnership Between India and the EU: A Critical Appraisal", *European Law Journal*, vol. 13, no. 6, November 2007, pp. 747–748.
45 Interview with R. Jain, Centre for European Studies, Jawaharlal Nehru University, New Delhi, 16.01.2019.
46 Government of India, Ministry of Commerce, Directorate General for Foreign Trade, 'Exim Policy 1997–2002', New Delhi, 1997; Government of India, Ministry of Commerce, Directorate General for Foreign Trade, 'EXIM Policy 2002–2007', New Delhi, 2002.
47 Ministry of Commerce. Export-Import Databank. Accessed 20.03.2021. Indian data refers to the fiscal year and not the calendar year. It lasts from the beginning of April of one year to the end of March of the following year, hence it may often not coincide with data reported for calendar years by international organisations or other countries.
48 Government of India, Ministry of External Affairs, *India-EU Relations: Perspectives in the 21stCentury. External Affairs Minister Shri Yashwant Sinha's Presentation at the Pantheion University, Athens*, January 16, 2003.
49 Government of India, Ministry of External Affairs, *EC Communication Titled "An EU-India Strategic Partnership" – India's Response*, New Delhi, August 27, 2004.
50 *Keynote Address by Prime Minister Dr. Manmohan Singh at the India-EU Business Summit*, September 07, 2005.
51 *Keynote Address by Prime Minister Dr. Manmohan Singh at the India-EU Business Summit*, September 07, 2005.
52 Government of India, Ministry of External Affairs, *PM's Keynote Address at India-EU Business Summit*, October 12, 2006.
53 Government of India Ministry of External Affairs, *Media Statement by PM During 12th India-EU Summit*, February 10, 2012.
54 "Report of the EU-India High Level Trade Group to the EU-India Summit", October 13, 2006, http://trade.ec.europa.eu/doclib/html/130306.htm.
55 See CARIS, *Qualitative Analysis of a Potential Free Trade Agreement Between the European Union and India*, Centre for the Analysis of Regional Integration at Sussex, CUTS International, 2006; Y. Decreux, C. Mitaritonna, *Economic Impact of a Potential Free Trade Agreement (FTA) Between The European Union and India*, Paris: CEPII-CIREM, 2007; T. Achterbosch, M. Kuiper, P. Roza, *EU-India Free Trade Agreement: A Quantitative Assessment*, 2008; Ecorys, *Trade*

Sustainability Impact Assessment for the FTA Between the EU and the Republic of India, 2009.
56 Government of India, Ministry of External Affairs, *Statement at the Press Conference at 7th India-EU Summit*, October 13, 2006.
57 D. Khullar, "India-EU Bilateral Trade and Investment Agreement: Process, Issues, Prospects", [in:] R. K. Jain (ed.), *India and the European Union in a Turbulent World*, Singapore: Palgrave Macmillan, 2020, p. 111.
58 D. Khullar, "India-EU Bilateral Trade and Investment Agreement: Process, Issues, Prospects", [in:] R. K. Jain (ed.), *India and the European Union in a Turbulent World*, Singapore: Palgrave Macmillan, 2020, p. 112.
59 B. Mukherjee, *India and EU: An Insider's View*, New Delhi: Vij Books, 2018, p. 135.
60 D. Khullar, "India-EU Bilateral Trade and Investment Agreement: Process, Issues, Prospects", [in:] R. K. Jain (ed.), *India and the European Union in a Turbulent World*, Singapore: Palgrave Macmillan, 2020, s. 116.
61 Government of India, Ministry of External Affairs, *Joint Statement Issued After the 8th India-EU Annual Summit*, New Delhi, November 30, 2007, paragraph 6.
62 Government of India, Ministry of External Affairs, *India-EU Joint Press Communique*, New Delhi, September 29, 2008, p. 3.
63 Government of India, Ministry of External Affairs, *India-EU Joint Statement*, New Delhi, November 06, 2009, paragraph 23.
64 Government of India, Ministry of External Affairs, *EU-India Joint Statement*, New Delhi, December 10, 2010, paragraph 3.
65 Government of India, Ministry of External Affairs, *EU-India summit*, New Delhi, February 10, 2012, paragraph 4.
66 D. Khullar, "India-EU Bilateral Trade and Investment Agreement: Process, Issues, Prospects", [in:] R. K. Jain (ed.), *India and the European Union in a Turbulent World*, Singapore: Palgrave Macmillan, 2020, p. 116.
67 Government of India, Ministry of External Affairs, *Media Statement by PM during 12th India-EU Summit*, New Delhi, February 10, 2012.
68 D. Khullar, "India-EU Bilateral Trade and Investment Agreement: Process, Issues, Prospects", [in:] R. K. Jain (ed.), *India and the European Union in a Turbulent World*, Singapore: Palgrave Macmillan, 2020, p. 113.
69 *Trade Invaders: How Big Business is Driving the EU-India Free Trade Negotiations*, Corporate Europe Observatory and India FDI Watch, Brussels/Delhi, September 2010, p. 4.
70 Government of India, Ministry of External Affairs, *Annual Report 2012–2013*, New Delhi, 2013 p. 70.
71 Government of India, Ministry of External Affairs, *Annual Report 2013–2014*, New Delhi, 2014, p. 72.
72 Government of India, Ministry of Commerce and Industry, *India's Current Engagements in RTAs*, https://commerce.gov.in/international-trade-trade-agreements-indias-current-engagements-in-rtas/india-eu-broad-based-trade-and-investment-agreement-btia-negotiations/ (Accessed 15.09.2021).
73 European Commission, *Trade, Policy, Countries and Regions, India*, https://ec.europa.eu/trade/policy/countries-and-regions/countries/india/ (Accessed 20.01.2021).
74 European Commission, *Trade, Policy, Countries and Regions, India*, https://ec.europa.eu/trade/policy/countries-and-regions/countries/india/ (Accessed 20.01.2021).
75 Government of India, Ministry of Commerce and Industry, Department of Commerce, *Annual Report 2021–22*, New Delhi, 2022, pp. 98–99.
76 European Parliament, *An EU-India Free Trade Agreement*, European Parliament Resolution of 26 March 2009 on an EU-India Free Trade Agreement (2008/2135(INI)), P6_TA (2009)0189, Article 7, pp. 36–47.

77 G. Sachdeva, "India-EU Economic Ties: Strengthening the Core of the Strategic Partnership", [in:] L. Peral, V. Sakhuja (eds.), *The EU-India Partnership: Time to Go Strategic?*, Paris: EU Institute of Strategic Studies, 2012, pp. 42–43.
78 R. K. Jain, "EU India Free Trade Deal to be Game-changer", *Business Standard*, October 01, 2015.
79 Government of India, Ministry of Commerce and Industry, Trade Statistics, Export Import Data Bank, https://tradestat.commerce.gov.in/ (Accessed 10.01.2020).
80 Government of India, Ministry of Commerce and Industry, Department of Promotion of Industry and Internal Trade, *SIA Newsletter Annual Issue 2014, Chapter 6.1.(B)*, https://dipp.gov.in/sia-newsletter/sia-newsletter-annual-issue-2014; Table No. 6.1.(B): *FDI Synopsis on country European Union. (as on 31.12.2014)*
 https://dipp.gov.in/sites/default/files/SIA_NEWSLETTER_AnnualIssue_2014_Chapter6.1.B.pdf
81 Government of India, Ministry of Commerce and Industry, Trade Statistics, Export Import Data Bank, https://tradestat.commerce.gov.in/ (Accessed 10.01.2020).
82 G. Sachdeva, "India-EU Economic Ties: Strengthening the Core of the Strategic Partnership", [in:] L. Peral, V. Sakhuja (eds.), *The EU-India Partnership: Time to Go Strategic?*, Paris: EU Institute of Strategic Studies, 2012, p. 42.
83 Eurostat, Comext data, International Trade, own elaboration. Data retrieved 10.01.2021.
84 Government of India, Ministry of Commerce and Industry, Trade Statistics, Export Import Data Bank, https://tradestat.commerce.gov.in/ (Accessed 10.01.2020).
85 P. Kugiel, D. K. Upadhyay, "India and Central and Eastern Europe: Post-Cold War Engagement", *International Studies*, vol. 54, no. 1–4, 2017, s. 132.
86 European Commission, Eurostat, International trade in services (since 2010) (BPM6), Last update: 26-04-2021, https://appsso.eurostat.ec.europa.eu/ (Accessed 17.09.2021).
87 Eurostat does not provide data on Germany's imports of services from India until 2016, hence the total trade in services was probably higher.
88 Ifo Institute, 'Europe and India: Relaunching a Troubled Trade Relationship, Study of the Ifo Institute on Behalf of the Bertelsmann Foundation', Final Report on September 13, 2016, p. 36.
89 Government of India, Ministry of Commerce and Industry, Department of Promotion of Industry and Internal Trade, *SIA Newsletter Annual Issue 2014, Chapter 6.1.(B)*, https://dipp.gov.in/sia-newsletter/sia-newsletter-annual-issue-2014; Table No. 6.1.(B): FDI Synopsis On Country European Union. (as on 31.12.2014); https://dipp.gov.in/sites/default/files/SIA_NEWSLETTER_AnnualIssue_2014_Chapter6.1.B.pdf.
90 Government of India, Ministry of Commerce and Industry, Department of Promotion of Industry and Internal Trade, *Fact Sheet on Foreign Direct Investment (FDI) from April, 2000 to January, 2015*, (updated up to January, 2015).
91 IfO Institute, 'Europe and India: Relaunching a Troubled Trade Relationship, Study of the Ifo Institute on Behalf of the Bertelsmann Foundation', Final Report on September 13, 2016, p. 43.
92 Government of India, Ministry of Commerce and Industry, Department of Promotion of Industry and Internal Trade, *Fact Sheet on Foreign Direct Investment (FDI) from April, 2000 to January, 2015*, (updated up to January, 2015).
93 S. A. Wulbers, "Identity Configurations in India-Europe Relations", [in:] S. A. Wulbers (ed.), *EU-India Relations: A Critique*, New Delhi: Academic Foundation, 2008, p. 133.
94 See D. K. Giri, "Indians in Europe", [in:] B. Vivekanandan, D. K. Giri (eds.), *Contemporary Europe and South Asia*, New Delhi: Concept Publishing Company, 2001, pp. 179–196.

95 P. P. Chaudhuri, "India Migration and Europe", [in:] R. K. Jain (ed.), *India, Europe and South Asia*, New Delhi: Radiant Publishers, 2007, pp. 147–148.
96 IfO Institute, 'Europe and India: Relaunching a Troubled Trade Relationship, Study of the Ifo Institute on Behalf of the Bertelsmann Foundation', Final Report on September 13, 2016, p. 45.
97 See P. Kugiel, K. Pędziwiatr, "Indian Diaspora in Central Europe", [in:] R. K. Jain (ed.), *India and Central Europe*, Singapore: Macmillan, 2021.
98 C. Tumbe, "EU-India Bilateral Remittances", *Research Report Case Study* CARIM-India RR 2012/10, Robert Schuman Centre for Advanced Studies, San Domenico di Fiesole (FI): European University Institute, 2012, p. 6.
99 *EC Country Strategy Paper – India*, European Commission, September 10, 2002.
100 *EC Country Strategy Paper – India*, European Commission, September 10, 2002, p. 23.
101 *INDIA. Country Strategy Paper 2007 – 2013*, European Commission, Brussels, 2007.
102 *INDIA. Country Strategy Paper 2007 – 2013*, European Commission, Brussels, 2007.
103 S. Chaturvedi, "India, the EU and Development Aid: New Context and New Realities", [in:] R. K. Jain (ed.), *India and the European Union in a Changing World*, New Delhi: Aakar Books, 2014, p. 132.
104 Data from OECD.Stat, Aid (ODA) disbursements to countries and regions [DAC2a] Total ODA Gross disbursements, Constant prices, USD million. https://stats.oecd.org/ (Accessed 22.12.2022).
105 *EC Country Strategy Paper – India*, European Commission, September 10, 2002, p. 20.
106 A. Coulon, European Union Development Cooperation in India, [in:] S. A. Wulbers (ed.), *EU-India Relations: A Critique*, New Delhi: Academic Foundation, 2008, p. 10
107 J. Amin, "EU Development Cooperation with India", [in:] R. K. Jain (ed.), *India and the European Union in a Changing World*, New Delhi: Aakar Books, 2014, pp. 125, 126.
108 Government of India, Ministry of External Affairs, *EC Communication Titled "An EU-India Strategic Partnership" – India's Response*, New Delhi, August 27, 2004, paragraph 77.
109 *EU-India Summit. Lisbon, 28 June 2000, Joint Declaration. Conseil/00/229*, Brussels, June 28, 2000, 9552/00 (Press 229).
110 B. Mukherjee, *India and EU: An Insider's View*, New Delhi: Vij Books, 2018, ss. 175–178.
111 Government of India, Ministry of External Affairs, *Joint Declaration on Research and Innovation Cooperation*, February 10, 2012.
112 B. Mukherjee, *India and EU: An Insider's View*, New Delhi: Vij Books, 2018, s. 157.
113 D. K. Upadhyay, "Coping with Climate Change: India-EU Cooperation on Renewable Energy and Clean Technology", *India Quarterly*, vol. 70, no. 3, 2014, pp. 241–256.
114 Council of the European Union, *The India-EU Strategic Partnership: Joint Action Plan*, Brussels, September 07, 2005.
115 Government of India, Ministry of External Affairs, *Sustainability Through Technology & Innovation. Joint Statement EU – India Business Summit*, New Delhi, November 29, 2007.
116 D. K. Upadhyay, "EU-India Energy Cooperation: Promoting Renewable Sources and Widening Commitments", [in:] L. Peral, V. Sakhuja (eds.), *The EU-India Partnership: Time to Go Strategic?*, Paris: The European Union Institute for Security Studies, 2012, p. 82.

117 Government of India, Ministry of External Affairs, *EC Communication Titled "An EU-India Strategic Partnership" – India's Response*, New Delhi, August 27, 2004.
118 Government of India, Ministry of External Affairs, *EC Communication Titled "An EU-India Strategic Partnership" – India's Response*, New Delhi, August 27, 2004, paragraphs 77–87, pp. 16–17.
119 European Commission, *Erasmus – Facts, Figures & Trends. The European Union Support for Student and Staff Exchanges and University Cooperation in 2013–14*, Luxembourg: Publications Office of the European Union, 2015, p. 23.
120 B. Mukherjee, *India and EU: An Insider's View*, New Delhi: Vij Books, 2018, pp. 157–159.
121 Council of the European Union, *The India-EU Strategic Partnership: Joint Action Plan*, Brussels, September 07, 2005, p. 1, pp. 6–7.
122 *Address by Mr. Atal Behari Vajpayee, Prime Minister of the Republic of India*, United Nations General Assembly, Fifty-third session, Thursday, September 24, 1998, New York, A/53/PV.13, p. 17.
123 *Speech by A. B. Vajpayee, Prime Minister of India*, United Nations General Assembly, Fifty-fifth session, Friday, September 08, 2000, New York, A/55/PV.7, p. 28.
124 *Speech by A. B. Vajpaee, Prime Minister of India*, United Nations General Assembly, Fifty-sixth session, Saturday, November 10, 2001, New York, A/55/PV.7, p. 31.
125 *Speech by A. B. Vajpayee, Prime Minister of India*, United Nations General Assembly, Fifty-fifth session, Friday, September 08, 2000, New York, A/55/PV.7, p. 28.
126 *Speech by A. B. Vajpaee, Prime Minister of India*, United Nations General Assembly, Fifty-sixth session, Saturday, November 10, 2001, New York, A/55/PV.7, p. 31.
127 Council of the European Union, *The India-EU Strategic Partnership: Joint Action Plan*, Brussels, September 07, 2005, pp. 6–7.
128 Council of the European Union, *The India-EU Strategic Partnership: Joint Action Plan*, Brussels, September 07, 2005, p. 5.
129 P. Kugiel, "EU-India Counter-terrorism Cooperation: Limitations and Prospects", *PISM Bulletin*, no. 5 (1578) January 15, 2018.
130 R. Prodi, "Drawing the World Together", [in:] R. K. Jain (ed.), *India and the European Union in the 21st Century*, New Delhi: Radiant Publishers, 2002, p. 272.
131 P. Chaudhuri, "Decline of Kashmir in India-EU Relations", [in:] R. K. Jain (ed.), *India, Europe and Pakistan*, New Delhi: Knowledge World Publishers, 2018, pp. 58–66.
132 G. Khandekar, "EU-India Cooperation on Counter-terrorism", [in:] L. Peral, V. Sakhuja (eds.), *The EU-India Partnership: Time to Go Strategic?*, Paris: The European Union Institute for Security Studies, 2012, p. 122.
133 B. Mukherjee, *India and EU: An Insider's View*, New Delhi: Vij Books, 2018, pp. 184–185.
134 Council of the European Union, *EU-India Joint Declaration on International Terrorism*, Brussels, December 10, 2010.
135 Government of India, Ministry of External Affairs, *India-European Union Joint Statement*, February 10, 2012, New Delhi.
136 G. Khandekar, "EU-India Cooperation on Counter-terrorism", [in:] L. Peral, V. Sakhuja (eds.), *The EU-India Partnership: Time to Go Strategic?*, Paris: The European Union Institute for Security Studies, 2012, p. 114.
137 G. Khandekar, "EU-India Cooperation on Counter-terrorism", [in:] L. Peral, V. Sakhuja (eds.), *The EU-India Partnership: Time to Go Strategic?*, Paris: The European Union Institute for Security Studies, 2012, p. 122.

138 B. Mukherjee, "India, the European Union and Counter-terrorism: Shifting Paradigms, New Cooperation", [in:] R. K. Jain (ed.), *India and the European Union in a Turbulent World*, Singapore: Palgrave Macmillan, 2020, p. 137.
139 G. Price, "Counter-terrorism and Radicalisation", [in:] S. Saran, E. Pejsova, G. Price, K. Gupta, J. J. Wilkins (eds.), *Prospects for EU-India Security Cooperation*, New Delhi: Observer Research Foundation, 2016, pp. 33–40.
140 B. Mukherjee, "India, the European Union and Counter-terrorism: Shifting Paradigms, New Cooperation", [in:] R. K. Jain (ed.), *India and the European Union in a Turbulent World*, Singapore: Palgrave Macmillan, 2020, p. 134.
141 V. Sakhuja, "India-EU Cooperation in the Indian Ocean: Strategic Thinking, Policy Framework and Challenges Ahead", [in:] L. Peral, V. Sakhuja (eds.), *The EU-India Partnership: Time to Go Strategic?*, Paris: The European Union Institute for Security Studies, 2012.
142 T. S. de Swielande, "Piracy in the Indian Ocean: An Area where the Interests of the European Union and India Converge?", [in:] L. Peral, V. Sakhuja (eds.), *The EU-India Partnership: Time to Go Strategic?*, Paris: The European Union Institute for Security Studies, 2012, p. 169.
143 Government of India, Ministry of External Affairs, *EU-India Joint Statement*, New Delhi, December 10, 2010.
144 Government of India, Ministry of External Affairs, *India-EU Joint Statement*, February 10, 2012, para. 10, s. 2.
145 B. Mukherjee, *India and EU: An Insider's View*, New Delhi: Vij Books, 2018, p. 205.
146 E. Pejsova, J. J. Wilkins, "Maritime Security", [in:] S. Saran, E. Pejsova, G. Price, K. Gupta, J. J. Wilkins (eds.), *Prospects for EU-India Security Cooperation*, New Delhi: Observer Research Foundation, 2016, pp. 33–40.
147 V. Sakhuja, "India-EU Cooperation in the Indian Ocean: Strategic Thinking, Policy Framework and Challenges Ahead", [in:] L. Peral, V. Sakhuja (eds.), *The EU-India Partnership: Time to Go Strategic?*, Paris: The European Union Institute for Security Studies, 2012, ss. 178–182.
148 *EU-India Summit. Lisbon, 28 June 2000. Joint Declaration*. Conseil/00/229, Brussels, June 28, 2000.
149 Government of India, Ministry of External Affairs, *Joint Communique, Indo-EU Summit*, New Delhi, November 23, 2001.
150 Government of India, Ministry of External Affairs, *EC Communication Titled "An EU-India Strategic Partnership" – India's Response*, New Delhi, August 27, 2004.
151 Council of the European Union, *The India-EU Strategic Partnership: Joint Action Plan*, Brussels, September 07, 2005.
152 *The EU-India Joint Action Plan (JAP): Global Partners for global challenges*, EU-India Summit, Marseille, September 29, 2008.
153 L. Klossek, "'Training for Peace' – A Universal Practise? How Micro Processes are Impacting the Likelihood of an EU-India Cooperation in Peacekeeping", *European Security*, vol. 29, no. 4, 2020, pp. 506–523.
154 Government of India, Ministry of External Affairs, Annual Report 2012–2013, New Delhi, 2013, p. 70.
155 A. Bendiek, Ch. Wagner, "Prospects and Challenges of EU-India Security Cooperation", [in:] S. A. Wulbers (ed.), *EU-India Relations: A Critique*, New Delhi: Academic Foundation, 2008, p. 154.
156 L. Peral, V. Sakhuja (eds.), *The EU-India Partnership: Time to Go Strategic?*, Paris: EU Institute of Strategic Studies, 2012.
157 P. Winand, "A Partnership Between Two Large Elephants? Opportunities and Challenges in India-EU Relations", [in:] P. Gieg et al. (eds.), *EU-India Relations*.

The Strategic Partnership in the Light of the European Union Global Strategy, Cheltenham: Springer, 2021, p. 128.
158 E. Kavalski, "The EU-India Strategic Partnership: Neither Very Strategic, Nor Much of a Partnership", *Cambridge Review of International Affairs*, vol. 29, no. 1, 2016, p. 204.
159 R. K. Jain, "EU India Free Trade Deal to be Game-changer", *Business Standard*, 2011, p. 230.
160 S. Wülbers, "EU and India – Goals, Challenges, Prospects", [in:] U. Liebert, J. Wolff (eds.), *Interdisziplinäre Europastudien [Interdiciplinary European Studies]*, Wiesbaden: Springer VS, 2015, pp. 417–431.
161 E. Kavalski, "The EU-India Strategic Partnership: Neither Very Strategic, Nor Much of a Partnership", *Cambridge Review of International Affairs*, vol. 29, no. 1, 2016, p. 193,194, 204.
162 P. Kugiel, "EU-India Strategic Partnership Needs a Reality Check", *PISM Policy Paper* No 37, 2015.
163 B. von Muenchow-Pohl, "India and Europe in a Multipolar World", *The Carnegie Papers*, May 2012, p. 2.

4 Reinforced partnership

India's foreign policy towards the EU under the Prime Minister Modi (2014–2025)

India's post-2014 policy towards the EU has undergone another transformation. The relationship, which had assumed greater political importance in the previous decade, has now acquired a strategic dimension. The partnership evolving with problems since 2004 has finally begun to fill with content. The crisis in relations with the Union felt since 2010 was soon overcome and cooperation regained momentum and expanded into new areas. Although the relationship was dominated by the economy, security and geopolitical issues took an increasingly prominent place.

The change of government in India played a huge role in this process. In May 2014, the general election was decisively won by the Indian People's Party (BJP) under Narendra Modi winning 282 seats in the 545-seat parliament, giving it an absolute majority. Modi's personal popularity and dominance on the national political scene gave the BJP another decisive electoral victory in May 2019, further consolidating its dominance in parliament (303 seats). In the spring of 2024, Prime Minister Modi led his party to a third victory, although the BJP's lost its absolute majority, which can be seen as a warning signal for the ruling party. However, Prime Minister Modi's strong political mandate and international activism since 2014 has allowed him to reinvigorate India's foreign policy in many dimensions, including towards the EU.

Although the new Prime Minister's foreign policy views were not strongly exposed during the 2014 election campaign, one would have expected an intensification of efforts to realize the country's superpower ambitions. The BJP's spring 2014 election manifesto devoted only one and a half out of 42 pages to international affairs, but indicated strong aspirations to play a more important international role. The starting point for India's place in the world was references to "the most ancient civilization" with "a much bigger role and presence in industry and manufacturing than any nation in Europe or Asia" and a high "level of progress and prosperity attained by India before the advent of the Europeans".[1] It was traditional and ancient values, forgotten by the leaders of independent India, rather than concepts taken from the British, to guide India to regain former greatness and wealth.

The BJP heralded a vision "to fundamentally reboot and reorient the foreign policy goals, content and process, […] so it leads to an economically

DOI: 10.4324/9781003688648-5

This chapter has been made available under a CC-BY-NC-ND 4.0 International license.

stronger India, and its voice is heard in the international fora". The most important objective of the new strategy was to "build a strong, self-reliant, and self-confident India, regaining its **rightful place** in the comity of nations".[2] The BJP proposed a policy based on national interest, web of allies, using all resources, and people to play a greater role, including a strong emphasis on soft power tools. The document stressed the paramount importance of regional cooperation and in global forums.

A key policy thrust of the new government became the immediate neighbourhood under the Neighbourhood First policy. Modi also sought to strengthen relations with partners in Asia (Japan, China, Act East Policy) as a priority, alongside traditional multilateral diplomacy (G20, BRICS) and frequent contacts with other power leaders (US, Russia). Europe and especially the EU initially occupied a distant place on Modi's foreign policy agenda. However, this soon began to change.

This chapter analyses this shift in India's approach to the EU post-2014 and the key reasons for this turnaround. The first section identifies three factors that influenced the rise of the EU in India's foreign policy – the country's modernization plans and India's relations with the US and China. This is followed by the evolution of the PM Modi government's approach to the EU and the deepening of political cooperation between 2014 and 2025. Finally, the main dimensions of economic cooperation are examined.

4.1 The rationale for growing role of the EU in Modi's foreign policy

The change of power in India and the EU in 2014 opened up new opportunities for cooperation and another chapter in bilateral relations. The BJP government's greater international ambitions and an increasingly uncertain international environment prompted the authorities to intensify cooperation with Europe. The most important conditions influencing the increased interest in the EU after 2014 include:

1 Reforms agenda and state modernization programmes.
2 The unilateral policy of US President Donald Trump's administration.
3 China's assertive policy.

4.1.1 India's modernization agenda

The Indian People's Party (BJP) won an electoral victory in 2014 with the slogan *Sabka Saath, Sabka Vikas* ("everyone's effort, everyone's development") promising rapid but "sustainable and inclusive economic growth" that put the "ordinary citizen" at the centre. Prime Minister Narendra Modi announced economic reforms, further liberalization and modernization of the country, fighting corruption, excessive bureaucracy, and unlocking human potential. Modi wanted to convey to the world that "India means business" and is determined to unlock economic development and regain its position as one of the major powers in the global system.³ Economic development became India's most important goal, leading to an even stronger economization of foreign policy.

The new government undertook a number of changes and initiatives in the coming years, marking the second stage of liberalization on the scale of the reforms initiated in 1991.⁴ The measures taken were aimed at improving the macroeconomic situation (including consolidating public finances and curbing inflation), opening up the economy more by liberalizing regulations, reducing bureaucracy, fighting corruption, and "red carpet",⁵ privatizing some enterprises, promoting e-government and the digital economy. The government was opening up more sectors of the economy to foreign investment, increasing limits on foreign ownership, and simplifying investment procedures. It introduces major tax reform in 2016 (uniform Goods and Services Tax), demonetization, and tried to push for an agriculture reform in 2020 (tough it had to retreat under the pressure from the farmers).

In addition to structural reforms, Prime Minister Modi also announced a number of flagship programmes and initiatives to address specific weaknesses of the Indian state and economy. The most important initiative of the new government announced back in 2014 was the *Make in* India campaign to make India a global hub for the design, production and export of goods, i.e. the new "factory of the world". This was later strengthened by the "Self-Reliant India" (*Atmanirbhar Bharat*) initiative in May 2020, supported by a special *Production Linked Incentive* (PLI) initiative to encourage investments in modern sectors of the economy. In addition, the Modi government has also pursued several other programmes and campaigns to respond to India's specific problems, such as the *Skill India* programme, *Clean India*, *Housing for All*, *Clean Ganga*, SAGAR MALA, the plan to build 100 *smart cities*, and the expansion of transport infrastructure – road, sea, and air, and green energy transformation. Indian politicians estimated in 2017 that $646 billion is needed for essential infrastructure investments alone in the next five years.⁶

Such an ambitious modernization programme for India required naturally massive capital investment, access to modern technology and foreign markets, and favourable international regulations. European countries were among the few potential partners, along with the US, Japan, China, or Korea, that had these necessary resources and influence in international organizations. While India continued to prefer bilateral cooperation with individual EU members, the Union's exclusive trade competence and its own resources also made the Community as a whole an indispensable interlocutor. As the largest economic bloc and a hub for technology and regulation, the Union could play an important role in Modi's plans.

The reforms undertaken by the BJP government simultaneously strengthened India's attractiveness as an economic partner and removed some of the historical hurdles in the relationship. Some of the changes, such as the liberalization of foreign investment rules in more sectors, the improvement of the business environment (evident in the improved ranking in the World Bank rankings), the increased transparency of the administration's activities, the reduction of bureaucracy and corruption through the digitalization of the economy, or finally the expansion of transport infrastructure made India an easier partner. However some decisions, like termination in 2015 almost all investment protection agreements (which also included 22 countries from the EU) or the increase in average tariffs during the BJP government and the protectionist nature of the *Make in India* or *Self-Sufficient India* programmes send a mixed signal to Europe and made cooperation harder.

4.1.2 Trump factor in India's policy towards the EU

The election of Donald Trump as US President in 2016 and his unilateral and unpredictable foreign policy in the following years was a key external factor influencing India's changing attitude towards the EU.[7] Trump's attacks on multilateral institutions during his first term or threats to impose unilateral tariffs on the EU and India at the beginning of his second term caused shock in Brussels and New Delhi and made the two partners look at each other with greater interest. While Donald Trump's first term ultimately proved good for India, it has discovered the utility of Europe.

US policy has highlighted the convergence of Indian and EU views on important international issues, including multilateralism and free trade. It demonstrated the dangers to the liberal international order positioned the EU, rather than the US, as a partner defending values and institutions important to India. Despite the US withdrawal from a number of international organizations and regimes, the EU and India continued to support the Paris Climate Deal, the JCPOA nuclear deal with Iran, or an open international trade regime with a central role for the WTO.

When analysing the impact of the Donald Trump administration's policies on India–Europe relations, it is important to note that the US factor has always played a huge role in them. At the same time, it is worth noting that this influence has been ambivalent, both positive and negative. On one hand, the American–Indian rapprochement since 2000 has created favourable conditions for closer cooperation with America's allies, including European countries in particular. It set directions and mobilized India for closer cooperation with the EU as well, while at the same time enhancing India's value as a partner.

The change in India's international strategy after the Cold War meant, in large part, a "return to the West" and a rapprochement with the US. The views put forward at the time that India–EU relations would benefit from improving India's relationship with the US were accurate.[8] It allowed the Cold War divisions and mistrust to be discarded, sanctioned improved relations with the West as a whole, and strengthened India's position in the liberal democratic camp.

Indeed, it is noteworthy the regularity that landmark events in India–US relations have guided and pre-empted similar decisions on the India–EU line.

The first India–EU summit in June 2000 came three months after the historic India–US summit during Bill Clinton's visit to Delhi in March. The upgrading of the relationship to a "strategic partnership", at a summit in The Hague in September 2004 came after India and the US announced their own "strategic partnership" initiative in January 2004. Indian Prime Minister A. B. Vajpayee had described India and the US as "natural allies" sharing democratic values as early as 1998, and it was only in 2004 that another Prime Minister M. Singh used a similar phrase ("natural partners") in relation to the EU. It was the surprising declaration by President Bush and Prime Minister Singh in Washington in July 2005 to start negotiations on a nuclear deal that made European countries think about changing their approach on the issue. France signed its own civilian nuclear cooperation agreement in September 2008, the UK did so in 2010, and the EU only in July 2020. Europe's 2021 Indo-Pacific strategy came several years after a new concept was promoted by Donald Trump in 2017.

The examples above prove the thesis that Europe, in its relations with India, followed the example of the US, which set what was permissible and desirable. This meant that Europe would not do anything in relations with India that was not already accepted in Washington or contrary to American interests. It is highly doubtful, for example, that European countries would accept Indian nuclear explosions and support the granting of a weaver at the IAEA in 2008 to allow them to trade in nuclear materials if they were to do so against the US position.

On the other hand, the comparison between the US and the EU's capabilities, international weight, and willingness to act decisively, worked against the Union and caused it to be undervalued as a political and security partner. Europe and especially the EU was seen in Delhi as a dependent actor and junior partner to the major superpower. As a result, Indo-European cooperation took place in the shadow of Indo-US relations, and Europe could not count on similar attention and interest – from Indian politicians, the media, and the public – as the US get.[9]

A leading Indian strategist admitted in the early 2000s that there is an "American bias" that India is "obsessed with the US, that it does not pay much attention to anyone else. ".[10] While the author compares rapprochement with the US to an affair with a new partner, where there is excitement and passion, Europe appears like the dowdy old lady that India has known for 400 years and where there is no such excitement anymore.[11]

The US was seen in India not only as a more attractive partner (in terms of power and position), but also more similar and easier to understand. For India, wrote the Indian expert on Europe, Prof Jain, "it is much easier to deal with the United States, which is characterized by effective leadership and a dedicated pursuit of interests, whereas the EU's foreign policy is considerably more problematic as it is driven forward by committees and compromises".[12] Despite a number of similarities between the EU and India, highlighted by politicians and diplomats, India saw itself as more similar to the US than to the EU.

When analysing the three actors along the three dimensions of the political dichotomy, first between *hard* and *soft power*, second, between the nation-state and the post-modern actor, and thirdly between the *revisionist-state* and the *status-quo state*, India has always been closer to the US. The Union, as a soft-power, a post-modern organization, and *status-quo power*, has been less attractive and less comprehensible to India than the US, a nation-state with *hard power* and a willingness to change international rules when its interests require it. The US as a rational and predictable hegemon of the international system was a much more important partner for India than the Union.

In this sense, the change in US policy introduced in Trump's first term affected India's approach to the EU in two dimensions. Firstly, it created incentive for Europe to become more independent and abandon its position as a junior partner in transatlantic relations. It reinvigorated expectations that had existed in India since the end of the Cold War that Europe could become an independent centre in a multipolar world and therefore an equal partner for India. These hopes were further reinforced at the start of Donald Trump's second term as US President in 2025, when his attacks on Europe became even stronger.

Uncertainty in the transatlantic relationship has prompted EU leaders to look at the world through geopolitical lens and openly speak the language of interests and power more than values and principles. In India, the adoption of a more realistic and pragmatic EU Security Strategy in 2016, the announcement of a new European Commission in 2019 as "geopolitical" and European discussions on the creation of "strategic autonomy" and the re-armament of Europe were all applauded. All this brought the Union, as an international actor, closer to India and made it a more attractive player.

Secondly, and perhaps even more importantly, America's unpredictability made the predictable and sometimes boring EU an alternative and more reliable and valuable partner for India on the international stage. Repeated for two decades assurances from the EU and India of support for multilateralism, the UN and free trade have taken on new meaning. Although India, as Pramit Chaudury notes, did not feel obliged to defend the present system that it perceived as "inherently discriminatory to emerging powers like India"[13] – it was not also in its interest to see a multilateral system that it saw as beneficial and necessary for its economic growth, destabilized. Hence, the US administration's attacks on globalization and multilateralism, on the WTO and the UN, the unilateral imposition of tariffs and sanctions, raised legitimate concerns in Delhi that this international system was not a given once and for all. Stopping globalization and reverting to protectionism in trade at a time when India had only recently begun to benefit from this system and needed it to continue its economic development would be a serious threat to its future and the realization of its strategic aspirations. It was only the undermining of the liberal international system by the US that made India appreciate other partners interested in preserving this order.

To an even greater extent, the search for "like-minded" global partners has become a priority for the EU, surprised by US policy. India's importance as an increasingly powerful power sharing democratic values and a belief in multilateralism and globalization has further increased. It is largely to Trump's credit that the European Commission prepared a new strategy towards India in November 2018, with the aim of working together "in defence of an international rules-based order". For the forces that would threaten this order were no longer just Russia or China, but increasingly the creator and promoter of this system and Europe's traditional ally, the US.

Faced with an unpredictable and transactional America focused on pursuing its own economic interests, India appreciated the value of diversifying its key relationship with the West. At this juncture, it is not the US, but Europe that has emerged as the champion of principles and mechanisms that benefit India – globalization, multilateralism, international organizations, and international law. Not without reason, it was during Trump's presidency that Indian diplomacy was most active in the European direction, both at the level of the EU and the member states. It is no exaggeration to say that it was Donald Trump who proved to be one of the godfathers of India's new policy towards Europe.

4.1.3 The China threat and India–EU strategic convergence

China is the second external factor, besides the US, that has most influenced India's policy towards the EU during this period, and Xi Jinping can be considered the second godfather of India–EU rapprochement. The northern neighbour represents a traditional rival and challenge to India, which suffered a painful defeat in the 1962 war. The dispute over the long Himalayan border is a fundamental, but not the only, problem in bilateral relations. China's growing influence in South Asia,[14] its support for Pakistan, its blocking of India's global aspirations, or the growing trade deficit and the increasing disparity in economic and military potentials to India's disadvantage are additional worries for Delhi. Attempts to normalize cooperation and resolve contentious issues in the spirit of a community of interests between emerging economies since the 1990s have ultimately failed to yield satisfactory results.[15]

Xi Jinping's assumption of power in China in 2012 began a new more confrontational phase in policy towards India. Increasingly frequent border crises, the Belt and Road Initiative implemented in parts of Pakistan-controlled Kashmir,[16] and which India regards as its own territory or ultimately the deadly clashes in Ladakh in June 2020 led to the biggest crisis in relations in four decades[17] and cemented the perception of China as India's "most serious security threat".[18] To reduce dependence on a difficult partner, India withdrew from negotiations of the China-dominated Regional Comprehensive Economic Partnership (RCEP) in 2019 and restricted Chinese investment opportunities and the presence of Chinese applications in its market in 2020.

Deteriorating Indo-Chinese relations meant that the EU gained in value as a potential partner for India to stabilize Asia. India began to see the EU as part of its policy to counterbalance China's disruptive influence in Asia.

"Delhi realized", wrote Raja Mohan, "that no one country could do this alone, not even the US, so a greater role for Europe in Asian security was critically important".[19]

At the same time, Xi Jinping's policies have caused a similar process of re-evaluation of relations with China to take place in Europe. The China factor, which had previously been a source of tension and distrust between India and the EU, soon began to play a beneficial role in their cooperation. Indian commentators had long complained that the EU did not recognize India as an important partner in Asia after the Cold War, focusing all attention on cooperation with China. The 1994 EU Strategy for Asia devoted most of its focus on opportunities for cooperation with China, and EU and European politicians travelled far more often to Beijing than to Delhi over the following decades. And this was despite China was an authoritarian state. EU–China relations consequently became a cause for accusing the EU of hypocrisy, double standards and preferring economic benefits over fidelity to principles. Indian experts accused Europe of succumbing to the "mirage of China's socialization" into the existing international order and warned against growing Chinese influence in Europe leading to the construction of a Sinocentric global order.[20] They also pointed out that Europe, with strong economic ties to China, does not share India's threat assessment.

However, China's increasing involvement with the Belt and Road project in regions where European countries played a dominant role (Africa, Middle East) and Xi Jinping's offensive actions and territorial claims in Asia (e.g. South China Sea, East China Sea) eventually began to raise growing concerns in Europe as well. Fears were also heightened by Chinese investments in Member States, including engagement in Central Europe, in the form of the 16+1 initiative. As a result, the EU noticeably tightened its stance towards Beijing in the following years, to the delight of Delhi.

Adopted in 2018 by the European Commission, the Europe–Asia Connectivity Strategy[21] was widely perceived as an alternative and response to China's Belt and Road Initiative (BRI). The EU approach shared many of the criticisms of the BRI made earlier by the Indian Foreign Ministry.[22] The consensus of both sides on a connectivity model that is transparent, law-based, fair, and balanced opened the way for closer strategic cooperation between India and the EU.[23] Further evidence that the EU is beginning to value India more than China was the adoption of a new India Strategy in November 2018. The document explicitly stated that it was in the EU's interest to have a "multipolar Asia", i.e. one in which India would be one of the poles.

The watershed moment was the Commission's March 2019 Communication, which described China for the first time simultaneously as a "cooperation partner", an "economic competitor", and a "systemic rival".[24] Indian observers read this as a long-awaited toughening of course towards Beijing, an end to naivety in European policy and an appreciation of the strategic risks posed by assertive Chinese policies. This gave rise to the expectation that defining China as a "systemic rival promoting alternative models of governance" would naturally increase India's importance as a natural partner in Asia.[25]

The outbreak of the COVID-19 pandemic in March 2020, followed by the India–China border clashes in Ladakh in June 2020, heightened expectations that India and the EU could jointly counter Chinese aggressive actions in Asia. While Chinese aggression in Ladakh has increased the need for international coalition building by Delhi, the Indian strategist recommended, "integrating Europe into India's new strategic calculus ought to be major objective".[26] The EU began to be described as a "non-obvious" but "useful" partner for India, "as attitudes in Europe shift decisively away from China, the EU can be a crucial partner for India on several fronts"..[27] In Europe, too, it was perceived that it was "thanks to China that India now sees the EU as a useful partner, while the EU has understood the importance of cooperating with Asia's largest democracy".[28]

Another proof of growing alignment of views on China in Europe and India was European Strategy towards Indo-Pacific released in September 2021. Though the document of the Commission stresses the importance of cooperation, it signalled EU's commitment to work with India for the prosperity of larger region where China is expanding its footprint.

In sum, the importance of the EU to India in the context of China stems from two factors – economic and normative. Firstly, India saw an economic opportunity in changing Europe's approach to China. The deteriorating political relations, as well as the increasingly critical attitude of European societies towards China, could prompt Europe to diversify its supply chains and move away from China, and closer to India. Indian diplomats stressed the need to build "resilient and reliable supply chains" in a sharply changed post-pandemic global reality.[29]

The inflow of European investments to India would become an important source of economic growth, help it to strengthen manufacturing, and reduce dependence on China. India hoped simply to benefit from deteriorating EU–China relations. At the same time, the weakening of economic ties between the EU and China would weaken the Chinese economy, hitherto benefiting from European technologies and markets, and make it easier for India to reduce its power disparity with its powerful neighbour.

Equally important was the second factor – joint pressure for China's compliance with international laws and rules and the co-creation of new regulations based on shared democratic values. Highlighting systemic similarities, Indian representatives pointed to India's unique advantage over its Chinese partner. They referred to a sense of trust and a common political code. India and the EU, as "natural partners", had a common interest in defending the Indo-Pacific liberal order, threatened by 'systemic rivals' promoting alternative models. It was emphasized that Chinese aggressive actions in Ladakh and on the India–China border were as much a threat to the international order as threats to Taiwan or the construction of artificial islands and territorial claims in the South China Sea.

4.2 Deepening the strategic partnership with the EU

All the factors mentioned above – the ongoing economic reforms, the uncertainty of US policy, the deterioration of India's relationship with China – have led India to take the EU more seriously as a political and strategic partner, opening a new opportunity for strategic engagement. The new quality of the partnership was marked by renewed political dialogue at the highest level and deepened cooperation on security, technology, and security issues. Cooperation in South Asia, the Indo-Pacific, and on the global stage also became an important dimension of the dialogue.

Three phases in India's policy towards the EU can be distinguished in the period under review:

1. 2014–2015 – a period of limited cooperation at working level
2. 2016–2019 – a period of intensified relations started with the successful India–EU summit in March 2016 in Brussels.
3. 2020–2025 – the stage of strengthening the strategic partnership, confirmed by a symbolic visit of the entire European Commission to India in February 2025.

4.2.1 Cold start in India's engagement with the EU: 2014–2015

The beginnings of PM Modi's government did not at all promise a special engagement with the EU. Europe, undergoing successive crises (financial, economic, migration),[30] appeared to Delhi as a declining power "even more preoccupied with itself".[31] India's attitude towards the EU was affected by the UK's vote to leave the EU in June 2016, which weakened the importance of the EU as India's economic and political partner. The whole series of crises sweeping Europe had the effect of reinforcing negative coverage in the Indian media and undermining the image of the EU as a norm and standard setter in international politics.[32] The Indian foreign minister, assessing these challenges in 2020, assessed that "Europe, with its increasing siege mentality, is finding it increasingly difficult to find a balance between interests and values".[33] The two sides also differed in their assessment of Russia's actions in Ukraine and the annexation of Crimea in 2014.[34]

Moreover, Prime Minister Narendra Modi took over in India during the prolonged impasse in India–EU relations. Bilateral summits had not been held since 2012, and negotiations of the Free Trade and Investment Agreement (BTIA) had been suspended since mid-2013. The dispute with one of the EU members, Italy, over the detention of Italian marines negatively affected the overall political relationship at EU level.

The EU was not mentioned at all among future foreign partners in the BJP's 2014 election manifesto, and Prime Minister Modi devoted absolutely no space to it in his first major foreign policy speeches. As recently as January 2017, while delivering a keynote address on India's priorities in the world, at the Raisina Dialogue conference in Delhi, Modi did not mention the EU, referring only to France as a bilateral partner in Europe.[35] Indian strategists and international relations experts, as well as the media, continued to pay equally little attention to the EU.

Prime Minister Modi also had personal reasons to be reluctant about Europe. His election victory in 2014 was not well received in many European capitals, where the far-right and nationalist BJP traditionally did not have a good reputation. The negative attitude stemmed from accusations of human rights violations and an unclear role in anti-Muslim pogroms in the state of Gujarat in 2002, when Modi was prime minister of the state government. He was denied visas by many European countries in subsequent years and European diplomats were informally banned from having contact with him.[36] As a result, the new Prime Minister had little knowledge of Europe, which he had never been to, unlike the many visits to China he had made as Prime Minister of Gujarat. Distrust of Europe meant that Modi first sought to strengthen cooperation with Asian partners, as demonstrated by welcoming the Chinese leader to India in September 2014 and visiting Japan and China in the first half of 2015.

Modi made his first trip to Europe only almost a year after becoming Prime Minister of India. In April 2015, he visited France and Germany. It was probably at the urging of European leaders that Modi agreed to renew contacts at the regional level with the EU. The rapprochement with the EU also enabled a positive resolution of the Italian seafarers' case and Italy's withdrawal of the blockade on bilateral summits in 2015.[37]

However, Prime Minister Modi's first meeting with the EU representative, European Council President Herman van Rompuy, took place already on the sidelines of the G20 Summit in Brisbane, Australia, on November 14, 2014, which was said to be the "first step in revitalizing relations".[38] Another opportunity to meet the new EU leaders emerging after the 2014 elections (RE President Donald Tusk and EC President Jean C. Juncker) was the G20 Summit in Antalya, Turkey, on 15 November 2015. A visit to the Europarliament in Brussels in June 2015 was paid by the Speaker of the Indian Parliament Sumitra Mahajan with a group of a dozen members. Deputy External Affairs Minister V.K. Singh also flew to Europe for the ASEM Ministerial Meeting in November 2015.[39]

In the absence of summits and with limited political contact between India and the EU, cooperation focused on economic issues during this initial period and the continuation of existing lower-level dialogue formats: the Joint Commission, working group meetings, and other sectoral mechanisms. Interestingly, there was also an exploratory meeting of the chief negotiators of the BTIA in Delhi in October 2014, but little came out of it.

During this time, the EU sought to modify its approach to India by responding to the BJP government's new priorities. The EU's new global strategy, finally presented in June 2016, indicated a willingness to play a greater role in Asia, while taking a more pragmatic approach to non-European partners.⁴⁰ The new EU ambassador in Delhi, Krzysztof Kozlowski, saw it as his task to focus on addressing specific development issues and preparing a detailed offer in areas of Indian interest, rather than general ambitious goals and declarations.⁴¹ Such a pragmatic approach was more responsive to India's needs and allowed the preparation of new initiatives tailored directly to India's modernization agendas to be presented at the leaders' meeting.

4.2.2 A new opening in India-EU partnership: 2016–2019

The Modi government's first summit with EU leaders, which finally took place on March 30, 2016, in Brussels, proved to be a breakthrough for unlocking bilateral cooperation. It was considered in both Europe and India to be very successful and to give a new dynamic to India–EU cooperation. It witnessed the adoption of seven documents, including a Joint Statement and an ambitious EU–India Agenda for Action-2020, which set out a blueprint for cooperation over the next five years.⁴² Other documents included two declarations on economic partnerships (water and energy and climate change), a declaration on migration and mobility, a declaration on combating international terrorism, and a €450 million agreement with the EIB for the construction of the Lucknow Metro.

The statement recalled that the India–EU Strategic Partnership is based on "shared values and principles".⁴³ The leaders discussed all major regional challenges and expressed support for a "stable, democratic, peaceful, and developing Afghanistan", a "stable and democratic Pakistan", an "inclusive solution to the constitutional crisis in Nepal". They also agreed a common position on North Korea, the nuclear programme in Iran, the civil war in Syria, the situation in Ukraine. On the latter, they expressed "strong support for a diplomatic solution to the conflict in eastern Ukraine through the full implementation of the Minsk Agreements by all parties in accordance with UN Security Council Resolution 2202 (2015)".

The fact that the Summit took place a few days after the terrorist attacks in Brussels on 22 March and a few months after the attacks in Paris in November 2015 made the security issue particularly important. Indian partners believed that such a serious threat in the heart of Europe would allow a better understanding of India's counter-terrorism policy and facilitate joint solutions. Prime Minister Modi visited the site of the attack to pay tribute to the victims there, and the leaders in the Joint Statement "strongly condemned the attacks in Brussels". The additional third-ever Declaration on Combating Terrorism was the strongest in form and language among the EU–India documents to date. It condemned the attacks in Europe (Brussels and Paris) and in India (Pathankot and Gurdaspur),⁴⁴ and called for decisive action against terrorist organizations, directly naming also those attacking Indian targets: the Islamic State (Da'esh), Lashkar-e-Taiba, Jaish-e-Mohammad, Hizbul Mujahideen, Haqqani Network, Al.-Kaida, and their affiliated groups.

The Agenda for Action 2020 announced increased cooperation bilaterally and in international fora on foreign policy, including in relation to Africa, Asia, the Middle East, or Europe.⁴⁵ Opportunities to strengthen development cooperation, including in third countries, were to be explored. Among other things, the plan indicated the possibility of information sharing between Europol and Indian counterparts on security threats, including terrorism. The document also introduced one important institutional change – the EU–India Security Dialogue and the Foreign Policy Consultations were to be merged into a single mechanism at the level of Foreign Ministers: The Foreign and Security Policy Consultations. Within this framework, four working groups were to continue their activities: (1) non-proliferation and disarmament, (2) counter-piracy, (3) counter-terrorism, and (4) cyber-security.

The Summit gave a new dynamic to cooperation with the EU. In the following months, political talks continued through a series of ministerial visits and working group meetings. In April 2017, EU High Representative for Foreign Policy Federica Mogherini arrived in Delhi for ministerial consultations and met with Indian Minister Sushma Swaraj and Prime Minister Modi. In early September, Deputy External Affairs Minister M.J. Akbar met Ms Mogherini once again in Slovenia to discuss preparations for the next summit. Sectoral and economic groups held their regular meetings. The positive trend in relations was noted by the European Parliament, which reported on political relations with India in June 2017. In a resolution finally adopted on September 13, 2017, Members of European Parliament expressed "full support for a stronger and deeper partnership between the EU and India".⁴⁶

4.2.2.1   14th India–EU summit: 2017

The 14th EU–India Summit was held on October 6, 2017, in New Delhi. It coincided with the 55th anniversary of the establishment of diplomatic relations between the two sides. The meeting, attended by European Council President Donald Tusk, EC Chief Jean Claude Juncker, and Indian Prime Minister Narendra Modi, was followed by a comprehensive Joint Statement and three declarations – on counter-terrorism, climate and energy, and smart cities and urbanization.

The leaders recalled that the EU and India are "natural partners" and their partnership is based on shared values such as "democracy, freedom, the rule of law and respect for human rights, and the territorial integrity of states".⁴⁷ They pointed to a "growing convergence on contemporary global issues" and announced closer cooperation among "largest democracies" to "support "a rules-based international order that upholds agreed international norms, global peace and stability, and encourages inclusive growth and sustainable development in all parts of the interconnected and multipolar world".

The leaders discussed a very long list of regional issues, including the situation in Afghanistan, Myanmar, Iran, the Korean Peninsula, Syria, the Middle East, Libya, and Ukraine, as well as cross-cutting issues such as counter-terrorism, maritime security, human rights protection, the migration and refugee crisis, non-proliferation, connectivity, and the role of ASEM. [48]

The summit finally pushed India's policy towards the EU into new directions. It emerged that cooperation with the EU, apart from economic issues, is also based on many similarities in strategic matters. Prime Minister Modi emphasized that as "two major democracies, India and the EU are natural partners" who share "a vision of a multi-polar, rules-based international order".[49] He assessed that since the 2016 summit, relations with the EU have "gained new momentum" and got "a good wind in their sails!. Some observed that bold decisions to engage stronger Europe meant that Modi rejected the historical hesitations and ideological constraints characteristic of National Congress governments, including the traditional distrust of the West.[50]

Personnel appointments in the Indian Ministry of External Affairs have also had an impact on the increased interest in the EU. In January 2015, Subramaniam Jaishankar, an experienced diplomat with an excellent experience in Europe, was appointed as Foreign Secretary. In Modi's second cabinet, he became External Affairs Minister from May 2019. This former Indian ambassador to China and the US, and earlier also in Prague (and in Budapest at a lower rank), appreciated the importance of Europe in pursuing India's interests. It was his personal commitment that can be attributed to the greater frequency of high-level visits to Europe, including to the middle states, hitherto mostly overlooked. As noted by one Indian expert, "Dr. Jaishankar is probably the first foreign minister in India to recognize the centrality and importance of Brussels for our future".[51] Also, another expert assessed at the beginning of 2019 that "the Modi government is one of the most pro-European governments in Indian history", which presents unique opportunities for enhanced cooperation.[52]

4.2.2.2 Intensifying India–Europe cooperation

There were no further summits with the EU in 2018 and 2019, but this was largely due to the electoral calendar (EU and Indian elections were held in May 2019). This did not mean a crisis or marginalization of Europe in India's foreign policy. Much more attention, the Indian side paid to revitalizing relations with member states during this period. Prime Minister Modi visited Sweden in April 2018 for a special first summit with the leaders of the five Nordic countries (Norway, Sweden, Finland, Denmark, and Iceland). He continued his stay in Europe with Germany and the UK. In August 2019, he visited France. President Nath Kovid visited Greece in June 2018, with additional visits to Cyprus, Bulgaria, and the Czech Republic in September. Vice President M. Venkaih Naidu travelled to the region shortly afterwards, visiting Serbia, Malta, and Romania (September 14–20, 2018). In 2019, the President of India also visited Slovenia and the Vice President made his first ever high-level government visits to Estonia, Lithuania, and Latvia.[53]

Foreign Ministers also travelled extensively: Sushma Swaraj visited four European countries in June 2018 – Italy, France, Luxembourg, and Belgium. During her stay in Brussels, she met the President of the European Commission to discuss progress in implementing the provisions of the last summit of October 2017. Europe has become a more frequented destination for the new Foreign Minister S. Jaishankar from May 2019. Only in one year - 2019, he visited France, Italy, the Netherlands, Finland, the UK, Bulgaria, Spain, Poland, and Hungary. The visits of European leaders and ministers to India were even more frequent. The intensive contacts were only interrupted by the outbreak of the COVID-19 pandemic in March 2020.

India's unprecedented diplomatic activity towards non-traditional partners is worth highlighting. Smaller countries, long overlooked and neglected in Indian politics, especially those in Central Europe, have gained attention. Minister Jaishankar's visit to Poland, for example, was the first by an Indian foreign minister for 32 years and since the end of the Cold War. In part, India's increased interest in this previously overlooked region was linked to China's growing engagement in this part of the world.[54] The impact of Brexit and the increasing geo-economic interests of India and China were also pointed to as reasons for looking at the region through a "more strategic prism".[55]

At the Raisina Dialogue conference in New Delhi in early 2020, Minister Jaishankar acknowledged that so far, India's relations with Europe have been "mainly concerned with individual countries, at the national level", and have paid less attention to the Union as a whole and smaller European countries. He admitted that he saw "huge potential to exploit" and that this was one of the reasons for his more frequent trips to Europe to "revitalize this relationship".[56]

The change in India's approach to the EU was also shown in the evolution of the flagship conference on international relations, co-organized by India's MEA, Raisina Dialogue. While at the first editions in 2016–2017, Europe did not appear either as a theme or as a participant in the discussions, in the following years, European themes and guests from Europe became central to the conference. The forum also served to invite European politicians, heads of government, ministers, and parliamentarians. Europe and the EU became important partners for India to talk about the world.

India also welcomed the change in the EU's approach to Asia. During this time, several important policy documents were adopted in Brussels, which were received positively in Delhi. In May 2018, European Council adopted Conclusions on Security Cooperation with Asia, in which the EU flagged its ambition to play a greater role in an area where it had not hitherto been seen as an important partner. The Council listed India as one of the "strategic partners in Asia" (along with China, Japan, and South Korea) with whom there is great potential for "deepening security cooperation" in areas such as "maritime security, cyber security, counter-terrorism, hybrid threats, conflict prevention, chemical, biological, radiological, and nuclear proliferation and the development of regional cooperative governance".[57] In September 2018, the Commission adopted the Europe–Asia Connectivity Strategy, which set out a vision for investment in connectivity across multiple dimensions.[58] Above all, the document emphasized the highest standards in such investments and coincided with India's position on this issue.

4.2.2.3 EU strategy on India – 2018

Most important, however, was the EU Strategy on India presented in November 2018. This was the first document of its kind since 2004 (and the third ever after the 1996 and 2004 documents) dedicated to relations with India, indicating the EU's new, more strategic approach to cooperation. It emphasized the importance of India as a partner of the EU and identified a number of convergences and opportunities for cooperation over the next 10–15 years.[59] The new document was consistent with the 2016 European Security Strategy and confirmed a more strategic approach to India.[60] The document was positively received in the Indian MEA, which even issued, rare in such cases, a statement. In it, the Indian side noted with satisfaction that the Commission's communication refers to India as "an emerging global power that plays a key role in the current multi-polar world and a factor of stability in a complex region".[61] Indian diplomats added that India is keen to engage with the EU and "looks forward to engaging with the EU not only on a robust bilateral agenda, but also on regional and global issues of shared concern and for reforming the multilateral system and institutions to better reflect contemporary global realities".

External Affairs Minister Sushma Swaraj was also positive about the document. A few months later, speaking at a closed-door meeting at the Ministry, she assessed that relations with the EU were "excellent", pointing to, among other things, the "EU India Strategy, which confirms India's growing importance", increasing trade or the first-ever India–Nordic summit in 2018.[62] Unlike the 2004 EU Strategy for India, however, this time India did not prepare its response in the form of an updated Strategy towards the EU.

Indian commentators appreciated that the EU had moved away from its earlier cautionary tone towards India".[63] Experts appreciated "holistic, long-term strategic vision" to help redefine and reinvigorate the partnership.[64] Others stressed that the strategy shows that "the EU's approach has become more mature".[65] The pragmatism and strategic approach was also evident in the change in language on human rights, which heralded a greater understanding to India's sensitivities and constraints on this issue and opened the way for more fruitful cooperation.[66]

One of the major weaknesses of the strategy was the lack of a clear statement on a fundamental issue – India's membership of the UN Security Council. Differences of opinion among member states meant that the EU remained the only global player besides China that did not support Indian aspirations.

The positive atmosphere of the relationship was not quickly translated into tangible results due to the beginning of the Indian and EU electoral periods and the subsequent period of formation of new authorities. While the Indian elections quickly led to the formation of Prime Minister Modi's second government in May 2019, bolstered by a decisive victory for the BJP, the transition period in Europe took much longer, with the new European Commission taking over only in December 2019. At the same time, the new Commission chief Ursula von der Leyen's announcement that the Commission would be more "geopolitical" and the EU would develop "strategic autonomy" gave hope that India and the EU would eventually speak a common language.

4.2.3 Rejecting strategic hesitations towards the EU: 2020–2025

Four events during this period reaffirmed the will to strengthen India's strategic partnership with the EU – an online summit in July 2020, a meeting between EU27 and Indian leaders in May 2021, a visit by the President of the European Commission to Delhi in April 2022 and a visit by the entire European Commission to Delhi in February 2025.

The first important signal was already sent by the new EC in January 2020, when EU High Representative for Foreign and Security Policy, Josep Borrell chose New Delhi as the destination for his first trip outside Europe. Among other things, Borrell attended the Raisina Dialogue conference, where he asserted his willingness to deepen relations with India, and held talks with his counterpart Jaishankar and Prime Minister Modi. The visit helped reinvigorate cooperation after a long hiatus and gave it more momentum. An opportunity to continue political talks soon followed during Foreign Minister S. Jaishankar's trip to Belgium and Germany in February 2020. In Brussels, he attended the Foreign Affairs Council (FAC), where he addressed the foreign ministers of the member states as the first ever Indian minister. He presented to them India's foreign policy priorities and perspective on regional and global issues, highlighting the commonality of values with the EU.[67] He discussed, among other issues, terrorism, climate change, and economic cooperation and preparations for the upcoming leaders' summit.[68] Interestingly, he also met a group of European Parliamentarians where a resolution was being prepared criticizing India's Citizenship Bill, seen as targeting India's Muslim minority. He sought to explain to them the objectives of the new law and influence them to change the critical stance of the Europarliament.

The India–EU summit scheduled for March 13 was postponed at the last minute due to the outbreak of the COVID-19 pandemic. The pandemic forced both sides to focus on fighting the coronavirus on their territory. Meanwhile, in February 2020, the UK finally left the EU, changing the balance of power between India and the EU. Contrary to fears, however, the event proved to have a positive impact on mutual perceptions between India and the EU. Paradoxically, Brexit prompted Indian politicians to rethink European policy and engage more strongly on the continent – both at the bilateral level with major countries like Germany and France, and smaller ones in Central Europe, and at the EU level.[69] A similar process has taken place in Europe, which for various reasons has become more interested in building close relations with new partners. As the Indian External Affairs Minister assessed, "After Brexit, a less confident Europe has also developed a greater interest in India as a force for stability and development in Asia".[70]

4.2.3.1 15th India–EU summit in 2020

Finally, the 15th India–EU summit took place via video conference on July 15, 2020, after the first wave of the COVID-19 pandemic had passed. It also took place a few weeks after the Sino-Indian clashes at the joint border in Ladakh, in which some 20 Indian soldiers were killed. For both reasons, the summit took on added significance for India.

The meeting was attended by Prime Minister Modi and representatives of the new EU authorities: the President of the European Council, Charles Michel and the President of the European Commission, Ursula von der Leyen. The main outcome of the summit was the adoption of a new action plan for the next five years – A Roadmap to 2025. An agreement between EUROATOM and India on cooperation in research and development for the peaceful use of nuclear energy was also signed on the occasion, and the Agreement on Scientific and Technological Cooperation was extended for another five years.

Clearly, a lot of space in the talks was devoted to countering the COVID-19 pandemic and it was announced that "cooperation on health security and pandemic preparedness and response will be intensified".[71] The leaders reaffirmed their willingness to promote effective multilateralism and a rules-based multilateral order built around the UN and WTO. The ritualistic references to shared democratic values as the basis of the partnership gain real meaning in the context of deteriorating Indian and EU relations with China.[72] The good atmosphere of this meeting contrasted with the EU–China Summit held three weeks earlier (22 June), which ended even without the adoption of a joint statement.

In addition to economic issues, opportunities for closer cooperation in the fight against climate change (including in the implementation of the Paris Agreement) and sustainable modernization, connectivity, or digitalization were identified. India finally agreed to the resumption of the Human Rights Dialogue (after a hiatus of 7 years), announcing the organization of such a meeting "as soon as possible". On security matters, it was agreed, among other things, to intensify cooperation on maritime security, including the launch of a regular dialogue on this issue, which was to replace the Working Group on Combating Piracy.[73]

The new, much more extensive and detailed A Roadmap to 2025 listed opportunities for cooperation in more than 20 areas, ranging from security and economic affairs to exchanges of parliamentarians and cultural cooperation.[74] It was largely a review of existing mechanisms and announced an intensification of cooperation bilaterally and in multilateral fora. Of the new ideas, it declared the start of negotiations for a cooperation agreement between

Europol and India's Central Bureau of Investigation, the launch of a special dialogue on multilateral issues, including UN reform. A lot of attention was given to security cooperation, including, among other things, announcing regular consultations on this issue, strengthening military exchanges and cooperation, and deepening the interaction between the European Atalanta Operation and the Indian Navy. A special Strategic Partnership Review Meeting was to be responsible for coordinating and guiding the implementation of the Roadmap to 2025. The decisions adopted and the concrete plans for cooperation in a number of areas proved that the "partnership is maturing".[75]

The implementation of the provisions was discussed by holding the seventh Foreign and Security Policy Consultation virtually on October 22, 2020.[76] All four forums of the Security Mechanism were also held soon: 12th Counter-Terrorism Dialogue (November 19, 2020); 6th Disarmament and Non-Proliferation Consultation (November 23, 2020); 6th Cyber Security Dialogue (December 14); and the first Maritime Security Dialogue (January 20, 2021). On April 27, 2021, the first Dialogue on Human Rights since 2013 was held.. This also showed India's willingness to discuss sensitive issues and give credibility to its democratic system, against increasingly strong voices indicating the deterioration of democracy.

4.2.3.2 EU–India leaders' summit in 2021

On May 8, 2021, the EU–India Leaders' Meeting was held in Porto. The unique format of the Leaders' Meeting (EU27-India), attended by the Heads of State or Government of all Member States, was a form of recognition for India as a special partner of the EU. Previously, such a format had only been proposed to the leader of China, but the meeting in Leipzig in September 2020 ultimately did not take place, due to rising tensions. Prime Minister Modi also did not finally make it to Portugal, due to the increase in Covid-19 infections and the difficult pandemic situation in the country, but the Summit was held in a hybrid format. It brought a joint statement from the leaders and another Connectivity Partnership.

The leaders recalled that the EU–India Strategic Partnership is based on shared values such as democracy, freedom, rule of law, and respect for human rights.[77] Apart from economic issues, they devoted a lot of space to the fight against COVID-19, the second wave of which was taking a deadly toll in India. Traditionally, the parties have supported cooperation in the fight against climate change, implementation of the Sustainable Development Goals, and digital transformation. They reaffirmed earlier agreements on "plans to establish a joint task force on artificial intelligence, organize a high-level digital investment forum, and enhance cooperation on high performance computing".[78]

The leaders appreciated the deepening of political and security cooperation including non-proliferation and disarmament, counter-terrorism, radicalization and extremism, maritime security, and cyber security threats. They announced the "imminent" signing of a working agreement between Europol and India's Central Bureau of Investigation and closer cooperation between the Indian Navy and EU Operation EUNAVAFOR Atalanta. For the first time, the joint document included a reference to "an open, free, inclusive and law-based Indo-Pacific region", anchored in respect for "territorial integrity and sovereignty, democracy and the rule of law, transparency, freedom of navigation and overflight, unimpeded lawful trade and the peaceful settlement of disputes, in accordance with international law, including the United Nations Convention on the Law of the Sea (UNCLOS)".[79]

India's foreign minister was very positive about the outcome of the summit, judging that the progress achieved was "political and it is strategic" and this is "the main difference that everyone should understand".[80] The summit triggered a series of favourable comments in Indian expert circles.[81]

The summit was followed by a high frequency of official contacts and consultations on current issues. President of the European Council Charles Michel called Prime Minister Modi in late August to discuss the dramatic situation in Afghanistan following the Taliban takeover.[82] Prime Minister Modi met the President of the European Council again in Rome on October 29, 2021, on the sidelines of the G20 Summit,[83] where bilateral and climate issues were discussed. He again held talks with EU leaders in Glasgow during the Climate Summit in November 2021.

Minister Jaishankar, in turn, attended an informal meeting of EU Foreign Ministers in the Gymnich format in Slovenia in early September 2021, where the EU's Indo-Pacific concept and opportunities for cooperation were discussed, as well as the power shift in Afghanistan.[84] The special meeting with EU ministers was the second such event, after attending the FAC in Brussels in February 2020, which also confirmed India's special position in the EU. During his trip to Europe in September 2021, the Minister also paid bilateral visits to Slovenia, Croatia, and Denmark.

4.2.3.3 *War in Ukraine*

The excellent atmosphere and momentum of cooperation collided in 2022 with the most serious challenge to India–EU relations since 1998, that is Russia's aggression against Ukraine on February 24, 2022.

Despite intense pressure from European capitals and at the EU level (as well as the US or UK), India adopted a cautious and neutral stance towards Russian aggression. It limited itself to calls for a cessation of hostilities and resolution of the dispute through diplomacy and dialogue. In the days and months that followed, it did not publicly condemn Russia's violation of international law and abstained in subsequent votes on the issue at the UN. It was critical of the sanctions imposed on Russia by the West and soon became a key importer of Russian oil itself. The most far-reaching criticism of Moscow's actions was Prime Minister Modi's statement at the Shanghai Cooperation Organization Summit in Samarkand in September 2022 that "this is not the era of wars".

In the first days after the outbreak of war, India focused on evacuating its own citizens from Ukraine and delivering humanitarian aid. In the years that followed, Prime Minister Modi sought to maintain direct dialogue (by phone and in person) with both Russian President Vladimir Putin and Ukrainian President Vladimir Zelenski. India's consistent position has been limited to calls to end the war and resolve the conflict through diplomatic talks.

India's attitude towards the war in Ukraine was a major disappointment and challenge to its European partners. The EU and its member states had a legitimate expectation that a country declaring its commitment to international law, the UN Charter, the sovereignty, and territorial integrity of states would condemn the unequivocal violation of these principles. India, however, chose to distance itself from the issue based on a calculation of its own national interest. Putin has put India in the difficult position of choosing between loyalty to its traditional partner Russia and the expectations of its new partners in the West. India, dependent on Russian armaments and appreciating the strategic importance of Russia in the context of balancing China in Asia, therefore chose not to take sides. It has also assertively rejected any criticism of the stance adopted by foreign partners and observers.

Indian ministers defended of buying Russian oil pointing at India's economic interests and European hypocrisy. Minister Jaishankar famously said in June 2022 at GLOBSEC conference in Slovakia, when asked about India's position on the war in Ukraine, that "somewhere Europe has to grow out of the mind-set that Europe's problems are the world's problems but the world's problems are not Europe's problems".[85] Though he ignored the fact that the EU is the largest donor of aid globally supporting people in all parts of the world, including in South Asia, his remarks were well taken back home and in the Global South. Again in May 2025, while referring to relations with Europe, he kindly reminded that India "needs partners, not preachers", especially when these "preachers do not practice what they preach at home" and suggested that Europe must show sensitivity and mutual interest to strengthen ties with India.[86]

India's policy undermined the trust it enjoyed in Europe and showed the illusory nature of their claim to be committed to common values and principles.[87] However, it did not ultimately harm its cooperation with the EU. European diplomats, after the initial shock, recognized the limitations and reasons of the Indian approach. They also decided that the relationship with India was too important to give up because of the war in Ukraine. It was appreciated that India was not providing such overt support to Russia's policies as China. In the end, there was agreement in Europe to disagree on this issue.[88] Instead of putting pressure on India, it was decided in Brussels that it would be more effective in terms of pulling India away from Russia to engage even more into the relationship.

Hence, after a brief moment of limbo, India–EU relations took on a new impetus. Already on March 7, the first ever Consultation on Africa was held (in online format), implementing the provisions of the 2021 Leaders' Summit. At the end of March, the EU's special envoy for Indo-Pacific made a visit to Delhi to reassure his partners that, while the EU was "not pleased" by India's votes of abstention at the UN on the Ukraine resolutions, he believed "that India and the EU continue to share the same values on the global order".[89] Instead of putting pressure on India, the EU decided to double down on strengthening cooperation.

4.2.3.4 Visit of the President of the European Commission to India – 2022

Ursula von der Leyen, President of the European Commission, did not abandon her previously scheduled visit to India on April 24–25, 2022. Delivering the opening lecture as chief guest at the Raisina Dialogue conference, she refrained from criticizing India's attitude, but emphasized the importance of the war in Ukraine for the international order. In meetings with Prime Minister Modi and Minister Jaishankar, it was decided to reinvigorate cooperation and launch new initiatives. The leaders announced the establishment of a Trade and Technology Council at ministerial level, only the second such mechanism that the Union had previously launched with the US alone. They also announced the decision to resume negotiations on a free trade agreement. Prime Minister Modi met EU leaders again on June 28 in Germany for the G7 Summit, where India was again invited despite its different approach to the war in Ukraine.

On June 10, a new format – Security and Defence Consultations – met for the first time in Brussels. On June 17, Minister of Commerce and Industry (Minister of Commerce and Industry, Consumer Affairs Food and Public Distribution and Textiles of India) Piyush Goyal arrived in Brussels to formally launch FTA negotiations. In September (7–8), Delhi was visited by European Commissioner for Energy Kadri Simson to meet Minister for Coal and Minister for Power and Non-Renewable Energy and participate at the first India–EU Hydrogen Forum.

In addition, 2022 saw the 9th round of Foreign Policy and Security Consultations (November 22, 2022, in New Delhi); 6th edition of the High-Level Dialogue on Migration and Mobility (October 27, 2022, in Brussels); 10th edition of the India–EU Human Rights Dialogue (July 15, 2022). Talks by several sectoral ministers continued throughout the year on the margins of multilateral meetings in the G20, WTO, or IMF.[90]

In 2023, the talks with the EU gained even more momentum, not least with India taking over the G20 chairmanship. EU diplomacy chief Josep Borell was in India for the G20 foreign ministers' meeting in March 2023 and attended the Raisina Dialogue conference again. He met with his counterpart Minister Jaishankar twice more in 2023 in Brussels and Tokyo. European Commission Chief Ursula von der Leyen and European Council President Charles Michel arrived in Delhi in September for the G20 Summit, where they also had a bilateral meeting with Prime Minister Modi.

President von der Leyen also attended a virtual G20 meeting organized by Prime Minister Modi on November 22. Sectoral ministers have met on several occasions on the margins of G20 ministerial meetings. On May 16, 2023, the inaugural ministerial meeting of the Trade and Technology Council format was held in Brussels. Sectoral dialogues continued with the Strategic Partnership Review Meeting (Delhi, May), the High-Level Dialogue on Trade and Investment (Delhi, August), the Maritime Security Dialogue and Cyber Dialogue (Brussels, October), the High Level Dialogue on Migration and Mobility (Delhi, October), and the Joint Working Group on Renewable Energy (Virtual, July).[91]

In 2024, the dynamics of cooperation weakened due to the elections taking place in the two largest democracies in spring – parliamentary elections in India (March–June) and elections to the European Parliament (June 6–9). While the emergence of new authorities in Delhi was already completed in June, in Europe the process took until December. Meetings of leaders took place on the margins of multilateral meetings (East Asia Summit in Laos on October 10, G20 Summit in Rio de Janeiro on November 19). In addition to several meetings between Minister Jaishankar and his counterpart, a number of dialogue mechanisms continued, including the Strategic Partnership Review Meeting in Brussels, the Foreign Policy and Security Consultations meeting in Brussels, and the Energy Panel in Brussels, in November, the High-Level Dialogues on Migration and Mobility was held in Brussels in November, and on Climate in New Delhi in October.[92] It was not until the completion of the formation of the new authorities in the EU that cooperation was to be restarted.

4.2.3.5 *European Commission visit to India in 2025*

The new European Commission established in December 2024 was again headed by Ursula von der Leyen, convinced of the importance of strengthening cooperation with India. In Mission Letters to as many as five new Commissioners, she identified India as an important priority, and a special India team was set up in the EEAS. Already in January, during a speech at the Davos Economic Forum, von der Leyen identified India as a priority focus, announcing a trip by the entire College of Commissioners to India.

The historic first visit of the European Commission outside Europe in this term and the first ever visit to Delhi took place on February 27–28. It was attended by 21 of the 27 Commissioners who met their Indian counterparts. This unprecedented move marked the recognition of India's special role for the EU at a time when Donald Trump has once again taken over in Washington. The meeting with PM Modi was followed by a leaders' statement reaffirming the EU and India's shared interest in "shaping a resilient multipolar global order" and describing both sides as "like-minded and trusted partners".[93] The leaders sent a strong political signal that "balanced, ambitious and mutually beneficial FTA" negotiations should be completed by the end of the year, with the main objective being "to enhance market access and remove trade barriers". In the area of economic cooperation, the need to develop trade and de-risking of supply chains, the development of clean hydrogen and other renewable energy technologies was highlighted. Further cooperation was announced in the implementation of the India-Middle East-Europe Economic Corridor (IMEC), the promotion of a "free, open, peaceful, and prosperous Indo-Pacific".

A new feature of this meeting was the special attention given to security issues. The President of the European Commission proposed India to sign Security and Defence Partnership similar to ones it just had concluded in 2024 with Japan and South Korea. She claimed that "security should be a core part of our new strategic partnership with India". India expressed interest in joining projects under the EU's Permanent Structured Cooperation (PESCO), undertaking Security and Information Agreement (SoIA) negotiations. The findings of the meeting were described as "the beginning of a new chapter in the history of the relationship".

The Commission's visit reaffirmed the political will on both sides to strengthen the strategic partnership and extend it to security issues. It provided an opportunity for India to strengthen defence industry cooperation and benefit from the rearmament plans of Europe, which could now rely less on the US. Economic and technological cooperation also assumed strategic importance in this situation. The visit saw the second meeting of the TTC to accelerate cooperation on critical technologies. The leaders' meeting enhanced the pace of FTA negotiations by setting a clear deadline for compromise.

In the months that followed, the escalation of tensions between India and Pakistan following the terrorist attacks in Kashmir at Pahalgam on April 22 and India's accusations of circumventing EU sanctions on Russia cast a shadow over the relationship. On the former, India was disappointed by the Union's lack of clear support for its strong response to terrorism, which it accused Pakistan of, leading to retaliatory attacks on terrorist camps in Pakistan as part of Operation Sindoor in May 2025. While the Union called for de-escalation, it ultimately recognized India's attacks in Pakistan as an exercise of its right of self-defence against terrorism. The resolution of misunderstandings in relations was confirmed by MEA Jaishankar's successful visit to Brussels on June 9–11.

Minister Jaishankar met with EC President Ursula von der Leyen, European Parliament President Roberta Metsola, and also several Commissioners. Together with the new Vice-President of the Commission and High Representative for Foreign Affairs Kaja Kallas, he chaired the first meeting of the EU–India Strategic Dialogue, a new mechanism to discuss security and defence, maritime security, counter-terrorism, and cyber threats, replacing the earlier annual Ministerial Meetings. During the meeting with European Commissioner for Defence Industry and Space Andrius Kubilius, issues of cooperation between the defence and space industries were discussed. With the Commissioner for Trade and Economic Security, progress in FTA negotiations was discussed, and with the Commissioner for International Partnerships, Jozef Sikela, an Administrative Agreement on establishing a framework for trilateral cooperation to promote development projects in third countries was agreed.[94] The meeting confirmed the growing role of security cooperation and strategic technologies in mutual partnerships.

4.2.4 Security cooperation

During Prime Minister Modi's government, security issues played an increasing role in policy towards the EU. Subsequent summits paid increasing attention to these issues and in 2025 Union proposed security as one of the three pillars of the strategic partnership (alongside trade and technology and global partnerships). The greatest progress was made in developing cooperation on maritime security and counter-terrorism. Cyber security issues played a growing role and, more recently, proposals for defence industry cooperation were added.

In October 2017, the Indian naval ship INS Trishul held a joint exercise with EU Operation Atalanta ships in the Indian Ocean for the first time (as part of Operation PASSEX with Italian ships).[95] In December 2018, Indian and EU Operation Atalanta (EU NAVFOR) ships took part in escorting WFP transport convoys in the Indian Ocean. Ships of EU countries (mainly France) made more frequent calls to Indian ports, and EU military delegations started to visit India to discuss cooperation in the Indian Ocean (the first in January 2019).[96] Deepening cooperation with India in this area was also announced in the EU Indo-Pacific Strategy adopted in September 2021.

During the summit in 2020, sides agreed to upgrade the counter-piracy dialogue into broader maritime security dialogue and explore opportunities for further maritime cooperation. In the Strategic Agenda, they called for deeper cooperation between the European Union Naval Force (EUNAVFOR) ATALANTA and the Indian Navy. Four rounds of Maritime Security Dialogue at the level of Joint Secretary at MEA and Director for Security & Defence Policy in EEAS were held on January 20, 2021, in virtual format, February 1, 2022 (Virtual), October 5, 2023, in Brussels, and March 21, 2025, in New Delhi. They discussed naval coordination between Indian and EUNAVFOR Operation ATALANTA, policy coordination on maritime domain awareness (MDA), llicit Maritime Activities (IMA), maritime law enforcement, safeguarding critical maritime infrastructure, regional maritime capacity-building, and joint naval activities.

In the following years, both sides continued mutual port calls and joint naval exercises. On June 18–19, 2021, the EU (NAVFOR Somalia – Operation Atalanta) and India conducted a joint naval exercise with Indian navy ship in the Gulf of Aden. On October 24, 2023, the EU and India conducted their first joint naval exercise in the Gulf of Guinea. Lastly, on June 1–3, 2025, the EU and India conducted another joint naval exercise – the first-ever full-scale counter piracy operation in the Indian Ocean. These operations expanded EU–India maritime cooperation beyond Indian Ocean reaching Atlantic.

They were relatively small (involving usually three to five navy assets) and rare and hold mostly symbolic and political significance. Yet, they were important for building mutual trust and confidence and to make a step towards better interoperability and to improve operational know-how between both navies. They also showed shared commitment to maritime security common determination to uphold the United Nations Convention on Law of the Sea (UNCLOS).

India continued its dialogue with the EU on counter-terrorism. Two more Declarations were signed in this regard in 2016 and 2017. Terrorism Working Group Dialogues were held regularly, deepening cooperation on information sharing, capacity building, and joint efforts to combat terrorism financing. After many years of work, finally on March 21, 2024, The Central Bureau of Investigation (CBI) signed with Europol – the EU's law enforcement cooperation agency – a Working Arrangement to allow for better information sharing and cooperation between services in the fight against terrorism. After the Pahalgam attacks in April 2024, the EU "unequivocally condemned the heinous terrorist attack", adding that "terrorism can never be justified" and those "responsible for the attack must be brought to justice".[97] At the last meeting of Indian and EU chief diplomats in Brussels in June 2025, Kaja Kallas, High Representative of the EU again condemned terrorist attacks in India and reiterated that "India has the right to protect its citizens in accordance with the international law".[98]

New opportunities for India are opening up for defence industry cooperation in relation to the European ambitious plans to rearm Europe. While India will do most of its defence cooperation at the bilateral level with member states, the Union's growing competence in this area also increases the attractiveness of this partner.

4.2.5 Summary

By mid-2025, India's political relations with the EU at the bilateral level were the best ever. This was evidenced by the intensity of contacts at various levels and the outcome of recent summits, as well as symbolic gestures – Prime Minister Modi's meeting with EU27 leaders, Minister Jaishankar's invitations twice to Union Foreign Ministers' meetings, and the visit of the entire Commission to India in February 2025. The scope of cooperation has been steadily expanded into new areas of maritime security, counter-piracy, security, and defence cooperation. The setting of ambitious goals was accompanied, importantly for India, increasingly by concrete joint actions (e.g. naval exercises with Operation Atalanta). Although the dynamics of cooperation were disrupted by the outbreak of the COVID-19 pandemic and the war in Ukraine, India remained interested in closer engagement with the EU. This also meant that strategic and security issues began to play an increasingly important role.

India and the EU have further strengthened the institutional framework of their multifaceted cooperation. While most of the existing mechanisms continued their work after 2014, some were discontinued and others were upgraded to a higher level, with new formats also being added. By June 2025, the list of different forums for bilateral engagement between India and the EU had grown to over 40 (see Table 4.1) The most important mechanism, the EU–India summits at leaders level, was augmented by several ministerial-level mechanisms, with different ministries engaging in regular talks on strategic

Table 4.1 Institutional framework of India–EU strategic cooperation (as on June 30, 2025)

Leaders' Level	1 Annual EU–India Summits (started in 2000, last meeting in July 15, 2020)
Ministerial Level	2 Ministerial Meetings (2000, in 2025 replaced by Strategic Dialogue) 3 Strategic Dialogue (2025) 4 High-Level Dialogue on Trade and Investment (2020, 3rd in 2023) 5 Trade and Technology Council (TTC) – (Feb 2023, 2nd February 28, 2025)
Senior Officials' Level	6 Joint Commission (1993, 15th Meeting on November 26, 2019) 7 Strategic Partnership Review Meetings (2020, 5th in 2024) 8 Foreign Policy and Security Consultations (2011, 10th on November 21, 2024) 9 Security and Defence Consultations (2022, 2nd on May 6, 2024) 10 Anti-piracy Dialogue (2011, in 2020 replaced by Maritime Security Dialogue) 11 EU–India Maritime Security Dialogue (2020, 4th on March 21, 2025) 12 Cyber Dialogue (2012, 8th on March 20, 2025) 13 Counter Terrorism Dialogue (2001, 14th on May 7, 2024). 14 Dialogue on Disarmament and Non-Proliferation (2011, 7th on February 10, 2022) 15 Dialogue on Space (planned in 2025) 16 EU–India Human Rights Dialogue (2004, 11th meeting on January 8, 2025) 17 High-Level Dialogue on Migration and Mobility (HLDMM) (2016, 7th on October 20, 2023) 18 EU–India Senior Officials' Dialogue to deepen bilateral cooperation on WTO issues (2021)
Working level	Sub-Commissions of the Joint Commission: 19 Sub-Commission on Trade 20 Sub-commission on Development Cooperation 21 Sub-commission on Science and Technology (S&T) Working groups under the Trade and Technology Council (TTC) 22 Working Group on Strategic Technologies, Digital Governance and Digital Connectivity; 23 Working Group on Green and Clean Energy Technologies; 24 Working Group on Trade, Investment and Resilient Value Chains Other 25 Joint Committee on S&T Cooperation (2001, 14th meeting in 2024) 26 Joint Customs Cooperation Committee. 27 EU–India Joint Working Group on pharmaceuticals, biotechnology and medical devices, 28 EU–India Joint Working Group on Sanitary and phytosanitary measures and technical barriers to trade (SPS-TBT) 29 Agricultural and Marine Joint Working Group

(*Continued*)

Table 4.1 (Continued)

Working level	30	Intellectual Property Rights (IPR) Dialogue (2020, 1st on January 14, 2021)
	31	Regulatory Dialogue on Public Procurement
	32	EU–India Policy Dialogue on employment and social policy (2020)
	33	EU–India Climate Change Dialogue (2020)
	34	Joint Working Group on Water (2016)
	35	Joint Working group on Urbanization (2019, 3rd on February 13, 2023)
	36	Joint Working Group on Environment (2020, n.a.)
	37	Joint Working Group on sustainable digital infrastructure, services, norms, and regulatory frameworks,
	38	Joint Working Group for comprehensive space collaboration (2020)
	39	EU–India Annual Review on Development partnership in third countries (2020)
	40	Joint working group to intensify regulatory cooperation on goods and services (2021)
	41	Joint Working Group on resilient supply chains (2021)
Civil society level	42	EU–India Think Tanks Twinning Initiative (2015–2023)
	43	EU–India Water Forum (2016, 6th on September 18, 2024)
	44	India–EU Urban Forum (2019, 3rd on February 13, 2023)
	45	Environmental Forum (2020, n.a.)
	46	EU–India Green Hydrogen Forum (2022, 2nd on May 25, 2025)

and political issues, trade and investment, and technology. Dialogue at senior official level (usually joint secretaries in Indian ministries and directors from the European External Action Service or European Commission directorates general) regularly considered cooperation in the most important areas. Specialized discussions were also held at working level by dozens of joint working groups, as well as consultations among junior officials, professionals, and specialists in various sectors. This structure was supplemented by a growing network of engagements between civil society representatives from business, academia, and think tanks.

4.3 India's economic cooperation with the EU

Economic cooperation has invariably been the cornerstone of India's relationship with the EU. The EU has continued to be a major trading partner and source of investment, with high-tech cooperation playing an increasingly important role. Several key goals of India in economic and social cooperation with the EU can be listed for the period 2014–2025:

1 EU participation in India's modernization and reform plans
2 Increasing access to the EU market through free trade agreement negotiations
3 Increasing trade
4 Attracting EU investment
5 Technological cooperation and the role of the Trade and Technology Council

6 Improving connectivity and implementation of the IMEC project
7 Facilitating migration and mobility in the EU for Indian citizens
8 Development cooperation

4.3.1 EU support for the modernization agenda

Political declarations of the Union's cooperation and support for India's modernization plans have become an enduring feature of Prime Minister Narendra Modi's meetings with EU leaders. Already at his first Summit in Brussels on March 30, 2016, the joint declaration included provisions for "support and willingness to cooperate more" in the implementation of several flagship programmes: *Make in India, Skill India, Digital India, Clean India and Clean Ganga.*[99] The simultaneously adopted "Agenda for Action 2020" focused on economic themes and reiterated many ideas for cooperation on India's flagship programmes, investment and collaboration across a range of sectors.[100] Among other things, it highlighted the existing synergies between India's *Digital India* programme and the EU's *Digital Single Market* and called for the finalization of a Joint Declaration on the next generation of communication networks (5G). The summit also agreed to extend until 2020 Science and Technology Cooperation Agreement. From an economic perspective, the adoption of two declarations establishing new partnerships was significant for India: (1) *Clean Energy And Climate Partnership* and (2) *Water Partnership*.

Indian diplomats, in assessing the outcome of the meeting, were "pleased to note that the EU has become a leading partner in India's socio-economic transformation agenda" and the EU and its member states are "actively working with us on our ambitious flagship initiatives – whether it is building smart cities in India, creating *Digital India, Make in India, Skill India, Start Up India, Maritime India* or the *Clean Ganga* initiative".[101]

India's modernization agenda and cooperation on climate change, trade, research, and innovation were among the main themes of the 14th EU–India Summit in New Delhi on October 6, 2017. A joint statement described India and the EU as "partners in India's modernization" and announced the EU's "continued interest in participating in India's flagship initiatives such as 'Make in India', 'Digital India', 'Skill India', 'Smart City', 'Clean India,' and 'Start-Up India'".[102] The summit adopted two important declarations on economic issues: Joint Declaration on Climate and Energy and Declaration on Partnership for Smart and Sustainable Urbanization.

The Union's willingness to cooperate in a practical way to address India's development challenges meant that India "is beginning to realize that partnerships with the EU can be helpful in building the domestic resilience and capacity needed to achieve domestic and foreign policy goals".[103] While this did not automatically lead to access to the EU's vast funds, it seemed to set the stage for practical and useful cooperation.

Although the next bilateral summit had to wait for as long as three years, cooperation in India's modernization continued regularly at various levels.

Noteworthy are the visit of the EU Commissioner for Environment, Maritime Affairs and Fisheries, Karmenu Vella to India from September 3 to 7, 2018, to discuss cooperation on a circular economy; the meeting of the 9th Session of the Working Group on Pharmaceuticals, Biotechnology and Medical Devices (September 27–28, 2018) or the signing of a cooperation agreement between the respective sanitary services (Food Safety and Standards Authority of India and the European Food Safety Agency) on September 14, 2018, to facilitate mutual access of agricultural crops to both markets.[104]

An important and unequivocal confirmation of the EU's support for India's modernization and development was the strategy for India prepared by the European Commission in November 2018. The document already announced in its subtitle that one of the EU's objectives was a partnership for "the sustainable modernization of India".[105] It listed more than a dozen areas of possible cooperation and identified a number of actions, including, among others, supporting India's modernization through technical expertise and resource mobilization at EU level, including through EIB funds, public and private investment resources, and cooperation with Member States. In doing so, the Union was reinforcing its position as a major partner sharing India's economic objectives and ready to cooperate in achieving them.

The 15th India–EU Summit of July 15, 2020, in the form of a videoconference, was dominated by the issue of the response to the COVID-19 pandemic. The Indian side was then particularly keen to highlight India's attractiveness as a location for relocating production as part of the diversification of global supply chains – a phenomenon that has taken priority in the wake of the coronavirus pandemic and the realization of the risk of over-dependence on China for many markets. An important objective was also to allay partners' concerns about the "Self-Reliant India" (*Aatmanirbhar Bharat*) campaign and present the initiative in a favourable light. The Indian Prime Minister encouraged European companies to seize opportunities in India and explained that *Aatmanirbhar Bharat* aims to integrate India's domestic production into global supply chains.[106]

Also at the special EU–India leaders' meeting on May 8, 2021, the Union assured support for India's reforms and modernization, and in the fight against the pandemic and its consequences. The main outcome was the decision to resume negotiations on a trade agreement and adoption of Connectivity Partnership. Also important for India's economic interests was the creation of three new dialogue mechanisms: (1) a joint working group to intensify regulatory cooperation on goods and services, including, inter alia, green, and digital technologies; (2) a joint working group on resilient supply chains, drawing on lessons learned from the COVID-19 pandemic; and (3) a senior officials' dialogue to deepen bilateral cooperation on WTO issues.

Also, during the recent visit of Commission President Von der Leyen to Delhi in February 2025, the Union assured support for India's economic development and modernization. All these declarations created a favourable atmosphere and incentives for companies interested in the Indian market.

On a more practical level, the five partnerships established since 2016, which addressed specific problems diagnosed by the Indian side and identified concrete cooperation mechanisms, were relevant: (1) *Clean Energy And Climate Partnership* – established in March 2016, (2) Water Partnership – 2016; (3) *India-EU Smart and Sustainable Urbanization Partnership*, 2017; (4) *Partnership for Resource Efficiency and Circular Economy, 2020; and* (5) the Connectivity *Partnership – 2021.*

The Partnerships were meant to be a step forward from the successive dialogue groups created in the previous decade. They were to become a practical forum for regular contacts and discussions, the exchange of experiences, and sector-specific expertise. They also identified key areas for bilateral cooperation in support of India's modernization. Though they are little know, they continued they day-to-day collaboration under consecutive work programmes and numerous activities. These Partnerships were instrumental in driving practical cooperation between EU and India at the working level, exchanging ideas, transferring knowledge, and supporting specific development projects.

For instance, under the India–EU Water Partnership, EU and India are collaborating on river management on Tapi and Ramganga River Basins. Under Phase III, the partnership will extend its efforts to other key basins like the Brahmaputra. Both regions have co-jointly funded seven research and innovation water projects with €37.4 million (EU €23.4 M + India €14 M), bringing together 743 participants from the EU and India. These projects focus on drinking water purification, wastewater treatment, and real-time monitoring and control systems, and the IEWP will further provide support for market uptake of these cutting-edge water technologies in India.[107] Through the partnerships, however, the Union offered technical assistance, contacts, and help in accessing external funding including from the European Investment Bank.

4.3.1.1 Support from the European Investment Bank

The European Investment Bank (EIB) has played a special role in supporting India's modernization. Although it had already been operating in India since 1993, it was only after 2014 that it intensified its activities in this market in strategic sectors. The EIB was identified by the EU as the institution to support two areas in India in particular: energy transition and the development of a low-carbon economy. In 2016, the EIB opened a Regional Representative Office for South Asia in New Delhi and signed the first agreement for a large low-interest loan (for €450 million) for the construction of the Lucknow metro. In the following years, the EIB also supported metro projects in Pune, Bangalore, Bhopal, Kanpur, Agra, and Nagpur.

In total, from 2014 to 2025, EIB has signed 36 loan agreements totalling €5.1. Since 1993, it has supported a total of 25 different projects with loans worth €5.46 billion.[108] Most of the funding went to transport development (67.8%) and energy transition (23.8%). The EIB's activities became the main instrument for the implementation of the Connectivity Partnership and the EU's Global Gateway Strategy in India. The EIB also supported, among others, projects for the development of solar energy and micro-lending to small and medium-sized entrepreneurs. The development banks of the largest Member States also strengthened their lending activities, further increasing the influence of European partners in key sectors.

4.3.1.2 EU joining ISA and CDRI

As an expression of the EU's support for India's initiatives and India's leadership in transforming developing countries, the EU joined two international initiatives set up by Prime Minister Modi – the International Solar Alliance, ISA (together with France at the Paris Climate Summit in 2015) seeking to develop investment in solar power in 123 countries around the world, and the Coalition for Disaster Resilient Infrastructure (CDRI). The 2017 India–EU Summit saw the signing of a Cooperation Agreement between the Delhi-based Interim Secretariat of the International Solar Alliance (ISA) and the European Investment Bank (EIB). Subsequently, on December 11, 2018, the EU signed a Joint Declaration with the International Solar Alliance at COP24 in Katowice, officially becoming a partner organization of ISA. This strengthened the credibility of the organization and encouraged more European countries to join.

Coalition for Disaster Resilient Infrastructure was launched by India in 2019 to promote infrastructure resilience against climate and disaster risks. COVID pandemic and launching of EU strategy on Indo-Pacific make CDRI an interesting platform to foster EU–India cooperation on resilience building in the Indo-Pacific. On March 18, 2021, the EU while accepting India's invitation has officially joined as a member of the Coalition for Disaster Resilient Infrastructure (CDRI), following its endorsement of the charter of the CDRI earlier.

4.3.2 Resumption of FTA negotiations

India's second key objective was to boost trade and make the European market more open to Indian exports. This issue depended heavily on the resumption of FTA negotiations. Also at the summits in 2016, 2017, and 2020 leaders reassured only about their "willingness to explore the possibility of resuming talks" on a free trade agreement and their opposition to protectionism. In 2020 Summit, decision was made to establish a regular High-Level Dialogue on Trade (at ministerial level) to review, provide guidance and resolve emerging contentious issues in this area. Only at the Leaders Meeting in Porto in the May 2021, the parties "agreed to resume negotiations of a balanced, ambitious, comprehensive, and mutually beneficial trade agreement".[109] But it was also announced to "launch negotiations on a stand-alone investment protection agreement" and to launch stand-alone talks on *Geographic Indications* (GIs), which could be adopted in the form of a separate agreement or incorporated into a trade agreement if progress went smoothly.

In practice, the decisions of the 2021 Summit marked the end of the negotiations since 2007 for an ambitious and comprehensive BTIA covering trade and investment, and breaking it down into three independent negotiations. This was also the result of greater pragmatism and a willingness to facilitate talks by carving out separate areas where progress was easier to achieve. Despite a declared breakthrough, negotiations did not get off the ground until the end of the year. Only in March 2022, the European Commission finally appointed its FTA negotiator, something it had delayed for months. In April, EU and Indian leaders at meeting in Delhi announced the rapid resumption of negotiations, indicating that they should be completed by the end of 2023, before the parliamentary elections scheduled in India and Europe in spring 2024.

Finally, on June 17, European Commission Executive Vice-President Valdis Dombrovskis and Indian Commerce Minister Piyush Goyal met in Brussels to formally relaunch EU–India negotiations on a balanced, ambitious, comprehensive, and mutually beneficial free trade agreement. This was after nine years break in negotiations over former BTIA deal. Ministers on the same date also launched EU–India negotiations on an investment protection agreement and on an agreement on geographical indications.

FTA negotiations were divided into 23 chapters covering crucial areas of cooperation, including Trade in Goods, Trade in Services, Investment, Sanitary and Phytosanitary Measures, Technical Barriers to Trade, Trade Remedies, Rules of Origin, Customs and Trade Facilitation, Competition, Trade Defence, Government Procurement, Dispute Settlement, Intellectual Property Rights, Geographical Indications, and Sustainable Development. While India wanted mainly better access to highly valued European market, EU pushed for more ambitious deal covering also sustainability issues and strong intellectual property regime. It aimed at significant duty cuts in automobiles and medical devices, and tax reduction in products such as wine, spirits, meat, and poultry.

The first round of negotiations was concluded in July 2022. Two more rounds took place by the end of the year in October in Brussels, and in Delhi from November 28 to December 9, 2022. Little progress achieved and low intensity of contacts indicated that ambitious deadline would be hard to meet.

In 2023, negotiators meet three times: for the fourth round of negotiations in Brussels concluded on March 18, 2023; the fifth round in mid-June 2023 in New Delhi; and sixth round of negotiations in October 2023 in Brussels. By then, it was clear that talks must be prolonged beyond 2023 and may be more difficult than originally assumed. By then only two chapters were concluded – on SMEs and government procurement (during the fifth round in Delhi in June), some progress on technical issues was reported, but most issues were facing little breakthrough.

Despite election campaign gaining momentum in India and Europe in Spring 2024, negotiations on FTAs continued throughout the year. The seventh round took place in February 2024 in New Delhi, when for the first time Chief Negotiators played a more active role in the negotiations on several chapters, to reduce the list of pending divergences. The eighth round took place in Brussels in June 2024, again with an active engagement of Chief Negotiators. The ninth round took place in New Delhi in September 2024. Three rounds held in 2024 made only some progress on Rules of Origin, Intellectual Property Rights, and Dispute Settlement, but the parties recognized that their respective positions still diverged on several issues.

In early 2025, the new European Commission travelled to India to speed up the negotiations and send a strong political signal to revive the momentum in talks. On February 28, Prime Minister Narendra Modi and the European Commission President set a new ambitious deadline for the conclusion on an FTA – end of 2025. This has helped to make substantial progress and intensify discussions in following months. In addition, US President Trump's threats of high tariffs on both India and the EU gave another reason to strengthen trade relations to fend off against US unilateral pressure.

The tenth round took place in Brussels in March 2025. Both sides agreed to intensify their efforts, and focus on market access. The eleventh round took place in New Delhi already in May 2025. This one marked the biggest progress thus far as five chapters were successfully closed. They included Transparency, Good regulatory practices, Customs and trade facilitation, Intellectual Property Rights, as well as Mutual Administrative Assistance provisions. Negotiators agreed to intensify coordination through a two-phased approach (separate timelines for mutually agreeable and harder-to-resolve areas). Next rounds were to take place in July 2025 in Brussels and September in New Delhi.

Strengthened political will to conclude the deal, more flexibility in approach and increasing progress suggest that some form of an FTA seems increasingly within the reach. By mid-2025 at least 8 chapters have been closed, including transparency, customs, regulatory cooperation, IPR, and trade facilitation, while substantial progress have been made on many others.[110] Still many contentious issues are waiting to be solved, like tariff reductions, non-tariff barriers, services, rules of origin (ROO), and technical measures like SPS and TBT. Securing consensus on most important sticking points, like sustainability measures (like CBAM), and market access for sensitive goods-especially autos and spirits-remains difficult.

A new phased-approach in which India and the EU are aiming to formalize easier chapters now and tackle sensitive issues later, together with a strong political push towards the deal suggests there is an increasing chance of signing kind of a more limited deal (Phase-1 or Early Harvest), instead of over ambitious agreement the EU has for long sought. This would fit better Indian traditional position and reflect similar deals it concluded recently with Australia, EFTA, or UK. Anyway, signing of the FTA with the EU would be a major breakthrough for their relations going far beyond trade and economic cooperation. As consequences of still possible failure of talks would also be detrimental to the overall partnership, the stakes of the talks are high. In the meantime, economic cooperation has grown remarkably in this period.

4.3.3 Trade in goods and services

At the beginning of Prime Minister Modi's rule in 2014, the EU was India's largest trading partner, with total trade (in goods and services) with the 28-member EU bloc amounting to €95.51 billion, of which trade in goods was worth €72.52 billion and in services €22.99 billion.[111] The EU was the largest partner for India, while India was the 9th largest partner for the EU. India's merchandise exports in 2014 were €36.8 billion, while imports were slightly less at €35.9 billion.

Despite the emphasis on economic cooperation, trade has not seen much improvement in many years. According to European data, trade in goods with the EU was worth €62.8 billion in 2020 – 10 billion less than six years earlier.[112] This meant a share of 11.1% of India's trade and a drop in the EU's importance to third place among major trading partners, behind China (12%) and the US (11.7%). India was the EU's 10th largest partner, accounting for 1.8% of EU trade, but far less important than China (16.1%) or the US (15.2%) and the UK (12.2%). Trade in services developed slightly better, rising to €32.7 billion in 2020 (10 billion more than in 2014). Overall, therefore, total trade remained at a similar level in 2020 as in 2014 – reaching €95.5 billion.

Such a surprising result, however, is primarily the result of the UK's exit from the EU, which accounted for a significant part of the Union's trade with India. After Brexit, the Union simply became a smaller trading partner. Another reason for the decline in trade in 2020 was also COVID-19 and the then universally occurring reduction in economic activity.

However, even if one excludes the UK from trade statistics the picture of trade development since 2014 does not look impressive either. The longer trend of trade with the smaller Union of 27 is shown in Chart 4.1, prepared on the basis of Indian data relating to the fiscal year, i.e. between April and March. Also according to this data, India's trade with the EU27 remained at similar levels for many years until 2020 when it declined as a result of the COVID-19 pandemic. It was only the rebound of the economies after the pandemic and especially the changes brought about by Russia's war in Ukraine in 2022 that gave a new dynamic to India's trade with the EU.

The data shows that it was only from 2021 onwards that trade started to grow rapidly from $81 billion in 2020 to $116 billion in 2021, $136 billion in 2022, $137 billion in 2023, and $135 billion in 2024. Indian exports to the EU grew particularly fast, almost doubling over this period – from $40.2 billion in 2014 to $76 billion in 2024. Over the same period, imports from the EU increased from $44.2 billion to almost $60 billion. As a result, trade, which was hitherto very balanced, has started to show a significant surplus on the Indian side, amounting to about $15 billion over the last three years.

This has resulted in the fact that while the EU's share as a source of imports of goods to India has declined over the period from about 10% in 2014 to 8.3% in 2024, its share in exports from India has increased from about 13%

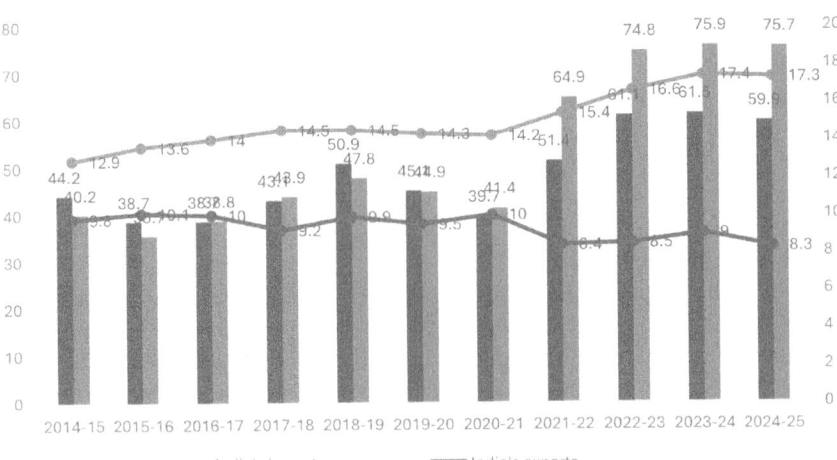

Chart 4.1 India's merchandise trade with the EU from 2014 to 2025 ($billion, %)

Source: Own compilation based on data from Department of Commerce and Industry, Government of India, FTPA- System on Foreign Trade Performance Analysis (FTPA), https://www.commerce.gov.in/trade-statistics/ (accessed 22.07.2025)

in 2014 to over 17% a decade later. This has reinforced the importance of the Union as a trading partner, especially as a destination for Indian products. In fiscal 2024–2025, the Union (with a share of 17.3%) was the second most important export destination behind the US (19.8%), but ahead of the UAE (9%), the UK (3%), or China (3%) (see Chart 4.2.). This is all the more important for India as its overall trade deficit has been growing steadily, mainly driven by a negative balance in trade with Asian partners, including China. Hence, increased exports to the EU were important for deficit reduction.

The EU's share of imports to India remained relatively similar over the period, fluctuating between 9.8% in 2014 and 10% in 2020. However, it started to decline in the following years to drop to 8.3% in 2024. The EU27 countries were the fourth main source of imports for India, behind China, Russia, and the UAE (Chart 4.3).

Overall by the early 2025, the EU is India's second-largest trading partner, accounting for 11.5% of India's total trade. India is the EU's 9th largest trading partner, accounting for 2.4% of the EU's total trade in goods in 2024, well behind the US (17.3%), China (14.6%), or the UK (10.1%).[113]

The total trade volume was complemented by an increasing trade in services. According to European data, this reached €59.7 billion in 2023, and India also recorded a surplus of €7.9 billion here. In total, bilateral trade in goods and services reached €184 billion in 2023.

Reflecting on the sudden increase in the value of trade and especially exports to the EU, it must be said that it is only partly the result of growing economic

Reinforced Partnership 173

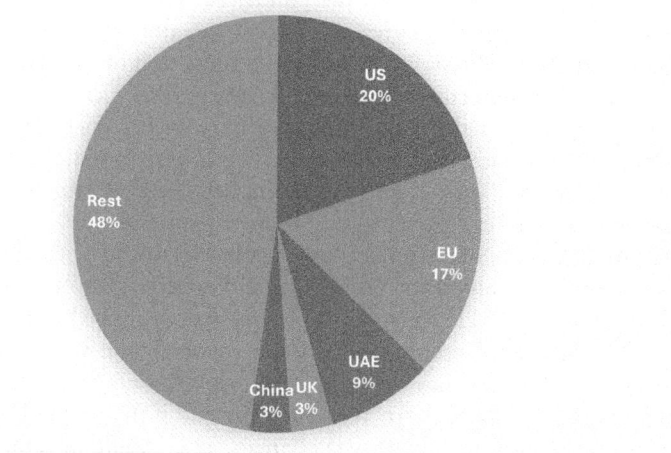

Chart 4.2 India's major export partners in 2024–2025

Source: Own compilation based on data from Department of Commerce and Industry, Government of India, FTPA-System on Foreign Trade Performance Analysis (FTPA), https://www.commerce.gov.in/trade-statistics/ (accessed 22.07.2025)

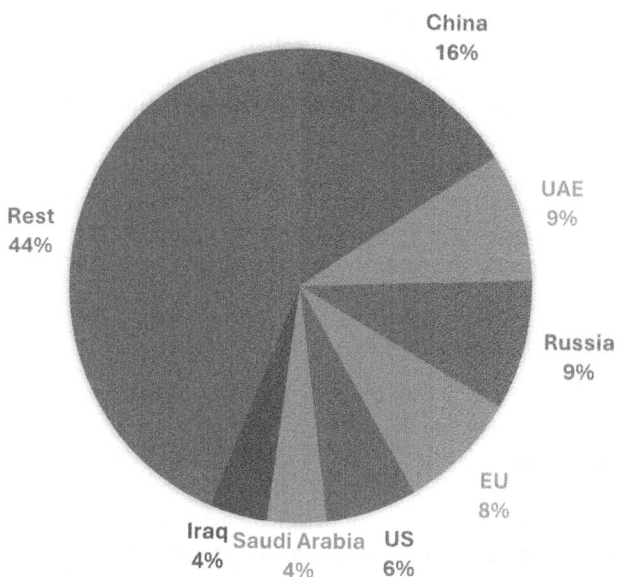

Chart 4.3 India's major import partners in 2024–2025

Source: Own compilation based on data from Department of Commerce and Industry, Government of India, FTPA-System on Foreign Trade Performance Analysis (FTPA), https://www.commerce.gov.in/trade-statistics/ (accessed 22.07.2025)

ties or a reaction to the end of the pandemic. For it is mostly related to the aftermath of the Russian aggression against Ukraine, including the imposition of EU sanctions on Russia, which meant a reduction in Russian oil imports to the EU. Some of this crude began to enter Europe via a circuitous route via India. This is shown by the sudden increase in exports of petroleum products to Europe, and especially the Netherlands. The country's share of India's exports has jumped from 2% in 2015 to 5.1% in 2023 and is largely driven by purchases of processed energy resources. In April–September 2024, almost 25% of India's total exports of petroleum products went to the Netherlands, which at the same time accounted for 66% of all Indian exports to the Netherlands.[114] In this sense, the development of trade happened somewhat by accident as a side-effect, or even sometimes unwanted effect, of the war in Ukraine. This means that it does not show a lasting change. There is a risk that the increase in exports from India is short-lived and may end if the war in Ukraine ends or the sanctions regime against Russia changes. This should prompt India and the EU to take other measures to facilitate access to each other's markets.

Rather, India's longstanding stagnation in trade and the EU's declining trade position confirm the existence of a number of trade constraints – difficulties in market access or the absence of a free trade agreement. The European Commission indicated in 2021 that "India's trade regime and regulatory environment remains relatively restrictive".[115] It pointed to "technical barriers to trade (TBT), sanitary and phytosanitary (SPS) measures, deviations from international standards and agreements, and discrimination based on legislative or administrative measures" as the main impediments, which "affect a wide range of sectors, including goods, services, investment, and government procurement". India, on the other hand, singled out the Union for a number of protectionist measures, such as "sanitary and phytosanitary standards, technical barriers, complex quota/tariff regime, anti-dumping/protection measures against Indian products, etc".[116] This shows that the liberalization of mutual trade through the FTA remains a very important condition for the sustainable development of trade cooperation.

4.3.4 Foreign direct investment (FDI)

Another key objective of India vis-à-vis the Union has been to attract European capital and investment. In 2014, EU countries invested €4.956 billion in India. In contrast, India's FDI in the EU28 amounted to €1.078 billion that year. While the EU remained the most important investment partner during the BJP government, its relative importance has declined.

Investment inflows from the EU remained at a similar level of around USD 8 billion per year for several years to start increasing in 2019 to USD 9.1 billion and to USD 13.376 billion in 2020 (Chart 4.4). In 2014, the EU accounted for 26.75% of India's total cumulative FDI ($64.07 billion).[117] By 2020, FDI from the EU had doubled to $117.43 billion, but despite this, the market share had declined to 22.49%.[118] At the same time, the UK – traditionally a major

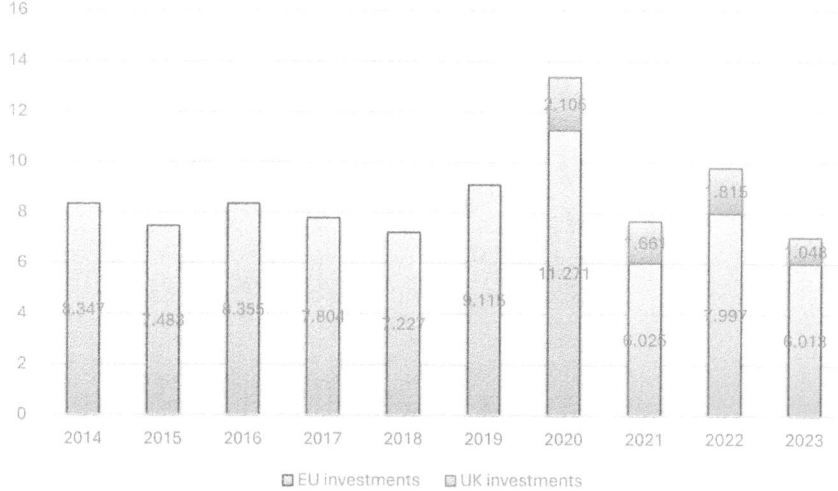

Chart 4.4 EU direct investment inflows to India from 2014 to 2023 (US$billion)
Source: Own elaboration based on: Foreign Direct Investment in India – Annual Issue 2023, Ministry of Commerce and Industry, Government of India, 2024.

investor in India – formally ceased to be part of the EU from February 1, 2020. This means that after subtracting all UK investment ($30.056 billion), total EU investment by 2020 falls to $87.37 billion, which already accounted for only 16.7% of total investment in India. In the following years, investment from the EU27 remained at a modest $6-8bn. In total, by the end of 2023, the total cumulative value of FDI from the EU was $107.43 billion. This represented 16.10% of India's total inward investment.[119]

This therefore meant a reduction in the role of the EU from a share reaching 26.75% in 2014 to 16.1% ten years later. Not only did EU investment inflows fail to increase, but the role of EU companies declined even further. The EU was the third largest source of investment capital (16.2%) in 2023, after Mauritius (26%) and Singapore (23%) (Chart 4.5). In the top ten largest investors, there were now only three member states: the Netherlands (4th place and 6.9%), Germany (9th place and 2.18%), and Cyprus (10th place and 2%).

EU investments went most often (in the period 2000–2023) to the following sectors: Services Sector – 15%, Automobile Industry – 8%, Computer Software & Hardware- 9%, and Trading – 6%, Metallurgical Industries - 5%.[120] The states that have attracted the most investment in the EU during 2019–2023 are traditionally Maharashtra (39%), Karnataka (16%), Delhi (10%), Tamil Nadu (8%), and Jharkhand (8%).

Investment from the EU came mainly from a few countries. Only four countries – the Netherlands (42%), Germany (14%), Cyprus (12%), and France (10%) – were responsible for 78% of all cumulative investment in India by 2023. (see Chart 4.6.)

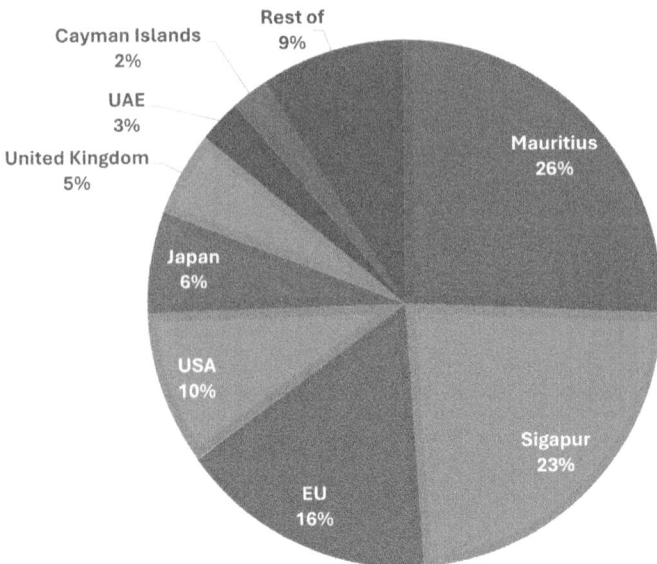

Chart 4.5 Largest foreign investors in India (billion dollars, cumulative value of investments over the period 2000–2023)

Source: Own elaboration based on: Foreign Direct Investment in India – Annual Issue 2023, Ministry of Commerce and Industry, Government of India, 2024.

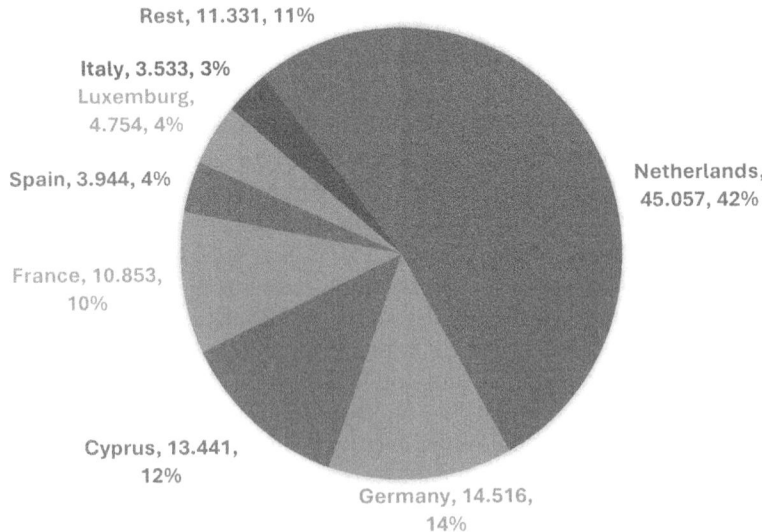

Chart 4.6 Largest investors in India among EU members (cumulative value 2000–2023, US$billion, % in total)

Source: Own elaboration based on: Foreign Direct Investment in India – Annual Issue 2023, Ministry of Commerce and Industry, Government of India, 2024.

At the same time, it is worth adding that EU statistics differ slightly from India's in this regard. According to Eurostat, the value of EU cumulative investment in India was at the end of 2023, EUR 140.1 billion.[121] This was still significantly less than EU investment in China (€231.6 billion) or Brazil (€312.1 billion). European figures also indicate that there are some 6000 European companies operating in India, directly creating 1.7 million jobs and indirectly supporting 5 million jobs. One can also point to growing, but nevertheless much smaller, Indian investment in the EU. The cumulative value of Indian direct investment in EU countries stood at the end of 2023, EUR 10.3 billion. The balance is therefore clearly positive for India (€130 billion).

4.3.5 Scientific and technological cooperation and the role of the TTC

The rapid technological development and burgeoning rivalry between the superpowers over the last decade has meant that technological cooperation has taken on a strategic importance. This has also meant that it has become increasingly important in India's policy towards the EU.

The formal basis for cooperation in this field is the 2001 Scientific and Technological Cooperation Agreement, which was renewed for a further five years on the occasion of summits in 2016 and 2020, and in 2024. A Steering Committee met regularly (the last time at its 14th meeting in 2024), which set the directions and plans for joint research for the following years. The agreement also allowed Indian entities to participate in research projects funded by EU sources. According to EU estimates, under Horizon 2020 and Horizon Europe, 88 collaborative projects worth over €452 million have been implemented by 2024, covering areas such as water, vaccines, and smart grids.[122] Moreover, India ranks 1st globally with over 2,700 Indian researchers funded by Marie Sklodowska-Curie Actions since 2014 and ranks 3rd globally with 77 European Research Council grantees.[123]

Educational and academic cooperation, including student and teacher mobility, developed dynamically. India emerged as the largest beneficiary of the Erasmus + programme, with over 2,200 students having received the prestigious Erasmus Mundus Scholarship since its inception in 2004 to pursue full master's programme at European Universities. Only in 2025 another 101 Indian students got fully funded scholarships to study in the EU. When all other shorter-term activities are included over 6,000 short and long-term Erasmus+ scholarships have been awarded to Indian students since the programme opened to international students. This is in addition to some 90,000 Indian students, who study at the EU as a higher education destination in 2025.[124]

Another significant development is the unblocking of cooperation on nuclear technology. After many years of talks and negotiations (the first announcements were as early as 2005), an Agreement between the European Atomic Energy Community (Euroatom) and the Government of the Republic of India for research and development cooperation in the field of the peaceful uses of nuclear energy was finally signed at the Summit in July 2020. The Commission has concluded Implementing Arrangements with the Indian

Science and Engineering Research Board (SERB) and with the Indian Council on Social Sciences Research (ICSSR) facilitating short-term mobility to be hosted by European Research Council grants. Cooperation between India's space agency ISRO and the European Space Agency ESA is growing. In June 2025, the EU and India decided to launch a dedicated Space Dialogue to accelerate research in this area. The development of scientific cooperation has been fostered through established sectoral partnerships, mechanism meetings (e.g. Energy Panel) and science and business events such as the Environment Forum, Green Hydrogen Forum, etc.

Crucial to fostering collaboration in critical technologies was the announcement in April 2022 of the creation of the Trade and Technology Council as a strategic coordination mechanism at ministerial level to tackle challenges at the nexus of trade, trusted technology, and security.[125] It formally began operations on February 6, 2023. Three working groups were established:

1 Working Group on Strategic Technologies, Digital Governance, and Digital Connectivity;
2 Working Group on Green and Clean Energy Technologies;
3 Working Group on Trade, Investment, and Resilient Value Chains

In May 2023, the first TTC meeting took place, attended by three ministers from the Indian side and their European counterparts. They discussed the work of the three working groups and announced closer co-operation on issues such as quantum and High-Performance Computing, trustworthy Artificial Intelligence, strategic semiconductors, digital skills, 5G, telecoms and Internet of Things standardization, interoperability of their respective digital public infrastructures, waste water management, recycling of batteries for e-vehicles as well as on resilient value chains, market access issues, and foreign direct investment screening.[126] First results of their work was signing of a Memorandum of Understanding on semiconductors during a stock-taking call of TTC in November 2023 to build robust semiconductor supply chains and work together on innovation. A year earlier already, in November 2022, the EU and India signed an "Intent of Cooperation on High Performance Computing and Quantum Technologies" aimed at establishing collaboration on HPC applications using Indian and European Supercomputers in the areas of Bio molecular medicines, COVID therapeutics, mitigating climate change, predicting natural disasters, and Quantum Computing.[127]

Despite commitment to annual meetings, TTC was not held in 2024. The second ministerial meeting took place in Delhi only in February 2025 during the visit of the European Commission to India. Among other things, they agreed to work towards the interoperability of digital public infrastructures (DPIs), to deepen cooperation in the field of AI between the European AI Office and the India AI Mission and to start joint investment of around €60 million on research cooperation on marine plastic litter, waste-to-renewable hydrogen, and recycling of batteries for E-vehicles.[128] While the TTC has not

Reinforced Partnership 179

yet produced many tangible results and is less well advanced than similar initiatives India has with the US (ICET) or the UK, it has identified new directions for technology cooperation in critical sectors.

4.3.6 Connectivity partnership and IMEC

Another area of cooperation of increasing strategic importance is in connectivity. The EU announced greater engagement in this area in its connectivity strategy September 19, 2018, which was to be an alternative to China's Belt and Road Initiative. Cooperation was to be based on the highest international standards and cover four areas: transport corridors, energy grids, digital links, and people exchange. The Union's approach was very similar to India's position, which was critical of China's BRI and emphasized the need to maintain high-quality investments while respecting international law.

This became the basis for the launch of a special Connectivity Partnership at the India–EU leaders' meeting in May 2021. It aims to develop connectivity networks across the digital, transport, energy, and people-to-people sectors. India and the EU pledged to emphasize social, economic, fiscal, climate, and environmental sustainability, as well as transparency, viability, good governance, and a level playing field for economic players. The partnership is also expected to include cooperation in the development of normative regulations, standards, and physical projects, and will encourage private sector action and investment in all dimensions of sustainable connectivity.

Both sides pledged to support bilateral connectivity, but also joint projects and initiatives in third countries, including Africa, Central Asia, and the Indo-Pacific. The partnership did not, however, create any new institutions or allocate any specific funds for this purpose. It was to be developed within the framework of other existing dialogue formats, and the overall oversight of the implementation of cooperation was entrusted to the EU–India Strategic Partnership Review Meeting.

The main vehicle for the implementation of connectivity projects was to be the EU's Global Gateway Strategy announced in December 2021, which promised to mobilize €300 billion for global infrastructure projects by 2027. The Union was also to work more closely with Member States under the Team Europe approach. The weakness of the initiative was the lack of new sources of funding. As a result, existing initiatives and projects already funded by the EIB or the Commission were pulled under the new brand. Neither the Connectivity Partnership nor Global Gateway resulted in a qualitative change in cooperation with India. Though there are not many details available, the EU claims that Team Europe (Commission plus Member States) invested in Global Gateway projects in India over nine billion euro between 2021 and 2025.[129] This included support for EU–Africa–India Digital Corridor and South Asia Energy Connectivity projects.

A new impetus for the expansion of strategic connectivity came with the announcement of the IMEC – India-Middle East – Europe Economic

Corridor initiative at the G20 Summit in Delhi on September 9, 2023. It is designed as a multimodal transport corridor linking India to Europe through the Middle East, aiming to enhance economic integration and supply chain resilience across three major regions. At the launching ceremony took part Prime Minister of India, President of European Commission and leaders from Germany, France, Italy, along with US, Saudi Arabia, and UAE. IMEC was not only a transport and trade corridor but was seen as initiative to enhance energy connectivity (to carry clean hydrogen, electricity) and digital connectivity (to transfer data) through undersea and terrestrial cables and pipelines. Though terrorist attacks in Israel on October 7, 2023, and Israel's attack on Gaza Strait worsened geopolitical context for its implementation, the EU and India stay committed to the project.

Despite little progress and serious doubts about its financial sustainability IMEC remained as a geopolitical vision that can bring Europe and India together. This was well reflected during the last visit of President of the European Commission to India in 2025. Von der Leyen in her lecture in Delhi described IMEC as a "historic opportunity", "a modern golden road – directly connecting India, the Arabian Gulf and Europe" and something much more "than 'just' a railway or a cable – "a green and digital bridge across continents and civilizations". She reaffirmed that this "can be a win-win-win for Europe, India and our partners" and promised that the EU is ready "to invest in concrete projects that can already start making these connections happen" and to "invest in our common future with India".[130] Though it is still unclear how and if IMEC will be implemented in future, it will certainly play a role as an idea that animates closer alignment between India and Europe.

4.3.7 Migration and mobility

Migration and greater access to the EU labour market has been an issue raised by India for a long time, but has been particularly highlighted by the BJP government in recent years. The issue was already widely discussed at the first Modi's Summit in Brussels in 2016. The "Declaration of the Joint Programme on Migration and Mobility" adopted then established a framework for closer cooperation on migration targets, recommendations, and actions. It set out concrete proposals for action in four areas: (1) better organizing and promoting legal migration; (2) increasing the developmental effect of regular migration; (3) preventing and combating irregular migration, including human trafficking; and (4) promoting international protection of migrants' rights.[131]

From India's point of view, there were several important European commitments in the document, including improving the visa issuance process; cooperating on the social security of migrants; increasing the mobility of skilled workers, entrepreneurs, researchers and students; matching the needs of labour markets with migration; or making progress on mutual recognition of qualifications. The parties also announced, among other things, to enhance border control capabilities, strengthen cooperation between relevant agencies from India and the EU, and "explore the possibility of adopting a Readmission Agreement". The Indian side read the declaration as "a step towards facilitating legal migration" to the EU.[132] The annual EU-India High Level Dialogue on Migration and Mobility, and supporting working-level meetings, is responsible for implementing the programme.

Even before the summit, during a meeting with MEPs in Brussels in March 2016, Modi pointed out that India has one of the youngest populations in the world and said that India was keen to build closer relations with the EU in areas such as trade, technology, and tourism. In this context, he noted that "the EU has the resources and technology, we have the manpower, so it can be a win-win partnership".[133] The Indian Deputy Minister went on to elaborate that "the EU can clearly benefit from the services of young Indian workers and professionals who are recognized globally for their scientific, engineering, and managerial skills, work ethic and ability to integrate seamlessly into all societies".[134]

However, despite the establishment and subsequent meetings of the Migration Dialogue in the following years, little progress has been made in regulating the mobility of Indian workers at EU level. The accessibility of the European labour market is in the competence of the Member States and it was up to individual governments to offer specific concessions to India. Also as a result of the so-called migration crisis in Europe in 2015, the issue became so politically sensitive that it was not possible to develop a common position towards India within the Union.

However, despite the lack of progress in formal arrangements, Indian migration to the EU has gained considerable momentum in recent years. According to available (albeit incomplete) Eurostat data, the number of Indian nationals in the 27 constituent countries of the EU has increased from 64,000 in 1998 to 730,000 in 2024 and thus more than 10 times! (Chart 4.7). This trend has particularly intensified during the Modi government since 2014 when 291,000 Indian citizens lived in Europe. According to the available data (the Eurostat database omits data from, for example, France or Poland), the largest number of Indus legally living in 2024 was in Germany with 224,500 (up from 36,600 in 1998), in Italy with 170,600 (up from 17,000 in 1998), in Spain with 56,100 (8,200 in 2002), in the Netherlands with 55,600 (3,400 in 1998), and also in Ireland with 59,600.[135]

In addition to the rapidly growing workforce, students and professionals were a large group of Indians in the EU. It appeared that even in the absence of formal agreements, increased migration of Indians to the EU had become a reality. The presence of a growing Indian diaspora in EU countries was a new phenomenon and an additional link bringing India closer to European countries. It is worth mentioning here that the number of Indian nationals in the UK was in 2021. 362,000 (up from 162,000 in 2000), which is less than that of EU countries. Although, in the case of the UK, account must be taken of the large number of people of Indian origin who have lived there for a

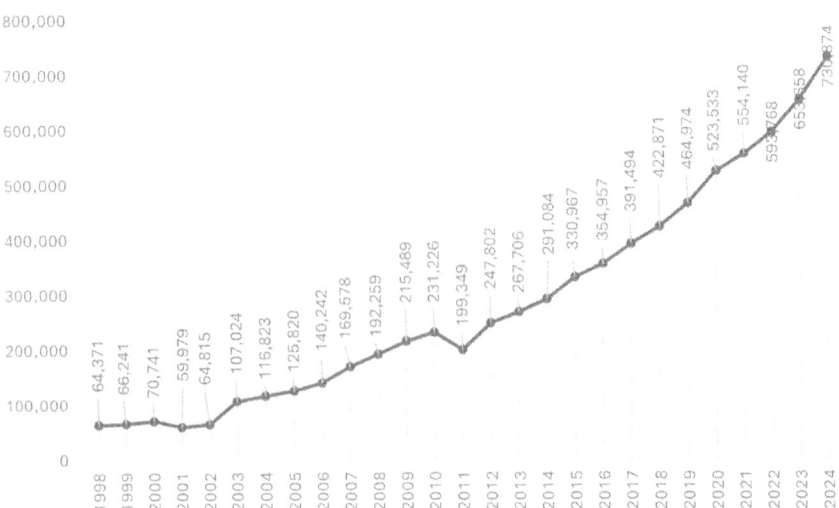

Chart 4.7 Number of Indian nationals living in the EU27 between 1998 and 2024

Source: Own compilation based on Eurostat, European Commission, "Population on 1 January by age group, sex and citizenship", https://ec.europa.eu/eurostat/ as of 22.07.2025.

long time, for the first time continental Europe has become a more important destination for Indian migration.

Indian high-skilled workers receive highest number of EU Blue Cards in 2023/2024. Also, the EU has opened up to Indian tourists and visitors. Indians emerged among top nations receiving the highest number of visas to travel to the EU in the last decade. Only in 2024, over 1 million Schengen visas were issued to Indians.[136]

4.3.8 International development cooperation

In 2014, the European Commission formally ended its development assistance in India and withdrew from its aid activities in the country. However, this does not mean that India stopped receiving EU aid. The Commission was no longer channelling aid under its main *Development Cooperation Instrument* (DCI) and had not prepared a *Country Strategy Paper* (CSP) for India for the new Financial Perspective (IFF) 2014–2021. This expressed a more partnership level of relations with India as an emerging power. However, funds from the previous perspective could still flow to India as part of the completion of earlier projects and programmes. Cooperation with India, including for activities envisaged in joint action plans and summit resolutions, was to be funded from the new Partnership Instrument (PI), created to pursue EU strategic interests and develop selected partnerships. Indian actors could also apply for funding from horizontal programmes, such as for support to civil society from the European Instrument for Democracy and Human Rights (EIDHR).

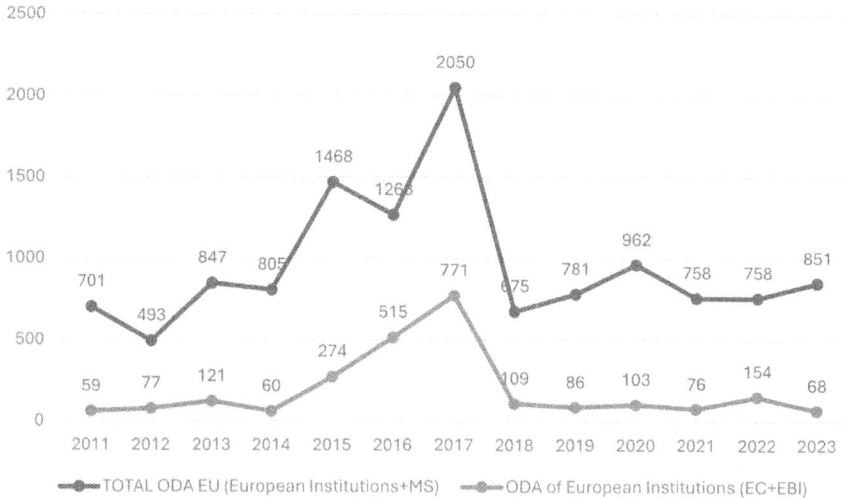

Chart 4.8 EU Official Development Assistance to India, 2011 to 2023 (€m, net disbursements)

Source: Own compilation based on: European Commission, EU Aid Explorer, https://euaidexplorer.ec.europa.eu/ (accessed 20.07.2025)

Most importantly, however, as Official Development Assistance (ODA) also counts as part of the concessional loans provided by the European Investment Bank (EIB), which has developed extensive financing activities in India for infrastructure projects and green transformation. As a result, even more, not less, aid money has started to flow to India (see Chart 4.8). According to the European Commission (EC), between 2014 and 2023, €2.22 billion of ODA-eligible funds went there from the European Institutions (IE), of which €1.9 billion came from the EIB (in the form of loans) and €316 million in grants from the European Commission.[137] This was at the same time four times more than the €547 million provided in the previous budget (2007–2013), when the majority was Commission grants (€457 million) and the EIB was just starting to lend (€89 million).

When MSs aid is taken into account, EU aid as a whole seriously gains in importance. It turns out that ODA provided to India after 2014 was much higher than in the earlier period, often amounting to more than €1 billion per year (at its peak in 2017, it was even more than €2 billion). In total, net aid disbursements to India amounted to €10.4 billion between 2014 and 2023.[138] India was the fifth largest recipient of European aid during this period after Turkey (€30 billion), Ukraine (€26 billion), Syria (€11.8 billion), and Morocco (€11.7 billion), receiving more funds than Afghanistan (€10.3 billion) or Ethiopia (7.3 billion). Germany (€6.65 billion), the European Institutions (€2.22 billion), France (€1.21 billion), and Italy (€140 million) provided by far the most aid during this period.

This means that despite the formal end of bilateral development assistance and the marginalization of this topic in the bilateral dialogue, European support for India's development objectives remained an important source of funding for projects in India. For comparison, it is worth mentioning that according to OECD data, total ODA (gross disbursements) to India in 2023 was 2.3 billion dollars.[139] The EU as a whole was the second largest donor of ODA to India behind Japan, and ahead of the US or UK.

4.3.9 Summary

The balance of India's economic goals vis-à-vis the EU during the Modi government is mixed. On the one hand, India has made progress in all areas of economic cooperation with the EU – supporting the country's modernization programmes, doubling exports to the EU market, attracting additional investment, remaining an important recipient of EU development assistance, enhancing cooperation in critical technology and infrastructure projects, increasing access to EU labour markets and education. On the other hand, trade has long stagnated and current growth is built on fragile foundations, investment flows from Europe have slowed, and many joint projects remain in the realm of declarations and plans. The importance of the EU as a source of investment and trade partner has also declined.

This means that there is certainly still a lot of untapped potential for economic and technological cooperation. An opportunity to exploit it would be the adoption of a free trade agreement, negotiations for which have gained momentum. Also, the international context related to the Trump administration's US policy and the will for independence from China may push India to deepen its cooperation with the EU. Prime Minister Modi has opened the door to a strategic economic partnership with Europe. The next years will show whether he is willing to go through them.

Notes

1 Bharatiya Janata Party, *Election Manifesto 2014; Sabka Saath, Sabka Vikas*, New Delhi, 2014, p. 1.
2 Bharatiya Janata Party, *Election Manifesto 2014; Sabka Saath, Sabka Vikas*, New Delhi, 2014, pp. 39–40.
3 J. D. Pedersen, "India as an Emerging Power in the Global Order: On Geopolitics and Geo-economics", [in:] S. F. Christensen, L. Xing (eds.), *Emerging Powers, Emerging Markets, Emerging Societies*, International Political Economy Series, London: Palgrave Macmillan, 2016, s. 111.
4 See P. Kugiel, "India in the Reform Process: Opportunities for Poland", *PISM Report*, Warsaw, February 2017.
5 "PM Modi to extend red carpet for investors, launch Make in India campaign tomorrow", *The Economic Times*, September 24, 2014, http://economictimes.indiatimes.com.
6 "India needs Rs. 43 trillion of investment in infrastructure over next 5 years: Jaitley", *Livemint*, April 01, 2017.

7 P. P. Chaudhuri, "India, the European Union and the World Order", [in:] R. K. Jain (ed.), *India and the European Union in a Turbulent World*, Singapore: Palgrave Macmillan, 2020, p. 3.
8 A. N. Ram, "India and the European Union in the New Millennium", [in:] R. K. Jain (ed.), *India and the European Union in the 21stCentury*, New Delhi: Radiant Publishers, 2002, p. 3.
9 J. Luc-Racine, "The India-Europe Relationship in the US Shadow", [in:] R. K. Jain (ed.), *India and the European Union. Building a Strategic Partnership*, Delhi: Radiant Publishers, 2007, pp. 41–62.
10 R. C. Mohan, "India, Europe and the United States", [in:] R. K. Jain (ed.), *India and the European Union in the 21stCentury*, New Delhi: Radiant Publishers, 2002, p. 58.
11 R. C. Mohan, "India, Europe and the United States", [in:] R. K. Jain (ed.), *India and the European Union in the 21stCentury*, New Delhi: Radiant Publishers, 2002, p. 62.
12 R. K. Jain, "India and EU: Parameters and Potentials of Strategic Partnership", [in:] R. K. Jain (ed.), *India and the European Union, Building a Strategic Partnership*, Delhi: Radiant Publishers, 2007, p. 73.
13 P. P. Chaudhuri, "India, the European Union and the World Order", [in:] R. K. Jain (ed.), *India and the European Union in a Turbulent World*, Singapore: Palgrave Macmillan, 2020, p. 17.
14 P. Kugiel, "China's Growing Engagement in South Asia", *PISM Bulleiyn*, no. 46 (1794), April 17, 2019.
15 See K. Bajpai, *India versus China: Why They Are Not Friends*, New Delhi: Juggernaut Publishers, 2021; G. Bambawale, V. Kelkar, R. Mashelkar, G. Natarajan, A. Ranade, A. Shah, *Rising to the China Challenge: Winning Through Strategic Patience and Economic Growth*, New Delhi: Rupa Publications India PVT, 2021.
16 P. Kugiel, "Growing Rivalry in Asia: India Steps Away from China's Silk Road Project", *PISM Bulletin*, no. 61 (1503) June 26, 2017.
17 S. Jaishankar, "Situation in Ladakh the 'Most Serious' After 1962 Conflict, Says Jaishankar", *The Business Standard*, August 27, 2020.
18 "China biggest security threat to India, says CDS chief Bipin Rawat", *Wion*, wionews.com, November 12, 2021.
19 R. C. Mohan, "A Power Shift in the Making", *The Indian Express*, January 25, 2022.
20 R. K. Jain "India and EU-China Relations: Perceptions and Misperceptions", [in:] R. K. Jain (ed.), *India, Europe and Asia*, Singapore: Palgrave Macmillan, 2021, pp. 45–73.
21 European Commission, *Connecting Europe and Asia – Building Blocks for an EU Strategy. Joint Communication to the European Parliament, the Council, the European Economic and Social Committee, the Committee of the Regions and the European Investment Bank*, Brussels, 19.9.2018.
22 *Official Spokesperson's Response to a Query on Participation of India in OBOR/BRI Forum*, Ministry of External Affairs, Government of India, New Delhi, May 13, 2017.
23 M. Singh, "India, Europe and Connectivity: From Shared Views on BRI to Mutual Cooperation?", [in:] R. K. Jain (ed.), *India, Europe and Asia*, Singapore: Palgrave Macmillan, 2021, pp. 133–159.
24 European Commission, *EU-China – A strategic outlook. Joint Communication to the European Parliament, the European Council and the Council*, Strasbourg, 12.3.2019.
25 R. K. Jain "India and EU-China Relations: Perceptions and Misperceptions", [in:] R. K. Jain (ed.), *India, Europe and Asia*, Singapore: Palgrave Macmillan, 2021.
26 R.C. Mohan, "India's New Europolitik", *The Indian Express*, December 22, 2020.

27 G. Mohan, "Europe can be a Key Ally for India", *The Hindustan Times*, July 14, 2020.
28 S. Benaglia, "EU-India Relations Set for a New Era", *Policy Biref*, CEPS, July 17, 2020.
29 *External Affairs Minister's Remarks at the Annual Meeting of Romanian Diplomacy*, Ministry of External Affairs, Government of India, September 08, 2021.
30 See S. Sharma, "Indian and European Responses to Migration and Refugee Crises", [in:] R. K. Jain (ed.), *India and the European Union in a Turbulent World*, Singapore: Palgrave Macmillan, 2020, pp. 205–217.
31 S. Jaishankar, *The India Way. Strategies for an Uncertain World*, New Delhi: Harper Collins Publishers India, 2020, p. 77.
32 G. Sachadeva (ed.), *Challenges in Europe: Indian Perspectives*, Singapore: Palgrave Macmillan, 2019, p. 11.
33 S. Jaishankar, *The India Way. Strategies for an Uncertain World*, New Delhi: Harper Collins Publishers India, 2020, p. 12.
34 See P. Kugiel, "India vis-à-vis the Ukraine Crisis: Watching and Waiting", *PISM Bulletin*, no. 54 (1166), May 06, 2014.
35 Inaugural Address by Prime Minister at Second Raisina Dialogue, New Delhi (January 17, 2017), January 17, 2017.
36 Interview with a European diplomat in India, New Delhi, July 22, 2014.
37 Transcript of Media Briefing by Official Spokesperson in Brussels on visit of Prime Minister to Belgium (March 30, 2016), Ministry of External Affairs, Government of India, New Delhi, March 31, 2016.
38 *Annual Report 2014–2015*, Ministry of External Affairs, Government of India, New Delhi, 2015, p. 94.
39 *Annual Report 2015–2016*, Ministry of External Affairs, Government of India, New Delhi, 2016, p. 103.
40 "Shared Vision, Common Action: A Stronger Europe a Global Strategy for the European Union's Foreign and Security Policy", European External Action Service, June 2016.
41 Interview with Krzysztof Kozlowski, EU Ambassador to India at the EU-India think-tank forum, New Delhi, November 03, 2015.
42 *Annual Report 2016–17*, Ministry of External Affairs, Government of India, New Delhi, 2017, p. 127.
43 European Commission, *Joint Statement 13th EU-India Summit*, Brussels, March 30, 2016.
44 Ministry of External Affairs, Government of India, India-EU Joint Declaration on the Fight Against Terrorism, New Delhi, March 30, 2016.
45 EU-India Agenda for Action-2020, EU-India Summit, Brussels, March 30, 2016.
46 European Parliament Resolution of 13 September 2017 on EU Political Relations with India (2017/2025(INI)), September 13, 2017 – Strasbourg.
47 India – EU Joint Statement 14th India-EU Summit, New Delhi, October 06, 2017.
48 P. Kugiel, "14th EU-India Summit in New Delhi Strengthens Partnership", *PISM Bulletin*, no. 111 (1553), November 16, 2017.
49 English Translation of Press Statement by Prime Minister during India-EU Summit (October 06, 2017), Ministry of External Affairs, Government of India, October 06, 2017
50 R. C. Mohan, *Raja Mandala: Reconnecting with Europe*, Carnegie India, September 2018.
51 S. Saran, *ORF 'In-Conversation' – External Affairs Minister and Portuguese Foreign Minister on the Future of India-EU relations (June 23, 2021)*, Ministry of External Affairs, Government of India, New Delhi, June 23, 2021.
52 H. Pant, Observer Research Foundation, interview with the author in Delhi, 21.02.2019.

53 *Annual Report 2018–2019*, Ministry of External Affairs, Government of India, New Delhi, 2019; *Annual Report 2019–2020*, Ministry of External Affairs, Government of India, New Delhi, 2020.
54 P. P. Chaudhuri, "India and Central Europe: From the Margins to the Centre in Three Stages", [in:] R. K. Jain (ed.), *India and Central Europe*, Singapore: Palgrave Macmillan, 2021; P. Kugiel, "India and Central Europe: A Road More Travelled?", [in:] R. K. Jain (eds), *India and Central Europe*, Singapore: Palgrave Macmillan, 2021.
55 D. Jaishankar, "Here's Why Central and Eastern Europe may Become an Area of Promise for India", *Brookings India*, September 05, 2018.
56 *External Affairs Minister in Conversation at Raisina Dialogue 2020: The India Way*, Ministry of External Affairs, Government of India, New Delhi, January 16, 2020.
57 Council of the European Union, *Enhanced EU Security Cooperation in and with Asia – Council conclusions* (May 28, 2018), Brussels, May 28, 2018.
58 European Commission, High Representative of the Union for Foreign Affairs and Security Policy, *Connecting Europe and Asia – Building blocks for an EU Strategy. Joint Communication to the European Parliament, the Council, the European Economic and Social Committee, the Committee of the Regions and the European Investment Bank*, JOIN(2018) 31 final, Brussels, 19.9.2018.
59 European Commission, High Representative of the Union for Foreign Affairs and Security Policy, *Joint Communication to the European Parliament and the Council, "Elements for EU's Strategy on India – Partnership for sustainable modernisation and rules-based global order"*, Brussels, 20.11.2018 JOIN(2018) 28 final.
60 See H. C. Aspengren, A. Nordenstam, "What Strategies Can Do for Strategic Partnerships: Lessons from the EU's Strategy on India", [in:] P. Gieg, T. Lowinger, M. Pietzko, A. Zürn, U.S. Bava, G. Müller-Brandeck-Bocquet (eds.), *EU-India Relations. Contributions to International Relations*, Cham: Springer, 2021.
61 *India welcomes Joint Communication by the European Commission on India-EU partnership – "A Partnership for Sustainable Modernisation and Rules-based Global Order"*, Ministry of External Affairs, Government of India, New Delhi, November 26, 2018.
62 Sushma Swaraj, lecture to participants of Kautliya Fellowship Programme, New Delhi, 20.02.2019.
63 C. R. Mohan, A. Atmakuri, "The European Union's New Strategy towards India", *ISAS Brief*, no. 625, December 03, 2018.
64 A. Dutta, "EU's Strategy on India: Time to Revitalise the Natural Partnership", *Issue Brief*, Indian Council on World Affairs, February 01, 2019.
65 Interview with Harsh Pant, Observer Research Foundation, Delhi, 21.02.2019.
66 B. Mukherjee, "India and the European Union: A Dialectical Approach to Human Rights", [in:] R. K. Jain (ed.), *India and the European Union in a Turbulent World*, Singapore: Palgrave Macmillan, 2020, pp. 167–185.
67 Ministry of External Affairs, Government of India, *Visit of External Affairs Minister to European Union*, February 18, 2020.
68 Ministry of External Affairs, Government of India, Economic Diplomacy division, *EAM Jaishankar Meets EU Leaders in Brussels*, February 19, 2020.
69 P. P. Chaudhuri, "Brexit and India-UK Relations", [in:] R. K. Jain (ed), *India and the European Union in a Turbulent World*, Singapore: Palgrave Macmillan, 2020, p. 101.
70 S. Jaishankar, *The India Way. Strategies for an Uncertain World*, New Delhi: Harper Collins Publishers India, 2020, p. 40.
71 European Commission, *Joint Statement – 15th EU-India Summit*, July 15, 2020.
72 P. Kugiel, 'EU-India Summit-the Democracy Linchpin', *Spootlight PISM* no. 55/2020, July 20, 2020.

73 European Commission, *Joint Statement – 15th EU-India Summit*, July 15, 2020.
74 European Commission, *EU-India Strategic Partnership: A Roadmap to 2025*, July 15, 2020.
75 U. S. Bava, "India and the European Union: A Partnership for Joining Forces on the Global Scene-Concluding Remarks and Outlook", [in:] P. Gieg, T. Lowinger, M. Pietzko, A. Zürn, U. S. Bava, G. Müller-Brandeck-Bocquet (eds.), *EU-India Relations. Contributions to International Relations*, Cham: Springer, 2021.
76 *Annual Report 2020–2021*, Ministry of External Affairs, Government of India, New Delhi, 2021, p. 126.
77 Ministry of External Affairs, Government of India, Joint Statement on India-EU Leaders' Meeting (May 08, 2021), New Delhi, May 08, 2021.
78 European Commission, *India-EU Working Group Advances Joint Commitment for Digital Collaboration*, Publication, News Article, 23 April 2021.
79 Ministry of External Affairs, Government of India, Joint Statement on India-EU Leaders' Meeting (May 08, 2021), New Delhi, May 08, 2021.
80 S. Jaishankar, *ORF 'In-Conversation' – External Affairs Minister and Portuguese Foreign Minister on the Future of India-EU relations (June 23, 2021)*, June 23, 2021.
81 G. Singh, "India-EU: Everything is in Place", Gateway House, May 13, 20121.
82 Ministry of External Affairs, Government of India, *Telephone Conversation Between Prime Minister Shri Narendra Modi and President of the European Council, Charles Michel*, August 31, 2021.
83 Ministry of External Affairs, Government of India, *Prime Minister's Meeting with President of European Council and President of European Commission*, October 29, 2021.
84 European Union External Action Service, Informal meeting of Foreign Affairs Ministers (Gymnich): *Remarks by High Representative Josep Borrell at the Press Conference*, Brussels, 03/09/2021.
85 S. R. Barman, "Europe has to Grow Out of Mindset that its Problems are World's Problems", Jaishankar, *The Indian Express*, 02.06.2022.
86 'We look for partners not preachers': Jaishankar says Europe must show sensitivity to strengthen India ties, *The Indian Express*, 05.05.2025.
87 P. Kugiel, "End of the Illusion: EU Partnership Holds Firm Despite India's Stance on Russian Aggression", PISM Strategic File No. 10 (118), July 2022.
88 S. Benaglia, "The EU and India Agree to Disagree on Ukraine. and That's Ok", *CEPS Blog*, July 11, 2022.
89 S. Haidar, "Not Pleased with India's Votes on Ukraine, but Confident we Share Same Values: EU Envoy", *The Hindu*, March 29, 2022.
90 Ministry of External Affairs, Government of India, *Annual Report 2022–2023*, New Delhi, 2023, pp. 142–143.
91 Ministry of External Affairs, Government of India, *Annual Report 2023–2024*, New Delhi, 2024, pp. 115–116.
92 Ministry of External Affairs, Government of India, *Annual Report 2023–2024*, New Delhi, 2025, pp. 154–155.
93 Leaders' Statement: Visit of Ms. Ursula von der Leyen, President of the European Commission and EU College of Commissioners to India (February 27–28, 2025), Ministry of External Affairs, Government of India, February 28, 2025.
94 Visit of External Affairs Minister to the European and Belgium (June 9–11, 2025), Ministry of External Affairs, Government of India, June 11, 2025.
95 *Annual Report 2017–2018*, Ministry of External Affairs, Government of India, New Delhi, 2018, p. 133.
96 D. R. Chaudhury, "French Navy Displays Commitment to Balance China in Indian Ocean through Port Call in Mumbai", *The Economic Times*, January 25, 2019.

97 India/Pakistan: Statement by the High Representative on behalf of the European Union on the latest developments, Council of the EU, Press Release, Brussels, 08.05.2025.
98 EU-India Strategic Dialogue: press remarks by High Representative/Vice-President Kaja Kallas at the joint press point, EEAS, Brussels, 10.06.2025.
99 European Commission, *Joint Statement: 13th EU-India Summit*, Brussels, March 30, 2016.
100 European Commission, *EU-India Agenda for Action-2020 EU-India Summit*, Brussels, March 30, 2016.
101 *Speech by Minister of State for External Affairs on "What next for EU-India Relations?" at the Horasis India Meeting, Cascais (July 04, 2016)*, Ministry of External Affairs, Government of India, New Delhi, July 05, 2016.
102 European Commission, *India – EU Joint Statement. 14th India-EU Summit*, New Delhi, October 06, 2017.
103 G. Mohan, "A Turning Point for Europe and India", *Insights, Transatlantic Take*, German Marshal Fund, May 04, 2021.
104 *Annual Report 2018–2019*, Ministry of External Affairs, Government of India, New Delhi, 2019, p. 178.
105 European Commission, High Representative of the Union for Foreign Affairs and Security Policy, *Joint Communication to the European Parliament and the Council, "Elements for EU's Strategy on India – Partnership for sustainable modernisation and rules-based global order"*, Brussels, 20.11.2018 JOIN(2018) 28 final.
106 *Transcript of Virtual Special Media Briefing on India-EU Summit by Secretary (West) (July 15, 2020)*, Ministry of External Affairs, Government of India, New Delhi, July 17, 2020.
107 EU and India agree to deepen cooperation in Sustainable Water Management, EEAS, Press Release, 18.09.2024.
108 *India and the EIB*, European Investment Bank 2022, https://www.eib.org/en/projects/regions/ala/india/index.htm (Accessed 22.12.2021).
109 European Commission, *Joint Statement EU-India Leaders' Meeting*, May 08, 2021.
110 India and Europe agree on nearly half of trade deal 'chapters', *Financial Time*, June 03, 2025.
111 *Annual Report 2015–2016*, Ministry of External Affairs, Government of India, New Delhi, 2016, p. 103.
112 European Commission, Directorate-General for Trade, European Union, Trade in goods with India, 02.06.2021.
113 EU trade relations with India. Facts, figures and latest developments. European Commission, (Accessed 22.07.2025).
114 Monthly Bulletin on Foreign Trade statistics: October 2024. Government of India, Ministry of Commerce and Industry, Department of Commerce, New Delhi October 2024.
115 European Commission, Trade, Countries and regions: India, September 10, 2021, https://ec.europa.eu/trade/policy/countries-and-regions/countries/india/.
116 Government of India, Ministry of Commerce and Industry, Department of Commerce, *Annual Report 2021–22*, New Delhi, 2022, p. 98.
117 Foreign Direct Investment in India – Annual Issue 2014, Table No. 6.1. (B): FDI Synopsis on Country: European Union, (As on 31.12.2014), Ministry of Commerce and Industry, Government of India, 2015.
118 Foreign Direct Investment in India – Annual Issue 2020, Table No. 6.1. (B FDI Synopsis on Country: European Union, (As on 31.12.2020), FDI Newsletter, Ministry of Commerce and Industry, Government of India. https://dpiit.gov.in/sites/default/files/European_Union_B_2020.pdf (Accessed 29.12.2021).

119 Foreign Direct Investment in India – Annual Issue 2023, Table No. 6.1. (B): FDI Synopsis on European Union Countries, (As on 31.12.2023), Ministry of Commerce and Industry, Government of India, 2024.
120 Foreign Direct Investment in India – Annual Issue 2020, Table No. 6.1. (B): FDI Synopsis on European Union Countries, (As on 31.12.2023), Ministry of Commerce and Industry, Government of India, 2024.
121 European Commission, DG Trade, *EU trade relations with India. Facts, figures and latest developments*, https://ec.europa.eu/trade/policy/countries-and-regions/countries/india/ (Accessed 22.07.2025).
122 India-EU Joint Committee on S&T Cooperation Sets Strategic Agenda for 2025–27, EEAS, Brussels 26.09.2024.
123 EU-India Towards a New Strategic Agenda, Factsheet, EEAS, Brussels, June 2025.
124 Indian students continue to excel: 101 Indian Students Awarded Prestigious Erasmus+ Scholarships for Higher Education in Europe, EU Delegation to India, Press Release, New Delhi, 07.07.205.
125 EU-India: Joint press release on launching the Trade and Technology Council, European Commission, Press Release, New Delhi, April 25, 2022.
126 First EU-India Trade and Technology Council focused on deepening strategic engagement on trade and technology, European Commission, Brussels, 16.05.2023.
127 EU-India signed an 'Intent of Cooperation on High Performance Computing and Quantum Technologies', Delegation of the European Union to INDIA and BHUTAN, New Delhi/Brussels, 21.11.2022
128 EU and India deepen strategic engagement in second Trade and Technology Council, European Commission, Press release, New Delhi 28.02.2025.
129 EU-India Towards a New Strategic Agenda, Factsheet, EEAS, Brussels, June 2025.
130 Speech by President von der Leyen: 'The Consequential Partnership: Reimagining and Realigning EU and, India Ties for Today's World', European Commission, February 28, 2025.
131 European Commission, *Joint declaration on a common agenda on migration and mobility between India and the European Union and its Member States*, Brussels, March 29, 2016.
132 *Annual Report 2016–2017*, Ministry of External Affairs, Government of India, New Delhi, 2017, p. 127.
133 *Transcript of Media Briefing by Official Spokesperson in Brussels on visit of Prime Minister to Belgium (March 30, 2016)*, MEA, Government of India, New Delhi, March 31, 2016.
134 *Speech by Minister of State for External Affairs on "What next for EU-India Relations?"* at the Horasis India Meeting, Cascais (July 04, 2016), July 05, 2016.
135 Eurostat, European Commission, *Population on 1 January by age group, sex and citizenship*, https://ec.europa.eu/eurostat/databrowser/view/migr_pop1ctz/ (Accessed 22.07.2025).
136 EU-India Towards a New Strategic Agenda, Factsheet, EEAS, Brussels, June 2025.
137 European Commission, EU Aid Explorer, https://euaidexplorer.ec.europa.eu/ (Accessed 22.07.2025).
138 European Commission, EU Aid Explorer, https://euaidexplorer.ec.europa.eu/ (Accessed 20.07.2025).
139 Data from OECD.Stat, Aid (ODA) disbursements to countries and regions [DAC2a] Total ODA Gross disbursements, Constant prices, USD million, https://stats.oecd.org/ (Accessed 22.07.2025).

5 India, the EU, and the liberal international order

Cooperation in multilateral forums was an important element of India's post-Cold War policy towards the EU. The EU as an economic and diplomatic power and normative actor played an important role in many international negotiations and organizations where India saw its vital interests. Support and cooperation with the EU was an important condition for India to gain influence over the shape and nature of the international system.

Commitment to cooperation at the multilateral level has been a constant feature of India's partnership with the EU since its inception. Already in the 1993 Cooperation Agreement, the parties reaffirmed "the importance they attach to the **principles of the United Nations Charter** and the respect of democratic principles and human rights".[1] The Political Declaration, adopted on the same day, emphasized "a common commitment to safeguarding peace and establishing **a just and stable international order** in accordance with the UN Charter".[2] In turn, in the Joint Statement of the first Lisbon Summit in 2000, India and the EU declared they are "important partners in the shaping of the **emerging multipolar** world".[3] In 2003, the EU recognized India as one of its 10 strategic partners with whom it wanted to promote "effective multilateralism".

Over the years, the EU has been increasingly viewing India, especially since the first Donald Trump's term in the White House, as a valuable partner in saving multilateralism and stabilizing global order. Therefore, one of main goals of the EU Strategy towards India adopted in 2018 was to "join forces to **consolidate the rules-based global order**, based on multilateralism with the UN and the WTO at its core".[4] In the joint action plan adopted in 2020 – A Roadmap to 2025, two sides were "equally convinced of the necessity to **preserve the rules-based international order** and effective multilateralism".[5]

Despite the divergences concerning the war in Ukraine, during the latest highest level engagement in Delhi in February 2025 President of the Commission Ursula von der Leyen observed that "India is a like-minded friend" and EU and India are "bound by shared convictions and values".[6] In the joint Leaders Statement, "India and EU underscored their commitment and shared interest in shaping **a resilient multipolar global order**" and "agreed that shared values and principles including democracy, rule of law, and the

DOI: 10.4324/9781003688648-6

This chapter has been made available under a CC-BY-NC-ND 4.0 International license.

rules-based international order** in line with the purposes and principles of the UN Charter make India and the EU like-minded and trusted partners".[7] Deeper cooperation on "global partnerships" was recognized as one of key aims of the European Commission.

This overview shows that India and the EU attached much importance to multilateral cooperation and both were committed to multilateralism and international law, at least at rhetorical level. The Union has hoped that India can help it save liberal international order, increasingly under attack from all sides. But has India shared the same goal? What did India want from the EU at international and regional level? And what has it gained from growing engagement with the EU at the multilateral fora in practical terms?

This chapter examines the India's position on global order and locates the EU in this larger context. It evaluates the evolution of cooperation with the EU and its practical outcomes at regional and global levels. To better understand similarities and differences between the two partners, it looks at six particular case studies – functional regimes seen as crucial elements of the Liberal International Order. In conclusion, it tries to explain why the India–EU cooperation at the global level has brought so little so far.

5.1 The EU in India's vision of reformed multilateralism

5.1.1 India's difficult relationship with the LIO

India has had an ambivalent attitude towards the Liberal International Order (LIO), the system that the Western powers created after World War II and which became the dominant global system after 1991.[8] During the Cold War, India remained on the margins of the Western-created international system and was largely critical of it. Though it participated in the formation of most global international institutions such as the UN, World Bank, and GATT, it was not given a prominent position in them. The rapid emergence of the two-bloc division of the world led India to initially try to chart a "third way" by promoting separate global solutions within the Non-Aligned Movement, only to move increasingly closer to the bloc of communist states led by the USSR after 1971. At the time, it was among the loudest critics of established Western principles and policies on economic issues, trade, non-proliferation, or political institutions.

Only the end of the Cold War and the collapse of the bipolar division of the world prompted India to gradually integrate into the liberal international order led by the US, which at the same time became the dominant system with universal reach. The liberalization of the economy and the revision of foreign policy objectives enabled India to integrate more fully into the international economic circuit and the system of global governance. Over the past 30 years, it has gradually adapted and integrated itself into successive international regimes (e.g. non-proliferation, climate). By coming closer to Western countries and reaping the increasing benefits of globalization, India has shifted from a position of a contestant to an engaged participant in the system.

While Indian leaders do not use the term "liberal international order", they have repeatedly declared a commitment to and support for a *"rules-based international order"*, which is often considered synonymous with the LIO. At the heart of its strategy was an adherence to international law, both in letter and spirit. Prime Minister Manmohan Singh, for example, at the UNGA in 2011, when NATO countries intervened in Libya, called for a cooperative rather than confrontational approach in addressing global challenges and asserted: "We will succeed if we embrace once again the principles on which the United Nations was founded – internationalism and multilateralism. More importantly, we will succeed if our efforts have legitimacy and are pursued not just within the framework of law but also the spirit of the law".[9]

A commitment to international law and multilateralism is an enduring feature of Indian foreign policy. It is worth recalling that India is arguably one of the few countries in the world whose Constitution (adopted in 1949) almost explicitly directs the central government to promote *rules-based order*. Article 51 says that "the State shall endeavour" to "promote international peace and security" and "foster respect for international law and treaty obligations".[10]

At the same time, however, India's attitude towards the LIO remained ambiguous. Despite its increasing engagement, India was highly critical of the existing distribution of power and wealth and selected international organizations or regimes. As in many other countries of the Global South, "the LIO is often seen as a narrow ideological, economic, and strategic framework reflecting and supporting the interests and identities of US-led Western nations".[11] India's attitude can be described by what researchers describe as the practice of "representational contestation", i.e. challenging who establishes and oversees adherence to international rules, as opposed to "normative contestation", i.e. challenging the very rules and norms of the international order.[12] As an Indian journalist explained in 2019, "India is not a revisionist state, unlike China, because it does not want to overthrow the current system, only modify it".[13] Rather than trying to undermine the system from outside, India has rather contested it and sought to change it from within. Hence, its attitude towards the LIO was characterized by a desire for reform.

In effect, India was balancing between criticizing Western-dominated institutions and trying to adapt them to its needs. Hence, it joined groups and coalitions, such as the RIC or BRICS, proposing changes and alternatives, while seeking inclusion in existing regimes (e.g. non-proliferation). While opposing a unipolar world with the hegemonic position of the US, it sought a multipolar system, where it would gain a privileged position as one of its centres.

In order to more fully reap the benefits of participation in the LIO, it sought greater influence in shaping the rules of this system. Hence, India's key objective within this order was to gain greater power in key international institutions. Getting a permanent seat on the UN Security Council became the most important strategic aim.[14] To this end, it has often used the liberal argument of "democratization" but applied at global rather than national level. Calls for the inclusiveness and representativeness of the UN, including the Security Council, were meant to persuade other participants in the system, particularly Western states, to support its aspirations.

For example, Indian Prime Minister Atal B. Vajpayee, in his very first speech to the UN General Assembly in 1998, called for the "democratization of the UN itself" and warned that "[an] international body that does not reflect and change with changing international circumstances will inevitably suffer from a credibility deficit".[15] The same arguments were presented by the next Prime Minister, from a different political party, indicating a continuity in pursuit of a goal widely regarded as India's *raison d'etat*. During his first speech at the UN in 2004, Manmohan Singh directly pointed to the problem of a "democratic deficit" in the UN, "which prevents effective multilateralism, a multilateralism that is based on a democratically evolved global consensus".[16] While pointing to the "urgency" of reform of the UN, he observed:

> An overwhelming majority of the world's population cannot be excluded from an institution that today legislates on an increasing number of issues, with an ever-widening impact. The expansion of the Security Council, in the category of both permanent and non-permanent members, and the inclusion of countries like India, as permanent members, would be a first step in the process of making the United Nations a truly representative body.[17]

The same rhetoric returned with renewed vigour after Prime Minister Narendra Modi of the BJP took power. In his first General Assembly speech in September 2014, he appealed: "We must reform the United Nations, including the Security Council, and make it more democratic and participative".[18] During a speech in the General Assembly in 2020, Modi highlighted the mismatch between the UN created under different circumstances in 1945 and the realities of the modern world and the 21st century, and pointed to the growing disillusionment and impatience of millions of Indians:

> It is a fact that the faith and respect that the United Nations enjoys in India are unparalleled. But it is also true that the people of India have been waiting for a long time for the completion of the reforms of the United Nations. Today, people of India are concerned whether this reform-process will ever reach its logical conclusion. **For how long will India be kept out of the decision-making structures of the United Nations?** A country, which is the largest democracy of the world, a country with more than 18% of the world population, a country, which has hundreds of languages, hundreds of dialects, many sects, many ideologies, a country, which was a leading global economy for centuries and also one which has seen hundreds of years of foreign rule.[19]

5.1.2 India's call for change

Such a tension between partial adaptation to the dominant order and a strong desire to change it meant that from the end of the Cold War onwards, there was a strong belief in India that the current international arrangement was "transitional", "temporary", and "changing". The main reason for this change would be the relative weakening of the West and the rise of Asia, with a particular role for India.

Hence, it reacted differently to the successive international crises that emerged in the West (financial in 2008, migration in 2015, the rise of populist sentiment, COVID-19, the war in Ukraine). While it feared the backlash against globalization and the increasing political instability and unpredictability of superpower politics, it also saw opportunities in the chaos.[20] As an emerging power, India hoped to use the changes and the period of turmoil in the international system to improve its political and economic position. A time of global transition, loosened structures, and tensions make the world more willing to accommodate new players and offer some opportunities for middle powers like India, Minister Jaishankar argued.[21]

The fact that India did not feel that it was a beneficiary of the current system also meant that it did not feel obliged to come to its defence. For this reason, it also assessed the behaviour of revisionist states like Russia and China differently than the West. While the rise of China's power is a factor of concern for India, MEA Jaishankar seemed to find a positive element in this as well, writing that China today is a "great disruptor" whose emergence "cannot be accommodated in the old framework".[22] India's rise is only set to accelerate change. As French scholar Christophe Jaffrelot observed while reviewing Jaishankar's book: "Dismantling Western dominance must occur by attacking the architecture of the international system", and here, China can play a helpful role.[23] According to Amitav Acharya, such a post-American "multiplex" world, in which the US had lost its ability to shape the world order according to its own interests and image, presented new opportunities for new powers, especially China and India.[24]

The optimism with which India looked to the future was also due to the change of leadership in the country and the formation of a stable BJP government in 2014. Prime Minister Modi made India's foreign policy more dynamic and set it an ambitious international role expressing openly its superpower aspirations. Early on in office, during a meeting with Indian ambassadors in February 2015, he directed them to support India's positioning as a *"leading power"*,[25] and not just an *"emerging power"*, *"bridging power"*, or *"balancing power"*. Foreign Secretary S. Jaishankar, while speaking in Singapore in July 2015, confirmed that India aspires "to be a leading power, rather than just a balancing power", but consequently, it is more willing to "shoulder greater global responsibilities".[26] In practice, this expressed India's aspiration to become a "global power" capable of influencing the shape of the entire international system.[27]

India was to be more ready to contribute to global discussions and solutions, to influence international outcomes. India would like to become "more of a shaper or decider rather than just be an abstainer".[28] As Indian President Kamal Nath expressed it in 2018: " As a responsible power, India seeks to be a rule framer and rule custodian".[29] In doing so, it does not relinquish its moral leadership among developing countries – On the contrary, "India must be a just and fair power as well, consolidating its position as a standard bearer of the Global South".[30]

India was thus to propose its own solutions, promote an alternative models of cooperation, and be a "force for good" in an increasingly uncertain world. Indian scholars were proposing the *Pax Indica* – democratic global system as an alternative to the hegemonic *Pax Americana* or *Pax Britannica*,[31] and to formulate a *New Delhi Consensus*, though not fully defined, but alternative and superior to the liberal *Washington Consensus* and the authoritarian *Beijing Consensus* model.[32] India was to be the Lighthouse in the Tempest, as the title of the 2023 Raisina Dialogue conference proclaimed.

To take advantage of emerging opportunities, however, India needed more proactive and multi-sectoral diplomacy. In this more fluid and unpredictable world, Dr Jaishankar explained, "India must reach out in as many directions as possible and maximize its gains" and to avoid problems with partners and forge new alliances. The ultimate goal is clear: "Many friends, few foes, great goodwill, more influence. That must be achieved through the India way".[33] This meant maintaining good relations with all the major powers (US, China, EU, or Russia) at the same time. As Jaishankar asserted: "This is the time for us to engage America, manage China, cultivate Europe, reassure Russia, bring Japan into play, draw neighbours in, extend the neighbourhood, and expand traditional constituencies of support".[34]

In essence, this is a policy of "multi-alignment" pursued with greater conviction in line with the traditional principle of Indian international strategy – strategic autonomy. It is worth recalling here, for example, the statement of the Foreign Secretary in the 2004–2006 National Congress government, Shayam Saran, who reiterated that India should "engage with all powers and ally with none".[35]

The growing crisis of the liberal international order has provided an opportunity for India to intensify its efforts to reform the international system. The watchword for Indian diplomacy has become "reformed multilateralism". Minister Jaishankar observed that resurgent nationalisms weaken multilateral cooperation and lead to a dangerous situation where we have "prospect of multipolarity with less multilateralism".[36] In his view, we are not facing a "binary choice between defending the order and inviting disorder". The solution to the problem would be "reformed multilateralism", – "one that is relevant for the age in which we live, not when this architecture was erected".[37] Minister Jaishankar stressed that "multipolar world requires actually more not less multilateralism".[38] Speaking at the Alliance for Multilateralism in September 2020, he stressed that as a result of the pandemic, "the demand for reformed multilateralism is stronger than ever in the past".³⁹ But in order to succeed, the "current anachronistic order must be ushed to change, along with its outdated agenda".⁴⁰

Another Indian diplomat, Harsh Shringla stressed in 2021 that despite the weaknesses of the system exposed by the pandemic, "there is no turning back from multilateralism or globalization. Multilateralism must be strengthened. Where needed, it will be complemented and supported by plulilateralism, and new governance structures to address contemporary threats and non-traditional challenges will have to be created".⁴¹

5.1.3 India's offer to the EU

India was aware that reforming multilateralism required the cooperation of the West, including the EU. Therefore, it did not count on undermining the West too much, unlike Russia or China. It needed Europe as a partner in building a multipolar order and reforming the system. The Indian Minister at the 2020 Munich Conference argued that "non-western democratic societies have an interest in the West. They would not like to see the West weaken" because the West is "still an integral indispensable part of our global multiple society".⁴² Hence, the West shall build new coalitions, plurilateral formats in various fields with countries interested in multilateralism, as a way to rebuild and strengthen it. Another Indian diplomat argued that "India believes that the continued influence and prosperity of the EU is important for India's development and for the emergence of an inclusive and multipolar world".⁴³ Rejecting Western criticism of India's cooperation with BRICS, Minister Jaishankar explained that India is "not-West but it is also not anti-West", not necessarily like the other members of the organization.⁴⁴

Instead of a confrontation with the West as adopted by Russia or by China, India chose to engage in order to gain support for its own demands. The European Union was India's natural partner in this task. The EU was itself an example of the effectiveness of multilateralism and was itself using this language in its communications. As early as 2003, in its first European Security Strategy, the Union identified the promotion of "effective multilateralism" as a foreign policy objective. In its subsequent 2016 Security Strategy, it announced support for "reformed global governance" noting that: "A commitment to global governance must translate in the determination to reform the UN, including the Security Council, and the International Financial Institutions (IFIs). **Resisting change risks triggering the erosion of such institutions** and the emergence of alternative groupings to the detriment of all EU Member States".⁴⁵

And commitment to global reforms has strengthened over time as ineffectiveness of the current system became more apparent in recent years. It is well understood by the new Commission of the European Union formed in late 2024. Its president, Ursula von der Leyen while presenting plan for the next five years reminded that "Europe will always defend the international rules-based order, in which laws and norms are stronger than might and conflict". But she also added that Europe must also "recognize the legitimate concerns of partners around the world who believe the current system was neither designed by them nor works for them". And called the EU "to **play a leading role in reforming the international system**".[46]

Hence, not surprisingly, assertions of support for a "rules-based order" with a central role for the UN have been repeated in most of the joint documents adopted by India and the EU since 2000. Perhaps the fullest expression of this is the declaration in the preamble of the latest joint plan "Roadmap to 2025":

> In a complex international environment, the Republic of India and the European Union, both "unions of diversity", sharing values of democracy, rule of law and human rights, are equally convinced of the necessity **to preserve the rules-based international order** and **effective multilateralism**. India and the EU have a common interest in each other's security, prosperity and sustainable development. They can contribute jointly to a safer, cleaner and more stable world.[47]

Faced with the unpredictability of the US and the assertiveness of China, it was the Union, despite its weaknesses, that was the most serious partner ready to stand up for multilateralism and international law, free trade, the fight against climate change, or poverty. Moreover, Europe, conflicted with the US, itself began to appreciate India as a "like-minded partner". As an Indian diplomat assessed in 2020: "As two large Unions of diversity, sharing values of democracy, pluralism and rule of law, and a commitment to a rules-based international order and effective multilateralism, **the India–EU partnership is a force for good** in our complex world".[48]

At the same time, it must be remembered that India was not interested in simply stabilizing the existing order, but was inviting the European Union to reform it to make it fairer, more effective and more attuned to contemporary realities. As an Indian diplomat pointed out in 2016, India believed that after Brexit, as the EU redirects its foreign policy, it "will find more complementarity in India as a partner to work towards a stable multilaterally oriented global governance architecture".[49]

One of the keynote speeches by Indian representatives, which the Indian press described as a presentation of European policy and an offer to Europe, was presented by President Ram Nath Kovind, during a visit to Greece in June 2018.[50] During a lecture on "India and Europe in a Changing World", the Indian President emphasized shared values and inter-civilizational contacts, noting that "the era of empires is over", the 21st century "will belong to democracies like ours", and Europe will find no better partner than India in achieving its goals.[51] India's offer was to cooperate in promoting peace, realizing sustainable development and building a less unequal world. He pointed to cooperation in the fight against climate change, terrorism and radicalization, digital threats and in regulating the internet. Highlighting similarities in visions of the world, he stated that "India and Europe must work together to ensure that the **multilateral mechanism remains resilient and serves future generations** – as well as accommodates new actors with a merit-based claim for a seat at the table".

Minister Jaishankar explained in 2021 that what is currently happening between India and the EU is the search for a new level of relationship – a "new compact" – that would "reflect a more multipolar world with more centres of power".[52] This would also include the climate agenda, connectivity issues, digital matters, and technology cooperation. The Indian minister suggested the West to "sit down together and work out a new Pact". India would like to work with the EU in reforming existing global institutions, but also in creating new rules and principles in new unregulated areas. There has been no shortage of voices among observers of India–EU relations that the current crisis of multilateralism also presents opportunities for India, which needs to build coalitions with other like-minded partners for the implementation of its own proposals.[53]

Talks on reforming multilateralism were put on hold after the Russian aggression against Ukraine in 2022. India's unwillingness to condemn the apparent violation of international law and Ukraine's sovereignty undermined India's credibility as a country defending a rules-based order and eroded mutual trust. While dialogue was quickly resumed at the highest level, both sides also had other priorities in their neighbourhood. However, the European Commission's visit to Delhi in February 2025 shows that Europe is regaining confidence in India as a natural partner. The leaders' joint statement reiterated that both sides share a commitment to "the rules-based international order in line with the purposes and principles of the UN Charter".[54] The challenges to a number of international organizations and regimes posed by the policies of the US administration of Donald Trump make the role of India's cooperation with the EU on issues of reform of the international system fundamental at the same time. This opens up strategic opportunities for future cooperation in changing the liberal international system.

5.2 The EU as India's regional partner

The EU was, after the Cold War, the largest trading partner, source of development aid and investment for most South Asian countries. It seemed a natural partner and an inevitable direction for India to develop cooperation. While India had in the past been reluctant to accept the presence of other powers in its neighbourhood, this time it saw the benefits of Union involvement – financial, diplomatic, developmental – which could stabilize the region, reduce the risk of security threats, strengthen democratic systems, and promote economic growth. By engaging the EU on regional issues, India wanted also to strengthen its position beyond South Asia, in the geopolitical Indo-Pacific region.

5.2.1 India, the EU, and SAARC

As a successful example of a regional organization, the Union was sometimes seen as a model or source of inspiration for the South Asian Association for Regional Cooperation (SAARC), which was established in 1985. This approach is well reflected in a statement by Christopher Patten, EU Commissioner for External Relations, who, praising the EU's achievements in Delhi in January 2001, said that "[d]eveloping our experience of regional integration is probably one of the most important international achievements that Europe can offer" to India and South Asia, and added that "the EU believes that SAARC can replicate this success".[55] Some Indian politicians viewed the European example of liberal peacemaking through regional cooperation and integration favourably. In January 2003, Indian Foreign Minister Yaswanth Sinha assessed that the European Union "has become the United States of Europe" and as such "is indeed an example of regional cooperation that we in Asia can emulate".[56] In another speech on South Asian cooperation in Dhaka, he made direct reference to the European experience by even suggesting the creation of a larger organization than SAARC – the South Asian Union – which "will not just be an economic entity, but will also get a political dimension in the same way that the European Union got its political and strategic dimension".[57]

However, not everyone was positive about the potential for meaningful inter-organizational cooperation. As problems within SAARC grew, there was a growing perception that European experience was of little use in South Asia. One Indian expert in 2007 listed a dozen differences between SAARC and the EU, making a comparison between the two "a comparison of the incomparable, as the former is probably the most successful experiment in human history and the latter is closer to the other end of the spectrum".[58]

Nonetheless, initially, it seemed that EU could provide valuable support to SAARC. Already in 1996, the European Commission and SAARC Secretariat signed Memorandum of Understanding on Cooperation, which has provided the basis for technical assistance on trade matters. The topic of inter-regional and institutional cooperation with SAARC was discussed at the first EU-India Summit, but actually found a lot of attention at the Hague Summit in 2004, where the EU expressed its "readiness to cooperate and share experiences in regional cooperation with SAARC".[59] In 2005, India supported the EU's efforts to become an observer in SAARC. Finally, in 2006, the Union was formally granted such status. In May 2007, EU participated for the first time as an Observer at the SAARC Summit in New Delhi. On the other hand, India was supported by the EU to join the ASEM dialogue and became a member of this intercontinental initiative from January 1, 2007.

The EU has supported regional integration in SAARC as part of its development assistance. This "integration through trade" approach included support for harmonizing standards in trade, raising awareness of the benefits of regional cooperation, and promoting business contacts across borders.[60]

However, this did not quite match the expectations of regional partners and the specificities of SAARC, which did not aim at all for EU-like integration. Apart from all the other problems, the progress of SAARC was held hostage to tensions between states in the region, particularly between India and Pakistan. The deterioration of these relations after the 2008 Mumbai terrorist attacks destined SAARC to paralysis and marginalization. It also ended opportunities for cooperation with the EU at the inter-regional level.

5.2.2 India–EU cooperation in South Asian States

More opportunities for cooperation were offered by some countries in the South Asian region. The EU was politically and economically involved in the stabilization of Afghanistan from 2002, supported Norway's mediation in the civil war in Sri Lanka from 2003, supported the democratization of Nepal from 2005, and the transition in Myanmar from 2011. India had serious interests of its own in these countries and often convergent objectives with the Union. The diplomatic and developmental presence created favourable conditions to coordinate activities and undertake joint-aid projects and initiatives.

Afghanistan, after the overthrow of the Taliban in 2001, presented particular opportunities, as it was of great importance to both the EU and India, and two had huge development programmes there.[61] Despite discussing the situation in the country at successive summits and declaring support for the transitional authorities and announcing "intensified cooperation in the reconstruction of Afghanistan",[62] there was never any closer cooperation. Even despite the planned withdrawal of international troops and the transfer of all responsibility to the Afghan authorities, with the growing risk of a Taliban takeover, India and the EU have not engaged in any joint practical initiative in Afghanistan. The most tangible result of their cooperation was only the issuance of a joint statement on Afghanistan in April 2021, thus at a time when NATO was withdrawing its last troops and the Taliban was intensifying its march for power.

In a relatively comprehensive joint document, Minister S. Jaishankar and High Representative J. Borrell reaffirmed, among other things, "that any political settlement in Afghanistan must protect the human rights and fundamental freedoms of all Afghans, including women, youth, and minorities", called on the Taliban to "ceasefire", "stop the violence", and warned that India and the EU "will not support the re-establishment of the Islamic Emirate of Afghanistan".[63] However, when the Emirate was effectively established following the Taliban's takeover of Kabul on August 15, 2021, both sides adopted a similar policy of pragmatic engagement with them, but without official recognition of the new authorities. They sought to consult and coordinate their positions on Afghanistan in the following months at the UN,[64] during the leaders' phone calls on 31 August, the foreign affairs ministers' meeting on 3 September in Slovenia, or the meetings of the special envoys on Afghanistan.[65] In the years that followed, India and the EU maintained a convergent stance towards the Taliban, but each on their own increasingly normalized contacts with the new Afghan authorities.

India's and the EU's cooperation towards other countries in the region have not brought any more results. Joint statements showed a converging position towards events in Sri Lanka or Nepal, but this did not translate into actual cooperation and joint initiatives. The parties also failed to take advantage of a short window of opportunity to provide stronger support for democratic transition processes in Myanmar after 2011.[66] The subsequent military coup in the country in 2021 and the adoption of a different approach to relations with the junta by the EU and India has again become a source of misunderstanding and disappointment. As one Indian strategist noted: "While the West has made democracy the sole prism of its Myanmar policy, India doesn't have that luxury".[67]

These examples show that the situation in the South Asian region has been an important topic of discussion between India and the EU, and very often, the parties have agreed on the overall policy and objectives in the region. However, despite a high degree of convergence in their assessment of the situation and interests, they were unable to translate this into practical action. India and the EU, in effect, conducted their activities independently and in parallel. India was not interested in cooperation as it did not see the added value of working with the EU and followed a different model of development assistance. There was probably also a lack of mutual trust and the more pragmatic India did not always understand the overly ideological approach of its European partners.

However, regular dialogue on regional issues with the EU provided India with an opportunity to exchange information and explain its perspective on the situation in individual countries. Closer dialogue with the EU at the same time allowed Indian authorities to reduce European criticism by explaining the complexities of its own approach. The talks with the EU also reinforced India's role as a leader in South Asia, which was particularly important in the context of China's growing influence in the region.

India hoped that greater European involvement and presence in the region would balance the Chinese presence. Economic and strategic cooperation was also intended to strengthen India's own position vis-à-vis the rising power. It was thus part of their strategy to build a balance of power in Asia. Cooperation with the EU in the Indo-Pacific became even more important in this context.

5.2.3 *India, the EU, and the Indo-Pacific*

The Indo-Pacific has become very important in India's international strategy in recent years. The strong endorsement of the Indo-Pacific concept and the adoption of its own vision for the region can also be read in the context of India's ambition to assert its leading role beyond South Asia.[68] Recognizing its role as a major force in the larger geopolitical arena and in a key region of the world would thus be another step towards global power status. Increasing engagement in the Indian Ocean and expanding the navy was an important priority for the BJP government and was partly a response to China's growing influence in the area, traditionally considered India's sphere of influence.[69]

Hence, Indian Prime Minister Modi presenting, in the fullest form yet, India's vision for the Indo-Pacific at the Shangri La conference in Singapore in June 2018, portrayed India as a leading actor in the region. In doing so, he called for building an inclusive, open and rules-based order, open to all nations that respect international law.[70] In May 2019, a new Indo-Pacific department was established in the Indian Ministry of External Affairs to coordinate policy in the region. In turn, at the East Asia Summit in Thailand on November 4, 2019, Prime Minister Modi announced the Indo-Pacific Oceans' Initiative (IPOI), which proposed cooperation in seven areas for a secure and stable maritime domain.[71] While the concept was only explained in very general terms, it appeared to be India's way of developing a mechanism for cooperation with "like-minded" countries to build a "free, open, inclusive, and rules-based Indo-Pacific".[72] It signalled more coherent strategy towards the area and reaffirmed India's ambition to play a leading role.[73]

The growing rivalry with China, particularly the June 2020 clash on the India–China border, prompted the adoption of a more proactive policy in the Indo-Pacific and increased cooperation with "like-minded partners".[74] The policy of balancing China's influence has intensified.[75] While some scholars show that the approach towards China was more nuanced and included an element of cooperation and engagement, India's goal remained "to prevent China's hegemony in Asia" and to prepare a place for itself as a power in a multipolar Asia.[76] As the Indian minister explained, "creating a stable balance in Asia is India's foremost priority. It is only a multipolar Asia that can lead to a multipolar world. Equally important, it would put a premium on India's value for the global system".[77]

The success of these plans would be influenced not only by the support of partners in the region, but also by the acceptance of India's role and the support provided by other countries outside the region. While the priority for India are partners with adequate security resources, this also opens up scope for closer cooperation with the EU, in areas such as diversification of supply chains, digital cooperation, 5G network expansion, or connectivity.[78] The attitude of the EU – as a key economic power – towards India's aspirations and positioning in the region was therefore closely followed in Delhi.

Already, the EU's 2018 India Strategy recognized India as an "emerging global power with an increasingly active foreign policy" that will leave a strong impact "on the development of Asia and the world".[79] Moreover, the EU stated that it "has an interest in India playing a greater role in a multipolar world, which requires a multipolar Asia". EU–India cooperation was intended to strengthen an open and inclusive rights-based order in the region, but also globally. The Union also declared that a "strong partnership with India is key for a balanced EU policy towards Asia as a whole", thus acknowledging that the policy to date had been too focused on one partner – China. This meant recognizing India as a regional power in Asia and a stabilizing force on the continent. India was no longer seen only in the context of South Asia or its relationship with Pakistan, but as a strategic player with a much greater responsibility and role. The EU strategy was therefore an important step towards realizing India's ambitions.

Even more important was the launch of a new EU policy towards the Indo-Pacific. While initially the European Commission did not see the need for a separate document towards the region, the adoption of a relevant strategy by the main countries in the Indo-Pacific and eventually also by the largest EU members – France (June 2019), Germany (September 2020), and the Netherlands (November 2020) – prompted the Commission to change its approach. At the end of 2020, the member states called on the Commission to prepare an EU vision, abroad vision was presented by the EU Council already in April,[80] and a more detailed official Strategy was published by the Commission in September 2021. India was recognized as a "key partner of the EU in the region, alongside Japan and ASEAN". This was most clearly expressed by the EU's top diplomat Josep Borrell, who in March 2021 recognized closer engagement with India as one of three reasons why the EU needs an Indo-Pacific strategy, observing that "India certainly plays a pivotal role" in this region and there is a need to "intensify relations with such a heavyweight country".[81] The Indo-Pacific was already discussed at the EU27–India Leaders' Summit in May 2021 and included into priorities of announced then EU–India Connectivity Partnership.

The EU strategy for the Indo-Pacific reaffirmed the emphasis on cooperation, openness, and inclusiveness of the region and the centrality of ASEAN.[82] It highlighted a commitment to a rules-based order, multilateralism, equal economic opportunities, and the protection of human rights and democracy. The document listed seven priority areas for EU engagement with the region: Sustainable and inclusive prosperity; green transition; ocean governance; digital governance and partnerships; connectivity; security and defence; and human security. These were areas largely overlapping with the pillars of India's IPOI.

The document reaffirmed the will to resume FTA negotiations with India, build more resilient and sustainable supply chains and develop technological standards and regulations, implement the Connectivity Partnership, develop digital partnerships, increase security cooperation through, inter alia, more frequent joint naval exercises, ship visits, joint patrols in the Indo-Pacific, information sharing and capacity building of countries in the region in exploiting marine resources.[83]

The EU's increased interest in the Indo-Pacific was well received in India.[84] It was assessed that despite limited resources, the EU could be helpful in strengthening stability and development in the region.[85] For Indian strategists, this was an argument for further deepening the partnership with the EU. EU signalled its willingness to become a partner in building a sustainable balance of power in the Indo-Pacific. India and the EU were not interested in the emergence of a bipolar system in the region, but a more multilateral order based on cooperation and compliance. Accordingly, India should engage more strongly in building "a strong coalition of Asian and European middle powers" that would become "an indispensable element of geopolitics in the East".[86] The researchers pointed out that India and the EU, as "normative powers", should better exploit the potential for cooperation in the Indo-Pacific maritime domain.[87]

The Indo-Pacific has already become a regular topic of bilateral and multilateral political consultations. India participated in successive EU-organized Ministerial Forums on Indo-Pacific in 2022 in Paris, 2023 in Stockholm, and 2024 in Brussels. This reinforced the shared belief that "the security of Europe and the Indo-Pacific are increasingly interlinked".[88]

India welcomed the growing naval presence of EU countries in the Indian Ocean and initiatives enhancing the EU's ability to operate in the region, such as CRIMARIO II – Critical Maritime Routes in Indo-Pacific, CMP – Coordinated Maritime Presence in the North West Indian Ocean, and ESIWA – Enhancing Security Cooperation in and with Asia. EU and Indian naval exercises, have been occurring with increasing regularity. In 2024, the Union joined India's Indo-Pacific Oceans Initiative (IPOI) and became a Dialogue Partner of the Indian Ocean Rim Association (IORA), where India plays a key role. At the first Strategic Dialogue meeting in Brussels in June 2025, Minister Jaishankar and European High Representative Kallas reaffirmed "shared strategic interests in the Indo-Pacific and underlined the importance of a **free, open, and rules-based** Indo-Pacific region".[89]

From India's point of view, the EU's adoption of an Indo-Pacific strategy heralded greater European involvement in a more volatile and geopolitically contested region of the world. In a sense, Europe was "returning as a geopolitical actor to Asia and the Indo-Pacific" and India was rejecting its traditional reluctance to accept again such a role for European powers in its neighbourhood.[90] Adopting this strategy also meant that the EU accepted that the Indo-Pacific was becoming the most important geopolitical area, replacing the Euro-Atlantic. This reinforced India's position as a power occupying a strategic position in the region. It was another sign that the EU's Asia policy was becoming less China-centric. The strategy opened up new opportunities for deeper cooperation on security, trade, or connectivity. The overall convergence of the Indo-Pacific vision offered an opportunity for joint participation in building a more resilient and cooperative region, mitigating the negative impact of the US–China rivalry.[91] Ultimately, it reaffirmed India's role as an emerging global power with influence far beyond South Asia.

5.3 Cooperation with the EU at the global level

Multilateral cooperation was important topic of India's conversation with the EU since the first summit in 2000. Subsequent India–EU declarations indicated the convergence of India's and the EU's goals and support for institutions and processes based on multilateralism. This subchapter analyses the practical cooperation and concrete actions taken within the six selected "functional orders" that are part of the liberal international order. The selection of the examples analysed has been made so as to address (a) relevant elements of the LIO, (b) issues of importance to India and/or the EU, and at the same time (c) represent the diverse attitudes and models of cooperation undertaken by the partners. In this way, it will help to assess the actual degree of convergence of perspectives and differences in India's and the EU's attitudes towards the liberal order and identify factors affecting cooperation.

5.3.1 Reform of international institutions

Cooperation in international organizations, including in the reform of the UN and financial organizations, was one of India's key strategic objectives vis-à-vis the EU. This task became more important as its material resources and conviction of its growing international role increased. Hence, since the end of the Cold War, India was eager to look at its relations with the EU as a "partnership of major democracies" and "global actors in a multipolar world".[92] In practical terms, this translated into an expectation that the EU would support changes in global governance institutions, as well as co-create new rules and norms governing international relations. India's primary objective was to gain EU support in its efforts to join as a permanent member of the UN Security Council and to increase its influence in financial organizations. These expectations were openly expressed in response to the EU's 2004 Strategic Partnership proposal:

> We also appreciate the fact that the EU has noted in its document India's position on UNSC reform, including India's candidacy for the post of permanent member of the UNSC. Taking into account all objective criteria such as population, size, GDP, economic potential, civilisational heritage, political system and contribution to UN activities (especially peacekeeping operations), **India has all the qualifications to be a permanent member of the UNSC.** We hope to be able to work closely and coordinate our efforts with the EU to this end.[93]

Getting real EU support in this regard, however, was a very difficult task. The EU is not a member of the UN, it can facilitate coordination of its 27 member states. However, the EU was seen by many in India precisely as a pillar of the existing system, a "conservative force and defender of the existing order"[94] and as a "satisfied power", in contrast to India which "seeks to change the *status quo* in global governance".[95] Indeed, any major reform of the system established after World War II, when European powers played a leading role, and adapting it to the new realities of the 21st century would have to mean a deterioration of the position of an obviously over-represented Europe.[96]

Hence, the Indian authorities adopted a pragmatic approach of consequently putting forward their demands and cooperating with the EU in selected areas and initiatives, hoping to change the existing system step by step in an evolutionary manner. The EU's declared support to strengthen the multilateral system with a central role for the UN was seen as a good starting point. India also welcomed the EU's general statements of support for UN reform, including its most important body the Security Council.

Therefore, India's ultimate lack of unequivocal support from the EU for its efforts to obtain a permanent seat on the Security Council can be seen as a major disappointment and failure. Of the five permanent members of the current Security Council, only China has not officially supported India's aspirations. Also, most of the EU members have more or less formally expressed support for India's permanent seat on the Security Council. However, the Community as a whole has not been able to reach a common position on this issue. Neither the 2018 EU Strategy for India nor any of the joint statements following the bilateral summits contained a clear statement of support.

This was due to the diverging interests and ambitions of different member states (e.g. similar claims were made by Germany and Italy), disagreements on the shape of the UNSC reform and doubts about the level of European representation in the revised forum. India therefore had to convince individual member states to its arguments in order to gain broad support within the EU, and it took concrete action bilaterally – e.g. with Germany in the G4 (which also included Brazil and Japan) proposing a joint proposal for UNSC reform in 2004.

The lack of a common position on this key issue for India was further evidence of the weakness of the EU, which is unable to "speak with one voice" and influence strategic international issues. At the same time, it confirmed that bilateral relations with individual countries are more tangible and more important than cooperation at the level of the whole Union. This reduced the importance of the EU as a strategic partner.

Few more results can be pointed out in the case of India's cooperation with the EU in other organizations and structures within the UN. Subsequent India–EU summits and declarations have promised more frequent consultations at the UN, cooperation in the Human Rights Commission, exchange of views on peacekeeping operations, etc., but these provisions have not produced tangible results and have not translated into concrete action.[97] India joined the Franco-German Alliance for Multilateralism initiative in 2020, but this remained just another forum to discuss and present its own assessment of the international system.

Serious differences in perspectives on many of the issues debated at the UN were shown by the votes in the General Assembly. According to the researchers, the convergence of India's votes with the EU as a whole in the UNGA (when all member states voted unanimously) between 2004 and 2010 was only 43%, falling to 25% for votes on human rights resolutions.[98] It is noteworthy that India was much more likely to vote together with China or Russia at the UN than with the EU and the US. This showed not only the differences in approach to many detailed issues, but also the convergence with other "emerging powers" on a critical assessment of the design of the international system and the privileged position of Western states. In the absence of the will to seriously reform the international system, India, together with its BRICS partners, not only criticized the existing Western-dominated system, but also challenged the "hegemony of the Western discourse" in international relations promoted by the EU and the US.[99]

Differences with the EU were evident, for example, in the approach to the Arab Spring in 2011 and the NATO intervention in Libya, the attitude towards the civil war in Syria, towards the Russian annexation of Crimea in 2014, and full-scale aggression against Ukraine in 2022. Differences were evident, for example, during its tenure as a non-permanent member of the UNSC in 2021–2022, when India stood, inter alia, against the EU's position, that the Council should not encroach on the areas of climate change, democracy promotion, human rights, or gender justice, which would be a transgression of its original mandate to act.[100]

India has had more success working with the EU in reforming the global financial architecture – the Bretton Woods institutions (IMF, World Bank) and within the G20. Particularly important for India was the creation of the G20 (first at the level of finance ministers and then at the level of heads of state and government) as the main forum for coordinating the response to the 2008 financial crisis, and then an increasingly wide range of economic and political issues. From an Indian perspective, this was a step towards building a more democratic and equitable system.[101] Cooperation with the EU during India's chairmanship of the G20 in 2023 played a special role. It was also thanks to the support of the Union and its member states for Indian initiatives (e.g. the admission of the African Union to the forum) that India's chairmanship was successful.

India's cooperation with the EU within the global financial institutions also developed with some success. India has traditionally been among some of the loudest critics of the Bretton Woods institutions, including because of its over-representation on the governing bodies of European countries and the low influence of developing countries. However, despite the inherent differences between a developing country and a group of developed countries (the EU), the two sides have been able to forge common ground on some issues, including supporting "multilateral financial governance mechanisms or selected international standards and regulations".[102]

A good example is the reform of the IMF. Working closely with the EU – the organization's largest shareholder – India won its support for reform increasing the voice of developing and emerging economies, despite the fact that this was mainly at the expense of European countries. As a result, in 2010, IMF members approved reforms that, among other things, reduced the share of European countries from 30% to 26% and increased (albeit slightly) India's share from 2.4% to 2.7%. Although the unwritten rule that the head of the

World Bank had to be an American and the head of the IMF had to be a European remained intact, it was India that was able to record a small success in 2010.

However, the slow pace of reforms, controlled still be the West, invited criticism in India. The former deputy foreign minister noted that "There was an effort to preserve the existing architecture while catering to new players", which he compared vividly to a situation where "more and more tenants are living in a house, but the owner, who sets the rules of the house, remains the same".[103] Indian experts added that "while Europe recognizes the need to make changes in international institutions and give more voice and space to emerging powers, it sees their role more in terms of co-opting them into the Western-dominated system and ensuring that they behave according to the rules already set by the dominant players".[104]

However, despite their declared support for reform of the international system, in practice the EU and India have not played a major role in this matter. Their assurances of closer coordination of positions within the UN have so far not translated into serious joint reform proposals. The Union's lack of a clear position on supporting India's aspirations in the Security Council remains disappointing. While the Union has played a positive role in improving India's position in the IMF or its effective chairmanship of the G20, India remains dissatisfied with its position in international organizations. Realistic cooperation in reforming global institutions therefore remains an important task for the India–EU partnership.

5.3.2 International trade negotiations

The multilateral international trade regime centred around the GATT/WTO is most often regarded as one of the core elements of the liberal international order. The decision to become more involved in global economy after 1991 made the issue of increasing influence in this regime even more important for India. The fact that European countries played a key role in the international institutions regulating trade gave priority to cooperation with the EU in this regard. India was among the founding members of the General Agreement on Tariffs and Trade (GATT) of 1947 and its successor, the World Trade Organization (WTO) established in 1995. India has traditionally taken a defensive stance in GAAT/WTO, trying to protect the interests of developing countries and to create favourable international trade rules for them, which positioned it in opposition to developed countries.[105]

This made India and the EU "pitted against each other" in successive WTO Ministerial Conferences in the 1990s in Singapore, Geneva, and Seattle.[106] Against the EU, India was opposed to expanding the scope of WTO regulations to include more "non-traditional" and "non-trade" issues such as investment, environment, competitiveness policy, information technology, e-commerce, government procurement, trade facilitation, or labour rights. On most of these issues, the Indian position was "diametrically opposed" to the EU's.[107] Instead of adding new topics, India emphasized the "implementation problem", i.e. the need to fully implement the Uruguay Round arrangements, such as on agriculture, market access, or the services sector. They were therefore opposed to starting another round of negotiations at the WTO before these issues were settled first.

Despite greater openness to globalization after 1991, the view was still popular in India that the WTO "is an instrument of exploitation of developing countries by developed countries",[108] and that the arrangements so far have been unfavourable and have led to "unequal distribution of the benefits of trade liberalization".[109] Attempts by the EU and other developed countries to condition access to their market with concessions on labour, social, or environmental rights were judged to "reinforce protectionism", "undermine the natural competitive advantage of developing countries", and as a "Trojan horse" tactic to make India's economy uncompetitive.[110]

Despite strong opposition, India was ultimately unable to block the launch of a new so-called Doha Development Round in 2001. However, it was not satisfied with the comprehensive negotiating agenda promoted by the EU. As the Indian representative assessed the Ministerial Declaration after the conference, "it is neither right nor fair" and proves that "developing countries have little influence on the formation of the WTO work programme".[111] India made it clear to the European side that "it needs space for development" and therefore "its priorities and views on multilateral trade issues may not always coincide with those presented by the EU".[112] It stressed that "the centrality of the development component" lies at the heart of the Doha Round and recalled its expectations: access to developed markets, removal of agricultural and other trade-distorting subsidies, and veto against linking trade to any non-trade and social issues. In this context, it wanted the rejection of the three "controversial" so-called Singapore issues – relating to investment, competition policy, and government procurement – in the Doha Round. Instead, it stressed the importance of liberalizing services in relation to the movement of people and preserving the special status and treatment of developing countries.

The different approaches to global trade within the WTO framework has become one of the main points of contention between India and the EU and a reason to strengthen dialogue. Stronger engagement with the EU provided an additional channel to present India's concerns and expectations, against one of the main forces driving international negotiations. Following the failure of the 1999 Seattle conference, India was visited in March 2000 by EU Trade Commissioner Pascal Lamy, who urged the partners to change their stance and suggested more flexibility and support from the EU on the implementation of earlier provisions.[113] In April 2001, the EU Troika–India ministerial meeting was largely devoted to forging a compromise on the WTO issue.

It had already been agreed at the first bilateral summit in June 2000 that "multilateral trade issues" would be discussed in a new high-level dialogue on the WTO. The commitment to closer consultation on WTO issues has been emphasized in all bilateral summits and Joint Action Plans: of 2005,

2008, 2016, and 2020. However, despite regular assurances of commitment "to further strengthening the multilateral trade regime in the WTO",[114] both sides have shown no willingness to compromise and, as a result, have contributed to the deadlock in the Doha Round negotiations since 2008. From Europe's point of view, the rise of countries such as India and Brazil has made it more difficult for the EU to pursue its own goals in the WTO and make decisions on the basis of consensus.[115] Trade, despite the stated compatibility of overall objectives, ultimately became one of the most important challenges in the India–EU relationship.

WTO cooperation with the EU also did not improve significantly during Prime Minister Modi's reformist government. Despite being seen as a leader who favoured liberalization, India's negotiating position in the WTO did not change, and in some areas became even tougher.[116] India stalled trade agreement negotiations for many years and did not sign any trade liberalization agreement until 2021. In 2019, India pulled out at the last minute from signing a regional FTA – the Regional Comprehensive Economic Partnership (RCEP) bringing together 15 countries in Asia. Modi also terminated most of the 86 bilateral investment protection agreements, and few countries agreed to new agreements on unfavourable Indian terms. It was only after the pandemic that India changed its approach to trade agreements and in recent years has written off a few, albeit not very ambitious agreements – with Mauritius (in 2021), the UAE (2022), Australia (2022), EFTA (2024), and UK (2025). It resumed a number of other negotiations, including with the EU and New Zealand.

Despite criticizing protectionism as a global threat, India under the Modi government has increased protection of its own market, with average applied tariffs rising from 13% in 2014/15 to 14.3% in 2020/21 and 15.6% in 2024.[117] India has become the leading user of anti-dumping measures, initiating 233 new investigations in the 2014–2019 period (compared to 82 in 2011–2014).[118] The main flagship programmes of the government were protectionist in nature: *Make in* India and *Self-Sufficient* India, which were supposed to make India an export powerhouse. This adversely affected the ability to converge with the EU in international institutions.

Meanwhile, the impasse in the Doha Round trade negotiations and the paralysis of the WTO Appellate Body as a result of the policies of US President D. Trump's administration necessitated closer cooperation among the remaining actors, and the EU and India could play a key role in this. The fact that such a rapprochement did not occur was one of the reasons for the failure of the 2017 WTO Ministerial Conference in Buenos Aires. While India and the EU shared the overall goal and interest in revitalizing the multilateral trading system and improving the efficiency of the WTO, they were "proposing divergent solutions".[119]

While India cooperated with the EU and even joined December 2018 proposals on Appellate Body reform aimed at resolving the crisis and restoring the functioning of this key WTO body, it generally rejected the EU's plan for comprehensive WTO reform put forward in September 2018.[120] It was particularly critical of the EU-backed US proposals to reduce privileges for developing countries. In the WTO talks, India reverted to its traditional negotiating strategy by presenting itself as a poor country and a representative of developing countries.[121]

In its own reform proposal ("Strengthening the WTO to promote development and inclusivity"), supported by a number of developing countries, presented in August 2019 and extended in December 2020, India included several key demands: the retention of core values and the voting system through consensus; the unblocking of the Appellate Body and the normal functioning of the dispute settlement system; the retention of the "*Special and Differential Treatment*" (SDT) of developing countries as a "non-negotiable and treaty-based right of developing and least developed countries"; the need to take into account the limited capacities of developing countries in the approach to transparency and notification requirements.[122] India also rejected the EU's October 2021 proposal to set up a Working Party on WTO reform, being of the view that it "seeks fundamental changes in the institutional architecture of the WTO and most of the proposed solutions may not be in India's interest and would be against the interests of developing countries".[123]

In addition, the Buenos Aires conference clearly highlighted the differences between India and the EU in their approach to the scope and modalities of negotiations in new trade areas. India did not join any of the groups of countries pushed by the EU willing to negotiate on digital services, small and medium enterprises and e-commerce. Another point of contention in the course of the COVID-19 pandemic in 2020 has become patents for coronavirus vaccines. India, together with South Africa, made a proposal to partially suspend patent protection so that preparations could reach those in need in developing countries more quickly, but the EU blocked such a solution for a long time.

India's stance towards the WTO is largely due to the fact that it is the only international institution in which it is relatively satisfied with its position and the shape of the organization. Consensus voting, where each member has one vote, gives India a position on par with the major powers, and the ability to form broad coalitions of developing countries gives it a real say in the rules that are set. Hence, India is intrigued to defend this status quo.

In fact, one gets the impression that India and the EU have traded places in their approach to WTO reform in the sense that it was India that stood for the *status quo* and the traditional role of the organization, while the EU along with the US were the *revisionist* powers demanding sweeping changes in the rules and functioning of the WTO.[124] Moreover, India's defensive and protectionist stance in the WTO is proving more suited to the changed international context after the COVID-19 pandemic. In a world where attention has begun to turn to the phenomenon of "*weaponized interdependence*", India's policy of reducing dependence and securitizing economic and trade policies is proving to be an asset rather than a problem.[125]

Nevertheless, trade differences within the WTO have been one of the main concerns for the EU. This is well illustrated by the Strategy towards India at the end of 2018 where the generally very friendly tone of the document only changes in one place to a more assertive and critical towards India when it states that "the EU expects India to play a more constructive role in the WTO in order to identify long-lasting solutions, to contribute to addressing the deep causes of existing trade tensions and to help restore balance in the international trading system".[126]

An indication of the divergent approaches to trade issues and serious tensions is the number of reciprocal trade investigations at the WTO and bilateral restrictions imposed by both sides. Since the establishment of the organization, India has brought a case against the EU at the WTO seven times, the third highest after the US (20 cases) and Canada (8 cases), while the EU has initiated a dispute with India at the WTO 11 times, fewer than only with the US (35) and China (14).[127] Even more often, both sides retaliated unilaterally. At the end of 2021, the EU had anti-dumping measures imposed on imports from India in four cases (out of 140 globally on all Union partners) and anti-subsidy measures in three cases (out of a total of 20), and had initiated in 2021 three new proceedings (out of 66).[128] In contrast, India was one of the countries most frequently using defensive trade measures against the EU, after the US and China. At the end of 2021, it had 12 such instruments in force (down from 15 in 2020) and initiated two new anti-dumping cases in 2021 alone.[129]

The divergent stance of India and the EU in the multilateral trading system remains one of the most serious challenges in India's policy towards the Union. To mitigate these tensions and seek opportunities for compromise, the May 2021 leaders' meeting in Porto agreed to establish an additional India–EU Senior Officials' Dialogue on WTO issues.[130] The fact that similar initiatives and declarations have already been made many times over the past 20 years does not augur a quick breakthrough and significant convergence of positions. Progress on this issue will largely depend on the negotiation of a bilateral trade agreement, and possible success on this issue could unlock the prospects for cooperation in the multilateral forum.

5.3.3 *International non-proliferation regime*

Initially, an important objective for India in its dialogue with the EU was to gain acceptance of its status as a nuclear weapons state and to limit criticism. European states and the EU were the leading promoters of the non-proliferation and saw India's nuclearization as a serious threat to the entire regime. In turn, persuading European countries to change their approach was essential for India in 2000s to get the approval of the Nuclear Suppliers Group (NSG) to allow nuclear trade and implement the nuclear deal with the US. This was followed by India's desire to join the other organizations controlling cooperation and trade in this area.

India's starting point was extremely difficult because it was one of only a handful of countries that had not signed the Nuclear Non-Proliferation Treaty (NPT), and after the 1998 nuclear tests, it was the first (along with Pakistan) to openly declare itself a nuclear state undermining the entire non-proliferation regime. This put India in dispute with the EU, although in fact both sides agreed on the principle of non-proliferation of weapons of mass destruction (WMD). It is somewhat ironic, note the Indian researchers, that the EU and India found themselves on opposite sides of the non-proliferation barricade and the issue divided them for many decades from the 1950s to the mid-2000s.[131]

On the one hand, European states, including the two officially recognized as "nuclear states" by the NPT, benefiting from the US nuclear umbrella supported non-proliferation but were not exactly interested in nuclear disarmament. The EU had since the 1990s become an active promoter of the non-proliferation regime, including the NPT and the Comprehensive Nuclear Test Ban Treaty (CTBT).

India, on the other hand, was a strong advocate of universal nuclear disarmament and supported WMD non-proliferation in principle, but not in its then current form. Above all, it rejected the NPT, dividing states into those that can legally possess nuclear weapons and the rest who are deprived of this capability, regarding this as a discriminatory treaty imposing a kind of "nuclear apartheid".[132] As a result, it opposed the indefinite extension of the NPT advocated by European countries and the EU itself at the 1995 Review Conference. Noting in turn that the CTBT was primarily intended to lead to a strengthening of the non-proliferation regime rather than to nuclear disarmament, it changed its own position on the agreement, ultimately refusing to sign it. Increased pressure on India from, among others, the US and Europe to sign the NPT and the CTBT eventually accelerated India's decision to fully nuclearize and carry out five nuclear explosions in May 1998.[133] As a result, at the turn of the millennium, India rejected the core international non-proliferation agreements that the EU strongly supported and was not a member of the core non-proliferation regimes where European countries sat.

It was not until the nuclear tests and the start of dialogue in bilateral summits from 2000 and the 2004 Strategic Partnership that the positions were brought closer. The 2005 Joint Action Plan indicated that India and the EU "have a common interest in pursuing the goals of universal disarmament and non-proliferation of weapons of mass destruction and their means of delivery".[134] While the parties agreed on the need to control the export of dual-use materials, "such measures should not impede international cooperation in trade in materials, equipment and technology for peaceful purposes". Non-proliferation issues were to be discussed within the newly established Security Dialogue. Subsequent declarations on this issue reiterated a position favourable to India. The main challenge became translating the growing understanding of India in the EU into support for favourable decisions in the Nuclear Suppliers Group.

India, which had concluded a preliminary nuclear agreement with the US in 2006, needed, as a non-signatory to the NPT, approval for its implementation from the Nuclear Suppliers Group (NSG), the most important non-proliferation regime, where EU members were in the majority. Some countries (e.g. Austria, Sweden, Ireland) did not want to support India on this issue, taking the principled position that creating an exception for one country would jeopardize the entire regime. It was only the efforts of Indian diplomacy, indicating its full support for the non-proliferation regime and its responsible behaviour in the past (especially when juxtaposed with the evidence revealed in 2003 of the transfer of nuclear technology abroad by A.Q. Khan's network in Pakistan), and probably also pressure from the US, overcame the resistance of last European states and India obtained a *"waiver"* from the NSG from the general rules of the non-proliferation regime in September 2008. Although the decision was taken by individual states, the increasingly cooperative atmosphere between India and the Union as a whole probably also had some influence. Suffice is to note that the vote on India's case in the NSG in Vienna took place a few days before the India–EU Summit in Marseille on September 29, 2008. The favourable outcome of the vote for India contributed to the successful conduct of the India–EU talks.

The NSG decision amounted to a *de facto* recognition of India as a nuclear weapons state and integrated it (though partially) into the existing non-proliferation regime. It thus solved an important problem in EU–India relations. It opened the way for closer cooperation between India and the EU on civilian nuclear technology and dual-use trade, from which India had been excluded since 1974. France quickly became the first country (even before the US) to sign a nuclear cooperation agreement with India in 2008, with the UK signing a similar agreement in 2010. The EU promised a similar deal at the level of the EU institutions, which did not happen, however, until 2021.

The favourable change in the EU countries' position on NSG has allowed India to engage in non-proliferation cooperation with greater confidence. India and the EU expressed a common position on the nuclear programme of Iran and North Korea. In the years that followed, European countries agreed to accept and sometimes actively supported India in joining key agreements regulating trade and use of nuclear technology: Missile Technology Control Regime (joined in 2016), Wassenar Agreement (2017), and Australia Group (2018). European countries also supported India joining the most important of these mechanisms, the NSG, but China's opposition stands in the way.

Having accepted India's special position in the system, it has become a responsible participant keeping an eye on others' compliance. This is well illustrated by the example of India's policy towards Iran. Although India had been developing its own partnership with Iran since 2003 and was interested in importing Iranian oil, it supported the policy of Western countries to stop Iran's nuclear programme. It complied with the Western sanctions on Iran imposed between 2008 and 2012, and voted against Iran at the International Atomic Energy Agency and the UN. It supported negotiations and signing of nuclear agreement with Iran (JCPOA) in 2015 opening the way for closer cooperation with the EU on Iran.[135] Even when Donald Trump withdrew the US from the agreement India, like Europe, continued to support the JCPOA and hoped for a return to the agreement.

The non-proliferation regime is a very interesting example of India's integration into the liberal international order and cooperation with the EU in this regard. Although India and the EU continue to take different positions on the NPT or the CTBT, it is a major achievement to take the topic of non-proliferation off the list of contentious issues. It is important to note that this was made possible by India's integration into the existing regime, but on India's terms. It therefore required more of adaptation and more compromise on the part of the European partners than India. This example shows also that India is more ready to defend elements of the liberal international order when it is recognized as an important part of it, without compromising its interests and expectations.

5.3.4 International climate-change negotiations

Climate change and environmental issues have become a new and increasingly important element of India's dialogue with the EU in the 21st century. India wanted to reduce pressure from the EU for costly economic change and preserve the privileges of the poorest countries in this regard. At the same time, climate protection was becoming an increasingly important international regime centred around the Conference of the Parties (COP) to the United Nations Framework Convention on Climate Change (UNFCCC) and reinforced by the annual COPs.

India's position towards international climate policy was conditioned by two factors. On the one hand was the imperative of rapid economic growth and lifting millions of citizens out of poverty and improving their living conditions. Climate change was, for the Delhi in this context, a secondary concern to be addressed by the developed countries that contributed most to adverse change. Furthermore, the Indian side took the view that as long as India had such a low per capita national income, "it cannot be expected to prioritize international concerns for future survival over domestic concerns that deal with survival in the present day".[136]

On the other hand, unsustainable growth has resulted in increasingly visible environmental destruction and a dynamic surge in greenhouse gas emissions. Rapid economic growth after 1991 made India a leading emitter of CO_2. In doing so, it was one of the countries most vulnerable to the effects of climate change. Possible rising sea levels, deforestation and desertification of large areas, melting glaciers in the Himalayas, and increasingly scarce water resources or increasingly destructive monsoons – all of these directly threatened the lives of tens of millions of Indian citizens and also damaged the economy.

The tension between the need to catch up quickly economically and the fear of climate change also resulted in a strongly ambivalent attitude towards the EU – the global leader in the fight against climate change. India saw the EU as both an opportunity (as a source of funding and technology) and a threat (as a source of international pressure). This factor complicated cooperation with the EU bilaterally and in the global arena.

India rejected proposals promoted by the EU in global climate negotiations for universal and legally binding commitments to reduce greenhouse gas emissions. While the EU proposed to set common targets and obligations, India, invoking principles of equity and fairness, argued that the burden of tackling climate change should fall on the developed economies, including the EU members that have contributed the most to climate change and have the highest per capita emissions. It was largely under pressure from India that the principle of "common but differentiated responsibilities" (CBRD) for climate change was finally adopted in international climate negotiations in the 1990s.[137] In the 21st century, India stuck to the 1997 Kyoto Protocol, which clearly demarcated the responsibilities and obligations of industrialized and developing countries. It feared that imposing binding climate targets on developing countries would limit their ability to grow their economies and lift millions of citizens out of poverty and that climate policy would become a form of "green imperialism".

Environmental issues emerged as early as 2000 among the themes of the bilateral summits, to occupy more and more attention in subsequent years. An analysis of the language of the Joint Statements shows the strong influence of the Indian perspective. Indian representatives ensured that the Joint Communiqués incorporated their position on addressing the "twin challenges: protecting the environment and promoting sustainable development".[138] The joint document from the first summit indicated that India and the EU should respond to global climate issues according to the principle of "common but differentiated responsibilities". In its 2004 position paper, the Indian government indicated that climate policy must "be consistent with the respective needs and concerns of countries at different levels of economic development" and warned:

> Given that the EU and India are not at the same level of economic development, engagement strategies on this issue must take into account Indian development needs. Attempts have been made in the past to link trade and environmental issues. India is principledly opposed to linking non-trade issues with trade issues as such a linkage can be used for protectionist purposes. The key to thinking about trade and environment is the concept of sustainable development, which includes both environmental protection and poverty eradication.[139]

This position was reflected in the 2005 Joint Action Plan, which expressed a commitment to "sustainable development", affirmed the principle of "common but differentiated responsibilities", called on countries to meet their Kyoto Protocol commitments and announced "working together in future climate negotiations".[140] As the topic became more important to the EU, it was announced that the work of the *Joint Working Group on Environment, Energy Panel, India–EU Environment Forum* would be intensified and new opportunities for cooperation and financing of clean technologies would be created. In the Joint Cooperation Programme on Energy, Clean Development and Climate Change adopted at the Marseille Summit in 2008, the EU and India set out a series of targets and new initiatives in this area and reaffirmed their "determination to reach an ambitious and comprehensive agreement" by 2009 in the UNFCCC climate negotiations, with "common but differentiated responsibilities and respective capabilities".[141] At the November 2009 summit – just before the Copenhagen Climate Summit in December 2009 – climate issues took centre stage and were identified as the main common challenge.

In order to fend off criticism and pressure from foreign partners, including the EU, the Indian government had earlier adopted a *National Action Plan for Climate Change* (NAPCC), detailing various measures to reduce CO_2 emissions and minimize the negative environmental impact of economic development. This step was not perceived as sufficient by the EU side, which pressured India to accept joint climate commitments. In the end, India and the EU agreed to work together for "an ambitious and agreed globally equitable outcome" of the conference.[142] However, India succeeded, among other things, in including in the declaration provisions of importance to it that "equal weight will be given to climate change mitigation–adaptation" in the negotiations and "increasing financial and technological support to developing countries in this regard is critical".

Nonetheless, this did not bring the positions of the two sides sufficiently closer and, as a result, there was a major dispute between the EU and India and other developing countries (BASIC) at the Copenhagen Summit, which ultimately led to the failure of the negotiations. India's tough stance, however, meant that the EU had to take its proposals more into account in subsequent years. This made it possible, among other things, to forge a compromise agreement at COP-19 in Warsaw in 2013 on setting voluntary and non-legally binding climate targets (*Nationally Determined Contributions*) as a goals by all countries to the fight against climate change.

A breakthrough in India's approach to climate issues and cooperation with the EU came at the Paris Summit in 2015 (COP-21), where India abandoned its defensive approach in favour of a more constructive one. The new Prime Minister Narendra Modi announced India's climate goals for the first time, and on the margins of the conference, the establishment of the Indo-French-initiative: the *International Solar* Alliance (ISA), a Delhi-based international organization to promote investment in solar energy in developing countries, was announced. It was the first international organization set up by India, giving it an important tool in climate policy.

In the following years, climate issues disappeared from the list of India–EU disputes and the Paris Agreements became the new reference point. Already at the next EU–India summit in 2016, the two sides announced closer cooperation to achieve the Sustainable Development Goals (SDGs) and the UN 2030 Agenda and reaffirmed their willingness to fully implement the Paris Climate Agreement. The parties expressed support for the International

Solar Alliance (ISA),[143] which soon led to the EU joining the organization and the development of cooperation between the ISA and the EIB. Union's position gave credibility to the ISA as one of the organizations fighting climate change through fundraising and financial support for investment in solar energy worldwide. Climate change and clean energy issues became one of the priority areas of bilateral cooperation with the Union, which financially supported projects promoting pro-environmental investments in India (e.g. the construction of metros in several cities).

Co-operation in international forums was somewhat less successful. Despite their declared support for full implementation of the Paris Agreement, India and the EU pursued their own climate targets independently and remained at different levels of ambition. Despite pressure from the EU and the US ahead of the Glasgow climate summit in 2021, India did not adopt an ambitious target of climate neutrality by 2050, although Prime Minister Modi announced that India would achieve such a target by 2070. He also put forward new but unambitious commitments. Rather, India sought to defend the interests of developing countries and the responsibilities of the richest countries. Hence, Modi in Glasgow criticized developed countries for not keeping their promises to contribute to the Climate Fund and called for an increase in this funding from $100 billion to $1 trillion if developing countries are to develop in a sustainable manner.[144] It was also India's opposition that largely determined the relaxation of the final commitment to "move away" from coal power to only "reduce" it in one of its final declarations, to the disappointment of the EU.

Shortly thereafter, India voted with Russia at the UNSC against the EU-backed initiative to declare climate change a threat to international security. Explaining its opposition to the 113-country-sponsored resolution, India pointed out that it was an attempt by developed countries to "distract" the world from failing to fulfil its UN environmental justice commitments.[145] The EU's ambitious climate plans, such as the Carbon Border Adjustment Mechanism (CBAM), soon became a new source of contention with India, which sees CBAM primarily as a form of protectionism.

Nevertheless, the turnaround in India's approach and the adoption of climate commitments at the Paris Summit in 2015, and improved overall partnership with the EU helped to change the perception of India in Europe and opened up new opportunities for cooperation. The EU has recognized India's limitations in this regard and has increased support for energy transition through the EIB and other instruments. Despite remaining differences in the level of ambition in emissions reductions and disagreements around financing the green transition, India recognized the EU as a key partner in overcoming its own challenges in this area. This has allowed for a dynamic development of practical business and technology cooperation with the EU to enhance India's capacity to reduce GHG emissions.

At the same time, India's and the EU's continued support for the implementation of the Paris Agreement, at a time when the Donald Trump administration has withdrawn from it, has provided important stabilizing support to the climate regime. India went from being a brake on climate negotiations, to becoming one of the leaders proposing new solutions and seeking closer international cooperation.

This change can be pointed to as one of the most important examples of a positive transformation in India–EU relations. An issue that was among the most sensitive and difficult in the past has now become an important area of multilateral and bilateral cooperation. India has also muted the international criticism it faced from the EU in previous years. The change in rhetoric, and the adoption of a more offensive strategy, has allowed India to assume a leadership role on climate issues, despite the very limited emission reduction targets adopted.

Importantly, however, the change in India's position towards the climate negotiations was not the result of European pressure, nor did it mark the end of disagreements. It was primarily the result of a number of internal factors – the growing negative impact of pollution and climate change on Indians' health and economy; falling costs of renewable energy sources, perceived economic and strategic opportunities (e.g. independence from raw material imports), or a desire to play a greater role and shape new international regulations.[146] At the same time, it may have stemmed from the personal views of the Indian Prime Minister, who is known for his pro-environmental stance. His personal commitment and leadership skills also helped explain the change of approach to the Indian public as a religiously understood and economically beneficial step.

5.3.5 Promotion of democracy and international protection of human rights

The international protection of human rights and the promotion of democracy are a key element of the liberal international order. The promotion of democracy in other states is even seen as a necessity, inherent in the nature of the liberal order.[147] Hence, it can be expected that this area should be an important part of the cooperation between the world's two largest democracies, India and the European Union. Participation in this activity would be a proof of India being a "responsible power".[148] Using India's experience and potential to support democracy in other developing countries was an attractive prospect for the EU, which was keen to cooperate in this area.

A commitment to respect for democratic principles and values was considered a so-called essential element of the 1993 CAPD agreement with the EU and has been a constant reference point of all India–EU summits since 2000. Already at the second summit in 2001, it was announced that the partners would "intensify efforts to promote democracy and support human rights at bilateral and multilateral levels".[149] At the third summit in 2003, India and the EU expressed their readiness "to promote pluralistic democracy in the world".[150] The first Joint Action Plan adopted in 2005 identified democracy promotion as an important element of the strategic partnership, with the parties declaring that they would "explore possible synergies and initiatives for the promotion of human rights and democracy" and announced consultations and discussions on human rights issues and the possibility of joint draft resolutions within the UN Commission on Human Rights and the General Assembly".[151] Although in subsequent years this theme was no longer so prominent in the joint documents, India and the EU continued to declare their support for democratic transitions in Afghanistan, Nepal, Myanmar, Bangladesh, or even Pakistan.

Apart from this, India and EU countries have become members of several major multilateral initiatives aiming to support democratic principles, norms, and institutions in the world. India was one of the founding members of the Community of Democracies, an intergovernmental coalition established in 2000 at the initiative of the US and Poland. Indian External Affairs Minister Jaswant Singh travelled to the first EU–India Summit in Lisbon on June 28, 2000 directly from Warsaw, where he attended the first Ministerial Conference of the Community of Democracies. In 2005, India joined another US initiative and became one of the founders of the UN Democracy Fund. It also supported the establishment of the UN Commission on Human Rights and became a member. In addition, it has itself become increasingly involved in projects strengthening democratic institutions in countries in the region, such as training parliamentarians in Afghanistan and members of the Election Commission in Nepal after 2005.

However, despite these ambitious declarations, India has not undertaken any real cooperation with the EU to support democracy in third countries. One cannot point to a single example of a joint EU–India diplomatic initiative or development project aimed at democratization. And this despite the fact that in many countries, both India and the EU were simultaneously engaged in similar activities on their own. Even in South Asian countries where India had an interest in strengthening democratic systems and where the EU was developing its own aid programmes, there were no instances of closer cooperation.[152]

Democracy promotion, unsurprisingly, instead of being an important element of India's policy towards the EU, became a sensitive topic and a source of tension. Instead of being an example of cooperation in strengthening the liberal international order, democracy support turned out to be an example of differences in approach to this system. Leaving aside the issue of respect for human rights and democratic standards at the bilateral level (in India or the EU),[153] India has been critical and distrustful of Western democratization initiatives abroad.

Looking at the impact of Western interference in the Middle East or Africa, India became one of the louder critics of the concept of democracy promotion. It was critical about conditioning aid or making trade conditional on human rights concessions or political change. It itself did not impose sanctions on other states and maintained normal relations with authoritarian regimes that violated human rights (e.g. Iran, Myanmar), which astonished Europe.[154]

In India, on the other hand, the method of supporting democracy without the consent and cooperation of the local authorities, and sometimes against them, was viewed negatively as meddling in the internal affairs of other states. Sometimes, as in the case of support for democratic protests in Ukraine in 2013, this was seen as part of a policy of *regime change*. As one Indian expert graphically commented on such actions, "if the American ambassador had turned up at anti-government protests in Delhi, supporting the demonstrators and handing out sandwiches, as happened in Ukraine, he would have had to leave India the next day".[155]

Indian experts were particularly critical of actions taken without a UN mandate and in violation of international law, and carried out as a result of military intervention, which they saw as a source of problems and destabilization of more regions.[156] They took a negative view of combining democratization efforts with Responsibility to Protect (R2P) operations or humanitarian interventions.[157] They pointed out that such operations are often misused, serve interests other than those declared, are misguided, and ultimately lead to negative consequences.

The turning point in India's rejection of the R2P concept was the 2011 NATO intervention in Libya, which exposed the possible abuses and risks of its use by the superpowers.[158] Following this event, Prime Minister Singh reminded the UN General Assembly in 2011 that:

> The observance of the rule of law is as important in international affairs as it is within countries. Societies cannot be reordered from outside through military force. People in all countries have the right to choose their own destiny and decide their own future. The international community has a role to play in assisting in the processes of transition and institution building, but the idea that prescriptions have to be imposed from outside is fraught with danger. Actions taken under the authority of the United Nations must respect the unity, territorial integrity, sovereignty and independence of individual states.[159]

In fact, it can be said that the basic principle that defines India's attitude in this matter is the rejection of the possibility of "exporting" or imposing any ideology or political system.[160] As the Foreign Secretary explained in 2005: "As a flourishing democracy, India would certainly welcome more democracy in our neighbourhood, but it is something that we can encourage and promote, and it is nothing of the sort that we can impose on others".[161] Similarly, the Indian Ministry of Defence reported in 2006 that India's security policy "is fully committed to dual priorities: 1) no territorial ambitions and 2) not exporting any ideology".[162] Indian External Affairs Minister Pranab Mukherjee reaffirmed in 2007 that his country is not interested in "exporting ideology" based on international norms and values to third countries.[163]

Interestingly, such a policy shows great continuity in Indian history. It is worth quoting the opinion of Indian Prime Minister Indira Gandhi delivered in 1972: "India's foreign policy is a product of the values we have cherished over the centuries and the concerns we have today. We are not committed to traditional foreign policy concepts designed to protect overseas possessions, investments, carving out spheres of influence or erecting cordons sanitaires. Nor are we interested in exporting any ideologies".[164]

Despite such principled assertions, it is worth noting that the Indian stance towards democracy promotion and human rights is more nuanced. Indeed, supporting democratic systems in other countries has traditionally been part of India's foreign policy.[165] Even during the Cold War, India was committed to democracy support, mainly through its ITEC (Indian Technical and Economic Cooperation) technical assistance programme for sharing Indian experience with developing countries through the training of officials and experts. The beneficiaries of this programme were often members of electoral commissions, parliamentarians, and officials from developing countries, who could thus learn how Indian democratic institutions worked. After the Cold War, India developed this programme and launched additional projects in the area of strengthening democratic structures. At the same time, the approach to supporting democratic processes and human rights in India and the EU was markedly different.

India took a more pragmatic approach to democracy support than the West in trying to balance values with interests.[166] Therefore, it felt uncomfortable with Western pressure to condemn authoritarian governments in their neighbourhood when cooperation with them was important for their security (Myanmar) or economic interests (Iran). According to the researchers, India adopted a "middle way" in this regard, seeking to combine – in a normative sense – the value of human rights and democracy with the defence of the principle of state sovereignty.[167]

India distanced itself from the Western model of action and emphasized its own distinct approach also in the nomenclature adopted. Hence, the term *"democracy assistance"* was used in India rather than *"democracy promotion"* associated with the US and the EU.[168] In contrast to the EU directly supporting civil society and NGOs (*bottom-up approach*), India worked through government institutions (*top-down approach*), with the consent and cooperation of local authorities.[169] The Indian approach is more subtle and passive – India has supported democracy more by the force of its own example than by taking active action in other countries.

While Indian scholars have allowed for the promotion of democracy and the democratization of other societies, they have criticized the means by which Western states have supported such changes. The fundamental difference and criticism of the EU would therefore be more about the manner of "democracy promotion" than its desirability. Nevertheless, fundamental differences on this issue kept India from working more closely with the EU in this area.

Some scholars believe that India may develop a more open and "cooperative" approach to cooperative human rights and democracy promotion as it increases its confidence in Western countries and the threat from China grows.[170] Another author points out that a change in India's policy in this regard will be linked to the development and growth of its international standing, not ruling out that "a richer and stronger India may become a more active defender of human security in the world and even a leader of liberal democracy".[171] However, given the somewhat compromised nature of the idea of democracy promotion in recent decades, it seems unlikely that India will engage in this activity in a manner similar to EU practice. Rather, it will point to the effectiveness of its own model and offer support on its own terms.

An example of such a proactive stance is the conception of India as "*Vishawaguru*" (Teacher of the World) that Prime Minister Modi's government has promoted in recent years. It has portrayed India as a civilization-state, possessing ancient wisdom, philosophy, and knowledge that can help better arrange relations between states in the modern world. India is also presented as the "mother of democracy", with its own knowledge and model that it can pass on to the world. This means that India wants to play the role of a normative power that should define what is good and desirable in the modern world.[172] Thus, not only India does not want to join the Western model of democracy promotion, it began to promote its own and better system of values and principles of international cooperation. Instead of adopting to this the normative element of the liberal order promoted by the EU, it seems to be creating an alternative proposal for the ordering of the international system. It does not subscribe to the values promoted by the EU, but itself wants to be a source of norms for others. This opens an interesting space for cooperation with the EU, but also for competition.

5.3.6 International development cooperation

A specific regime adding to a liberal international order is also international development cooperation. It was created by Western industrialized states that provided development assistance during the Cold War and are treated as traditional donors. The main institution of this regime is the Paris-based OECD Development Assistance Committee (OECD DAC), which set the standards, objectives, and rules for the provision of Official Development Assistance (ODA), and collect statistics to analyse and compare financial flows between ODA donors and recipients. As new sources of development funding from outside the Euro-Atlantic area have emerged, attempts have been made to create a more inclusive architecture for international development cooperation through the so-called Global Partnership for Effective Development Cooperation, established in 2011 at the Busan Conference. However, little engagement with this format from new players from the Global South and little progress from the organization itself have kept this regime relatively underdeveloped.

While India was for a long time primarily a recipient of development assistance from the EU, the increasingly visible transformation of the country from recipient to a donor opened up a new area of cooperation as partners in action in the international forum.[173] This ranged from cross-cutting issues such as architecture, standard-setting, and rule-setting in international development cooperation, to opportunities for direct cooperation between India and the EU in third countries. While until 2000, aid emerged in the context of bilateral EU support for poverty alleviation in India, in the 21st century, it has increasingly become a topic of multilateral discussion on the global stage.

For the first time at the 2005 Summit, development cooperation emerged in the context of partnership and cooperation in third countries. The Joint Plan of Action noted that "India is itself becoming an increasingly active actor in changing development policy: It is both a recipient and a donor of aid, a user of development innovations and an exporter of new ideas".[174] Its position as an "emerging bilateral donor" could pave the way "for a fruitful EU-India dialogue on how best to implement development assistance in third countries".[175] The plan recommended exploring such possibilities for the future. The renewed 2008 Joint Action Plan included a commitment to "join efforts in multilateral fora in using expertise in global development policy to promote the achievement of the Millennium Development Goals and aid effectiveness" and to "pursue dialogue on issues of relevance to cooperation with third countries".[176] Increasingly, discussions on the matter have addressed the objectives and architecture of the global development cooperation system.

The 2016 Joint Agenda for Action once again recommended "exploring the possibility of undertaking joint projects in third countries".[177] Although no action was taken in the coming years, the new Roadmap to 2025 adopted in 2020 Summit tried to stimulate parties to cooperate by recommending to implement joint "pilot development projects" in Africa or Asia.[178] By mid-2025, however, such initiatives had still not materialized. Though in recent years, India has started such cooperation and joint trilateral aid projects in Africa and Asia with the US, UK, and even Germany. It was only in March 2022 that the first India–EU consultations on Africa took place. In June 2025, during Minister Jaishankar's visit to Brussels, two sides signed An Administrative Arrangement on establishing a framework for Trilateral Cooperation, which aims to leverage strengths and expertise of both sides to promote developmental projects in third countries.[179] Despite a number of complementary competencies, twenty years of deliberations and assurances about "exploring the possibilities" of implementing projects in third countries, it is difficult to see the achievements to date as satisfactory.

Serious ideological, methodological, and practical differences in the provision of support have stood in the way of closer cooperation under the emerging development cooperation regime and the implementation of trilateral projects.

India had been providing development assistance to neighbouring countries almost since the beginning of its independence, and in 1963 launched its flagship technical assistance programme, ITEC (*Indian Technical and Economic Cooperation*). In the 21st century, however, this activity has taken on a much more ambitious scale, a new formal framework, and a more strategic dimension. A special programme for development assistance (*Indian Development and Economic Assistance Scheme*) was first created within the Ministry of External Affairs and in 2012 a separate department *Partnership Development Administration* was established to oversee policy in this regard. Indian aid, traditionally focused on its immediate neighbours in South Asia, has also started to reach new recipients in Africa or Central Asia.[180]

India provided support in three main forms – technical assistance (e.g. the ITEC programme, or scholarships to study in India), financial assistance (soft loans), and project assistance (grants for development projects). While accurately counting the value of Indian aid is not easy, due to the different methodologies in India and OECD countries, it is suffice to say that India emerged as one of the biggest "donors" from outside OECD. India did not shy away from tying up development aid, with loans and other mixed financial instruments accounting for the lion's share, in essence allowing for the financing of Indian investments in third countries.

Unlike in the West, aid is not treated as a form of charity, focused on poverty alleviation, but as mutually beneficial support for economic development and infrastructure development, allowing economic catch-up. At the same time, India rejects the practice of conditioning aid on the fulfilment of specific political or social reforms, seeing this as a form of interference in the internal affairs of other countries. Another feature of Indian development cooperation has been close cooperation with partner governments, regardless of their political system, and less emphasis on supporting civil society. The provision of aid emanates from India's traditional identity as a country of the Global South, which sets it in opposition to traditional donors, including the EU. To differentiate itself from Western aid donors, India also rejected the dominant discourse in the West and spoke of "development partnerships" instead of "development aid", and used the term "partners" instead of divisions between "recipients" and "donors". India's Foreign Secretary characterized Indian aid at the 2013 Delhi conference as follows, clearly distinguishing it from the approach of Western countries:

> Our engagement is needs-driven and responsive to the development needs of our partners. We do not condition our aid, impose any policy or undermine national sovereignty. We promote a mutually beneficial exchange of development experiences and resources.[181]

Thus, while India provided significant support in countries where the EU also had a large presence (e.g. Afghanistan, Nepal), it did not engage in any triangular aid projects with the EU. Moreover, India has been reluctant to co-operate with Western donors clustered in the OECD DAC in terms of setting common standards for aid delivery, reporting of statistics, or modalities of support. It has not joined the Paris Declaration on aid effectiveness of 2005, promoted by the EU, and agreed within the OECD DAC. Nor did it join the global effort to reform the international aid architecture post the 2011 Busan Conference. Though there are intensified contacts between DAC OECD and Indian partners in the past, two still look at development cooperation through a different prism.

India has emphasized the distinctiveness of the aid delivery system of the rich North from that of the South and has promoted itself as a leader in development cooperation of developing countries (*South–South Cooperation*). Hence, while India may be interested in sharing experiences and learning from each other about different models of development cooperation, it does not have the resources to engage in complex trilateral projects, especially with a bureaucratic and complicated partner like the EU.

According to the British researcher, Western partners also underestimated how many normative assumptions about international development cooperation are openly questioned and rejected by India.[182] This implies that the country did not want to be associated with traditional donors and does not have sufficient incentives to give up its distinct "southern" identity in exchange for cooperating with the EU on development issues.

In the end, therefore, despite the rhetorical consensus on the importance of international development cooperation, India avoided constructive dialogue with the EU on the transformation of the international development regime and was not interested in concrete joint action in third countries. While this issue did not become a source of serious dispute with the EU, India preferred to maintain its full independence and carry out aid activities according to its interests and in the spirit of solidarity of developing countries and often in opposition to Europe. India has therefore preferred to act in parallel, rather than together with the EU in this area for a number of reasons.

Nevertheless, the lack of significant tensions on this issue, the importance of implementing the Sustainable Development Goals in developing countries and the more pragmatic changes in EU development assistance mean that development cooperation may yet become an important area of the India-EU global partnership. The first concrete steps taken in this direction recently suggest the possibility of concrete projects in third countries. Even more importantly, the EU and India, as the leading providers of development assistance among developed and developing countries, can play a key role in undertaking a comprehensive reform of the development cooperation regime, which has come under additional crisis due to the US policies.

5.4 Challenges and constraints in multilateral cooperation with the EU

The above review of practical outcomes in India's cooperation with the EU at the regional level and in the multilateral forum shows a limited list of successes. The gap between the ambitious goals and declarations and the limited results of regional and multilateral cooperation is telling.

India's gains have mostly been of an image and political nature. It gained acceptance and support from Europe as an emerging power and the new centre of the multipolar world. This allowed it to reinforce its message as a "force for good" seeking to strengthen and improve the international system. The Union supported India as part of the reforms of the quota and voting powers in the IMF and G20 chairmanship. Member states eventually supported India's admission to international non-proliferation regimes. In its 2016 Global Strategy, the Union acknowledged the need to reform global institutions and multilateralism. This built an international atmosphere conducive to India's growing stature and relevance on the global stage.

Climate policy emerged as a promising area of cooperation for the future, but the parties had diametrically opposed approaches to trade negotiations or international development cooperation. Although India's objectives were most often generally aligned with those of the EU, and often both partners had their own activities in third countries, joint projects and initiatives were not taking place. Problems limiting progress in bilateral relations appeared to hinder multilateral cooperation as well. This points to serious challenges and limitations of India's partnership with the EU.

It appears that the similarities between the EU and India highlighted in contemporary joint documents or policy speeches in fact conceal much more serious differences that shape India's approach to the EU. In assessing the effectiveness and limitations of India's policy towards the EU, it is therefore worth taking a closer look at the factors that more openly or implicitly influence the limited results. The main determinants include historical (colonial and Cold War legacies), economic (difference in potentials), political (different nature and understanding of sovereignty), and structural (different positions in the international system) factors.

5.4.1 Historical differences: The legacy of colonialism and Cold War

Despite the passage of years, colonial history continues to influence India's worldview and basic foreign policy assumptions. These experiences have left a deep distrust of the West that persists to a large extent to this day. Policy towards the EU as an emanation of former colonial powers is still tinged with colonialism. A sense of injustice and a desire to make amends for years of domination and exploitation is still strong in India. This is reflected in the increasing number of studies by Indian authors on the crimes and costs of British colonial exploitation of India and the increasingly vociferous demands for reparations for the losses suffered.[183] Colonialism is being held responsible for striping India of its past glory and wealth. Some estimates suggest that between 1765 and 1938, Britain took the equivalent of $45 trillion out of India.[184]

Moreover, despite decolonization, the international system created by the Americans and Europeans after World War II is seen as petrifying rules that disadvantage post-colonial states. Traditionally, criticism has been levelled at

India, the EU, and the Liberal International Order 229

the inequitable distribution of wealth and power, an economic system that serves developed countries, or a non-proliferation regime that gives privileges to a handful of states. India, as a country seeking to change these rules, and Europe, as a beneficiary of this system, see the world from opposite historical perspectives.

5.4.2 Economic divergence: Asymmetry in the socio-economic development

An unjustifiably underestimated or consciously ignored premise in India's policy towards the EU is the significant difference in economic potential. Many of the problems in economic cooperation or India's intransigence in negotiating a free trade agreement stem precisely from its significantly lower level of socio-economic development. As a result, the solutions or standards proposed by the EU, for example in the area of labour rights or environmental protection, are ill-suited to Indian conditions and are perceived as imperialist imposition. India expects its difficult situation to be taken into account and unilateral concessions to be granted by its richer partners.

At the end of the Cold War and even before India embarked on economic reforms (in 1989), India's gross domestic product per capita was $272, and after taking into account the purchasing power of money (PPP), this figure rose to $1,053.[185] At that time, West Germany's GDP per capita was $14,890 in absolute terms (55 times more!) and $14,730 calculated in PPP (14 times more than in India), and in Italy, for example, $6,146 and $10,682 respectively. Even Central European post-communist countries started their transition from a much better level. The GDP per capita for e.g. Poland ($6,493) or Hungary ($7,054) was still several dozen times higher than India's. Although India's rapid economic growth in subsequent years has significantly raised income levels, the disparity between it and EU members remains huge. For example, in 2018. India's GDP/capita exceeded $2,000 in nominal terms and $7,700 in PPP. The average GDP/capita for the Union as a whole at that time was at $38.6k or $43.7k in PPP.[186] Although India had made significant progress (almost a tenfold increase in absolute terms), the gap with the EU was still huge – 19 times in absolute terms and 6 times when the PPP ratio was taken into account.

In the early 1990s, as much as almost half of the India's population (45.9% in 1993) lived in extreme poverty, i.e. on less than $1.9 a day.[187] This affected a total of 425 million citizens of the country. The life expectancy of India's population in 1989 was 55 years for women and 56 years for men, while a statistical German from West Germany could live almost 20 years longer (70 years for men and 77 years for women). India fared equally badly in most other indicators examining quality of life. This naturally gave rise to enormous social challenges and economic problems. It also meant that stimulating rapid economic growth was not only a matter of improving quality of life, but even survival for millions of citizens. The lack of understanding of the scale of these challenges by Europeans was a source of disappointment for Indian partners.

The different levels of development between India and the EU meant that the power relationship between them was highly asymmetrical. At the end of the Cold War, Western European countries accounted for almost half of world merchandise trade (48.3% of global exports and 48.7% of imports in 1990; falling to 39.5% and 39.6%, respectively, in 2000), while India's share was 0.5% of global exports and 0.6% of global imports (in 1993, rising to 0.9% and 1.0%, respectively, in 2000).[188] In 1990, EU countries accounted for 27.4% of global GDP (adjusted for purchasing power of money, PPP), while India accounted for 3.62% (PPP). These ratios changed in 2000 to 23.52% and 4.16%, respectively, and in 2018 were already: 16,27% and 7,74%.[189]

Such large disparities in potentials have given the EU a significant advantage in any bilateral or multilateral discussions with India. India's main economic advantage in such unequal circumstances was access to its own huge market and this asset it did not want to easily deprive itself of. With little to offer in other areas, India adopted a defensive posture, blocking access to its own market or impeding progress in international negotiations. Being too weak to push through a favourable solution for itself, India was at the same time strong enough to resist pressure from larger partners.

5.4.3 Political and institutional differences

Another obstacle to India's rapprochement with the EU was the difference in the political nature or structure of the two entities – a traditional nation-state on the one hand and a kind of post-modern entity, neither an international organization nor a state, on the other. The peculiar nature of the Union posed a conundrum for the Indian partners, a source of much misunderstanding and a reason for a different approach to many challenges. Central to this was the difference in approach to issues of state sovereignty, the use of force, or human rights.

India has a maximalist, or even dogmatic, approach to sovereignty, where any attrition or limitation in this dimension is strongly rejected. This is evident in the foreign policy principle of non-interference in the internal affairs of other states and respect for their territorial integrity. In the economic dimension, this has taken the form of the idea of self-sufficiency, as any form of economic dependence on external partners could lead to a restriction of sovereignty. In foreign policy, this in turn gave rise to the concept of "strategic autonomy", according to which India should have maximum freedom of decision-making, not being constrained by formal alliances and guided solely by its own national interest. A commitment to absolute sovereignty also explains the state's critical approach to phenomena such as humanitarian interventions, Responsibility to Protect (R2P), or democracy promotion. India has also not joined the International Criminal Court, seeing this as a threat to sovereignty.

In this sense, the specific nature of the European Union as a *sui generis* entity with shared sovereignty seemed very difficult for Indian partners to understand. Despite the progressive integration in Europe, Indians perceived the EU as a regional organization, where decision-making ultimately remains with the nation-states – the members of the Union. The fact that the EU is not a stand-alone entity, but a collection of 27 states and a bundle of their national interests also reduces the attractiveness of the Union, as the principle of consensus in foreign police definitely limits the ability to act quickly and effectively. Outside areas where the Union has its own competences (such as trade negotiations), the EU is not an equal partner. The complicated framework for the functioning of the various institutions and leaving the most important competences at the level of the European Council has reinforced the perception in India that "real business" still needs to be done with individual states. Therefore, without further institutional changes in the EU towards fuller integration and a common foreign and security policy, the Union will remain a secondary partner, complementing relations with member states.

On a second level, this gives rise to a sometimes dismissive approach to the Union in the security field. An entity that has no army or police of its own and cannot defend its territory is simply not a serious interlocutor. According to Bhaswati Mukherjee, it is the difference between India as a nation-state (*modern state*) and the EU as a *post-modern entity* that makes the two sides "have different approaches to security issues, which gives rise to a fundamental challenge".[190] Moreover, the fact that the Union acts as a "civilian" or "normative power" is responsible for the "fundamentally different way in which the Union views the world, different from India's global vision". This can be seen in a number of specific areas where the EU and Indian approaches to national security have been fundamentally incompatible because very different *realpolitik* guides their policies.

Finally, the nature of the EU as a post-modern entity is also sometimes seen in India as a source of looking at many issues differently and setting a different hierarchy of goals. This particularly causes disputes around liberal values such as human rights, environmental protection, etc. Union and Indian politicians operate in different realities and consider other issues important. The problems of liberal, post-modern Europeans regarding exorbitant standards of labour law, environmental protection, animal rights, or the protection of individual privacy seem, from an Indian perspective – where hundreds of millions of people had no access to electricity, where it is a problem to find any kind of job to survive, and where terrorist attacks have been a regular occurrence – to be completely absurd. While post-modern Europe is solving the problems of the rich 21st century world, significant parts of India were still stuck in the 19th century. These two perspectives could not meet and agreement was a long way off. Therefore, the solutions proposed by Europe or the imposition of conditions on them aroused strong emotions in India.

As an Indian professor assessed: "India sees many of the EU's foreign policy priorities as infringing on the sovereignty of other states. The EU – as a post-modern entity that is not responsible for establishing law and order within its member states – is unable to understand the complexities and economic, social and cultural challenges inherent in Indian society".[191]

5.4.4 Structural differences in the international system

Finally, the possibilities of multilateral cooperation between India and the EU were negatively affected by the diametrically opposed positions of the two partners in the international system. While India is most often described as an *emerging power*, Europe can be described as a *status quo power*. India's perspective as a state with growing power and resources, wanting to change some of the rules and parts of the international order, will be different from that of the Union, which is one of the main architects, beneficiaries, and privileged forces in the current order. Clearly, one's advantage (e.g. increasing India's influence in the IMF) must come at the expense of the other (Europe's surrender of some power).

This difference set India in opposition to Europe during the Cold War and not much has changed after it ended. While the EU wanted India to conform to the existing liberal order, India sought to change it to its own advantage. Just as during the Cold War India found no reason to join the West, so too in the new reality it did not seek an alliance with the dominant powers. In a sense, India's structural position in the system meant that India could not be interested in its stability, only in change. As one Indian author notes:

> Contrary to popular belief, India was not a status quo power. It fought against colonialism and apartheid, resisted pressure to join the Western bloc, and did not sign the NPT and CTBT. It is in India's long-term interest to effect a change in the status quo of the current international system. Understandably, the West would like to make India a 'responsible player' in the current system, designed and dominated by the West. But there is no reason for India to get involved as long as major changes are not made to fit the system to India.[192]

This structural tension puts India against the Union on many issues and makes it difficult for India to find common ground on global issues. If it is recognized that India should play a greater international role (and this is what Indians wants), then this must come at the great cost of reducing Europe's role and influence. This is well demonstrated by the situation around UN Security Council reform. In today's reality, it is increasingly incomprehensible why two European countries, representing some 130 million people sit at the highest global body, while most populous state representing 1.4 billion people is kept outside. Despite even the right arguments, no European country will voluntarily give up its privileges and reduce its influence. The interests of nation states have, in effect, blocked discussions about a common seat on the UNSC for the EU and preclude unequivocal EU support for granting India a permanent seat.

Notes

1 Cooperation Agreement Between the European Community and the Republic of India on Partnership and Development, Official Journal of the European Communities, L. 223, August 27, 1994.
2 European Union-India Political Statement, 1 1390/93 (Press 246 – c), European Community, Brussels, 20.12.1993.

3 European Commission, EU-India Summit. Lisbon, June 28, 2000, Joint Declaration. Conseil/00/229, Brussels, 9552/00 (Press 229), June 28, 2000.
4 European Commission, High Representative of the Union for Foreign Affairs and Security Policy, Joint Communication to the European Parliament and the Council, 'Elements for EU's Strategy on India – Partnership for sustainable modernisation and rules-based global order', JOIN(2018) 28 final, Brussels, 20.11.2018.
5 EU-India Strategic Partnership: A Roadmap to 2025, Ministry of External Affairs, Government of India, July 15, 2020.
6 Statement by President von der Leyen at the joint press point with Indian Prime Minister Modi, EEAS, Press Release, New Delhi 28.02.2025.
7 Leaders' Statement: Visit of Ms. Ursula von der Leyen, President of the European Commission and EU College of Commissioners to India (February 27–28, 2025), Ministry of External Affairs, Government of India, New Delhi, 28.02.2025.
8 On the concept of Liberal International Order see G. J. Ikenberry, "Liberal Internationalism 3.0: America and the Dilemmas of Liberal World Order", *Perspectives on Politics*, vol. 7, no. 1, 2009, pp. 71–87; G. J. Ikenberry, "The End of Liberal International Order?", *International Affairs*, vol. 94, no. 1, 2018, pp. 7–23; G. Allison, "The Myth of the Liberal Order: From Historical Accident to Conventional Wisdom", *Foreign Affairs*, vol. 97, no. 4, 2018, July/August, pp. 124–133.
9 Address by Mr. Manmohan Singh, Prime Minister of the Republic of India, General Assembly. United Nations, Sixty-sixth session, 22nd plenary meeting, New York, 24.09.2011.
10 Government of India, Ministry of Law and Justice, *The Constitution of India* [As on May, 2022] 2022, New Delhi 2022, Article 51(a), (c).
11 Amitav Acharya Hegemony and Diversity in the 'Liberal International Order': Theory and Reality Written by E-International Relations, January 14, 2020.
12 E. Newman, B. Zala, "Rising Powers and Order Contestation: Disaggregating the Normative from the Representational", *Third World Quarterly*, vol. 39, no. 5, 2018, pp. 871–888.
13 Interview with Pramit Pal Chaudhuri, Foreign Editor, Hindustan Times, New Delhi, 08.01.2019.
14 See A. Nafey, "Permanent Membership in the UN Security Council: India's Diplomatic Initiatives and Strategies", *India Quarterly*, Vol. 61, no. 4, 2005, pp. 1–38.
15 *Address by Mr. Atal Behari Vajpayee, Prime Minister and Minister of Foreign Affairs of the Republic of India*, United Nations, General Assembly, Fifty-third session, 13th plenary meeting, September 24, 1998, p. 17.
16 *Address by Mr. Manmohan Singh, Prime Minister of the Republic of India, United Nations, General Assembly*, Fifty-ninth session, 7th plenary meeting, Thursday September 23, 2004, New York, p. 14.
17 *Address by Mr. Manmohan Singh, Prime Minister of the Republic of India, United Nations, General Assembly*, Fifty-ninth session, 7th plenary meeting, Thursday September 23, 2004, New York, p. 15.
18 *English rendering of Prime Minister's Statement at the General Debate of the 69th Session of the UNGA*, Ministry of External Affairs, Government of India, 27.09.2014.
19 *English translation of Prime Minister's address at 75th United Nations General Assembly*, MEA, Government of India, 26.09.2020.
20 R. Mukherjee, "Chaos as Opportunity: The United States and World Order in India's Grand Strategy", *Contemporary Politics*, vol. 26, no. 4, 2020, pp. 420–438.
21 S. Jaishankar, *The India Way: Strategies for an Uncertain World*, HarperCollins India, 2020, p. 34.
22 S. Jaishankar, *The India Way: Strategies for an Uncertain World*, HarperCollins India, 2020, p. 113.
23 C. Jaffrelot, "Christophe Jaffrelot reviews 'The India Way: Strategies for an Uncertain World' by Dr S. Jaishankar", *SouthAsiaSource*, Atlantic Council, May 26, 2021.

24 A. Acharya, *The End of American World Order*, Cambridge UK: Polity, 2014.
25 Indian Press Information Bureau, Prime Minister's Office "PM to Heads of Indian Missions", press release, February 07, 2015.
26 *IISS Fullerton Lecture by Dr. S. Jaishankar, Foreign Secretary in Singapore*, Ministry of External Affairs, Government of India, July 20, 2015.
27 A. J. Tellis, *India as a Leading Power*, Carnegie Endowment for International Peace, April 04, 2016.
28 S. Jaishankar, *The India Way: Strategies for an Uncertain World*, New Delhi: HarperCollins India, 2020, p. 211.
29 "Address by the Hon'ble President of India Shri Ram Nath Kovind at the Event Organised by Hellenic Foundation for Europe and Foreign Policy Athens", Indian Embassy in Athens, June 19, 2018.
30 S. Jaishankar, *The India Way: Strategies for an Uncertain World*, New Delhi: HarperCollins India, 2020, p. 211.
31 S. Tharoor, *Pax Indica. India and the World of the 21st Century*, New Delhi: Penguin Books, 2012.
32 S. Saran, *Building a New Delhi Consensus, Reflections*, New Delhi: Observer Research Foundation, March 08, 2017.
33 S. Jaishankar, *The India Way: Strategies for an Uncertain World*, New Delhi: HarperCollins India, 2020, pp. 42–43.
34 S. Jaishankar, *The India Way: Strategies for an Uncertain World*, New Delhi: HarperCollins India, 2020, p. 10.
35 S. Saran, "India and Multilateralism: A Practitioner's Perspective", [in:] W. P. S. Sidhu, P. B. Mehta, B. Jones (eds.), *Shaping the Emerging World. India and the Multilateral Order*, Washington D.C.: Brookings Institution Press, 2013, p. 53.
36 S. Jaishankar, *The India Way: Strategies for an Uncertain World*, HarperCollins India, 2020, p. 32.
37 "EAM's remarks during the Virtual Ministerial Meeting of Alliance for Multilateralism", Ministry of External Affairs, Government of India, New Delhi, June 26, 2020.
38 Transcript of Panel Discussion Westlessness in the world Multilateralism in a Changing International Order, Ministry of External Affairs, Government of India, New Delhi, March 06, 2020.
39 *EAM's Remarks at Alliance for Multilateral Meeting*, Ministry of External Affairs, Government of India, New Delhi, September 28, 2020.
40 S. Jaishankar, *The India Way: Strategies for an Uncertain World*, New Delhi: HarperCollins India, 2020, p. 32.
41 Harsh Vardhan Shringla, Foreign Secretary, India: *Concluding Remarks*, Rasina Dialogue, Observer Research Foundation, April 16, 2021.
42 Ministry of External Affairs, Government of India, *Transcript of Panel Discussion Westlessness in the world Multilateralism in a Changing International Order*, March 06, 2020.
43 Ministry of External Affairs, Government of India, *Keynote Address by Secretary (West) on India-EU Cooperation in Security and Global Governance Domains*, Carnegie India, New Delhi (03 November 2016), November 04, 2016.
44 C. R. Mohan, India's New Alignment: "Non-West" but Not "Anti-West", ISAS Brief, Singapore, 19.02.2024.
45 European External Action Service, *Shared Vision, Common Action: A Stronger Europe a Global Strategy for the European Union's Foreign And Security Policy*, June 2016, p. 39.
46 Europe's Choice political guidelines for the next European Commission 2024–2029 Ursula von der Leyen Candidate for the European Commission President, Strasbourg, July 18, 2024.
47 India-EU Strategic Partnership: A Roadmap to 2025, MEA, Government of India, New Delhi, July 15, 2020.

48 *Transcript of Virtual Special Media Briefing on India-EU Summit by Secretary (West)* (July 15, 2020), July 17, 2020.
49 *Keynote Address by Secretary (West) on India-EU Cooperation in Security and Global Governance Domains*, Carnegie India, New Delhi (November 03, 2016), November 04, 2016.
50 I. Bagchi, "President Ram Nath Kovind to Deliver India's Europe policy in Athens", *The Times of India*, June 17, 2018; K. Bhattacherjee, "India for Rules-based World Order: Ram Nath Kovind", *The Hindu*, June 19, 2018.
51 Ministry of External Affairs, Government of India, *Address by the Hon'ble President of India Shri Ram Nath Kovind at the Event Organised by Hellenic Foundation for Europe and Foreign Policy, Athens*, Indian Embassy in Athens, June 19, 2018.
52 S. Jaishankar, *ORF 'In-Conversation' – External Affairs Minister and Portuguese Foreign Minister on the Future of India-EU relations* (June 23, 2021), Ministry of External affairs, Government of India, New Delhi, June 23, 2021.
53 A. Narlikar, *Harnessing New Opportunities in a World of Declining Multilateralism: What India Can Do for Itself and Others, India @75: Aspirations, Ambitions and Approaches*, New Delhi: Observer Research Foundation, January 26, 2022.
54 Speech by President von der Leyen: 'The Consequential Partnership: Reimagining and realigning EU and India ties for today's world', European Commission, New Delhi 28.02.2025.
55 C. Patten, "The Role of the European Union on the World Stage", [in:] R. K. Jain (ed.), *India, Europe and South Asia*, New Delhi: Radiant Publishers, 2007, pp. 4–5.
56 Government of India, Ministry of External Affairs, *India-EU Relations: Perspectives in the 21stCentury. External Affairs Minister Shri Yashwant Sinha's Presentation at the Pantheion University*, Athens, January 16, 2003.
57 Government of India, Ministry of External Affairs, *Yashwant Sinha, Seminar on South Asia Cooperation Organized by the South Asian Centre for Policy Studies*, Dhaka, January 10, 2003.
58 R. K. Jain, "European Integration and South Asian Regionalism: Lessons and Relevance of European Experiences", [in:] R. K. Jain (ed.), *India, Europe and South Asia*, New Delhi: Radiant Publishers, 2007, p. 88.
59 Council of the European Union, *Joint Press Statement, Fifth India-EU Summit*, The Hague, November 08, 2004, 14431/04 (Press 315), p. 8.
60 G. Mohan, 'EU Regional Strategy in South Asia: Moving Beyond the Role of a Trade Partner', *LSE IDEA*, 2016.
61 See A. B. Roy, "India-EU Cooperation on Afghanistan: Context, Constraints and Prospects", [in:] L. Peral, V. Sakhuja (eds.), *The EU-India Partnership: Time to Go Strategic?*, Paris: The European Union Institute for Security Studies, 2012, pp. 135–146; G. Sachdeva, "The European Union and Conflict Resolution in Afghanistan", [in:] R. K. Jain (ed.), *India, Europe and Conflict Resolution in South Asia, New Delhi*: Knowledge World Publications, 2015.
62 European Commission, *3rd EU-India Summit, Joint Press Statement*, Copenhagen, October 10, 2002, 12994/02 (Press 321), p. 5.
63 Ministry of External Affairs, Government of India, Joint Press Statement on Afghanistan by the External Affairs Minister, Dr. S. Jaishankar and the EU High Representative for Foreign Affairs and Security Policy/Vice-President of the European Commission, Mr. Borrell, New Delhi, May 04, 2021.
64 *Resolution 2593 (2021) Adopted by the Security Council at its 8848th meeting, on 30 August 2021*, United Nations Security Council, August 30, 2021.
65 N. Basu, 'India, EU discussed need to engage with Taliban but no recognition yet: EU special envoy', *The Print*, December 07.
66 P. Kugiel, "The EU, India and Conflict Resolution in Myanmar: Is there a Space for Cooperation?", [in:] R. K. Jain (ed.), *India Europe and Conflict Resolution in Asia*, New Delhi: KW Publishers, 2015, pp. 119–144.

67 H. V. Pant, 'India cannot take a black-and-white approach to Myanmar', *The Indian Express*, December 24, 2021.
68 J. Zajączkowski, "Indie - mocarstwo regionu Indo-Pacyfiku" ["India: An Indo-Pacific Power"], *Stosunki Międzynarodowe – International Relations*, vol. 51, no. 4, 2015, pp. 67–92.
69 J. Zajączkowski, "Strategie morskie Indii, Chin i USA w regionie Oceanu Indyjskiego: analiza w kategoriach realizmu ofensywnego' [Maritime Strategies of India, China and the US in the Indian Ocean Region: An Analysis in Terms of Offensive Realism]", Stosunki Międzynarodowe-*International Relations*, vol. 51, no. 2, 2015, pp. 37–70.
70 S. Banerjee, "Special Report on Indo-Pacific and the Shangri La Dialogue 2018", Indian Council of World Affairs, New Delhi, June 22, 2018.
71 *"Indo-Pacific Division Briefs"*, Ministry of External Affairs, Government of India, New Delhi, February 07, 2020.
72 P. Saha, A. Mishra, "The Indo-Pacific Oceans Initiative: Towards a Coherent Indo-Pacific Policy for India", *ORF Occasional Paper No. 292*, Observer Research Foundation. December 2020.
73 P. Kugiel, "India as a Key Indo-Pacific Country – Lessons for the EU", *PISM Bulletin* No. 153 (2572) September 22, 2022.
74 H. V. Pant, P. Saha, "India, China, and the Indo-Pacific: New Delhi's Recalibration is Underway", *The Washington Quarterly*, vol. 43, no. 4, 2020, pp. 187–206, p. 193.
75 Y. Joshi, "India's Radical Reimagination: No More Bandwagoning, for Real", *The Washington Quarterly*, vol. 45, no. 4, 2022, pp. 133–156.
76 M. S. Pardesi. "India's China Strategy Under Modi Continuity in the Management of An Asymmetric Rivalry", *International Politics*, Vol. 59, 2022, pp. 44–66.
77 S. Jaishankar, *The India Way: Strategies for an Uncertain World*, New Delhi: HarperCollins India, 2020, p. 11.
78 G. Mohan, "A European Strategy for the Indo-Pacific", *The Washington Quarterly*, vol. 43, no. 4, 2020, pp. 171–185.
79 *Elements for an EU strategy on India. Joint Communication to the European Parliament and the* Council, European Commission, Brussels, 18.11.2018, p. 11, p. 1.
80 *Council conclusions on an EU Strategy for cooperation in the Indo-Pacific*, Council of the European Union, Brussels, April 16, 2021.
81 J. Borrel, 'The EU needs a strategic approach for the Indo-Pacific', European External Action Service, HR/VP blog, March 12, 2021.
82 *Joint Communication to the European Parliament and the Council. The EU strategy for cooperation in the Indo-Pacific*, European Commission, Brussels, September 16, 2021.
83 *Joint Communication to the European Parliament and the Council. The EU strategy for cooperation in the Indo-Pacific*, European Commission, Brussels, September 16, 2021.
84 See P. Saha, *"What does an EU Indo-Pacific Strategy Entail?"* Observer Research Foundation, September 17, 2021; P. Basu, R. Saha, S. Bhowmick, "Connecting Distant Geographies: The EU in the Indo-Pacific". *ORF Occasional Paper No. 329*, Observer Research Foundation. September 2021.
85 G. Luthra, "An Assessment of the European Union's Indo-Pacific Strategy", *ORF Issue Brief*, no. 504, Observer Research Foundation, November 2021.
86 R. C. Mohan, "Delhi Now Sees European Powers as Natural Partners in Constructing a Durable Balance of Power in Indo-Pacific", *The Indian Express*, December 22, 2020.
87 T. Łukaszuk, "Normative Powers in Maritime Affairs: India-EU Cooperation in the Indian Ocean Region", *The Copernicus Journal of Political Studies*, vol. 56, 2020, pp. 231–254.

88 'Boosting EU-Indo-Pacific Partnerships: Chair's Press Release following the EU Indo-Pacific Ministerial Forum', EEAS, Press Release, 02.02.2024.
89 India: High Representative/Vice-President Kaja Kallas holds first EU-India Strategic Dialogue with Minister of External Affairs Dr. Subrahmanyam Jaishankar, EEAS, Press Release, Brussels 10.06.2025.
90 C. R. Mohan, "Indo-Pacific and Delhi's New Europolitik", [in:] C. Echle, J. Klien (eds.), *Panorama – Insights into Asian and European Affairs*, Singapore: Konrad-Adenauer-Stiftung, 2022, pp. 71–82, p. 76.
91 P. Kugiel, 'The EU and India in Indo-Pacific: Partners for a Resilient and Cooperative Order', EU-India Think Tanks Twinning Initiative 2020–22, March 15, 2021.
92 Government of India, Ministry of External Affairs, *Joint Communique, Indo-EU Summit*, New Delhi, November 23, 2001.
93 Government of India, Ministry of External Affairs, *EC Communication Titled "An EU-India Strategic Partnership" – India's Response*, New Delhi, August 27, 2004.
94 R. K. Jain, "The European Union as a Global Power: Indian Perceptions", *Perspectives*, vol. 20, no. 2, 2012, pp. 31–44.
95 U. S. Bava, "The EU and India: Challenges to a Strategic Partnership", [in:] G. Grevi, Á. de Vasconcelos (eds.), *Partnerships for Effective Multilateralism. EU Relations with Brazil, China, India and Russia*, Chaillot Paper no.109, Paris: Institute for Security Studies European Union, May 2008, p. 112.
96 R. K. Jain, G. Sachdeva, "India-EU Strategic Partnership: A New Roadmap", *Asia Europe Journal*, Vol. 17, September 2019, pp. 309–325.
97 See S. Prabhu, 'Enhancing EU-India Multilateral Cooperation at the United Nations High Table', EU-India Think Tanks Twinning Initiative 2020–22, 15.03.2021; P. Kugiel, 'Together at the High Table: Prospects for EU-India cooperation in the United Nations', EU-India Think Tanks Twinning Initiative, 6.11.2020; L. Klossek, S. Set, T. Lukaszuk, "Breaking Glass Ceiling? Mapping EU-India Security Cooperation", *ORF Issue Brief*, Observer Research Foundation, 2020.
98 S. Keukeleire, B. Hooijmaaijers, "EU-India Relations and Multilateral Governance: Where is the Strategic Partnership?", *FPRC Journal*, New Delhi: Foreign Policy Research Centre, no. 1, 2013, p. 120.
99 T. Wojczewski, "Global Power Shifts and World Order: The Contestation of 'Western' Discursive Hegemony", *Cambridge Review of International Affairs*, vol. 31, no. 1, 2018, pp. 33–52.
100 D. Mitra, 'UNSC Watch: India Continues to Draw a Line in the Sand on Security Council's Domain', *The Wire*, November 23, 2021.
101 S. Saran, *'The evolving role of emerging economies in global governance – an Indian perspective'*, Research and Information System for Developing Countries, RIS, June 07, 2012, p. 44.
102 K. Jedrzejowska, "The European Union and India in Global Financial Governance", [in:] R. K. Jain (ed.), *India and the European Union in a Turbulent World*, Singapore: Palgrave Macmillan, 2020, p. 86.
103 Sh. Saran, *'The evolving role of emerging economies in global governance – an Indian perspective'*, Research and Information System for Developing Countries, RIS, June 07, 2012, p. 26.
104 R. K. Jain, G. Sachdeva, "India-EU Strategic Partnership: A New Roadmap", *Asia Europe Journal*, Vol. 17, September 2019, pp. 309–325.
105 S. Baru, "The Economic Imperative of India's Multilateralism", [in:] W. P. S. Sidhu, P. B. Mehta, B. Jones (eds.), *Shaping the Emerging World. India and the Multilateral Order*, Washington D.C.: Brookings Institution Press, 2013, p. 84.
106 O. P. Sharma, "India, the European Union and the WTO", [in:] R. K. Jain (ed.), *India and the European Union in the 21st Century*, New Delhi: Radiant Publishers, 2002, p. 165.

107 B. Bassin, "India, the European Union and the WTO. Seattle and After", [in:] R. K. Jain (ed.), *India and Europe in the New Millennium*, New Delhi: Radiant Publishers, 2000, p. 69.
108 O. P. Sharma, "India, the European Union and the WTO", [in:] R. K. Jain (ed.), *India and the European Union in the 21st Century*, New Delhi: Radiant Publishers, 2002, p. 180.
109 B. Bhattacharya, "The European Union and India in WTO", [in:] R. K. Jain (ed.), *The European Union in a Changing World*, New Delhi: Radiant Publishers, 2002, p. 227.
110 R. K. Jain, "India and the European Union: Challenges and Opportunities", [in:] R. K. Jain (ed.), *India and Europe in the New Millennium*, New Delhi: Radiant Publishers, 2000, p. 96.
111 See O. P. Sharma, "India, the European Union and the WTO", [in:] R. K. Jain (ed.), *India and the European Union in the 21st Century*, New Delhi: Radiant Publishers, 2002, p. 185.
112 Government of India, Ministry of External Affairs, *EC Communication Titled "An EU-India Strategic Partnership"- India's Response*, New Delhi, August 27, 2004, para 57, p. 12.
113 B. Bassin, "India, the European Union and the WTO. Seattle and After", [in:] R. K. Jain (ed.), *India and Europe in the New Millennium*, New Delhi: Radiant Publishers, 2000, p. 66.
114 European Commission, *3rd EU-India Summit, Joint Press Statement*, Copenhagen, October 10, 2002, 12994/02 (Press 321).
115 A. Narlikar, "New Powers in the Club: The Challenges of Global Trade Governance", *International Affairs*, vol. 86, no. 3, 2010, pp. 717–728.
116 A. Narlikar, "India's Foreign Economic Policy Under Modi: Negotiations and Narratives in the WTO and Beyond", *International Politics*, vol. 59, 2022, p. 148.
117 World Trade Organization, *Trade Policy Review. Report by the Secretariat: India*, WT/TPR/S/403, November 25, 2020, pp. 9–10.
118 World Trade Organization, *Trade Policy Review. Report by the Secretariat: India*, WT/TPR/S/403, November 25, 2020, pp. 9–10.
119 A. Sparrow, "India, the European Union and Global Trade Governance", [in:] R. K. Jain (ed.), *India and the European Union in a Turbulent World*, Singapore: Palgrave Macmillan, 2020, p. 69.
120 A. Sparrow, "India, the European Union and Global Trade Governance", [in:] R. K. Jain (ed.), *India and the European Union in a Turbulent World*, Singapore: Palgrave Macmillan, 2020, p. 64.
121 A. Narlikar, "India's Foreign Economic Policy Under Modi: Negotiations and Narratives in the WTO and Beyond", *International Politics*, vol. 59, 2022, p. 157.
122 Government of India, Ministry of Commerce and Industry, Department of Commerce, *Annual Report 2021–22*, New Delhi, 2022, p. 102.
123 Government of India, Ministry of Commerce and Industry, Department of Commerce, *Annual Report 2021–22*, New Delhi, 2022, p. 102.
124 P. Kugiel, "India on WTO Reform: Defending the Status Quo", *PISM Bulletin*, no. 61, 16.05.2019.
125 A. Narlikar, "India's Foreign Economic Policy Under Modi: Negotiations and Narratives in the WTO and Beyond", *International Politics*, vol. 59, 2022, p. 166.
126 European Commission, *Elements for an EU strategy on India. Joint Communication to the European Parliament and the Council*, Brussels, 18.11.2018, p. 12.
127 World Trade Organisation, Disputes by member. www.wto.org (Accessed 20.07.2025).
128 European Commission, *Commission Staff Working Document. Accompanying the document Report from the Commission o he European Parliament and*

he Council. *40th Annual Report from the Commission to the Council and the European Parliament on the EU's Anti-Dumping, Anti-Subsidy and Safeguard activities and the Use of trade defence instruments by Third Countries targeting the EU in 2021*, SWD/2022/294 final, Brussels, 19.9.2022, p. 5.
129 European Commission, *Commission Staff Working Document. Accompanying the document Report from the Commission o he European Parliament and he Council. 40th Annual Report from the Commission to the Council and the European Parliament on the EU's Anti-Dumping, Anti-Subsidy and Safeguard activities and the Use of trade defence instruments by Third Countries targeting the EU in 2021*, SWD/2022/294 final, Brussels, 19.9.2022, p. 52.
130 Government of India, Ministry of Commerce and Industry, Department of Commerce, *Annual Report 2021-22*, New Delhi, 2022, p. 99.
131 M. Sethi, "India-EU Partnership for Security: Through the Prism of Nuclear Non-Proliferation", [in:] R. K. Jain (ed.), *India and the European Union in a Turbulent World*, Singapore: Palgrave Macmillan, 2020, p. 149.
132 J. Singh, "Against Nuclear Apartheid", *Foreign Affairs*, vol. 77, September-October 1998, pp. 41–52.
133 J. Singh, "India, Europe and Non-proliferation: Pokharan II and After", *Strategic Analysis*, vol. 22 no. 8, 1998, pp. 1111–1122.
134 Council of the European Union, *The India-EU Strategic Partnership: Joint Action Plan*, Brussels, September 07, 2005, p. 6.
135 See P. Kugiel, "India, the European Union and Iran", [in:] R. K. Jain (ed.), *India, Europe and Asia*, Singapore: Palgrave Macmillan, 2021, pp. 211–235.
136 A. Narlikar, "India's Role in Global Governance: A Modi-fication?", *International Affairs*, vol. 93, no. 1, January 01, 2017, p. 99.
137 N. K. Dubash, "Of Maps and Compasses: India in Multilateral Climate Negotiations", [in:] W. P. S. Sidhu, P. B. Mehta, B. Jones (eds.), *Shaping the Emerging World. India and the Multilateral Order*, Washington D.C.: Brookings Institution Press, 2013, p. 264.
138 European Commission, EU-India Summit. Lisbon, June 28, 2000, Joint Declaration. Conseil/00/229, Brussels, 9552/00 (Press 229), June 28, 2000.
139 Government of India, Ministry of External Affairs, *EC Communication Titled "An EU-India Strategic Partnership" – India's Response*, New Delhi, August 27, 2004, para 51, p. 11.
140 *Council of the European Union, The India-EU Strategic Partnership. Joint Action Plan*, Brussels, September 07, 2005, 11984/05 (Press 223), pp. 13–14.
141 Government of India, Ministry of External Relations, Joint Work Programme: European Union – India Co-operation on energy, clean development and climate change. Marseille, September 29, 2008. in: India's Foreign Relations – 2008: Documents, New Delhi, March 2009, p. 1033.
142 Government of India, Ministry of External Affairs, *Joint Statement issued after India-EU Summit*, New Delhi, November 06, 2009.
143 *Joint Statement 13th EU-India Summit*, Government of India, Ministry of External Affairs, March 30, 2016.
144 "National Statement by Prime Minister Shri Narendra Modi at COP26 Summit in Glasgow", November 02, 2021.
145 D. Mitra, "In India's Negative Vote in UNSC, a Long-Standing Advocacy Against Overlapping Mandates", *The Wire*, 14.12.2021.
146 P. Kugiel, "India's Climate Policy: From Lagging Behind to Leading the Way", *PISM Bulletin*, No. 82, 15.04.2021.
147 J. Mearsheimer, "Bound to Fail: The Rise and Fall of the Liberal International Order", *International Security*, vol. 43, no. 4, Spring 2019, p. 7.
148 X. Dormandy, "Is India, or Will It Be, A Responsible International Stakeholder?", *The Washington Quarterly*, vol. 30, no. 3, Summer 2007, pp. 117–130.

149 European Commission, *Joint Communique of the Second India-EU Summit*, New Delhi, November 23, 2001.
150 European Commission, *4th EU-India Summit – Joint Press Statement*, New Delhi, November 29, 2003, para. 4.
151 Council of the European Union, *The India-EU Strategic Partnership: Joint Action Plan*, Brussels, 11984/05 (press 223), September 07, 2005.
152 See R. K. Jain "The European Union and Democracy Building in South Asia". *IDEA Discussion Paper*, Stockholm: International Institute for Democracy and Electoral Assistance, October 2009; R. K. Nepali, "Democracy in South Asia", *IDEA Discussion Paper*, Stockholm: International Institute for Democracy and Electoral Assistance, 2009.
153 See more extensively R. K. Jain, "India, the European Union and Human Rights", *India Quarterly*, vol. 73, no. 4, 2017, pp. 411–429.
154 D. Twining, "India's Relations with Iran and Myanmar: 'Rogue State' or Responsible Democratic Stakeholder?", *India Review*, no. 1/2008, ss. 1–37.
155 Conversation with Indian expert, Observer Research Foundation, New Delhi, December 2014.
156 H. S. Puri, *Perilous Interventions: The Security Council and the Politics of Chaos*, New Delhi: HarperCollins, 2016.
157 Y. Choedon, "India on Humanitarian Intervention and Responsibility to Protect: Shifting Nuances", *India Quarterly*, vol. 73, no. 4, 2017, pp. 430–453.
158 C. R. Mohan, "India, Libya and The Principle of Non-intervention", *ISAS Insights, No. 122*, April 13, 2011, pp. 1–9; I. Hall, "Tilting at Windmills? The Indian Debate on Responsibility to Protect after UNSC 1973", *Global Responsibility to Protect*, vol. 5, no. 1, 2013, ss. 84–108.
159 Address by Mr. Manmohan Singh, Prime Minister of the Republic of India, United Nations General Assembly, Sixty-sixth session, Saturday, September 24, 2011, New York, A/66/PV.22, p. 10.
160 I. Hall, "Not Promoting, Not Exporting: India's Democracy Assistance", *Rising Powers Quarterly*, vol. 2, no. 3, 2017, pp. 81–97.
161 S. Saran, *India and Its Neighbours*, Speech given at the India International Centre, New Delhi, February 14, 2005.
162 *Annual Report 2005–06*, Ministry of Defence, Government of India, New Delhi, 2016, p. 12.
163 S. Varadarajan, India not interested in exporting ideology: Pranab, *The Hindu*, January 20, 2007.
164 I. Gandhi, "India and the World", *Foreign Affairs*, vol. 51, no. 1, 1972, pp. 65–77.
165 See S. D. Muni, *India's Foreign Policy: The Democracy Dimension*. New Delhi, Cambridge: University Press India Pvt. Ltd, 2009.
166 C. R. Mohan, "Balancing Interests and Values: India's Struggle with Democracy Promotion", *The Washington Quarterly*, vol. 30, no. 3, Summer 2007, pp. 99–115.
167 N. Pai, "R2P, Genocide Prevention, Human Rights, and Democracy", [in:] W. P. S. Sindhu, P. B. Mehta, B. Jones (eds.), *Shaping the Emerging World. India and the Multilateral Order*, Washington D.C.: Brookings Institutions, 2013, p. 305.
168 Y. Choedon, "India and Democracy Promotion: Cautious Approach and Opportunity", *India Quarterly*, vol. 71, no. 2, 2015, pp. 160–173.
169 P. Kugiel, "The European Union and India: Partners in democracy promotion?" Policy Paper No 25, Polish Institute of International Affairs (PISM), February 2012.
170 C. R. Mohan, "India's Changing Geopolitics and the New Humanitarianism", [in:] D. Lettinga, L. van Troost (eds.), *Shifting Power and Human Rights Diplomacy: India*, The Hague: Amnesty International, 2014, p. 25.

171 N. Pai, "R2P, Genocide Prevention, Human Rights, and Democracy", [in:] W. P. S. Sindhu, P. B. Mehta, B. Jones (eds.), *Shaping the Emerging World. India and the Multilateral Order*, Washington D.C.: Brookings Institutions, 2013, p. 317.
172 P. Kugiel, "India as the Vishwaguru and a Challenge to the Liberal International Order", *Polish Political Science Yearbook*, vol. 53, no. 4, 2024, pp. 65–77.
173 P. Winand, "The European Union and India: From Donor-recipient Relations to Partners in Development", *Global Affairs*, vol. 7, no. 4, 2021, pp. 579–595.
174 Council of the European Union, *The India-EU Strategic Partnership: Joint Action Plan*, Brussels, September 07, 2005, 11984/05 (press 223), p. 21.
175 Council of the European Union, *The India-EU Strategic Partnership: Joint Action Plan*, Brussels, September 07, 2005, 11984/05 (press 223), p. 21.
176 Government of India, Ministry of External Affairs, *Global Partners for Global Challenges: The EU-India Joint Action Plan (JAP), EU-India Summit*, Marseille, September 29, 2008, New Delhi, 2008.
177 European Commission, *EU-India Agenda for Action-2020, EU-India Summit*, Brussels, March 30, 2016.
178 European Commission, *EU-India Strategic Partnership: A Roadmap to 2025*, July 15, 2020.
179 Visit of External Affairs Minister to the European Union and Belgium (June 09–11, 2025), Ministry of External Affairs, Government of India, New Delhi, 11.06.2025.
180 See J. Zajączkowski, "Development Policy in India's International Strategy Towards Africa at the Dawn of the 21st Century", *Political Forum*, vol. 12, 2011, pp. 325–352.
181 R. Mathai, 'Development without strings attached', *The Hindu*, April 18, 2013.
182 E. Mawdsley, 'Development and the India-EU Strategic Partnership: Missing Incentives and Divergent Identities', *ESPO Policy Brief*, no. 14, October 2014.
183 See S. Tharoor, *Inglorious Empire: What the British Did to India*, London: C. Hurst & Co., 2017.
184 U. Patnaik, "Revisiting the 'Drain', or Transfer from India to Britain in the Context of Global Diffusion of Capitalism", [in:] S. Chakrabarti, U. Patnaik (eds.), *Agrarian and Other Histories: Essays for Binay Bhushan Chaudhuri*, New Delhi: Tulika Books, 2017.
185 World Bank World Development Indicators, GNI per capita, (25.03.2020).
186 World Bank data, GDP per capita, PPP (current international $) – (25.03.2020).
187 World Bank data, World Bank data, Poverty headcount ratio at $1.90 a day (2011 PPP) (% of population) (25.03.2020).
188 International Trade Statistics 2001, World Trade Organization, Geneva, 2001, p. 30.
189 IMF, GDP based on PPP, share of world, (25.03.2020).
190 B. Mukherjee, *India and EU. An Insider's View*, New Delhi: Vij Books India Pvt Ltd, 2018, p. 7.
191 R. K. Jain, "India, the European Union and Human Rights", *India Quarterly*, vol. 73, no. 4, 2017, p. 423.
192 R. Sikri, *Challenge and Strategy: Rethinking India's Foreign Policy*, New Delhi: Sage Publications, p. 281.

Conclusions and the way forward

In February 2025, at the India–EU relations conference in Delhi, Indian External Affairs Minister S. Jaishankr assessed that "India–EU relationship is more important than ever before".[1] A few weeks later in Delhi, a lecture was given by the President of the European Commission, Ursula von der Leyen, who acknowledged the EU–India relationship has a potential to be "one of the defining partnerships of this Century" and asserted that it would be "a cornerstone of Europe's foreign policy in the years and decades to come".[2] She proposed three areas where India and the EU can take their partnership to new levels: trade and technology, security and defence, connectivity and global partnership. At the same time, the visit of the entire Commission to India showed how much importance Europe places on this relationship and how long distance India's post-Cold War policy towards the EU has travelled.

The Union, which was seen only as an economic partner in the 1990s, became a political partner at the beginning of the 21st century and a strategic partner in the last decade. It has thus moved from the margins of India's vision of the world to its centre, becoming an important element in the plans for building a modern state and transforming the international order. This has meant both a broadening of the scope of the partnership and a deepening of the intensity and quality of cooperation. The rapprochement with the EU was part of India's broader and more active international multi-alignment strategy aimed at improving its position in different regions of the world and blocs of states. Given the potential and international role of these two major democracies, their cooperation will have a significant impact on international relations in the 21st century, including the resolution of global issues and the evolution of the global order.

However, this transformation of India's policy towards the EU has not been easy or without problems. The India–EU partnership has gone over the last three decades through different periods of high hopes and deep dives to re-emerge again to new opportunities and challenges. The new geopolitical and economic opportunities created by the end of the Cold War were not seized in the 1990s, despite the attempts at a new opening expressed in the Cooperation Agreement on Partnership and Development and the Political Statement of December 1993. This was hampered by the focus of both

DOI: 10.4324/9781003688648-7
This chapter has been made available under a CC-BY-NC-ND 4.0 International license.

partners on internal reforms and their own neighbourhood, political instability in India, disputes over the respect of human rights and finally the nuclear tests in 1998. However, the decision to launch annual EU–India Summits in 2000 gave the relationship a new momentum leading to the decision to establish a strategic partnership in 2004. Although cooperation with the EU expanded into new non-economic areas, the relationship lacked a truly strategic character. It was only Prime Minister Modi's more proactive foreign policy from 2014 onwards that helped to give the relationship with the EU a new meaning.

In recent times, India and the EU have built a strong foundation for an effective "strategic partnership". A multi-faceted and expansive network of cooperation has been created, involving more than 40 mechanisms at various levels discussing key challenges of today, from climate change to critical raw materials to space exploration. The parties share an unprecedented convergence of strategic interests and a common assessment of threats and challenges. India has long complained that the EU was too lenient on Pakistan and international terrorism and too naïve on China. Both of these constraints have disappeared in recent years, marred by the EU's own confrontation with the grave threat of terrorism and the risks posed by over-dependence on China. Today, the EU and India are stepping up the fight against international terrorism, seeking to de-risk and overhaul global supply chains. India and the EU speak with one voice on building connectivity based on the highest standards and respect for international law. The EU supports India's leadership role in a multipolar Asia. It has become India's partner in building a "free, prosperous and open Indo-Pacific". They plan to develop security cooperation and in green hydrogen or AI. The last major geopolitical divergence between them is the attitude towards Russia and Russian aggression against Ukraine. Here, however, the parties have learnt to de-hyphenate this difficult issue from other areas of cooperation, and the Union has accepted India's constraints on this issue.

The book sought to clarify the scale of its remarkable transformation, to understand the main effects of India's cooperation with the EU and to identify its limitations and prospects. The analysis allows us to indicate detailed answers to the research questions posed in the introduction: (1) What factors have most influenced India's decision to enter into close cooperation with the EU and the growing engagement in recent times?; (2) what benefits have been derived and objectives realized by India in its relationship with the EU?; and finally, (3) how does the India–EU partnership affect the liberal international order?

Why has India engaged the EU?

India's growing engagement with the EU after the Cold War was influenced by internal changes in Europe and India and the emergence of a new international context. The deepening of integration and the extension of the Union to new countries made it a more attractive economic and political partner. The Union itself began to pay more attention to the situation in Asia over time and appreciated the importance of India as a growing economy and emerging power. The issue of leadership and the personal views of leaders in India and Europe, especially in recent years of Prime Minister Narendra Modi and European Commission President Ursula von der Leyen, convinced of the need to strengthen the partnership, played an important role. This allowed historical prejudices, negative perceptions and bureaucratic constraints in the administrative and diplomatic apparatus, which slowed down progress, to be overcome. However, the greatest impact on the development of India–EU relations came from five strategic developments – two decisions made in India and three processes taking place outside the will and influence of the two partners.

Firstly, the very end of the Cold in 1991 and the collapse of the two-block division of the world removed political, economic and ideological barriers in India's engagement with the EU. The collapse of the USSR resulted in the loss of India's main political and economic partner and forced India to improve its relations with the US and its European partners. A unified Europe also began to be seen as a possible ally in building a multipolar world, in opposition to a system dominated by a single superpower – the US. The victory of democracy over communism gave new meaning to a community of values. The end of the Cold War also triggered economic changes prompting India to seek new economic partners and open up to globalization and international trade. Finally, the defeat of the communist states in the Cold War discredited socialism as an ideology pushing India to change its economic model.

Secondly, the decision to liberalize the Indian economy from 1991 onwards allowed India to become more involved in globalization processes, forced the economization of its foreign policy and the search for partners who could support its development. The rapid economic growth increased India's attractiveness as a huge market and opened up further sectors of cooperation.

Thirdly, the launch of the second phase of reforms and the adoption of ambitious modernization agenda for India by Prime Minister Modi's government in 2014 gave new impetus to the revival of cooperation with European partners. As the world's leading economy, the EU was a natural partner in supporting the implementation of India's plans.

Fourthly, the election of Donald Trump as US President in 2016 and his unpredictable and unilateralist policies during his first term (2017–2021) led India and the EU to look more intensively for alternative partners with whom to stabilize the international system and defend multilateralism, globalization and free trade. Actions taken at the beginning of the Trump's second term (from January 2025), including trade wars or attacks on international organizations, have further forced Europe to become more independent from the transatlantic superpower and seek solutions to reduce the negative effects of US policies. While in the past, the policy of US–India rapprochement set the direction for closer UE–India cooperation, this time the value of Europe was that it did not follow the American lead.

Fifth, and finally, China's more active and confrontational policy under President Xi Jinping since 2012 quickly alienated not only India but also the EU leading to a surprising closeness in the assessment of the strategic situation in Asia. India and the EU saw risks in over-dependence on China and opportunities in cooperation in rebuilding supply chains and the need to work together to defend the Indo-Pacific rules-based order. The EU's Asia policy, long focused on China, has diversified to include India as a key partner.

What has India achieved in cooperation with the EU?

The policy of engagement and cooperation with the EU, rather than isolation or confrontation, has been beneficial to India and has helped it achieve a number of key strategic objectives. In particular, the EU has played a positive role in advancing India's economic, political and strategic interests. It has contributed to strengthening India's position as a global power. It should be understood as India gaining the position and influence to shape the rules and principles of international cooperation so as to create conducive conditions for further economic growth and prevent interference by other countries in its own internal affairs.

In the economic dimension, a number of India's specific objectives vis-à-vis the EU have been identified: to increase exports through better access to the EU market; to attract foreign investment that creates jobs in India; to increase knowledge transfer and technological cooperation; to facilitate access to the EU labour market for Indian citizens; to support India's modernization by funding investment in infrastructure and in the energy transition. Politically and strategically, it was crucial for India to support counter-terrorism; gain support in joining non-proliferation regimes; accommodate Indian demands in international climate negotiations; support in the regional rivalry with China; strengthen India's role as a key power in the Indo-Pacific and one of the centres of a multipolar world; and support Indian demands for reform of international organizations and rules.

The assessment of the implementation of these objectives should be considered at three levels:

- bilateral economic cooperation
- bilateral political cooperation
- cooperation in a multilateral forum.

On the economic dimension, it is fair to say that India has succeeded in achieving most of the objectives set, although the level of satisfaction may vary from one area to another. In terms of improving access to the EU common market and increasing exports, it is worth highlighting the significant increase in merchandise trade from $2.5 billion in 1991 to $24 billion in

2000 and $134 billion in 2024. What is particularly important from an Indian point of view, it has managed to bridge the persistent negative trade balance during the Cold War and has even recorded a significant surplus in recent years. The EU has remained a major (first or second in different years) trading partner and destination for merchandise exports.

In terms of capital cooperation, EU companies have been an important source of foreign direct investment. Cumulative investment from EU countries increased from $0.5 billion in 2000 to $107 billion in 2024 (no longer including the UK, traditionally the largest investor). There were 6000 European companies operating in India in 2024, creating 1.7 million direct jobs and an additional 5 million indirect jobs.[3] Between 2000 and 2024, 16,1% of all FDI in India came from the EU, third only to Singapore (23%) and Mauritius (26%), but ahead of the US (10%), Japan (6%) or the UK (5%). In doing so, it should be borne in mind that some European companies invest in India via Mauritius and Singapore due to financial preferences. The EU has also become an important destination for acquisitions and *greenfield* investments for Indian corporations.

The EU also remains a major source of transfer of know-how and technology, with Indian players developing cooperation with European partners using EU funds (e.g. Horizon 2021–2027). Indian nationals have also become the largest group of foreign students under the EU's Erasmus Mundus and Erasmus+ academic mobility programmes.

EU countries have emerged as a new popular destination for Indians to travel for education, work or settlement. Despite the lack of ground-breaking agreements at EU level, the ongoing dialogue on migration and mobility allows for better coordination and understanding between the parties. At the same time, the demand for workers in the Union has resulted in the number of Indians living in the EU increasing almost tenfold in the last 20 years reaching almost 800 thousand people in 2023.

Finally, the EU has supported the country's reforms and modernization programmes implemented by Prime Minister Modi's government since 2014. The most important example is the assistance of the European Investment Bank, which has funded dozens of projects with loans totalling more than €5 billion, supporting transformation in critical sectors: transport infrastructure and renewable energy. Additional efforts are being made by Member States making the EU an indispensable partner in addressing India's development challenges.

Politically, rapprochement with the EU and regular dialogue has given India the opportunity to present its perspective on international issues and facilitated understanding in key areas. The parties have launched a number of consultation mechanisms on counter-terrorism, maritime security, non-proliferation or regional issues. India could count on EU condemnation of the terrorist attacks carried out there in recent years and a greater understanding of its threat perception. The four Declarations on Terrorism adopted and the cooperation mechanisms in place between the relevant services have facilitated the exchange of information and coordination in the fight against this threat. The EU has accepted India as a *de facto* nuclear state, and its member countries have supported India's admission to the four major non-proliferation regimes. India has also benefited from the increasing convergence in threat assessment arising from China's growing international role.

There have been some benefits for India in its cooperation with the EU at the multilateral level. Regular dialogue has allowed India to explain the EU – which plays a significant role in many international fora – its expectations and limitations on key international negotiations. This has allowed to ease tensions with the EU and seek compromises in climate, trade, or non-proliferation negotiations. The EU supported Indian leadership at the G20 in 2023 and recognized India as an important voice of the Global South.

Overall, the rapprochement with the EU helped to realize India's superpower ambitions by strengthening its international position. The EU's recognition of India as a "strategic partner" in 2004 or the convening of annual summits since 2000, hitherto reserved for China, were symbolic of India's move towards recognizing its growing role. The EU finally acknowledged India as a power in "multipolar Asia" and a key player in the Indo-Pacific region. Expanding the scope of relations and institutionalizing dialogue with the EU on key international issues strengthened India's position as a partner whose views and perspective must be taken into account. Emphasizing democratic values and openness to cooperation with the EU helped allay fears of India as an "emerging power". India's attitude of insisting on multilateralism, rather than isolationism, has convinced the European side to support its economic rise and growing position on the international stage. The EU is more willing than the US to co-operate with India in its proposal to "reform multilateralism", i.e. transform the institutions of global governance. India's cooperative strategy towards the EU has played an important role in the development of its economic and political power.

Of course, not all of India's interests have been realized, and cooperation with the EU has not just been a string of successes. The EU still means less to India than its largest members like France and Germany, not to mention other powers like the US and Russia. There is still considerable distrust and criticism of the Union in India, accused of double standards, green protectionism (e.g. CBAM) or meddling in the internal affairs of other countries. The Union is seen as a difficult, complicated, bureaucratic and ineffective actor, focused more on processes than on outcomes. Still, the list of cooperation mechanisms and partnerships may be longer than the list of concrete results of their actions.

Despite growing trade volumes, the EU's share of India's trade has been steadily declining from close to 30% in 1991 to 11,5% in 2024. However, this should be interpreted not so much in terms of the weakness of the India–EU relationship, but in terms of the success in diversifying trade destinations and integrating India into global economic ties with other partners. However, for a long time, trade has been stagnant, and India's recent robust growth and developed trade surplus with the EU in recent years is based on a fragile foundation (exports of refined Russian oil). In addition, the value of EU trade with India and EU investment in India are many times smaller than the EU's relationship with China. This shows that the economic relationship needs the structural change that an FTA can offer if the parties want to stop negative trends and realize the full potential of cooperation.

The EU has not been able to develop a clear position in support of India's aspirations to become a permanent member of the UN Security Council. The EU does not, in the perception of the Indian side, put enough pressure on Pakistan to stop supporting cross-border terrorism against India. The EU's response to India's clashes with China in the Himalayas in June 2020 or the conflict with Pakistan in May 2025 was disappointing to many as not sufficiently distinguishing who is the aggressor and who is the victim.

India has failed to convince the EU of its case in international trade negotiations, and recent disputes over the revocation of patent protection for COVID-19 vaccines, for example, show that there is still a long way to go before the positions of India and the EU converge. The partners differ on aid modalities and the shape of the architecture of international development cooperation, issues of democracy promotion or climate policy. The two sides have so far not been able to undertake any joint trilateral development projects in third countries, UN peacekeeping missions or a joint initiative to solve regional crises. Despite a similar assessment of the situation in Afghanistan or Myanmar, India has pursued a rather parallel policy in these countries to the Union's involvement and has been unable to use this presence to achieve its own goals. The divergence on multilateral issues also betrays more serious differences in attitudes towards the liberal international order.

What does the India–EU partnership mean for the liberal international order?

India's cooperation with the EU has so far had a limited and ambivalent impact on the liberal international order. It has proved important not so much in terms of defending and petrifying the existing *status quo* as modifying it. On the one hand, India's and the EU's declaratory endorsement of the "rules-based order" in successive joint declarations sent a political signal that increased the international legitimacy of the existing system and thus stabilized it. India shared the basic tenets of the liberal order – support for international law, free trade, multilateralism, cooperation between states and dialogue as a means of resolving disputes.

On the other hand, this did not translate into concrete joint action and compromise on many global issues. Difficulties in cooperation in the multilateral forum stemmed from India's incomplete integration into the system and India's differing approaches to its various components. Despite convergence at the general level, there are significant differences between India and the EU in practice and at the lower level. An analysis of six case studies of sub-systems of the liberal order in detail has shown this dissonance.

In only two of the six examples analysed is there an apparent convergence of objectives between the EU and India and real cooperation to strengthen and improve the functioning of these regimes: the non-proliferation regime and the climate protection regime. It is noteworthy that both have historically been among the major points of contention in the bilateral relationship, and it is only the evolution of India's approach and integration with both regimes in the last several years that has enabled the issue to turn into a field of cooperation. India has moved from being a serious critic of the two regimes to being their defender and even leader. India's integration into the non-proliferation order (though still incomplete) has, however, taken place on Indian terms and without having to abandon strategic achievements. Instead, the change in approach to international climate negotiations came only when India had sufficient financial and technological capacity to see its own benefits in a strong commitment to the system.

The most "revisionist" India is towards the existing system of global governance and major international organizations. It has been very vocal and relentless in demanding far-reaching changes in the way these institutions distribute influence and power to be more accommodative of its own position, interests, and ambitions. Operating more and more actively within the global economy and international system, India naturally wants to have a greater say in decision-making and the setting of international rules and laws. The EU, although claiming to support reform of multilateral institutions, has not been able to take the action expected by India due to its status (as an organization, not a state) and the differing views of its members (e.g. towards reform of the UN Security Council). However, the serious crisis of these institutions, greatly reinforced by the decisions of the Donald Trump administration, and the will expressed by the Commission in reforming international institutions give hope for closer cooperation in this regard in the future.

Much more serious differences exist with regard to the WTO trade regime. Here, the EU and India occupy diametrically opposed positions, with an unexpected swap of places – it is India that appears as a conservative power interested in protecting the "*status quo*" (the developmental nature of the WTO), while the EU is a "revisionist" power seeking changes to the scope and rules of the organization. As a result, unable to reach an agreement, both sides add to the paralysis of trade negotiations and WTO reform. It should be noted, however, that cooperation in unblocking the Appellate Body, or some concessions by India to the Trade Facilitation Agreement, suggests the possibility of more effective cooperation in the future.

Finally, the areas where India and the EU are furthest apart are the human rights and democracy regime and international development cooperation. In these areas, there has been no joint action or attempt to bring positions closer together, and India remains critical of the Western approach on both these issues. Not only does it not support the liberal approach of the EU and does not want to reinforce the prevailing practices of development assistance or democracy promotion, but it is actually building its own approach in opposition to the West as an alternative model for arranging cooperation with developing countries. India seems to be taking on an independent leadership role in this area also because it is the "regime" that is weakest, least institutionalized and at the same time most criticized. However, the EU's problems in both these foreign policy dimensions and India's growing international role may lead to a greater convergence of positions on these issues in the future. This will give India a greater say in shaping the rules and the character of these regimes.

An analysis of the examples cited suggests that India's attitude towards particular regimes and international institutions is a function of resources and capabilities on the one hand, and India's position in the system and degree of integration on the other. India is more willing and more strongly committed to defending existing norms, rules and ways of doing things in two cases. Firstly, when it has the material resources and does not see integration into a given international regime as a threat to its own development, but rather as an opportunity. This is demonstrated by India's changing approach to climate policy. Secondly, when it is integrated into a given regime on terms that it sees as beneficial, as evidenced by India's attitude towards the non-proliferation regime.

Joining the chosen regime not only gives India access to tangible resources and technology, but is also important in a symbolic sense, as a recognition of its status and prestige. As Rohan Mukherjee has shown, "international institutions are major sites of contestation between rising and great powers during power shifts", and the approach of rising powers that seek "symbolic equality" with great powers is defined by two variables "*the institutional openness and procedural fairness* of an international order's core institutions".[4] The example of India confirms Rohan's observation that "a rising power that is treated in an open and unbiased manner is more likely to cooperate with the rules and institutions of an order, even at the cost of short-term insecurity or material losses".[5] In addition, the example of the transformation of India's position from defensive to offensive in international climate negotiations also shows that it is more willing to take more responsibility when it has the opportunity to shape the agenda and priorities of international organization.

These observations suggest that it is possible to hypothesize that with further economic development and gaining a stronger foothold in international institutions and regimes – stronger integration into the LIO, India will act more as a stabilizing force and defend adherence to its rules. In other words, the richer and more integrated with the existing order India becomes, the more interest it will have in defending it. This would open the way for a more constructive and important cooperation between the EU and India for the stabilization of the international system.

In such a case, it would be in the EU's interest to support India's economic growth, e.g. by transferring investment there from China, increasing technology transfer or opening up its own market, as well as accelerating the reform of international institutions to give it more influence. Such thinking seems to be becoming dominant in Europe, looking at the growing interest of the EU and member states in strengthening political relations and gaining access to the Indian market. The need to see India as an alternative partner in Asia gets stronger as more difficult the EU's relationship with China becomes. A community of democratic values and skilful image-building of India as a "benign power" and a "force for good" facilitate the consolidation of this perception.

Such an approach, however, overlooks the fact that improving India's position will have to come at the cost of weakening the influence of European states, and there is no guarantee that a stronger India will work to strengthen the liberal international order. As pointed out by D. Malone and R. Mukherjee, there is a "paradox of attitude towards the international order" in the case of India because, contrary to theoretical expectations, India's attachment to maintaining the current multilateral security system is diminishing, rather than increasing, as its own position and strength improves.[6] A solution to this paradox may be possible in the long run and after the underlying security threats emanating from the region have subsided. But for now it would mean, however, that a better position of India in the system does not necessarily guarantee stronger integration.

India is first and foremost a force-seeking reform of the current system rather than protection of *the status quo*. At the same time, it is difficult today to define the limits of the expected changes. Certainly, India is not particularly interested in protecting the "liberal" character of the post-Cold War order, having the most serious doubts about democracy promotion and Western development aid. Arguably, it will also want the new order to be *"rules-based"* but to give greater rights and influence to developing countries. It is possible that the implementation of a number of Indian demands, on trade, climate change adaptation, etc., could improve the situation of the poorest and help build a fairer world. This should therefore become an important part of the EU's dialogue with India.

In all the examples analysed show that the overarching principle guiding India's approach to international regimes is alignment with national interests and the benefits achieved. This shows selective support for the liberal international order. India does not see the LIO as an end in itself and does not endorse it as a certain value worth preserving and maintaining. Rather, it is highly critical of many elements of it, while it is prepared to defend it where and when it is in its own national interests to do so. This attitude can be described as "selective multilateralism".

The analysis carried out supports the thesis that India is instrumental in using its relations with the EU to strengthen its own international position and to accelerate reforms in international institutions and regimes so that they are more conducive to the realization of its national interests and superpower ambitions.

India's main policy objectives vis-à-vis the EU were precisely to create the conditions and support for economic development and the realization of superpower aspirations. The EU has played an important role in both achieving economic objectives and recognizing India's status as a global power. The approach to the Union is based more on interests than values. Cooperation with the EU and frequent references to a "community of values" play an instrumental role in advancing India's core interests. For example, references to democracy have served not only to promote a "natural partnership" with the EU based on shared values, but also to cooperate in pushing for reforms of the international order ("democratization" of international institutions), combating the threat of international terrorism ("open societies are more vulnerable to attacks"), reducing the influence of authoritarian China (though no longer Russia or Myanmar) or creating a favourable atmosphere to support its economic development ("development and democracy can go hand in hand"). The Indian narrative was to convince its partners in the EU that its growth is not a threat to the global order, but is actually in the interest of humanity.

India appeals to a community of democratic values, economic interdependence and multilateral cooperation only insofar as it is convenient and helpful to its own national interest. For example, it is prepared to defend free trade in terms of increasing access to European markets, but is itself reinforcing protectionist measures.

Another example of a selective approach to the liberal international order is India's stance towards the war in Ukraine. Indeed, India has made it clear that the *rules-based order* must be respected when it concerns the Indo-Pacific and threats from China, its rival, while it is less valid in Europe and when it is violated by Russia, its partner. As shown in the book, India is prepared to defend the current global order only to the extent and in such areas where it sees its own benefits in doing so; otherwise, it allows its change and contestation. This confirms that India's commitment and support for the LIO is not driven by normative and ideological beliefs, but is an expression of pragmatism and political realism. At the same time, India's attitude towards the war in Ukraine shows how difficult it is in practice in politics to reconcile commitment to values with the defence of one's own interests, as India has often accused the West of doing.

What are the prospects for India–EU relations?

2025 could be a pivotal year for the EU–India partnership. Not only are FTA negotiations expected to conclude by the end of the year, The EU is also working on its new Strategy towards India. This will be the EU's fourth strategic document on India, following those adopted in 1996, 2004 and 2018, and certainly the most important. Both sides are also preparing the next multiannual plan, the Strategic Agenda, which is set to be announced at the forthcoming EU–India Summit. This will set a new level of ambition and confirm the more strategic nature of the EU–India partnership for the next five years. The forthcoming summit, the first since a five-year break, was originally planned for 2025, but will now take place in early 2026. It is likely

Conclusions and the Way Forward 253

to be a historic event, opening a new era in India–EU strategic and security cooperation.

Despite India's relationship with the EU having made progress over the past 30 years, it has not yet reached its full potential, in both economic and political terms. India has not yet realized many of its objectives, particularly with regard to regional and international issues. It has not gained the Union's support on key issues such as UN reform, counter-terrorism and development cooperation in third countries. Despite the establishment of several new dialogue mechanisms, cooperation has not progressed beyond mere discussions and the exchange of information on most issues. Now it is the time to move beyond consultations and focus on joint action, closer coordination and practical implementation of shared goals.

The positive trend in India–EU relations seems likely to continue in the future, reinforced by growing economic ties and converging assessments of international threats and changes to the global system. India's continued dynamic economic growth and integration into the international order will reduce the importance of differences between the partners, leading to greater convergence of worldviews and strategic interests. Growing technological and defence cooperation may create a new strong bond between two sides. Economic progress will make this market and its increasingly affluent consumer base more attractive to European partners. This will strengthen India's negotiating position with the EU, making it a more challenging partner for the Union to work with. Consequently, both sides will be compelled to coordinate their positions more closely and seek joint solutions to key contemporary challenges.

However, it should be noted that India's recent engagement with the EU is not necessarily permanent or irreversible. A change in the international environment (e.g. an improvement in India's relations with China, or a deterioration in its relations with the US), or the deepening of deglobalization and protectionism, could weaken India–EU ties once again. Furthermore, the deterioration of democratic standards and the strengthening of authoritarianism in India could intensify European criticism of India and undermine the partnership's normative basis. The four fundamental differences between India and the EU identified in this book – historical factors (colonial and Cold War legacies), economic factors (differences in potential), political factors (the different nature of actors) and structural factors (different positions in the international system) – will not dissipate any time soon. India's goals in international politics will often differ from those of Europe, hindering cooperation in certain areas.

At the same time, India's ambitions to become a "leading power" and a "teacher of the world" – the Vishwa Guru – mean that it will want to promote a different model of international relations that is more inclusive of the perspectives and interests of developing countries. India's increasingly vocal aspirations to become a normative power may foreshadow another area of tension with the EU. India's emergence as a leader of the Global South could help forge new solutions, but it could also be problematic for the EU. Moreover, the prevailing perception in India is that "its time has come", while Europe's time is running out and the future belongs to Asia and the Indo-Pacific. This could make finding compromises on contentious issues more difficult and make India an increasingly assertive partner that is resistant to external pressure, criticism, and influence.

Consequently, the most likely state of India's cooperation with the EU will be a "competitive partnership". This means India will continue to strengthen its relationship with the EU to use it for its own benefit, while competing with the EU for global influence and wealth. India will therefore be as much an indispensable partner as a difficult one.

The future of India's relationship with the EU hinges on decisions made in both India and Europe, as well as on external political and economic processes. Several final conclusions can be drawn about the prospects for this relationship and the key factors that will shape it.

Firstly, it is reasonable to assume that India will continue to seek close cooperation with the EU (and the West more broadly) for the same reasons as in the past 30 years: to support economic development and strengthen its international position. European countries, along with the US and Japan, will remain India's main source of investment, technology and export markets – all of which are necessary to sustain high economic growth and to help India become a developed country in the not-too-distant future. China and Russia cannot provide these resources. In addition, cooperation with the EU will be important in order to gain more influence within international organizations, as well as in order to establish new norms and standards in emerging areas, like artificial intelligence, 6G technology, connectivity, the use of digital data, or space exploration. Therefore, European politicians should recognize that India needs the EU more than the EU needs India. While India does not have many alternative partners to the West that can provide the necessary resources (capital, technology, etc.), the EU can pursue its economic and political goals with many other countries in Africa and Asia.

Secondly, "strategic autonomy" will remain the overriding principle of Indian policy as long as it brings the greatest economic and political benefits. India will therefore endeavour to maintain good relations with all powers and factions in international rivalries, using emerging tensions and crises to improve its own position. Consequently, India will not want to limit its options by forming formal alliances with the West and siding with it in the global confrontation with authoritarian regimes. However, this also means that the EU should not fear the formation of an anti-Western alliance between India, Russia and China. This would be hindered by the systemic India–China rivalry.

Thirdly, the China factor will remain the dominant rationale for developing India–EU relations. The worse China's relations with India and the EU become, the more India will be interested in moving closer to the Union. India will therefore keep a close eye on European–Chinese cooperation, support stronger Union engagement in the Indo-Pacific and expect political and economic support in its disputes with China. India is placing significant bets in the hope of benefiting from the European de-risking strategy and the relocation of some supply chains away from China. At the same time, an improvement in India–China relations cannot be ruled out in the years to come if China realizes that it needs allies in its rivalry with the US-led anti-China bloc. However, an improvement in India–China relations would require concessions from the PRC in areas that are important to India, which seems now unlikely. Nevertheless, India's distrust of China would remain greater than its distrust of the West, making it difficult to revive the concept of pan-Asian solidarity.

Fourthly, the US will remain India's most important and preferred global partner, and the EU–India relationship will continue to develop in its shadow. This factor will have an ambivalent impact: It will give the EU a secondary and complementary role in relation to the US, while also facilitating further rapprochement with the West as a whole. The EU's position in this arrangement will depend on economic developments in Europe, how autonomous the EU becomes from America and how far it progresses with internal integration. Unilateral US policies during Donald Trump's second term will help in closer strategic and economic cooperation between the EU and India.

Fifthly, the specific nature of the Union as an intergovernmental organization will remain the main constraint on EU–India relations. Unless the EU improves the efficiency and speed of its foreign policy decision-making processes, increases its security competencies, and becomes a more unified actor, India will continue to prioritize engagement with its largest member states, viewing the EU level as complementary. Only a united and more effective Europe with an independent foreign policy can be an equal and serious partner for India. Strengthening relations with countries such as India may be a compelling argument for deepening European integration.

Sixthly, the outcome of the FTA negotiations will be crucial for the future of the EU–India partnership. If the negotiations were to fail, it would have a serious negative impact on the relationship and mutual trust, as happened after the BTIA was suspended in 2013. Despite progress being made, there are still significant differences in expectations regarding key issues such as market access, labour rights, environmental protection and the use of digital data. Seeking to develop its own industry, India is not willing to ease market access too much, in the hope that European companies will be forced to relocate their production there. Consequently, if an FTA is signed, it is likely to be rather "shallow", covering few areas of importance to the Union (e.g. labour rights). However, the increasingly clear perception in both Delhi and Brussels of the strategic importance of economic cooperation means that both sides may be prepared to make more concessions. Regardless of the outcome of the negotiations, European companies should prepare to engage more with the growing Indian market. The example of cooperation with China, where an FTA was never signed, shows that this is not essential for dynamic economic cooperation.

Ultimately, it could be argued that India is not the EU's "like-minded partner" when it comes to the liberal international order. While it may be so in regard to specific issues and ad hoc situations, it does not endorse the LIO as a whole. This contradicts the increasingly widespread European view of India as a "natural partner" that shares European values and a vision of the international order. An overly naive understanding of India could lead to mistakes in EU policy towards this partner. Therefore, further research into Indian attitudes towards liberalism and the liberal international order is required. Therefore, it is crucial that EU policy towards India is guided more by an assessment of its own interests and less by the implicit idea of shared values.

EU policy towards India must be "pragmatic and ambitious",[7] but also realistic. While many shared values can facilitate cooperation, they will not be enough to establish an effective partnership. The EU's relationship with India should be based not only on a community of values, but also on a convergence of interests.[8] This therefore requires a better understanding of these interests. And they will not always be the same.

As an independent global power, India views the world from a different geographical, historical, geopolitical, and economic perspective to the EU, and the differences between the two are natural and understandable. It is simply unrealistic to expect India to agree with Europe on everything. Although their interests will not always align, there are still many fundamental areas in which they can collaborate.

Differences in their approach to the liberal international order mean that India is not an EU partner in defending that system. However, India could be a partner in reforming it. Also, the EU no longer wishes to defend the existing order, which is crumbling before our eyes. Both India and the EU are interested in making global institutions more effective and reflective of the realities and challenges of modern times, as well as giving countries like India their rightful place. To this end, they must strengthen their cooperation to break the deadlock in international trade negotiations and the reform of international financial institutions, or to find solutions to climate change and make development cooperation more effective. Even if they cannot save the liberal international order, they can still save multilateralism.

In a world of a destructive Russia, a disruptive China and an unpredictable America, India and the EU can lead the reform of global governance. As the leading voice of the Global South and the largest bloc of the Global North, respectively, they can help find compromises between developing and developed countries, creating solutions that will make the international system more effective, representative and just. While the new international order will not be as liberal, it can still be rules-based. And it must be founded on the force of law, not on law of the force. This could be a key priority for the emerging India–EU Global Strategic Partnership.

As India's power and international position grows, the need for further research on India's policy towards the EU and its role in the international order will increase. Many of the areas signalled here merit separate in-depth study – from cooperation in a selected area (e.g. high technology, security, combating asymmetric threats), to coordination in the face of major regional challenges (e.g. cooperation in Afghanistan, Indo-Pacific, Ukraine), to co-operation within a particular international regime (e.g. climate, democracy promotion). The strong need for reform of the international system calls for in-depth studies analysing the current approach and opportunities for practical cooperation between the EU and India in reforms of specific international organizations and institutions. India's partnership with the EU is entering a new phase and will also regularly provide new topics of analysis.

Notes

1 Remarks by External Affairs Minister Dr. S Jaishankar at IIC Bruegel Seminar, New Delhi (February 04, 2025), Ministry of External Affairs, Government of India, February 04, 2025.
2 Speech by President von der Leyen: 'The Consequential Partnership: Reimagining and realigning EU and India ties for today's world', New Delhi: European Commission, 28.02.2025.
3 *EU-India: A Broad trade and investment relationship*, EEAS, EU Delegation to India and Bhutan, 12.12.2024.
4 R. Mukherjee, *Ascending Order. Rising Powers and the Politics of Status in International Institutions*, Cambridge: Cambridge University Press, 2022, p. 287, p. 6.
5 R. Mukherjee, *Ascending Order. Rising Powers and the Politics of Status in International Institutions*, Cambridge: Cambridge University Press, 2022, p. 288.
6 D. Malone, R. Mukherjee, "Dilemmas of Sovereignty and Order: India and the UN Security Council", [in:] W. P. S. Sidhu, P. B. Mehta, B. Jones (eds.), *Shaping the Emerging World. India and the Multilateral Order*, Washington D.C.: Brookings Institution Press, 2013, p. 157.
7 Speech by President von der Leyen: 'The Consequential Partnership: Reimagining and realigning EU and India ties for today's world', New Delhi: European Commission, 28.02.2025.
8 R. K. Jain, "Engaging the European Superpower: India and the European Union", [in:] B. Gaens, J. Jokela, E. Limnell, (eds.), *The Role of the European Union in Asia: China and India as Strategic Partners*, The International Political Economy of New Regionalisms Series, Aldershot: Ashgate, 2009, p. 187.

Index

Note: – *Italicized* page references refer to figures and **bold** references refer to tables.

6th Cyber Security Dialogue 155
6th Disarmament and Non-Proliferation Consultation 155
12th Counter-Terrorism Dialogue 155

Acharya, Amitav 195
Agenda for Action 83, 148–149, 165, 225
Akbar, M.J. 149
Al.-Kaida 148
Andriessen, Frans 59
Armed Forces Special Power Act (AFSPA) 63
Asia-Europe Meetings (ASEM) 72, 90, 92, 147, 150, 200
Asian Union 16, 200
Australia Group 215

Babbar Khalsa 123
Bava, Salma Ummu 4–5
Beijing Consensus 196
Berlusconi, Silvio 83
Bharatiya Janata Party (BJP) 11, 22–23, 38–39, 50, 65, 78, 82, 203
Big Three 3
Bombay Consensus 31
Borrell, J. 42, 153, 201, 204
Broad-based Trade and Investment Agreement (BTIA) 90, 93–96, 100–104, 146–147, 169, 255
Busan Conference 224, 227

Carbon Border Adjustment Mechanism (CBAM) 170, 219, 247
cautious liberalization of economy 30–31
Central Bureau of Investigation (CBI) 162
Centre for United Nations Peacekeeping (CUNPK) 126

Centre for Western Europe 36
Chidambaram, P. 30
Clean Development and Climate Change 218
Clean Energy And Climate Partnership 165, 167
Clean Ganga 139, 165
Clean India 139, 165
climate change 3, 91, 99, 116, 125, 148, 153–155, 165, 178, 198, 208, 216–219
Coalition for Disaster Resilient Infrastructure (CDRI) 168
Cohen, Stephen 22
colonialism 16, 228, 232
Commercial and Economic Cooperation Agreement (CECA) 19, 20
Commercial Cooperation Agreement (CCA) 18–19
common but differentiated responsibilities (CBRD) 217
Comprehensive Nuclear-Test Ban Treaty (CTBT) 64–65, 214, 216
Confederation of Indian Industries (CII) 41
Conference of the Parties (COP) 216
connectivity partnership 167, 179–180, 204
Cooperation Agreement on Partnership and Development (CAPD) 60, 220
cooperation with European communities 17–18
Coordinated Maritime Presence (CMP) 205
Copenhagen Climate Summit 39, 91, 96, 218

Country Strategy Paper (CSP) 112, 182
COVID-19 pandemic 38, 151, 153, 154, 162, 166, 168, 171, 212
Critical Maritime Routes in Indo-Pacific (CRIMARIO II) 205
cross-border terrorism 63
Cyber Security Consultation 93

Datar, Poonam 4
de-bureaucratization 95
Declarations on Terrorism 246
democracy assistance 223
democracy promotion 208, 221, 223–224, 230, 240, 249, 251, 257
democratization 54, 78, 194, 201, 221, 222, 223, 252
Desai, Morarji 20
development aid 20, 33–34, 36, 96, 112–114, 226, 251
Development Cooperation Instrument (DCI) 182
development partnerships 226
Digital India 165
digital public infrastructures (DPIs) 178
Digital Single Market 165
Doha Round 39, 98, 210–211
Dombrovskis, Valdis 169
dual-use goods 65

economic and social cooperation 96–119; economic cooperation 104–114; free trade agreement with EU 99–104; India's economic objectives 96–99; socio-cultural contacts 116–119; technological cooperation 114–116
economic cooperation 104–114, 164–184; connectivity partnership and IMEC 179–180; development aid 112–114; EU support for the modernization agenda 165–168; foreign direct investment (FDI) 174–177; international development cooperation 182–184; investment cooperation 108–111; migration and mobility 180–182; migration and private remittances 111–112; resumption of FTA negotiations 168–170; scientific and technological cooperation and role of TTC 177–179; trade in goods and services 171–174; trade in services 33, 101, 108, 171–172

economic nationalism *(swadeshi)* 28–29
economic reforms: effects of 31–34; market-oriented reforms 32; pro-liberal 28–34
EEC-India Joint Commission 18
effective multilateralism 191, 198
emerging multipolar world 191
Energy Panel 53, 89, 116, 159, 217
enhanced partnership 61, 67
enhancing cooperation on anti-piracy efforts 125
Enhancing Security Cooperation in and with Asia (ESIWA) 205
EU–Africa–India Digital Corridor 179
EU as India's regional partner 199–205; India–EU cooperation in South Asian States 201–202; and Indo-Pacific 202–205; and SAARC 200–201
EU–India Business Summit 83, 97, 99, 118
EU–India maritime cooperation 161
EU–India Round Table 83
EU–India Security Dialogue 89, 149
EU-India Summit; *see also* India-EU Summits
EU–India Summit 4, 38, 82–83, 90, 98, 122, 149–150, 165, 218, 221, 243, 252; in Helsinki 90
EU–India Think Tanks Network 83
EU Institute for Security Studies (EUISS) 93, 119
EU Operation Atalanta 124, 161–162
European Business and Technology Centre (EBTC) 41, 91, 116, 118
European Commission (EC) 3, 20, 41–42, 60–61, 82, 87–88, 90, 92, 121, 142–144, 183; positive development 61; visit to India in 2025 159–160, 178
European Defence Community 15
European Economic and Social Committee (EESC) 118
European Economic Community (EEC) 2, 14–20, 34–35, 68; protectionist measures 19
European Instrument for Democracy and Human Rights (EIDHR) 182
European integration 15–16
European Investment Bank (EIB) 167–168, 183
European Parliament 20, 41, 59, 61–63, 67, 103, 149, 159–160

European Security and Defence Policy (ESDP) 119
European Space Agency (ESA) 115
European Union and India. Rehtoric or Meaningful Partnership, The 4
EU's Permanent Structured Cooperation (PESCO) 160
EU strategy on India 152–153
EU support for the modernization agenda 165–168

Federation of Indian Chambers of Commerce and Industries (FICCI) 41
fight against international terrorism 119–124
Financial Action Task Force (FATF) 91, 121, 123
first Maritime Security Dialogue 155
Fissile Material Cut-off Treaty (FMCT) 64
Foreign Affairs Council (FAC) 153
Foreign and Security Policy Consultations 149, 155
foreign direct investment (FDI) 174–177
foreign policy 24–26, 94; China threat and India–EU strategic convergence 143–145; goals after 1991 21–28; India-EU partnership 148–153; India's economic cooperation with EU 164–184; India's engagement with the EU 146–148; India's modernization agenda 138–140; objectives 24; overview 137–138; under the Prime Minister Modi (2014-2025) 137–184; role of EU in Modi's foreign policy 138–145; state-centric analysis of 9; strategic partnership with EU 146–164; strategy 2–3; Trump factor in India's policy towards the EU 140-143
Foreign Policy Consultations 79, 93, 149
free trade agreement (FTA) 103; with EU 99–104; European Commission 90; European Economic Area with 55; negotiations 11, 93, 99, 158–160, 168–170, 204, 211, 248, 252

G7 Summit 158
G20 Summit 147, 156, 158, 159, 180, 208, 247
Gandhi, Indira 25, 223
Gandhi, Mahatma 15
Gandhi, Rajiv 123

Ganguly, Sumit 6
General Agreement on Tariffs and Trade (GATT) 209
General Agreement on Trade in Services (GATS) 101
Geographic Indications (GIs) 168
Gieg, Philpp 4
Global Partnership for Effective Development Cooperation 224
global partnerships 161, 192
Goyal, Piyush 158, 169
green imperialism 217
Gucht, Karl de 102
Gulf of Aden 161
Gulf of Guinea 161
Gulf War 29
Guterres, Antonio 82

Hallstein, Walter 17
Haqqani Network 148
High-level Group on Trade (HLGT) 99–100
High Representative for Foreign Affairs and Security Policy 92
Hizbul Mujahideen 123, 148
Horizontal Civil Aviation Agreement 91
human rights in India 62–63

India: Asian neighbours 36; attitude towards liberal international order 5; call for change 195–197; difficult relationship with the LIO 192–194; economic objectives 96–99; engagement with the EU 243–245; export partners *173*; great power aspirations 26–28; import partners *173*; Indo-Pacific Oceans Initiative (IPOI) 205; international strategy of 1; merchandise trade with the EU *172*; nuclear programme and crisis 64–67; offer to the EU 197–199; as reformist power 5; as responsible stakeholder 6; "*Vishawaguru*" (Teacher of the World) conception of 224
India–EC Joint Commission 59
India–EC Troika meetings 59
India–EU Environment Forum 217
India–EU Information Centre 117
India-EU partnership 2, 7, 148–153, 198, 209, 242–243, 248–252; 14th EU–India summit 149–150; EU strategy on India 152–153;

intensifying India–Europe cooperation 150–152; prospects for 252–257
India–Europe cooperation 150–152
India-EU Smart and Sustainable Urbanization Partnership 167
India-EU Strategic Partnership 2–3, 7, 89, **163–164**
India-EU Summits 79, **84–86**, 89, 92–94; in Marseille 91; in New Delhi 91, 93; *see also* EU-India Summit
India–EU trade in goods 67–70, *68*
India for the new Financial Perspective (IFF) 182
India-Middle East-Europe Economic Corridor (IMEC) 160, 179–180
Indian Council for World Affairs (ICWA) 4, 93
Indian Council on Social Sciences Research (ICSSR) 178
Indian Development and Economic Assistance Scheme 226
Indian diplomacy 23, 28, 38–39, 41, 122, 143, 196, 215
Indian Foreign Ministry 60, 67, 144
Indian Foreign Service (IFS) 39
Indian Institute of Foreign Trade 57
Indian Ministry of External Affairs (MEA) 24, 39–40, 87, 150–152, 203
Indian National Congress (INC) 30, 38, 87
Indian Ocean 94, 124–125, 161, 203, 205
Indian Ocean Rim Association (IORA) 205
Indian policy towards EU 1–3, 8–10, 73; from 1991 to 1994 59; between 1995 and 1998 59; growing crisis in 92–94; rebuilding relations in 1998–2000 59
Indian School of International Studies (ISIS) 36
Indian Space Research Organisation (ISRO) 115
Indian Technical and Economic Cooperation (ITEC) 223, 226
India–Pakistan conflict 64
India's political cooperation with EU: institutionalization of 79–96, **80–81**
India's post-Cold War policy towards EU 14–42, 191; European integration 15–17; formalization of cooperation with European communities 17–18; India's foreign policy goals after 1991 21–28; India's perception of EU 34–38; institutional constraints of stronger engagement with EU 38–42; legacy of historical relations with Europe 14–21; lessons learned 20–21; period of intensified economic cooperation with EU 18–20; pro-liberal economic reforms 28–34
India's trading partners 105, *106*, *107*, 127, 164, 171–172
India–US rapprochement 65
Indo-Pacific 202–205, 245
Indo-Pacific Oceans' Initiative (IPOI) 203
Institute of Defence Studies and Analysis (IDSA) 4, 37
institutional openness 250
INS Trishul 161
international climate-change negotiations 216–220
international cooperation 8, 51, 214, 220, 224, 245; collective 51; complex issues of 40; liberal international order and uncertainty in 1; principles, norms, and rules of 26
international development cooperation 182–184, 224–227
International Financial Institutions (IFIs) 197
internationalism 193
International Labour Organisation 103
international law 8–9, 121, 143, 145, 156–157, 179, 192–193, 198–199, 203, 222, 243, 248
international non-proliferation regime 213–216
international protection of human rights 220–224
International Solar Alliance (ISA) 168, 218–219
international strategy 49–73; balance of first decade 71–73; development cooperation 70; EU as a key economic partner 67–70; EU as difficult political partner 58–67; India–Pakistan conflict 64; India's attitude towards deepening European integration and EU enlargement 54–58; India's nuclear programme and crisis 64–67; India's policy goals towards EU after the Cold War 49–54; India's position towards EU enlargement 57–58; India's reactions to establishment of EU 54–57; India's

strategy towards the EU (2004) 51–54; investment flows 70; overview 49; situation in Kashmir as a source of tensions with the EU 63
international system, structural differences in 232
International Thermonuclear Experimental Reactor Project (ITER) 89–90, 115
international trade negotiations 209–213
investment cooperation 108–111
investment flows 70
Islamic State (Da'esh) 148

Jaffrelot, Christophe 31, 195
Jain, Rajendra 4
Jain, R. K. 4, 16, 35, 58
Jaishankar, S. 40, 150–151, 153, 158–160, 195, 196–197, 201, 205, 225, 242
Jaish-e-Mohammad 148
Jenkins, Roy 20
Joint Action Plan (JAP) 89, 91, 95, 116, 119, 120, 126, 210, 217, 225
Joint Communiques 217
Joint Cooperation Programme on Energy 218
Joint Statements 217
Joint Working Group 164, 166; on Biotechnology 52; on Environment 217; Indian diplomat 123; on Phytosanitary Standards 52–53; on Renewable Energy 159; on Security Cooperation, 120; on Terrorism 53, 120
Joint Working Programme on Energy 116
Juncker, Jean Claude 149
just and stable international order 191

Kallas, Kaja 160, 162, 205
Kashmir 160; European criticism of situation in 122; fight against terrorists in 78; Pakistani organization active in 123; situation 63, 72; terrorist organizations in 82
Kerchove, Gilles de 121
Khalistan Zindabad Force (KZF) 123
Kohl, Helmut 59
Kovind, Ram Nath 198
Kubilius, Andrius 160
Kumar, Radha 24
Kyoto Protocol 217

Lall, Krishan Behari 17
Lamy, Pascal 119, 210
Lashkar-e-Taiba 91, 123, 148
legacy of colonialism and Cold War 228–229
liberal international order (LIO) 191–232, 248–252; benefits of participation in 193; challenges 227–232; constraints in multilateral cooperation with EU 227–232; cooperation with the EU at global level 205–227; EU as India's regional partner 199–205; EU in India's vision of reformed multilateralism 192–199; India's call for change 195–197; India's difficult relationship with 192–194; India's offer to the EU 197–199; overview 191–192
like-minded partners 203
Lisbon Treaty 92, 94, 96, 103, 119, 126

Make in India 139, 140, 165, 211
Mallone, David 25, 251
Marseille Summit 218
Menon, Krishna 17
Menon, Shivshankar 23
Metsola, Roberta 160
Michel, Charles 154, 156, 158
migration and mobility 180–182
migration and private remittances 111–112
Millennium Development Goals (MDGs) 112
Missile Technology Control Regime 215
Modi, Narendra 26, 39, 149–150, 155, 158, 165
Mogherini, Federica 125, 149
Mohan, Raja 6
Mukherjee, Bhaswati 4
Mukherjee, Pranab 222
Mukherjee, Rohan 27, 250–251
multilateral mechanism 199
Mutual Legal Assistance (MLA) 121

National Action Plan for Climate Change (NAPCC) 218
National Democratic Alliance (NDA) 78
Nehru, Jawaharlal 6, 15–18, 22, 25, 26, 58
neo-liberal institutionalism 8–10
New Delhi Consensus 196
New Economic Policy 30

Non-alignment Movement 22, 33, 192
Nuclear Non-Proliferation Treaty (NPT) 64–67, 213, 216
Nuclear Suppliers Group (NSG) 65, 213–215

Observer Research Foundation (ORF) 4
official development assistance (ODA) 70, 71, 113, 183–184, 224
Ollapally, Deppa 5
Operation PASSEX 161
Operation Sindoor 160
Ortoli, Francois-Xavier 20

Pandey, Shreya 4, 34, 35
Paris Agreement 218, 219
Paris-based OECD Development Assistance Committee (OECD DAC) 224, 226–227
Partnership Development Administration 226
Partnership for Resource Efficiency and Circular Economy 167
Partnership Instrument (PI) 182
Patten, Christopher 200
Paul, T.V. 27
Pax Americana 196
Pax Britannica 196
Pax Indica 196
political and institutional differences 230–231
political partnership 56, 73
post-modern entity 230, 231
Prodi, Romano 82
pro-liberal economic reforms 28–34; cautious liberalization of economy 30–31; economic reforms 29–30; effects of economic reforms 31–34
promotion of democracy 220–224
purchasing power parity (PPP) 33, 229–230

Raisina Dialogue 41
Ram, A. N. 62
Rao, N. 23, 27, 30, 59
Rao, Swasti 37
reformed multilateralism 192–199
reform of international institutions 206–209
regime change 222
Regional Comprehensive Economic Partnership (RCEP) 211
Regional Trade Agreements (RTAs) 100

reinforced partnership *see* foreign policy; India-EU partnership
remittances 111–112
resilient multipolar global order 191
Responsibility to Protect (R2P) 222, 230
resumption of FTA negotiations 168–170
Right to Public Information Act 98
Roadmap to 2025 154–155, 191, 198, 225
rules-based global order 191
rules-based international order 191–192, 193, 198
rules-based order 193, 198, 252

Sachdeva, Gulschan 4
sanitary and phytosanitary standards (SPS) 101, 174
Saran, Samir 6
satellite navigation programme 95
Science and Engineering Research Board (SERB) 178
Science and Technology Cooperation Agreement 83
Scientific and Technological Cooperation Agreement 177
Security and Information Agreement (SoIA) 160
security cooperation 119–126, 161–162; combating piracy 124–125; fight against international terrorism 119–124; UN peacekeeping missions 125–126
security of sea lanes of communication (SLOCs) 124
"Self-Reliant India" *(Aatmanirbhar Bharat)* 166
Shared Awareness and Deconfliction (SHADE) 124
Sharma, Annand 102
shock therapy 31
Sikela, Jozef 160
Sikh Youth Forum 123
Simson, Kadri 158
Singh, Jasjit 66
Singh, Jaswant 118, 221
Singh, Manmohan 18, 39, 87–88, 90–92, 97–100, 102, 193, 222
Singh, Natwar 88
Sinha, Yashwant 97, 200
Skill India 139, 165
socio-cultural contacts 116–119
socio-economic development 101; asymmetry in 229–230; in developing countries 91; indicators 33

socio-economic development, asymmetry 229–230
Solana, Javier 82
South Asia Energy Connectivity projects 179
South Asian Association for Regional Cooperation (SAARC) 200–201
Special and Differential Treatment (SDT) 212
strategic autonomy 25, 142, 153, 196, 230, 254
strategic hesitations towards EU 153–160; 15th India–EU summit 154–155; EU–India Leaders' Meeting 155–156; European Commission visit to India in 2025 159–160; visit of President of the European Commission to India 158–159; war in Ukraine 156–158
strategic partnership 38, 51–52, 66, 73, 78–128; criticism of 94–96; India's economic and social cooperation with EU (2000-2014) 96–119; institutionalization of India's political cooperation with EU 79–96; operationalization of 89–92; overview 78–79; security cooperation 119–126
Sustainable Development Goals (SDGs) 155, 218
Swaraj, Sushma 149, 151–152

Tamil Tigers 123
technical barriers to trade (TBT) 101, 174
technological cooperation 114–116
Terrorism Working Group Dialogues 162
Thorn, Gaston 20
Trade and Investment Development Programme (TIDP) 99
trade and technology council (TTC) 158, 177–178
trade in goods and services 171–174
trade in services 33, 101, 108, 171–172
Trump, Donald 1–2, 159, 191, 199, 211, 215
Tusk, Donald 149

UN Commission on Human Rights 221
United Nations Charter, principles 191
United Nations Convention on Law of the Sea (UNCLOS) 156, 162
United Nations Framework Convention on Climate Change (UNFCCC) 216
United Progressive Alliance (UPA) 83
UN peacekeeping missions 125–126
UN Security Council 72, 96, 193
Uruguay Round arrangements 210

Vajpayee, Atal B. 65, 78, 82, 120, 194
Vicziana, Marika 4
Vohra, N.N. 118
von der Leyen, Ursula 42, 153, 154, 158, 160, 166, 191, 244

war on terror 78
Washington Consensus 31, 196
Washington Consensus 196
Wassenar Agreement 215
Water Partnership 165, 167
weaponized interdependence 212
weapons of mass destruction (WMD) 214
Western-created international system 192
Western European Union (WEU) 15
Western Union/Brussels Treaty Organisation 15
Winand, Pascaline 40, 128
Winiand, Pascaline 4
World Trade Organization (WTO) 209
World War II 15, 105, 192, 206, 228

Xi Jinping 245

For Product Safety Concerns and Information please contact our EU representative GPSR@taylorandfrancis.com Taylor & Francis Verlag GmbH, Kaufingerstraße 24, 80331 München, Germany

Printed and bound by CPI Group (UK) Ltd, Croydon, CR0 4YY

23/12/2025

02024876-0002